DATE DUE	DATE RETURNED

examples for the study of
MUSICAL
STYLE

examples for the study of
MUSICAL STYLE

William R. Ward
San Francisco State College

WM. C. BROWN COMPANY PUBLISHERS

MUSIC SERIES

Consulting Editor
Frederick W. Westphal
Sacramento State College

Copyright © 1970 by
Wm. C. Brown Company Publishers

SBN 697–03541–7

Library of Congress Catalog Card Number: 69-13314

Printed in the United States of America

CONTENTS

CHAPTER 1

INTRODUCTION

With the advent of recorded music and the worldwide dissemination of published scores, the art of music can be studied as a body of literature. The ready availability of records and scores makes it possible for the study of Beethoven to be as vital humanistically and academically as the study of Shakespeare.

The student of music can now study the scores and hear the music of all ages of western civilization, and trace and compare trends and styles in musical composition. Because present techniques have roots in earlier styles, the student must have a comprehension of the evolution of western musical culture gained from the study of the music itself.

Most courses dealing with the structure of music —harmony, counterpoint, form and the like—begin with the eighteenth and early nineteenth centuries as a point of departure, a period of "common practice." Advanced courses then extend forward into late nineteenth- and twentieth-century techniques and back into pre-eighteenth-century music. The study of music history usually begins with a survey of the entire range of western music and is followed by advanced courses dealing with specific periods, composers or particular genres.

Throughout his theoretical and historical studies the student needs to have at hand examples of the music being studied. The purpose of this book is to supply a series of pertinent examples, comments, questions and suggestions which will illustrate salient features of the styles of important composers from the Viennese classical period to the present. The student needs to know more than how to connect chords and more than the design which sonata represents; he needs to know how important composers from Haydn to the present employ the concepts of harmony and form. The term *style* as used in this volume refers to all that makes a composer's music sound the way it sounds. What makes Mozart sound like Mozart or Stravinsky like Stravinsky? To help the student arrive at answers to these questions is an aim of this book.

Of course, it is not possible within the scope of a book of this type to deal comprehensively with all aspects of a composer's style. Also, because the music of the baroque period, especially the style of J. S. Bach, is well represented in most harmony texts and courses, this book is concerned with the two hundred years following J. S. Bach and the styles evolving after the baroque period.

A review of the evolution of musical styles over the past two hundred years reveals certain trends which help explain the present state of the art of music. The following list summarizes most of the significant steps in the evolvement of musical styles from the Viennese classical period to the present:

1. In the music of Haydn and Mozart we see the interpenetration or fusion of homophonic and polyphonic (or contrapuntal) textures in instrumental forms which exploit thematic contrast and/or derivation of thematic material and which are based on the pull, or tension among well-defined tonalities.

2. Already with Beethoven the preference for objective balance between formal design and emotional content found in Haydn and Mozart is modified by greater emphasis on personal, or subjective elements. With the addition of dramatic and descriptive functions to music's responsibilities the derivation of themes from a basic motive, the cyclic recall of themes, the transformation of themes, the *leitmotif* and the *idée fixe* all become more and more important as elements serving to unify large works which express a wide range of emotional, dramatic and descriptive qualities.

3. This element of a pervading idea, or motive used to unify movements or groups of movements or dramatic works persists into the twentieth century.

1

This procedure is hinted at in Haydn (For example, Symphony, no. 103, I), in Mozart (Symphony, no. 40 in g. I, m. 102-104 and IV, m. 117-119), and is further developed in Beethoven (Symphonies, nos. 5 and 9 and the late quartets). Then throughout the nineteenth and twentieth centuries this unifying procedure continues to be manifested in the following:

    a. The cyclic forms of Schumann, Franck, Tchaikovsky, Shostakovich, Hanson, Copland, Hindemith and Bartók;

    b. The integrated introduction and derivation of themes from basic, or "germ" motives in works of Brahms, Sibelius, Vaughan Williams, Walton and Bartók;

    c. The leitmotif of Wagner operas;

    d. Thematic transformation in symphonic poems of Liszt and Strauss;

    e. The *idée fixe* of Berlioz.

4. The element of folk music idioms is only suggested in the works of Haydn, Mozart and Beethoven, and elements of a national flavor are stronger in Schumann and Chopin. Then with the music of Mussorgsky the folk music idiom with its attendant emphasis on modality becomes important in the succeeding styles of Rimsky-Korsakov, Prokofiev, Shostakovitch, Copland, Harris, Stravinsky, Vaughan Williams and Bartók.

5. The burden of drama and description which music of the nineteenth century was required to carry and the introduction of modality into the tonal system resulted in a transformation of the conventional eighteenth-century concept of tonality. Rapidly shifting tonal centers, the expansion of key areas by inclusion of chromatic and modal harmonies, the building of chords in fourths and fifths, and the increasing prevalence of unresolved dissonance produced new attitudes toward tonal organization.

Already in the development sections of Haydn and Mozart symphonies distant key relationships are explored.

In Beethoven the tonic-dominant polarity is invaded by third relationship of keys.

Rapid shifts of tonality and passages in which the tonal center is indeterminate are found in Chopin.

Wagner, through constant chromatic shifting and deceptive resolutions, develops a cadenceless, continuous flow of sound to express such emotions as eternal longing for the unattainable.

Debussy, influenced by the free association of chords in Mussorgsky's music, exploits harmonic color independent of its function within conventional tonality.

By the early decades of the twentieth century the basic concepts of tonal organization include the following:

    a. The constant, unresolved dissonance and unrelieved emotional tension of late German romanticism embodied in the music of Wagner and Strauss evolved into the expressionistic, atonal styles of Schoenberg, Berg, Webern and Křenek. Theses styles manifest the deliberate avoidance of tonal center by embracing the twelve-tone row technique.

    b. The fusion of modality and tonality in the music of Mussorgsky and Debussy leads to a concept of tonality in which major, minor, modal and artificial scales are freely associated around a specific tone as center. A variety of styles evolving from this general concept includes the music of Ravel, Prokofiev, Walton, Bartók and Hindemith.

6. As a reaction to the emotional stress and tension of late romantic music several twentieth-century composers turned to the objectivity of musical expression associated with the baroque and classical styles. These composers include Hindemith, Bartók and earlier Stravinsky. On the other hand, those composers who did stem from late romanticism and who adopted the atonal approach have found it increasingly necessary to evolve tangible structural techniques on which to spin the twelve-tone row fabric. Therefore, such composers as Webern, Křenek, Stravinsky (of the 1940s and 1950s) and Babbitt have adopted stringent serialization of all musical components in a way that is reminiscent of the retrograde canons, hocket, isorhythm and numerical symbolism of medieval and Renaissance styles.

7. Now we find (at midtwentieth century) that techniques of tonal organization which were previously rather distinct are becoming more closely related and even blended in the styles of single composers. In addition, the elements of chance based on improvisation and the new media of electronic production and manipulation of sound represent new dimensions in the world of music.

The study of musical styles reveals that the various techniques and concepts of musical expression appear as unbroken strands which narrow and widen throughout the various periods of the history of music and are present in the styles of today.

Each following chapter of this book (except the last chapter) is concerned with the style of one specific composer. The order in which composers are presented results partly from chronology and partly from considerations of stylistic influences and relationships. For example, Mussorgsky and Debussy are presented after Rachmaninov because of their relationship to later trends and because Rachmaninov represents earlier stylistic influences. This order of presentation can be altered, however, to suit any course or text, or the book may be used as source material for a course or project without reference or adherence to any specific order.

Each chapter opens with a verbal generalization regarding the composer's style—the characteristics and influences in his music. The examples and the comments and questions then direct the student's attention to specific features which typify the composer's music. Broader aspects of formal design can be illustrated only in longer examples. Shorter examples involve concentration on details of texture.

The music itself is relatively free of analytical symbols. The few indications of chords, keys, nonharmonic tones, and the like, along with the remarks and questions concerning each musical example, are intended to draw attention to specific points and to be a challenge and guide to further study and analysis of the music.

The student is directed to additional works by the composer which he may study for a more comprehensive view and understanding of that style. This section of each chapter can be helpful as a partial catalog of the composer's works, the forms they represent and stylistic features to be found in them. Thus this volume with its examples, lists of works, suggested written assignments, bibliography and index of chords and devices can function as a source for analytical and research projects in both music theory and music history.

More space is devoted to some composers in order to emphasize fundamental harmonic or formal concepts which are met with later. For example, the chapter on Haydn is extensive because it deals with terms and procedures to be used later. The chapter on Debussy is an extended one because it deals with a departure from preceding techniques.

Some important composers, such as Mendelssohn, Liszt, Berg and Webern, are not represented by examples, and others which might be deemed less important are included; some composers get slight notice and others may seem to have undue emphasis. Several reasons can be given for this divergence of treatment:

1. Some composers, though important, do not represent techniques significantly different from those already exemplified; 2. some less significant branches form a broad influence which needs to be pointed out; 3. some works under copyright cannot be reprinted; 4. the author is human and cannot hide all his biases.

It is intended that the student will find this to be a profitable handbook for use from the beginning of his study of music theory and history through more advanced courses in form, analysis and stylistic studies. Examples from orchestral or ensemble music have been reduced, for the most part, to piano scores to facilitate their comprehension by students who have not studied orchestration or are not adept at reading open score. When appropriate, the student will want to consult the full score for the details of doublings and instrumental figurations not essential to the basic harmony, melody and form.

Definitions and Abbreviations

Chords are identified by the symbols as shown in the chord index. For the most part, these are comparable to the system of symbols used by Piston in his *Harmony.*

Nonharmonic tones are defined and identified likewise according to Piston, *Harmony,* Chapter 10.

a	=	appoggiatura
aux	=	auxilliary tone
an	=	anticipation
p	=	passing tone
e	=	échappée, or escape tone
s	=	suspension
c	=	cambiata

In general, any accented nonharmonic tone is an appoggiatura. Those tones sometimes called accented upper and lower neighbors (auxilliary tones) and accented passing tones are identified herein as appoggiaturas.

Those tones sometimes called upper and lower neighbors are herein identified as auxilliary tones.

In connection with keys and triads, capital letters refer to major, and lower case letters refer to minor. In reference to modes, capital letters are used with Lydian and Mixolydian, which are most nearly like major; and lower case is used with Dorian, Phrygian and Aeolian, which identify more with minor.

In connection with the formal designs, capital letters identify sections of larger forms such as sonata and rondo, and lower case letters refer to phrases or periods which form a part of a song form.

Roman numerals are used to identify movements of works which have more than one movement, such as sonatas, quartets, symphonies, suites and the like.

The lower case m. stands for measure or measures, and the hyphen between measure numbers means "through." Thus m. 4-12 means measures four through twelve inclusive. Phrases or other musical ideas which start with an anacrusis (upbeat or pickup) and are concluded on a partial measure will be identified from their first *full* measure through the final measure. Thus a phrase in 4/4 meter which starts on the third beat of m. 4 and concludes on the first beat of m. 8 would be identified as m. 5-8.

Forms are identified according to the following generalized designs:

Song form types:
Two part (binary)—ab
Three part (ternary)—aba

Rondo types:
First rondo—ABA
Second rondo—ABACA
Third rondo—ABACABA
Sonata-rondo—ABA Development ABA

The A section and often the C section and only occasionally the B section of a rondo are a song form type, a two- or three-part song form.

Sonata types:
Binary sonata refers to the preclassic form consisting of two parts, each repeated, in which the first part modulates from tonic to dominant or relative major and closes in that key and the second part modulates through various keys back to tonic.

Sonata cycle refers to a work of more than one movement for any medium in which at least one movement (usually the first) is in sonata form or design.

Sonata (or sonata-allegro) form or design refers to that form of a single movement which developed in the Viennese classical period of the late eighteenth century. During the classic and early romantic periods (c. 1760-1860) a predominant aspect of this form was the tension between the principal tonal center (tonic) and related tonalities, especially dominant, relative major or minor and subdominant. In the late nineteenth and early twentieth century the form became a framework for the presentation and development of themes or motives, and the pull among tonal centers degenerates because a strong sense of tonality is purposely avoided or is obscured by constant and rapid modulations or by chromatic alteration.

Sonata design, therefore, refers to the following general framework:

(Introduction optional)
Exposition: A theme or motive or group of themes (Theme 1) is stated in tonic and followed by a transition toward a new key. A theme or motive or group of themes is stated in the new key (Theme 2) and followed by a closing section involving cadential affirmation of the new key (closing theme).
Development: Previous material is modified (extended or fragmented) in a shifting tonal environment or new material may be introduced to form an episode replacing the development. The close of this section may include a hovering on the dominant or other effect to establish suspense for the return of the tonic key. This is the retransition.
Recapitulation: Themes 1 and 2 return with the connecting transition and closing section but modified to provide a strong reaffirmation of tonic for the close.
(Coda optional): The coda may be a short series of cadences or a further and extended treatment of thematic material in the nature of a terminal development.

Thus the sonata is basically a three-section form —exposition, development, recapitulation—and is expandable to four or five sections by the addition of an extended introduction or long coda (terminal development) or both.

A sonatina is an abridged form of sonata in which the development section is replaced by a short transition connecting the exposition and recapitulation.

The sonata design is constantly modified through the injection of the characteristics of other forms or types such as fugue, rondo and canon, and through the application of the cyclic principle, the arch design and motto theme.

The cyclic principle refers to the recall of a theme or themes from a previous movement or movements. It is a unifying factor which may influence the form of a later movement which is in sonata form.

The arch design refers to a symmetrical arrangement of movements or elements within a movement which tends to create a reflected relationship on either side of a central point (or keystone), for example, ABCBA.

The motto theme or motive is a trenchant rhythmic, melodic or harmonic idea which recurs in many guises as a unifying factor throughout a sonata cycle.

See the *Harvard Dictionary of Music* or other standard work for definitions of texture, tonality, modality, polytonality, bitonality, atonality, neoclassicism, motive, fugue and other such terms used herein.

Twelve-tone row music, row music and dodecaphony are generally synonomous. The term *serial* refers to that procedure, typical of twelve-tone music, in which a chosen numerical order of tones, intervals, rhythmic relationships or other components, is used as a pervasive pattern for organization of the musical fabric.

BIBLIOGRAPHY OF GENERAL HISTORICAL, THEORETICAL OR ANALYTICAL NATURE—A SELECTED LIST

ABRAHAM, GERALD, *A Hundred Years of Music*, London: Gerald Duckworth & Co., Ltd., 1949.

APEL, WILLI, *Harvard Dictionary of Music*, Cambridge: Harvard University Press, 1964.

BAKER, THEODORE, *Baker's Biographical Dictionary of Musicians*, New York: G. Schirmer, 1940.

BARLOW, HAROLD and SAM MORGENSTERN, *A Dictionary of Musical Themes*, New York: Crown Publishers, Inc., 1948.

BASART, ANN PHILLIPS, *Serial Music*, Berkeley: University of California Press, 1961.

COBBETT, WALTER W., ed., *Cobbett's Cyclopedic Survey of Chamber Music*, 2 vols., London: Oxford University Press, 1929-1930.

CHASE, GILBERT, *America's Music*, New York: McGraw-Hill Book Company, 1955.

DAVISON, ARCHIBALD T. and WILLI APEL, eds., *Historical Anthology of Music*, 2 vols., Cambridge: Harvard University Press, 1947-1950.

DENMUTH, NORMAN, *Musical Trends in the Twentieth Century*, London: Rockliff, 1952.

EDMUNDS, JOHN, *Some Twentieth Century American Composers*, New York: New York Public Library, 1959.

ESCHMAN, KARL, *Changing Forms in Modern Music*, Boston: E. C. Schirmer, 1945.

FERGUSON, DONALD N., *Masterworks of the Orchestral Repertoire*, Minneapolis: University of Minnesota Press, 1954.

————, *Piano Music of Six Great Composers*, Minneapolis: University of Minnesota Press, 1947.

GOETSCHIUS, PERCY, *Lessons in Music Form*, Boston: Ditson, 1904.

GOSS, MADELEINE, *Modern Music Makers*, New York: E. P. Dutton & Co., Inc., 1952.

GROUT, DONALD JAY, *A History of Western Music*, New York: W. W. Norton & Company, Inc., 1960.

————, *A Short History of Opera*, New York: Columbia University Press, 1947.

GROVE, SIR GEORGE, *Grove's Dictionary of Music and Musicians*, New York: St. Martin's Press, Inc., 1960.

HANSEN, PETER S., *An Introduction to Twentieth Century Music*, Boston: Allyn & Bacon, Inc., 1961.

HARTOG, HOWARD, *European Music in the Twentieth Century*, London: Routledge and Kegan Paul, Ltd., 1957.

HODEIR, ANDRÉ, *Since Debussy, A View of Contemporary Music*, New York: Grove Press, Inc., 1961.

HOWARD, JOHN TASKER and GEORGE KENT BELLOWS, *A Short History of Music in America*, New York: Thomas Y. Crowell Company, 1957.

LANG, PAUL HENRY, *Music in Western Civilization*, New York: W. W. Norton & Company, Inc., 1941.

LEICHTENTRITT, HUGO, *Musical Form*, Cambridge: Harvard University Press, 1959.

LOCKWOOD, ALBERT, *Notes on the Literature of the Piano*, Ann Arbor: University of Michigan Press, 1940.

MACHLIS, JOSEPH, *Introduction to Contemporary Music*, New York: W. W. Norton & Company, Inc., 1961.

MYERS, ROLLO, *Twentieth Century Music*, London: J. Calder, 1960.

NEWMAN, WILLIAM S., *The Sonata in the Classic Era*, Chapel Hill: University of North Carolina Press, 1963.

The Oxford History of Music, 8 vols., London: Oxford University Press, 1929-1938. (New edition being printed.)

PISTON, WALTER, *Harmony*, 3rd ed., New York: W. W. Norton & Company, Inc., 1962.

REIS, CLAIRE R., *Composers in America*, New York: The Macmillan Company, 1947.

RETI, RUDOLPH, *Tonality, Atonality, Pantonality*, London: Rockliff, 1958.

ROIHA, EINO, *On the Theory and Technique of Contemporary Music*, Helsinki: Suomalainen Tiedeakatemia, 1956.

SALZER, FELIZ, *Structural Hearing*, 2 vols., New York: Dover Publications, Inc., 1962.

SCHOENBERG, ARNOLD, *Structural Functions of Harmony*, New York: W. W. Norton & Company, Inc., 1954.

SEARLE, HUMPHREY, *Twentieth Century Counterpoint*, London: Williams & Norgate, 1954.

SLONIMSKY, NICOLAS, ed., *International Cyclopedia of Music and Musicians*, New York: Dodd, Mead & Company, 1949.

SLONIMSKY, NICOLAS, *Music Since 1900*, New York: Coleman-Ross, 1949.

STEIN, LEON, *Structure and Style*, Evanston, Ill.: Summy-Birchard Co., 1962.

TOVEY, DONALD FRANCIS, *Essays in Musical Analysis* 6 vols: vol. 1, *Symphonies*; vol. 2, *Symphonies, Variations, and Orchestral Polyphony*; vol. 3, *Concertos*; vol. 4, *Illustrative Music*; vol. 5, *Vocal Music*; vol. 6, *Miscellaneous Notes, Glossary, Index*; Supplement, *Chamber Music*, New York: Oxford University Press, 1935-1939.

ULRICH, HOMER, *Chamber Music*, New York: Columbia University Press, 1957.

————, *Symphonic Music*, New York: Columbia University Press, 1952.

————, and PAUL PISK, *A History of Music and Musical Style*, New York: Harcourt, Brace & World, Inc., 1963.

VEINUS, ABRAHAM, *The Concerto*, Garden City, N. Y.: Doubleday & Company, Inc., 1944.

VINCENT, JOHN, *The Diatonic Modes in Modern Music*, Berkeley: University of California Press, 1951.

CHAPTER 2

JOSEPH HAYDN

1732-1809

Haydn's greatest achievement was the development of an independent instrumental musical form and style. He did this by infusing the sonata form with content which lifted instrumental music from the plane of the decorative and ceremonial to an expression of inward spiritual significance.

Both he and Mozart represent the apogee of the Viennese classical style, with Beethoven representing the personalization of that classical expression which leads toward the romantic attitude.

Haydn's employment with the Esterhazy family placed him in relative musical isolation and placed at his disposal an excellent orchestra so that he could experiment over a period of years in solving the problem of combining homophonic and contrapuntal textures in a dynamic formal structure.

The development of his style can best be traced through his symphonies and string quartets.

Sonata form is flexibly handled by Haydn. The usual textbook definition of eighteenth-century sonata-allegro form cannot always be applied to Haydn sonata forms. His second-theme group often does not contrast with the first theme. Instead it will be derived from the first theme, or it may simply be the first theme repeated in the new key followed by closing material of new character or figuration. Occasionally, even the closing material may be derived from the original thematic material. In earlier works, instead of developing previous material, he may introduce new material (an episode) at the point of the usual development section.

The one unvarying aspect of the sonata form is the relationship of key areas. The introduction of material in the tonic, a transition to the dominant or other related tonality, followed by a section of shifting tonality and return to the tonic constituted the immutable tonal ingredients of sonata form for the classical composers.

Haydn also used a combination of rondo and sonata forms in finales to some of his symphonies and quartets. These finales are based on the third rondo form (ABACABA). Haydn imparts sonata character to the form by introducing a development of previous material in place of the C section where new thematic material would be expected in a rondo. Conversely those finales of Haydn which are in sonata form are given a rondo character by the use of typical rondo themes in two- or three-part song form. Thus Haydn gives the third rondo a sonata character by means of a development using the usual devices such as contrapuntal fragmentation and imitation, sequence, shifting key centers and rhythmic variation; and he gives the sonata a rondo character by using a theme having the form and character typical of a rondo.

Haydn's free treatment of form results in many unexpected and imaginative musical effects calculated to surprise, amuse or fascinate.

The usual instrumental figurations common to the period are found in Haydn's music. These include the Alberti pattern, repeated notes in the bass (drum bass), expressive appoggiaturas, measured tremolos or shakes, arpeggios and scale passages, and passages with broken thirds or sixths.

EXAMPLE 1 (pages 17-19)
Piano Sonata in G Major, H 27, I

This first movement of a relatively early piano sonata (composed c. 1775) is included as an illustration of early classical sonata style with clearly defined formal sections. Because of the unreliability of the opus numbers under which the Haydn piano sonatas were published, the numbering used in the Hoboken thematic catalog will be employed here, with an identifying prefix H.

This example contains all the elements of a three-part (ternary) sonata form except that in place of a development an expisode involving new material in

6

a shifting tonal pattern of modulations and sequences is introduced.

Items to note and questions to answer:

1. The first theme consists of twelve measures: an antecedent phrase of eight and a consequent phrase of four.

2. The second theme begins at m. 25 in the exposition. Where does it begin in the recapitulation? In what key is it in the recapitulation?

3. The transition from the first to the second theme is different in the exposition from the one in the recapitulation. The transition in the recapitulation is reminiscent of what previous material?

4. What key is emphasized in the transitions at m. 17-24 and 98-106?

5. Each transition ends on the D triad, V of G, in m. 24 and 106. In m. 24 it is treated as I of D, and in m. 106 it remains V of G. Why does the D triad tend to feel more like I of D in m. 24 than in m. 106?

6. From the beginning of the second theme to the close of the exposition there are thirty-three measures. In the recapitulation how many measures are there from the beginning of the second theme to the end of the movement? Why is there a difference?

7. What measures would you consider to be the closing theme?

8. There are two augmented sixth chords used in the episode which replaces the usual development section. One is in m. 71. Where is the other?

9. Notice the sequence of secondary dominants with roots descending by fifths in m. 73-76.

10. There is a change of mode to g minor at m. 79 to allow for passing through the key of B-flat major (relative major of g) on the way to the V^7 of G at m. 85 and the begining of the recapitulation at 86.

11. Locate the appoggiaturas in m. 5, 18, 20, 23-26, 41, 72, 84, 102, 104, 106 and 110. There are many more in addition to these.

12. Double auxiliary tones occur in m. 13 and 87.

13. In m. 80, 81 and 82 how would you explain the second eighth note in each measure in the right hand? Transpose the second and third eighths in each of these measures one octave lower to aid in defining these tones.

14. Turns occur in m. 43-45 and 48-50 as well as the respective measures in the recapitulation. Could the last four sixteenths in the right hand of m. 29, 31, 33, 115, 117 and 119 be considered turns?

15. M. 55-56 and 141-142 illustrate a drum bass forming a pedal over which V^7 and I are sounded.

16. The prevailing texture is three parts which is typical of the time for keyboard music. Even when the left hand has Alberti patterns, the accented notes form one harmonic voice and the unaccented notes form another voice producing with the right hand a total of three voices or implied three-part harmony. Such patterns, even though they appear visually as one part, actually produce an aural effect of two or three parts. Thus some examples of the texture in this movement may be analyzed as follows:

a. One part, unison or octave: m. 9-11, 95-97.
b. Two part: m. 7-8, 22-24, 29-35, 93-94, 105-106, 115-121. In measures such as 30, 32 and 34 the left-hand sixteenths produce simply an aural octave doubling of one part.
c. Written three parts: m. 1-6, 13-21, 55-57 and the related measures in the recapitulation.
d. Some measures which are written as two parts but which have the aural effect of three or four parts are 25-28, 36-45 and 58-85. Notice that in such measures as 42 and 128 the sixteenth-note pattern of broken thirds implies two parts.

17. How do you explain the sixth 16th-note in m. 53 (F♯) and 139 (B)?

EXAMPLE 2 (pages 20, 21)
Piano Sonata in G Major, H 27, II

This, the second movement of the same sonata, is included as an illustration of the song form with trio or minuet form. This form serves as the basis for nearly all minuets and scherzi as well as other dance movements and occasional pieces by composers of the classic and romantic periods.

The usual extensions found in most classical minuets are shown in marked degree here. Both the minuet and trio are full three-part forms. The overall form of the movement would thus be:

A	B	A
minuet	trio	minuet
‖:a:‖:ba:‖	‖:a:‖:ba:‖	aba

As indicated by the above diagrams and the letters in the score, the sequence of minuet, trio, minuet (da Capo) produces a large ABA form. The ABA rondo or first rondo form has much the same dimensions as the minuet and trio. The rondo however is a continuous movement which is more unified by transitions connecting the sections, whereas the minuet and the trio are two distinct song forms, unrelated thematically, and separated by conclusive cadences.

The ABA effect results simply from the repeat of the minuet after the trio.

The Minuet

1. In part a the antecedent phrase is four measures and the consequent phrase is ten measures. Extension is gained partially by four repetitions of V-I in D, m. 9-12. By numbering each measure according to the material it contains, the construction of part a, showing graphically the manner in which extension is accomplished, can be indicated as follows:

```
antecedent          consequent
1 2 3 4             1 2 2 3 2 2 2 2 3 4
G——V               ————————————D I
```

2. Part a modulates to D. Part b begins in D and modulates to G in the first phrase of four measures. The second phrase of part b is six measures (19-24). The inclusion of m. 19-20 or 21-22 produces this extension to six measures. Which pair of measures do you think sounds like extension?

3. The return of part a consists of the initial four-measure phrase of the minuet followed by a six-measure concluding (consequent) phrase, followed in turn by a codalike extending (or second consequent) phrase of eight measures, as follows:

```
antecedent     consequent     extension or second
                              consequent phrase
1 2 3 4        2 2 2 2 3 4    2 2 2 2 5 6 3 4
G——V          G————I         G————————I
```

The decisions regarding the thematic or motivic relationship of measures are a matter of interpretation in a phrase analysis like the one above, but even though some points may be open to argument, the procedure is nevertheless effective in helping explain structure.

4. A melodic characteristic of the m. 2 material is the initial appoggiatura which occurs also in m. 6, 7, 9, 11, 26, 29-32, 35 and 37. Appoggiaturas are also in m. 4, 13, 14, 16, 18-24, 28, 33, 34, 41 and 42. The G sharps in m. 3 and 27 as well as the second note of each triplet in m. 39 may be considered appoggiaturas. All but eleven of the forty-two measures of the minuet contain appoggiaturas.

5. The A♯ in m. 13 is simply an auxiliary tone between two B's an octave apart.

The Trio

1. The relationship of the key of the trio to the key of the minuet or scherzo is discussed on pages 13-14. Haydn more frequently places the trio in the same key as the minuet than any other key. The choice of parallel (or tonic) minor for a trio whose minuet is in major is also typical of Haydn as well as Mozart and Beethoven. Because the majority of Haydn's works are in major, the choice of tonic minor, as exemplified here, provides welcome contrast.

2. Each part of the trio is a conventional eight measures.

3. Notice the symmetry of the harmonization of part a:

```
meas.   1  2   3   4     5   6   7      8
chord   I V  I  V I     V   I V  V I  VI (II)  V
                (VI)
```

M. 1 and 3 of part a have the same melody, but F♮ is an appoggiatura to dominant harmony in one and to tonic (VI being a substitute for tonic function) in three.

4. Notice the augmented sixth in m. 49 approached through D as appoggiatura (accented passing tone) to C♯.

5. Part b is in the relative major (B♭) rather than dominant of g. The dominant of the minor key is seldom used in such situations. Notice that Haydn simply assumes the tonality of B♭ after the V of g, not an uncommon procedure.

6. The first four measures of part b have no appoggiaturas, but the next four (55-58) are full of of them.

7. In the return of part a Haydn introduces a new penultimate measure (65) which recalls part b and provides unity.

8. The final measure of every part of both the minuet and trio fulfills the harmony via an appoggiatura, another unifying device.

9. Two- and three-part textures prevail throughout the trio.

EXAMPLE 3 (pages 22-24)
Piano Sonata in E Minor, H 34, I

This sonata was written in 1783 shortly after the publication of the famous op. 33 quartets in which Haydn demonstrated his technique of development by using themes which could be separated into short motives of strong individual identity and developed contrapuntally. The opus 33 quartets and those symphonies and quartets which follow represent Haydn's solution to the problem of imbuing sonata form, a homophonic form, with contrapuntal or polyphonic texture and thus dramatizing the process of thematic development.

This example in sonata form includes a full development but without the contrapuntal display to be found in the quartets of this period of Haydn's writing.

The sectional nature heightened by the long pauses between sections, the minor key, and the sequential and repetitive nature of the treatment remind one of Haydn's earlier "sturm und drang" style of which the opus 20 quartets and Symphonies, no. 45 (Farewell) and no. 49 (La Passione) are examples.

1. The first theme is an instrumental motive with emphasis on rhythmic-harmonic interest rather than on melodic outline. This emphasis is common with later Haydn and with Beethoven.

2. The second theme which is introduced at m. 30 (key of G) is obviously based on the first. This relationship is so close that the movement has a mono-thematic quality. This results in a prevailing rhythmic motive which appears in about 60 per cent of the measures: the rhythm of the first measure and its variant which first appears in m. 14. It is not unusual for Haydn (or Beethoven) to base an entire movement on one predominant rhythmic pattern as he does in Symphony, no. 28, I; Symphony, no. 103, IV (see example 4); and Quartet, op. 50, no. 6, IV.

3. The development section beginning at m. 46 and continuing through 78 is based almost entirely on the one rhythmic motive and its variant.

4. The first theme consists of eight measures leading to a half cadence. The beginning of a repetition of the theme at m. 9 and 10 leads immediately into the key of G, the relative major and the usual second key for sonatas in minor. Although G is established by m. 14, the transition continues through m. 29 with a modulation to D beginning at m. 25 to point up the dominant of G preceding the entrance of the second theme in G.

5. Notice the three-measure sequence at m. 19-21 and the one measure repeated three times at m. 22-24.

6. The unison passage at m. 26-30 concluding with the D arpeggio is the typical ceremonial conclusion of the transition which heralds the entrance of the material of the new key area, be it a new theme (the second theme) or the first theme in new tonality. The arpeggio or several repetitions on the closing chord of the transition are a cliché which appears throughout most early classical styles. It is common in Haydn and Mozart but increasingly less so in Beethoven.

7. The structure of the second theme is simple enough: a six-measure phrase (30-35) followed by a repetition of seven measures (36-42) with the extra measure being m. 40.

8. The chromatic sixths in m. 40 are more typical of Mozart than of Haydn.

9. The closing section is only four measures (42-45).

10. The development is devoted to the first theme and transition material. Notice that the exposition ends in G and the development begins in a new key (a minor). Haydn frequently launches into the development in a key different from the close of the exposition. The expositions of sonatas in major close in the dominant so thas his choices of opening keys for the development are likely to be:

dominant as in Quartets, op. 3, no. 5, I; op. 17, no. 5, I; op. 33, no. 2, I; op. 64, nos. 2 and 4, I; op. 76, no. 1, I; op. 77, no. 2, I; in Symphony, no. 101, I; and in the first movements of most piano sonatas.

mediant (the major key a minor third above tonic) as in Quartets, op. 33, no. 6, I; op. 54, no. 2, I; op. 74, no. 1, I; and in Symphonies, nos. 97 and 100, I.

relative minor as in Quartets, op. 9, no. 2, I; op. 3, no. 3, I; op. 76, no. 3, I; in Symphonies, nos. 92, 99, and 104, I; and in Sonata, H33, I.

Less frequently or rarely will Haydn choose the following keys to open the development of sonata movements in major keys:

subdominant as in Quartet, op. 33, no. 3, I; Quartet, op. 54, no. 2, I; and Symphony, no. 94, I.

supertonic as in Quartets, op. 20, nos. 4 and 6, I; and Symphony, no. 102, I.

dominant minor as in Sonatas, H 27 (Example 1) and H 29.

tonic minor as in Quartet, op. 54, no. 1, I.
mediant: the major key a major third above tonic as in Quartet, op. 74, no. 2, I.

mediant: the minor key a major third above tonic as in Quartet, op. 76, no. 4, I.

submediant: the major key a minor third below tonic as in Sonata, H 52.

The expositions of sonata movements in minor close in the relative major so that Haydn's choices of opening keys for the development are likely to be:

relative major as in Quartet, op. 74, no. 3, I; Symphony, no. 45, I, and Sonata, H 36.

subdominant (minor) as in Quartet, op. 76, no. 2, I; Sonata, H 44, I; and Sonata, H 34 (the present example).

submediant (major) as in Quartets, op. 20, no. 5, I, and op. 64, no. 2, I.

Usually when the development opens in the same key as the close of the exposition, Haydn modulates quickly to a new key as in Sonata, H 52, I, where he moves from B♭ to C.

Occasionally he will insert a short transition between the final cadence of the exposition and the opening of the development as in Quartet, op. 54, no. 2, I, and Sonata, H 44, I.

11. Even though the present development opens in a, it moves suddenly to C (submediant) after five measures (measure 51).

12. The development section passes through the following sequence of keys: a, C, d, e, b. The key of b as dominant is prolonged from measure sixty to seventy-two at which point there is a return to e to establish the B triad as V of e leading to the recapitulation.

13. Measures 71-78 serve as a retransition building tension on the dominant for a natural return of the tonic key at the recapitulation. It consists of a sequence of five root movements descending by thirds followed by a descending fifth into the B triad. The series of roots is B G E C A F♯ B. (See Beethoven, Example 25 p. 125.)

14. Measures 67-70 introduce new melodic material.

15. The first theme and transition cover only sixteen measures in the recapitulation compared to twenty-nine measures in the exposition. How is this reduction accomplished?

16. On the other hand, the second theme is extended by two measures, and the closing theme leads into an extension having the character of a coda. This closing theme and coda total nineteen measures (109 to the end) compared to four measures in the exposition. This closing section begins in e, goes to C, passes through a and returns to e with a reference to the first theme in the last four measures.

17. The second theme is characterized by the suspensions in measures 32-34, 38-39, 97-99, 103 and especially the sequence of suspensive movement in measures 104-106 which serves to extend the second theme in the recapitulation.

18. The IV$_4^6$ from g minor used in G major appears in m. 39.

19. In m. 107 the E in the top voice acts as a pedal over the chromatic sixths in the lower voices.

20. The many ways in which the recapitulation varies from a literal return of the exposition material serve to point up the fact that a master composer such as Haydn uses form as a flexible, dynamic expression resulting from the musical consideration of thematic material rather than as a rigid framework on which to hang notes. The form serves the musical idea and not the reverse.

EXAMPLE 4 (pages 25-28)
Symphony No. 103 in E♭ Major, IV

For finales of symphonies Haydn employs sonata form with a rondo-type theme or sonata-rondo form. See the diagram of sonata-rondo form, p. 4. Finales of quartets are usually sonata form with rondo-type themes.

The finale of Symphony, no. 103 is unusual, even for Haydn, because:

1. It is monothematic, yet based on a sonata-rondo tonal design.

2. The theme consists of two contrasting motives (elements) which appear simultaneously and complementary to one another. The main motive is the upper melody in m. 5-8. This is the predominant material of the movement. The secondary motive is the horn call of the first four measures serving as an introduction and as harmonic undergirding of the main motive.

The sonata-rondo design of the movement may be outlined as follows:

Section A. Key of E♭ modulating to dominant. M. 5-28 plus dominant extension, m. 28-44, leading to

Section A repeated. Key of E♭ closing in E♭. M. 45-73. Do the first seventy-three measures constitute an a b a form?

Transition to section B. m. 73-90.

Section B. Two parts. Key of B♭ closing in B♭. M. 91-107 constitute the first part. Notice the horn-call motive, m. 91-98. M. 107-146 constitute the second or closing part of Section B.

Transition to return of A. M. 146-157.

Section A. Key of E♭ modulating to c minor and the beginning of the development or C section. M. 158-182.

Section C, development. It is difficult to state precisely where this section begins because the preceding section A does not close with a conclusive cadential effect. One could consider the beginning to be as early as m. 171, which closes fourteen measures in E♭, or m. 182 where c minor is reached, or as late as m. 196 inasmuch as the preceding six measures are in E♭ again. In any case, the modulating quality of this section imparts the sound of development. What keys are passed through in this section if we consider it to extend from m. 182 through 263?

M. 217-263 are comparable to the closing part of section B, m. 107-157.

Notice that the C section closes on a suspensive (half) cadence in the relative minor (on the V of VI chord) and that section A returns directly in the key of E♭ without the use of its dominant to precede it. It is not uncommon, particularly in early classical sonatas, for the development to close on a half cadence in the relative minor and for the recapitulation to begin with tonic with little or no further attempt to connect through the dominant. See Quartet, op. 74, no. 2, I, m. 173-174, for this effect. See also the Sammartini, Symphony in D Major, I, in the *Harvard Anthology*, vol. II, p. 283. This progression can be found in Symphony, no. 103, I, at the close of the slow introduction and the opening of the exposition.

Section A. Key of E♭. M. 264-299.

Section B. Key of E♭. M. 299-350. Notice that this is the same material as the earlier B section only in tonic instead of dominant and that the closing part of this section (316-350) is the same material as both the close of the first B section and the close of the C section.

Coda. Key of E♭. Measures 350 to the end. A full statement of the main theme does not appear, only the first five notes of the melody are used. It is not uncommon in third rondos and sonata-rondos of the classical period for the coda to replace a full statement of the main rondo theme.

Make a diagram of the form of this movement based on the preceding analysis. Could this movement be considered a sonata (instead of a sonata-rondo) with the development extending from m. 158 through 263?

Examples and Suggestions for Further Study of the Music of Haydn

first movements

The first movements of many of the symphonies and quartets are, to a greater or lesser degree, monothematic in character. This is true of some slow movements and finales also. Instead of introducing a contrasting theme on establishing the new key in the expositions of these movements, Haydn simply repeats the first or principal theme in this new key (dominant or relative major), and only toward the final or closing section of the exposition does he introduce contrasting material of thematic significance. This new material introduced at this late point has second-theme significance in Symphonies, nos. 99 and 100, I, but appears to be simply closing material in Symphonies, nos. 92 and 104, I.

Analyze the first movements of the following works which illustrate this monothematic character. Try to decide whether the new material toward the close of the exposition is a true second theme or the closing theme.

Symphonies: no. 45 (Farewell)
no. 85 (La Riene)
no. 92 (Oxford)
no. 99 (Imperial)
no. 100 (Military)
no. 104 (London)

This monothematic procedure appears in many first movements of quartets including the following:

op. 20, no. 5
op. 54, no. 1
op. 74, no. 1
op. 77, nos. 1 and 2

The second theme is obviously derived from the first in the following quartets:

op. 33, nos. 2 and 3
op. 50, no. 6
op. 64, nos. 2, 4 and 6
op. 76, nos. 3 and 4

Piano Sonatas, H 49 and 52 are monothematic. The second theme is derived from the first in Sonatas, H 21, 33 and 34.

When a sonata movement is in a minor key, the contrasting key is the relative major. This places the second theme in the major mode. In the recapitulation where the prevailing key would ordinarily be tonic minor throughout, the composer is faced with the choice of presenting the previously major-mode second theme in a minor version or of changing the key to tonic major at the entrance of the second theme to retain the major-mode character of that theme. Mozart usually chooses the former method and Haydn the latter. Quartet, op. 74, no. 3, I and IV, exemplify this method. Notice that Haydn even changes the key signature to tonic major.

slow movements

ABA rondos, sonata or sonatina forms, theme and variations, and song forms are Haydn's choice of forms for the slow movement of sonata cycles. The slow movement is commonly the second in a three- or four-movement cycle, although it is the third in several quartets such as op. 9, op. 17, the first four of op. 33 and an occasional later one.

Song form is used less frequently than the other slow movement forms. Quartets, op. 33, no. 2, III, and op. 54, no. 2, II, are three-part song forms. The latter one ends in a half cadence leading directly to the third movement.

Examples of two-part song form are quartets, op. 33, no. 3, III, and op. 64, no. 2, II. These might be classed as theme and variations because each is repeated with variation.

Theme and variations are more frequently used in the quartets and symphonies. Examples are:

Quartet, op. 20, no. 4, II. The theme is a two-part song form.

Quartet, op. 74, no. 2, II. The theme is a three-part song form.

Quartet, op. 76, no. 3, II. The theme is the well-known hymn, *Gott erhalte Franz den Kaiser*, which became the Austrian national anthem and was written by Haydn earlier. It is a two-part song form.

Symphony, no. 85, II. The theme is small three-part song form called a romance. It is a French song, known in Haydn's time, called *La gentille et la belle Lisette*. Notice the similarity of this theme to that of the Symphony, no. 100, II.

Symphony, no. 94, II. The theme is a two-part song form.

Symphony, no. 97, II. The theme is a two-part song form with the second part extended greatly.

Symphony, no. 103, II. This is a double theme and variations. Two three-part song forms

(the first in c and the second in C) are alternately varied, thus:

A (c minor), B (C major), A (Variation I), B (Variation I), A (Variation II), B (Var. II), etc.

Rondo form, nearly always three-part (ABA or first rondo) is frequently used by Haydn as a slow movement form. The theme or A section is always a closed two- or three-part song form. It is presented usually as an independent entity closing with an authentic conclusive cadence in tonic. It is always in major.

The second, or B section is almost invariably in tonic minor. In form it is not as well defined as A, having more the character of a transition. It is usually a phrase group based on the first part, a of A, or on the second part, b of A. Thus contrast is achieved in B through 1. change of mode, 2. change of dynamics (B is often louder), 3. transitional or modulatory character, and/or 4. rare use of new material.

The A theme (song form) is generally varied on its return as the third section. Often it is extended by repetition and/or a coda. This form diagrammed is:

Section:

A ab or aba song form in major	B phrase group or song form in tonic minor, usually based on A and leading back to	A extended and/or varied	Coda optional

The slow movements of all the following works are in the first rondo form as described. (All A sections are three-part song forms unless otherwise indicated:)

Quartets:
op. 54, no. 3, II
op. 64, no. 3, II (Both A and B are two-part song forms.)
op. 64, no. 4, III
op. 64, no. 5, II
op. 64, no. 6, II (A is a two-part song form.)
op. 74, no. 3, II
op. 76, no. 2, II
op. 76, no. 4, II (A is a two-part song form.)

Piano Sonatas:
H 49, II (B introduces new material.)
H 52, II

Symphonies:

> no. 92, II (B introduces new material.)
> no. 100, II (Could be considered a song form with trio but the long, pompous coda is typical of a rondo.)
> no. 101, II (The form is: ABA transition A-varied.)

Sonatina and sonata forms occur at least as frequently as rondo form for slow movements. Because of the brevity and transitional nature or the virtual absence of the usual development section in the following movements, they are best considered sonatinas:

Quartets:

> op. 3, no. 5, II (This is the famous "Serenade.")
> op. 17, no. 5, III (There is no development section. Notice the instrumental recitative and compare to Beethoven, Ex. 19, p. 91-97.)
> op. 33, no. 6, II
> op. 54, no. 1, II
> op. 76, no. 1, II (Monothematic)

Symphonies:

> no. 49, I (Note that the first movement is a slow movement.)
> no. 102, II (could it be a song form?)

The following slow movements are sonata forms:

Quartets:

> op. 3, no. 3, III
> op. 20, no. 5, III
> op. 50, no. 6, II (Monothematic)
> op. 74, no. 1, II
> op. 76, no. 5, II
> op. 77, no. 2, II (Where does the development begin?)

Piano Sonatas:

> H21, II
> H39, II (Monothematic)
> H34, II (Extended with a transition to III.)
> H36, II (Has a long coda involving harmonies from the tonic minor in the closing measures.)
> H19, II (What is unusual about the return of the first theme in the recapitulation?)

Symphonies:

> no. 45, II
> no. 99, II

minuet and scherzo movements

The minuet or scherzo of a sonata cycle is nearly always a song form with trio. (Exceptions are minuets which are the final movements of cycles such as piano sonatas or concertos when they may be cast in rondo form.) Both the minuet (or scherzo) and trio are three-part more often than two-part song forms. Rarely is a two-part trio coupled with a three-part minuet as in Quartets, op. 54, nos. 2 and 3, III; or a two-part minuet with a three-part trio as in Sonata, H29, II.

The minuet or scherzo movement is always in the tonic key of the work and the key of the trio has one of the following relationships to the main key.

Throughout all Haydn's works the most prevalent key for trios is tonic, the same key as the minuet, as in:

Quartets:

> op. 9, no. 2, III
> op. 20, no. 4, III
> op. 33, nos. 2, 3, II, and 6, III
> op. 50, no. 6, III (with greatly expanded trio)
> op. 54, nos. 1 and 3, III
> op. 64, nos. 3, 6, III, and 4, II
> op. 76, nos. 1, 4, and 6, III

Symphonies:

> nos. 85, 92, 94, 97, 100, 101, 102, 103, III

In works in a major key it is not uncommon for the trio to be in the tonic minor as in the following examples:

Quartets:

> op. 17, no. 5, II (The trio is a two-part song form.)
> op. 54, no. 2, III (The trio is a two-part song form.)
> op. 64, no. 5, III
> op. 76, no. 5, III

Sonatas:

> H 13, 14, 27, 28, 29

When the main key is minor, the trio is likely to be in the tonic major as in:

Quartets:

> op. 20, no. 5, II
> op. 64, no. 2, III
> op. 76, no. 2, III

and Symphony, no. 49, III

In Quartet, op. 74, no. 3, which is in g, Haydn placed the minuet in G and the trio in g. In Symphony, no. 45 in f♯, both the minuet and trio are in F♯.

There are several examples in Haydn's later works of a third relationship between the keys of the minuet and trio. In each of these cases there is a transition after the trio to provide a modulation to the original key for the da Capo of the minuet. The following examples anticipate Beethoven's effective use of a third relationship:

(The first key is the minuet, the second is the trio.)

Quartets:
    op. 74, no. 1, III, C to A
    op. 74, no. 2, III, F to D♭
    op. 77, no. 1, III, G to E♭
    op. 77, no. 2, II, F to D♭

Symphonies:
    no. 99, III, E♭ to C
    no. 104, III, D to B♭

(See page 15 for other examples of Haydn's use of third relationship.)

The trio is in relative minor in Quartets:
    op. 3, no. 3, III
    op. 76, no. 3, III

In Quartet, op. 3, no. 5, III, the trio is in subdominant.

The most frequent keys for trios are tonic, tonic of the opposite mode, or a major key which is a major or minor third below tonic. Dominant, subdominant and relative major and minor cannot be considered typical keys for trios in Haydn minuet movements.

Referring to Example 2 as a typical song form and trio of the classical period notice the following characteristics:

1. Part a consists of an antecedent phrase of conventional length (four measures) and a consequent phrase which is extended and closes with a conclusive cadence in the dominant or tonic.

2. Part b is a phrase or two usually based on part a material leading to a suspensive (half) cadence.

3. The return of part a is usually extended to more measures than the original part a.

4. The trio is the same form but generally of slighter nature and with less extension.

In the late symphonies and quartets Haydn expands the form by:

1. Increasing part a to a double period as in Symphonies nos. 101 and 102, III.

2. Expanding part b to a phrase group which is developmental in nature as in Symphonies nos. 100 and 104, III.

3. Injecting the character of extension and thematic development through extensive modulatory and nonconclusive phrase groups throughout the form as in Quartets:

    op. 64, nos. 3 and 5, III
    op. 74, no. 1, III
    op. 76, no. 4, III
    op. 77, no. 1, III

When the minuet and trio take the place of a finale in a piano sonata the form is usually rondo (ABACA) as in H 49, III, or variations are added as in H 29, III.

finales

The last movement of a Haydn sonata cycle will probably be in sonata, rondo or sonata-rondo form. These finales are fast movements usually marked *presto*. They are in two-four or six-eight meter and of a joyous, humorous and exuberant character.

Those finales in sonata form have a tuneful, rondo-like first theme in three-part song form, that is, an independent form with part a repeated and ba together repeated, thus, ‖:a:‖:ba:‖, as in minuets and trios. This theme may be a closed form with a conclusive cadence, or it may not have a definite close but instead move into a developmental transition to the contrasting key of the exposition.

The second theme in the dominant or relative major is usually derived from the first theme but is less well defined formally. New material may be introduced in the closing section. The development and recapitulation follow regular sonata form but with Haydn's usual variations in the recapitulation. Finales of this type are exemplified in Quartets:

    op. 50, no. 6
    op. 54, no. 3
    op. 64, nos. 2 and 6
    op. 74, nos. 2 and 3
    op. 76, nos. 1, 2, 3, and 5

Symphonies:
    nos. 45, 92, 97, 100 and 104

The first rondo (ABA) is rare in finales but does occur in Quartet, op. 64, no. 5.

The second rondo (ABACA) is fairly common in sonatas and occasionally appears in quartets and symphonies. Examples are:

Sonatas, H 19, 35, 37
Quartets, op. 33, no. 2 and op. 54, no. 1
Symphony, no. 101 is an interesting example
with variants as shown in the diagram:

Section:	A	long transition	B	trans.	A	C	A	Coda
Character:	aba		based on A		aba	like B	fugal	
Key:	D		A		D	d	D	

The second rondo based on only two themes or
key areas (ABABA) occurs in Sonata, H 34 and
Quartet, op. 33, no. 6. Because of the alternating of
two themes and the injecting of variation technique,
these movements have the characterter of double
theme and variations.

Instead of employing the conventional third
rondo form (ABACABA) Haydn is fond of giving it
a sonata character by using section C to develop previous material in place of introducing new ideas. His
employment of this sonata-rondo is limited almost
exclusively to symphonies, but it does appear in the
finale of Quartet, op. 33, no. 3. The finales of Symphonies nos. 85, 94, 99, 102 and 103 take this form.

Notice that the final A section in the sonata-
rondo does not usually return as a full statement but
is replaced by the coda which emphasizes a motive
or motives from A. Being monothematic the finale of
Symphony, no. 103, as discussed in Example 4, is a
subtle expression of that form.

Also, it is important to note that, on reaching
the dominant tonality for the first B section, Haydn
is likely to repeat motives from A before introducing
new material. This new material may in some cases
be construed to be a sort of closing theme.

The B sections in a sonata-rondo are comparable
to the second-theme area of a sonata in that the first
appearance of each is in dominant (or relative major)
and the second appearance in tonic. Thus the late appearance of new material in the B sections of Haydn
sonata-rondos gives even those movements a monothematic character, a character especially obvious in
the finale of Symphony, no. 103 (Example 4).

In the finale of Symphony, no. 102 the dominant
(F) is confirmed with V of F at the close of the
transition at m. 67. The next eleven measures (68-78)
are devoted to A material in the dominant; and not
until m. 79 is a new theme introduced. This new
theme is in turn followed by closing and transitional
material so that it sounds like a true B theme which
reappears in tonic at m. 235. The finale of Symphony,
no. 99 follows the same design. However, in Symphony, no. 94 the new theme is less independent and
appears at the close of the section like a closing theme
or codetta.

Because of those aspects of tonal and thematic
design which in Haydn's style are common to both
the sonata and the sonata-rondo form, it would appear
that Haydn regarded these two forms as very closely
related. Make a list of the ways in which these two
forms are related as a result of Haydn's handling of
them.

Additional Examples to Be Noted or Analyzed for Various Stylistic Features

for key relationships

Quartets:

op. 74, no. 3, I in g, II in E
op. 76, no. 6, I in E♭, II in B
op. 77, no. 1, I in G, II in E♭
op. 77, no. 2, I in F, II in D

Piano Sonata, H 52, I in E♭, II in B

In Quartet, op. 76, no. 1, the main key is G, but
the finale begins in g modulating to G in
the recapitulation. The same procedure is
used in Quartet, op. 76, no. 3, IV, the keys
being c and C.

for modulations, juxtaposition of keys and chord progression

Quartet, op. 54, no. 2, II. The main key is C, but
distant keys such as G♭ are used.

Sonata, H 52, I. Common tone modulation from
V of C to I of E.

Quartet, op. 50, no. 6, II. The main key is d, the
exposition closes in F, the development opens
in D♭.

Quartet, op. 54, no. 1, II. Analyze the unusual
modulatory progressions in m. 34-47 and 88-
101.

Symphony, no. 100, IV. Analyze the key changes
especially in the development section.

Quartet, op. 64, no. 2, II. Notice the Neapolitan
sixth at m. 27 and the gradual return to tonic
at the cadence (33-34).

Symphony, no. 92, I. Notice the prolonged augmented sixth chord at the close of the introduction and its resolution to V⁷ of G which
opens the first theme.

Quartet, op. 76, no. 6, II. The entire movement,
titled Fantasia, illustrates an unusual series
of keys and anticipates later nineteenth-
century procedure. The theme is a period
in which the consequent phrase modulates

to a new key and is followed by a transition which modulates to still another key. Because of the constant modulation in the first part of the movement, no key signature is given until m. 60, where the signature of B, the main key, is written. From this point keys closely related to B are maintained. What keys are used in this movement?

Symphony, no. 97, IV. The second theme is introduced in tonic (C) before the modulation to the dominant.

Quartet, op. 76, no. 5, II. Analyze m. 33-61 for change of mode and augmented sixths.

Quartet, op. 50, no. 6, I. Modulation from A to F by deceptive progression.

for nonharmonic tones

Quartet, op. 76, no. 6, II. Appoggiaturas in m. 89, 91, 101, 104, 107, 109.

Quartet, op. 54, no. 1, II. Unusual appoggiatura in m. 15.

for formal or thematic aspects

Quartet, op. 50, no. 6, IV. A sonata with the first theme fully stated in the coda, an unusual procedure for Haydn.

Quartet, op. 54, no. 2, IV. A movement consisting of an adagio section followed by a presto section in three-part song form, both sections framed between an adagio prelude and an adagio postlude. How would you identify this form?

Quartet, op. 64, no. 2, IV. Notice the employment of contrary motion in handling the thematic material.

Quartet, op. 50, no. 6, IV. Here is an interesting play on repeated notes alternating in tremolo fashion between open and stopped strings.

Quartet, op. 33, no. 2, IV. One of Haydn's jokes is in the coda. The pauses leave the listener bewildered as to when the piece really ends.

Symphony, no. 45, IV. This has the famous coda, like a fifth movement, during which the players one by one leave the orchestra.

Quartet, op. 76, no. 2, III. The minuet (not the trio) is a canon throughout.

Suggested written Assignments

1. Write a two-measure motive or a four-measure phrase and use it as a basis for a development section of approximately thirty measures employing sequences, imitative passages and modulations in the style of Haydn.

2. Write a slow movement in ABA rondo form with the B section in tonic minor.

3. Write a minuet and trio.

4. Write a finale-rondo-type of theme in three-part song form, two-four meter and presto tempo.

Bibliography

Geiringer, Karl, *Haydn, A Creative Life in Music*, Garden City, N. Y.: Doubleday & Company, Inc., 1963.

Haydn, Franz Joseph, *The Collected Correspondence and London Notebooks of Joseph Haydn*, ed. by H. C. Robbins Landon, London: Barrie & Rockliff, 1959.

Hoboken, Anthony van, *Joseph Haydn, Thematisch-bibliographisches Werkverzeichnis* (thematic catalog), Mainz: Schott, 1957.

Hughes, Rosemary, *Haydn*, London: J. M. Dent & Sons, Ltd., 1956.

Landon, H. C. Robbins, *The Symphonies of Joseph Haydn*, New York: The Macmillan Company, 1961.

EXAMPLE 1
HAYDN
PIANO SONATA IN G MAJOR, H 27
I
(Complete)

EPISODE

EXAMPLE 2

HAYDN
PIANO SONATA IN G MAJOR, H 27
II
(Complete)

Menuetto D. C.

EXAMPLE 3

HAYDN

PIANO SONATA IN E MINOR, H 34

I

(Complete)

EXAMPLE 4
HAYDN
SYMPHONY NO. 103 IN E♭ MAJOR
IV
(First 161 Measures)

CHAPTER 3

W. A. MOZART

1756-1791

To the superficial listener the music of Mozart seems to sound much like the music of Haydn. Certainly each composer had certain influences on the other: Haydn first influenced Mozart and then Mozart influenced Haydn. Also there are usually some stylistic traits common to all the composers of a specific period and locality. Yet there are many significant differences between Mozart's and Haydn's approach to the classical ideal of a balance of form and content. A comparison of the two composers' styles in some aspects should be helpful in analyzing Mozart and in gaining an insight into his style.

Haydn	*Mozart*
1. Essentiallly Germanic instrumental style, developed in relative isolation. Some Croatian and Austrian folk song influence.	1. The great assimilator. An eclectic, versed in the musical styles of the day but not an imitator. His was a universal expression.
2. Music full of humor, surprise, the unexpected as well as expressive.	2. Form always clearly delineated; no attempt to deceive the listener.
3. Predominantly major, optimistic and extroverted. Robust, essentially diatonic style.	3. More use of minor, a touch of melancholy, introspection. Restless, much use of melodic chromaticism.
4. Unity through monothematic procedure, derivation of themes.	4. Unity through contrast of themes, many themes, but themes which seem inevitable.
5. Influenced by Mozart's lyricism, harmonic boldness.	5. Influenced by Haydn's flexibility, logic, continuity.

Mozart believed that music should always be musical, should never excite or disgust. Mozart's music contains German formal logic and Italian lyricism. His formal structure is always made clear by cadences which define the formal sections.

EXAMPLE 5 (page 40)
String Quartet in D Minor, K 421, I

This and Example 6 are from the first movement of the second of the six quartets which Mozart dedicated to Haydn. In these quartets Mozart demon-

strates the technic of development he learned from Haydn, especially from the op. 33 quartets.

1. This example is the first theme, a balanced period consisting of a four-measure antecedent phrase and a four-measure consequent phrase.
2. Notice the expressiveness of the theme gained from octave and tenth leaps in the melody, the raised 7 to lowered 6 in minor (C♯ to B♭), expressive appoggiatura (B♭ as ninth of V^9 in m. 3, 7, 8) and chromatically altered chords (3).
3. Chords to note: V_2^4 of IV in m. 5; IV_6 with B♮ to the augmented sixth chord in m. 6.
4. All forms of the d minor scale appear:
    a. descending melodic in the bass of m. 1 and 2;
    b. ascending melodic in lower voice of m. 7;
    c. harmonic minor in m. 3 and 7 in the upper voice. Notice the close juxtaposition of B♭ in the upper voice and B♮ in the lower voice of m. 7.
5. The G♯ in m. 7 is an appoggiatura. What is the third (E-G♯) of m. 4?
6. How many suspensions can you locate? Where?

EXAMPLE 6 (pages 40-42)
String Quartet in D Minor, K 421, I

These are the opening measures of the development section. The opening key is E♭, one-half step above tonic d.

1. The first twelve measures move from E♭, through a♭, to establish a. The remaining measures (12-18) in the example are a contrapuntal development of the first two measures of the theme going from a to d to g. Elements of the third measure of the theme and the closing theme become similarly involved in the remainder of the development.
2. Measure four is interesting because the chord spelled F A C E♭ is really F A C D♯, an augmented

sixth chord resolving to I_4^6 in a. The E♭ (D♯) to E on the last beat is an anticipated resolution to I_4^6 of a, and drops to C instead of remaining on E in m. 5.

3. Measures 5-7 provide a series of appoggiaturas and suspensions over the dominant of a. Even this dominant pattern is the second measure of the theme.

4. What is the harmony in the first half of m. 8?

5. The lower auxiliary tone characteristic of the second measure of the theme is present in seven of the first eight measures.

6. Considering m. 5-12 to be in a, the harmony of m. 10 is VII_5^6 of IV.

7. Carefully analyze m. 13-14 and 16-17 for non-harmonic tones. This of course involves a careful definition of the harmonic content of these four measures.

EXAMPLE 7 (pages 41-45)
Piano Sonata in C Minor, K 457, I

This quotation, from the first movement of a sonata from Mozart's early mature period, illustrates the variety of thematic material typical of the composer.

1. The first theme itself contains two distinct ideas:
   a. the eight-measure period (1-8)
   b. the second half of the theme (9-18)

   A third idea is the connecting or transitional melody (23-30).

   A fourth is the real second theme beginning at m. 36.

   A fifth set of motives makes up the closing material (m. 59-70).

   The development includes no new material but the recapitulation (not quoted) introduces a new connecting or transitional melody (m. 121-126) replacing the one in the exposition (m. 23-30).

2. What is the form of the first eight measures?
3. The chromaticism in m. 10-12 is prevalent in Mozart.
4. The theme begins to repeat at m. 19 but a modulation to E♭ is immediately accomplished (m. 21-23).
5. The connecting theme beginning at m. 23 is repeated in the development section in f (m. 79-83), but is replaced by a new theme in the recapitulation.
6. The second theme beginning at m. 36 and closing at m. 59 consists of an eight-measure period (36-43) followed by a closing phrase, repeated and extended as follows:

   a. M. 44-48 constitute the closing phrase of five measures.
   b. M. 49-59 constitute the repetition and extension of the closing phrase. Extension is accomplished by the prolongation of the f chord (II of E♭) through m. 51-56 and by the addition of m. 57. A diagram of these measures illustrates this:

Phrase (m. 44-48)	Phrase (m. 49-59)
1 2 3 4 5	1 2 3 3 3 3 3 4 4 5
E♭: I———VI	I —————————— I

7. M. 59-71 consist of three phrases serving to confirm the key of E♭.
8. The development starts at m. 71 with the first theme in E♭ leading to C at 75.
9. Except for the transition or connecting theme in m. 79-82, the development consists simply of statements of the five-note arpeggio of the first theme moving through E♭, C, f, g, to c, leading into the recapitulation at m. 100 by V_5^6 of c at m. 99.
10. The recapitulation is unusual only for the new connecting theme in D♭.
11. There is a coda of eighteen measures based on the first theme.
12. Notice that Mozart indicates not only the usual repetition of the exposition but also the repetition of the development and recapitulation together, thus:

   ‖:Exposition:‖:Development, Recapitulation:‖

   This direction to repeat the development and recapitulation appears frequently in first movements of the sonatas and quartets but not in the symphonies. Is it possible that Mozart is thinking in terms of a two- rather than a three-part sonata form in such cases? It hardly seems possible because there is no significant difference in the design of movements with the repeats and those without them.

13. How do you define the third note of each triplet in m. 51-52?
14. Identify each appoggiatura.
15. Identify the harmony on the fourth beat of m. 68 and 70.

EXAMPLE 8 (page 46)
String Quartet in C Major, K 465, I

A slow introduction to a quartet by Mozart or Haydn is a rarity. This is the famous introduction which gives the quartet its nickname "Dissonant." This tonally devious preparation for a movement in C with its ambiguous and strange cross-relations in

m. 2 and 6 is a sample of Mozart's harmonic sophistication.

1. In m. 2, A♭ in the tenor is followed immediately by A♮ in the soprano. The same relationship exists between G♭ and G♮ in m. 6.

2. G changes to g in m. 4, and F changes to f in m. 8. Modulation through change of mode is common throughout Mozart's works (see Example 18).

The excessive chromaticism makes analysis of the first fifteen measures difficult, but m. 16-22 are simply prolongation of V of C leading to the first theme of the exposition.

3. M. 5-8 in F are a sequence of 1-4 in G.

4. Are there any Neapolitan sixths in this example?

5. What is the harmony on beat one of m. 3 and 7? The first note in the alto of each measure is in cross-relationship with the bass of the preceding measure.

EXAMPLE 9 (pages 47, 48)
String Quartet in C Major, K 465, III

This minuet illustrates a three-part song form expanded through contrapuntal imitation, sequence and repetition of short motives. Part a is twenty measures; Part b is nineteen measures; and the return of a is twenty-four measures.

1. The motive in the soprano of m. 8 is carried through each instrument in a different V-I relationship in four successive measures (8-11). Modulatory sequences of this type involving secondary dominants are a basic ingredient of the style of Mozart. M. 28-31 in Part b and 47-50 in the return of Part a are the same type of sequence.

2. Chromatic decoration at the cadence which is typical of Mozart occurs in m. 15, 35-38 (half-cadence) and 54.

3. The measures which extend and close Part a each time (16-20 and 55-63) involve the repetition of a melodic pattern with two different harmonizations so that the nonharmonic tones change from appoggiaturas (m. 17 and 56) to anticipations (m. 19 and 58). M. 62 contains double appoggiaturas and anticipations.

4. Mozart uses the first-measure motive throughout Part b and continues its use as counterpoint against the second and third measures of a on its return (m. 41-42). This gives Part b a developmental character.

5. Compare the tonal design, use of nonharmonic tones and contrapuntal technic of this minuet with the Haydn minuet, Example 2.

6. The trio of this movement is in c minor.

EXAMPLE 10 (page 49)
String Quarter in B♭ Major, K 458, IV

The theme of this finale is a period repeated. This example shows the first statement of the theme: antecedent and consequent phrases, each of four measures. This period is repeated an octave higher and extended by several repetitions of m. 7-8. This is the fourth of the six quartets dedicated to Haydn.

EXAMPLE 11 (pages 49, 50)
String Quartet in B♭ Major, K 458, IV

This finale is a sonata form with rondo characteristics. See p. 37-38 for a discussion of Mozart finales. These first thirty-two measures of the development section exemplify Mozart's marvelous technic of development through contrapuntal fragmentation and imitation combined with modulatory sequences based on the theme in Example 10. Elements of the theme are present in nearly every measure.

A two-measure modulating pattern ascending by thirds begins at m. 10 as follows:

> m. 10-11 in c
> m. 12-13 in E♭
> m. 14-15 in g

The material in m. 14-15 is repeated in 16-17, 18-19 and 20-21.

M. 20-21 begin a new modulating sequence descending by thirds as follows:

> m. 20-21 in g
> m. 22-23 in E♭
> m. 24-25 in c

M. 25 then becomes a one-measure sequence pattern descending as follows:

> m. 25 in c
> m. 26 in B♭
> m. 27 is II of g and leads to V of g

A detailed analysis of this excerpt is recommended.

EXAMPLE 12 (page 50, 51)
Symphony No. 39 in E♭ Major, K 543, II

This slow movement is in sonatina form. The theme is a three-part song form. This excerpt begins at m. 87 of the movement. This begins with the return of Part a of the main theme in the recapitulation and leads through the transition establishing E♭ as the V of tonic for the return of the second-theme material in tonic. Because a piano reduction cannot include a complete definition of all the instrumental lines, it is recommended that the orchestral score be consulted for more melodic detail.

1. The repetition of a phrase or motive in tonic minor to provide a new set of related keys is a common device of Mozart. Here the first phrase of four measures is in A♭. He changes the mode at m. 5 to a♭ which is enharmonic to the key of g♯, which in turn is the relative minor of B which he has established in m. 7-9. At m. 10 he again changes the mode to b (m. 10-12). The diminished seventh chord of m. 13 acts as a pivot to return the tonality to the "flat side" in order to establish A♭ again (m. 14-22).

2. There is an E♭ pedal in m. 20-21 under V and VII[7] of V.

3. What is the harmonic analysis of m. 13-19?

EXAMPLE 13 (pages 51-63)
Symphony No. 40 in G Minor, K 550, I

Symphonies 39, 40 and 41 were composed in the unbelievably short period of about two months in the summer of 1788 and represent the highest expression of the mature classical technic and universal quality of Mozart. An undercurrent of introspection expressing moods of melancholy, defiance and gloom seems to pervade the g minor symphony, especially in the first and last movements. These qualities are nevertheless an expression of universal rather than personal feeling.

1. The first theme is twenty measures long with the beginning of a repeat (m. 21) which ends in transition to the second theme.

2. The second theme is a regular period of two four-measure phrases (44-51). The repeat begins at m. 52, moves into an extension at m. 58 and closes at 66.

3. The phrase, m. 66-72, acts as an extending phrase to the second theme.

4. Beginning at m. 73 there follow three sections of closing material, each with its own theme. These may be called codettas as follows:

Codetta 1. M. 73-88. Sixteen measures consisting of an eight-measure period repeated and based on the head of the first theme. Mozart's closing material is frequently based on the first or main theme.

Codetta 2. M. 88-95.

Codetta 3. M. 95-99.

A four-measure transition leads to the development beginning in f♯.

5. The development may be divided into four sections as follows:

Section 1. M. 104-114. The first four measures of the first theme in sequence.

Section 2. M. 115-134. The first four measures of the first theme combined with a new countermelody in double counterpoint and in a modulating sequence, the themes inverting with each repetition. Thus:

	Modulating sequence			
Measures:	115-118	119-122	123-126	127-134
Themes:	Counter	Main	Counter	Main
	Main	Counter	Main	Counter
Keys:	e-a	d-g	C-F	B♭-g-d

Measures 129-134 constitute a sequence (three repetitions) of m. 3 and 4 of the first theme.

Section 3. M. 135-152. The first six notes of the first theme are developed through a series of harmonies leading to

Section 4. M. 153-164. Retransition. Dominant pedal based on the first-theme figure.

6. The recapitulation is regular except for the transition from theme one to theme two. Theme two is in g. Notice the alterations in theme two to form a minor version.

7. The transition from theme one to theme two is thirty-five measures (191-225) in the recapitulation compared to fifteen measures (28-42) in the exposition. Mozart often writes a more extensive transition in the recapitulation in order to make the tonality of the second theme (tonic) sound fresh on its return. In other words, in "modulating" from tonic (theme one) to tonic (theme two) in the recapitulation, Mozart goes further afield than when he modulates to a new key for the second theme as in the exposition.

8. A short coda (287 to the end) completes the movement.

9. The chromatic line in the second theme produces a sequence of dominants in m. 48-49, 56-57, 232 and 240.

10. Observe the extent of the closing sections of the exposition and recapitulation. This confirmation and reconfirmation of the tonality by much cadencing through I-IV-V-I is prevalent in Mozart's works, including the finales of scenes and acts of his operas.

11. Observe the quadruple appoggiaturas in m. 148, 150 and 152. The one in m. 148 forms another diminished seventh chord one-half step below the F♯ diminished seventh chord. But the other two form a highly dissonant effect rare in classical style. In m. 150 the middle voices a sixth apart move up a half-step while the outer voices a sixth apart move down a half-step forming the V_5^6. In m. 152 the voices are inverted.

12. The ostinato pattern on the dominant results in a highly dissonant sound in m. 155. How do you explain this?

EXAMPLE 14 (pages 63-69)
Symphony No. 40 in G Minor, K 550, IV

This is the usual design for a Mozart finale but the content is unusually concentrated and intense. It is a sonata with a rondo-type first theme much like a Haydn finale. The second theme is contrasted to the first, but the closing material is based on the closing measures of each part of the first theme (m. 7-8 and 15-16).

1. The first theme is an incipient three-part song form. It is incipient because only the last four measures of the first period (5-8) return to complete the second period (13-16).

2. The head (first two measures) of the theme is a "Mannheim rocket," so-called because the ascending tonic arpeggio was a favorite thematic figure of composers of the Mannheim school. Mozart was familiar with the music of these composers.

3. Notice the traditional accented chords, V of B♭, in m. 53-54, which proclaim the entrance of the second theme.

4. Nearly the entire transition is based on the figure of m. 7.

5. The second theme is a period repeated (m. 55-85).

6. The closing section is in two parts: m. 85-101 (eight measures and their repetition) and 102-108.

7. There is a wildly shifting transition which leads to the opening of the development at m. 109-118. Notice the sequence of diminished seventh intervals which are a diminished fourth apart, m. 110-116.

M. 117-118 are the same as Example 13, m. 102-103, and used at exactly the same relative position in the form and for the same purpose.

8. The development deals entirely with the head of theme one and is in four sections:

Section 1. M. 119-131. The arpeggio is altered to form a dominant ninth (minor) moving in a sequence: A^9, D^9, G^9, C^9 to f (m. 123-131).

Section 2. M. 131-159. The theme appears with a sometimes added scale passage in a modulating tonal design. The imitating voices enter with the theme overlapping one another in crowded, stretto texture, producing great intensity.

Section 3. M. 159-171. The arpeggio figure is increasingly expanded in the lower registers under a tremolo in the upper register. The key is c♯ throughout this section, which leads to a deceptive V^7-VI in c♯ (m. 170-171). Compare the range of the arpeggio figures in m. 159-162 to those in 163-166.

Section 4. M. 175-189. The arpeggio figure is altered so that it implies a dominant-tonic progression instead of a single harmony. It sounds rhythmically like the same theme but actually is considerably altered intervallically. The development closes with a rush of voices simultaneously upward and downward to the VII^7 of g followed by an intensely suspensive pause before the entrance of the first theme at the recapitulation.

9. The first theme reappears as in the exposition but without the repeats, and the remainder of the recapitulation is regular with the second theme in g.

10. Analyze the key changes in the development section.

EXAMPLE 15 (page 70)
Symphony No. 41 in C Major, K 551, IV

This remarkable finale is usually considered the apotheosis of Mozart's contrapuntal technic. The movement is cast in the tonal design of a sonata with a coda in which all five themes appear woven into a complex contrapuntal fabric. Themes A and B appear in the first-theme area, but B is ubiquitous throughout the movement. Both B and the first four notes of A appear in contrary motion (inverted) as well. The motive formed by the first four notes of A was used by Haydn in his Symphony, no. 13, IV.

Themes C, D and E are associated with the transitions and second-theme areas. Theme D acts as the real second theme. The closing sections are based on m. 5 and 6 of theme A. The development section is concerned with themes A and B. See Example 17 regarding the coda.

EXAMPLE 16 (pages 70, 71)
Symphony No. 41 in C Major, K 551, IV

This excerpt includes the last eight measures of the development and the opening measures of the recapitulation.

1. The first three measures show theme B in contrary motion in the key of e.

2. M. 3-8 constitute an interesting modulation consummated by a chromatically descending bass and diminished seventh and augmented sixth chords. Observe the unusual effect of m. 3.

3. M. 9-16 present theme A in its original form.

4. M. 17-36 are a developmental transition devoted to the first four notes of theme A in sequential modulations as follows:

Measures:	17-20	21-24	25-26
Keys:	C———	d———	e

Beginning with m. 27 there are five sequential repetitions of a two-measure pattern consisting of an augmented six-five-three resolving to a dominant seventh. Each succeeding pattern is a perfect fifth lower than the preceding one. Analyzed as secondary dominants and altered chords in C we would have:

Measure:	27	28	29	30	31	32
Chord:	aug $^6_5$ $_3$	V^7	aug $^6_5$ $_3$	V^7	aug $^6_5$ $_3$	V^7
		of		of		of
		VI		II		V

Measure:	33	34	35	36
Chord:	aug $^6_5$ $_3$	V^7	aug $^6_5$ $_3$	V^7
				of
				IV

The voice leading in the patterns varies to accommodate theme A (whole notes in the upper staff), but the harmonies are in sequence.

5. Observe the appoggiaturas (marked) resolving to the seventh of each of the dominant sevenths in the sequence (m. 28, 30, 32, 34, 36).

6. Observe the retrograde version of A in the bass of m. 11-14.

7. The bass pattern of ascending or descending sixteenths into the next downbeat in m. 17-36 is a typical Mozart idiom. See the first movement of this same symphony, m. 170-180.

EXAMPLE 17 (page 72)
Symphony No. 41 in C Major, K 551, IV

This example illustrates Mozart's intensive use of the thematic material in the coda. This coda which is as long as the development is in effect a further and even more exhaustive development of the thematic material. Codas of this type, though seldom so comprehensive as this one, are known as terminal developments. They appear frequently in the works of Beethoven but only occasionally in the music of Haydn and Mozart. (See the discussion of four-part sonata form, p. 4.)

EXAMPLE 18 (pages 72-78)
Piano Sonata in D Major, K 576, I

This sonata represents Mozart at his best in the medium of the piano sonata. The first movement is a brilliant work with an extensive development and interesting canonic writing.

1. Theme one is a regular eight-measure period which is repeated with variation. M. 9 and 13 with the free imitative effect anticipate the strict canonic imitation which appears later.

2. The transition begins at m. 16. One might expect the second theme to appear after the A triad at m. 27, but instead a passage in canonic imitation follows, based on the first theme. The canon is at the octave, but the lower voice enters only one-eighth note after the upper voice, an unusually close time interval. The imitation is exact from 28 into m. 33. M. 34-35 form a new melodic figure which is repeated in 36-37. M. 40-41 solidly establish the close of the first part of the second-

theme group. Here Mozart has, like Haydn, introduced first-theme material in the dominant before bringing in a new second theme.

3. The new second theme enters at m. 42. It is a period with a four-measure antecedent phrase (m. 42-45) and an extended consequent phrase of eight measures (46-53).

4. The six-measure closing phrase is reminiscent of theme one in the last two measures (53-58).

5. The development enters with a change of mode, A to a, which provides for smooth modulation to B♭ and g in the following fourteen measures (61-74).

The material developed includes:

a. the closing motive of the exposition, which is stated twice in m. 59-62 and is given extensive treatment in m. 81-97 at the close of the section;

b. the first theme which is treated to short canonic imitations within m. 63-74.

The keys involved in this section are a, B♭, g, a, b, e, A which becomes V of D.

6. Theme one is stated in its original form at the outset of the recapitulation, but the repetition of it becomes a developmental transition based on the scale figure first introduced in m. 10. The transition closes at m. 121.

7. Here, m. 122, Mozart presents the thematic material of the second-theme area (or group) in reverse order of its presentation in the exposition. The new second theme appears first (m. 122-137) and the section with canonic treatment of the first theme appears second (m. 138-155).

8. The second theme beginning at m. 122 is given more extensive treatment in the recapitulation. It is cast as a regular period of eight measures (122-129) and then repeated with variation, closing on a half cadence in b (130-137).

9. At 138-155 the entire section comparable to m. 28-41 in the exposition is presented. Notice that the cadence m. 153-154 is the same as 51-52 even though the order of the preceding themes has been reversed.

10. The closing phrase is comparable to the closing phrase of the exposition.

11. The decorative character of the sixteenth-note passages is idiomatic of Mozart and much of the classical period. There are many interesting uses of nonharmonic tones which should be analyzed in such passages as m. 7, 17-25, 47, 50, 134-135, 150-151.

12. Mozart's frequent ornamental resolution of I^6_4 to V is in m. 45, 51-52, 125, 133 and 153-154.

13. M. 76 has an augmented six-three combined with a trill.
14. M. 92-98 are a prolongation of the dominant, building tension for the return of the main key (D). Analyze the harmony of these measures.
15. Notice the heightened emotional effect of m. 150-152 in the recapitulation compared to their counterpart (m. 48-50) in the exposition.

Examples and Suggestions for Further Study of the Music of Mozart

The apparent multiplicity of thematic material in Mozart is a result of his innate lyricism. Passages of a transitional nature, closing passages and codettas have an independent lyric quality, a melodic significance which makes them sound thematic instead of like the instrumental "busy-work" found in much music of the period.

Movements of a monothematic character, when subsidiary themes are derived from a principal theme, have a quality of thematic variety because even the derived themes have a contrasting and independent character. Movements which illustrate this are:

> Piano Sonata in B♭, K. 498, I
> String Quartet, K. 464, IV
> String Quartet, K. 499, I
> String Quartet, K. 575, I
> String Quartet, K. 590, I and II
> Piano Quartet, K. 478, I
> String Quintet, K. 614, I
> Symphony, no. 35, K. 385, I
> Symphony, no. 39, K. 543, II and IV

In discussing Mozart's forms it is necessary to refer to theme groups or areas because of the many melodic ideas which may be in one section of a sonata or rondo form. The first theme may be a group of melodic entities as in the finale of the Linz Symphony (no. 36), K. 425, where there are seven phrases making up the first theme.

More often the greater number of melodic ideas falls in the second- and closing-theme group of a sonata or the second (B) section of a rondo. In sonatas the second theme (or themes) is set off with one or more codettas of new material or motives from theme one. These codettas involve much repetition of cadence formulae such as I-IV-V-I or I-II-I$_4^6$-V-I, becoming simply I-V-I as the close of the section or movement comes nearer. This is Mozart's way of expressing symphonic splendor. Identify each new closing phrase in Examples 7, 13, 14 and 18.

Mozart is also particularly lavish with themes in the piano concertos. He was quite adventuresome in regard to both form and orchestration in these works. Because of the added feature of the soloist the first-movement forms become longer and more diffuse with special interludes for the soloist, long closing sections and extended transitions. Concerto in C, K. 467, I, contains a theme in the second group which anticipates the first theme of Symphony, no. 40, K. 550. There are several themes in the second group of the Concerto in c, K. 491, I, which enter in a different order in the recapitulation.

first movements

Often the transition to the second-theme group does not modulate to the dominant key but simply closes on V, a half cadence, in the tonic. The second theme then begins on dominant simply by treating V of tonic as I of dominant. Examples of this procedure are:

> Piano Sonata in D, K. 284c, I
> Piano Sonata in C, K. 300h, I
> Piano Sonata in F, K. 547a, I
> String Quartet in D, K. 575, I

The second theme enters in tonic and modulates to the relative major in String Quintet in g, K. 516, I. See the discussion on Mozart rondos, p. 37-38.

Movements with two or more themes in the second-theme group are:

> Piano Sonata in F, K. 547a, I
> String Quartet, K. 465, I (3 themes)
> String Quartet, K. 590, I, both themes are derived from the first
> Piano Concerto, K. 466, I
> Piano Concerto, K. 491, I
> Symphony, no. 41, K. 551, I

The closing themes in most sonata forms, and particularly first-movement forms, are based on a first-theme motive or figure or an entire phrase of the first theme. This quoting of an entire phrase of the first theme at the close of the exposition and recapitulation gives a rondo character to the movement. Finales in sonata form often have rondo character resulting from this procedure. Examples of closing sections based on the first theme are many; a few follow:

> Piano Sonata in a, K. 300d, I
> String Quartets, K. 464, 465 (first theme in contrary motion), 575, 589, 590
> Piano Quartet, K. 478
> String Quintet, K. 516
> Symphonies, nos. 35, 38, 40 and 41

The development section often opens with a short "working over" of the final phrase of the exposition or of the transitional phrase inserted after the close of the exposition. The development as well as the coda of the Symphony, no. 36, K. 425, I, is devoted entirely to the short transitional phrase which leads into the development. This gives it the character of an episode. Other examples of this kind are:

Piano Sonata in D, K. 284c
Piano Sonata in D, K. 576 (Example 18)
String Quartet, K. 575, I
String Quartet, K. 589, I
Symphony, no. 41, K. 551, I

Episodes replace developments in Piano Sonata in C, K. 300h, I; and String Quartet, K. 458, I.

It is not unusual for Mozart to change the order of entrance of the various themes in the recapitulation, as in Piano Sonata in D, K. 284, I; Piano Sonata in D, K. 576, I (Example 18); and Piano Concerto, K. 491, I.

Mozart codas are generally more significant thematically or developmentally than Haydn codas, but they do not have as much importance in the formal design as Beethoven gives them in his works.

In the String Quartet, K. 458, I, the coda is a terminal development of themes one and two because the section following the exposition is an episode so that the order of sections is exposition, episode, recapitulation, (terminal) development.

In the String Quartet, K. 465, I, and the Piano Quartet, K. 478, I, the further development of the first theme in the coda anticipates Beethoven. The same effect is also in the finale of Symphony, no. 35, K. 385.

Many of the characteristics discussed in the preceding paragraphs under first movements can also be found in slow movements and finales which are in sonata form.

The influence of Haydn in some works written after 1783 can be seen in the monothematic character of some movements, the derivation of later themes from the first theme, the use of the first theme for closing material and the entrance of the first theme in the dominant before contrasting themes are introduced. This latter effect is seen in String Quartet, K. 499, I, and Piano Quartet, K. 478, I.

slow movements

The slow movement of a sonata cycle is usually the second, though in an occasional string quartet the minuet is second. The key of the slow movement of a work in major will most often be subdominant and less often dominant. An exception is the Piano Concerto in A, K. 488, with the slow movement in f♯.

The key of the slow movement of a work in minor will be the relative major or the submediant major.

Slow movements by Haydn are often stately adagio tempo, but those by Mozart are usually lyric andante. Two of the few adagio slow movements by Mozart are the String Quartet, K. 450, III, and String Quintet, K. 593, II.

The most frequently used forms for slow movements are sonatina or sonata. First or second rondo are next most frequently used, particularly in the piano concertos. Then there is an occasional theme and variations as in Piano Sonata in B♭, K. 498a, II, and String Quartet, K. 464, III; or extended three-part song form as in String Quartet, K. 575, II, and Piano Sonata in D, K. 576, II.

The sonatina movements seldom have the indication to repeat the exposition, but sonatas, which slow movements of symphonies are likely to be, have the exposition repeated and occasionally (as in Symphony, no. 36, II) the development and recapitulation together as well.

The Piano Concerto, K. 467, II, has the double exposition like the first movement.

The ABA rondo is less frequent in Mozart than Haydn, but examples are in Piano Sonata in C, K. 300h, II; String Quartet, K. 421, II; Piano Concertos, K. 488 and K. 595, II. Because Mozart transitions have a lyric character, the B sections of rondos seem to begin in tonic and in their course modulate to the new key. The Piano Concertos, K. 488 and 595, II, exemplify this. This is true in finale rondos also.

The ABACA rondo is found in Piano Sonata in c, K. 457, II; String Quintet, K. 614, II; and Piano Concertos, K. 466 and 491, II. In the Piano Concerto, K. 466, II, the B section starts in tonic (B♭) and modulates to dominant (F). In the String Quintet, K. 614, II, the B section is the theme of A in the dominant. In the Piano Concerto, K. 491, II, the woodwinds alternate with the soloist in the rondo as follows:

Instrument:	Soloist	Woodwinds	Soloist	Woodwinds	Soloist
Section:	A	B	A	C	A
Key:	E♭	c	E♭	A♭	E♭

The main rondo themes are usually three-part song forms. In ABA forms, the B section is occasionally in tonic minor but not as often as we find it in Haydn.

minuet movements

Mozart's handling of the minuet movement is generally more ingenious than Haydn's. It is possible that the latter learned much from the former in this regard.

Expansion of the song form boundaries through cadence avoidance, sequence and motivic development of a sonata-like theme is found in the following minuets:

String Quartet, K. 387, II, has sonata design.
String Quartet, K. 464, II, is highly extended.
String Quartet, K. 575, III, is highly extended.
String Quartet, K. 589, III, has an extra long trio. How is it extended?
String Quintet, K. 515, II, has an extra long trio.
String Quintet, K. 614, III. Notice the repeats in the trio.

The Quintet for Strings and Clarinet, K. 581, III, has two trios.

The key relationships of the trios to the minuets remain conventional: tonic, dominant, subdominant or tonic of the opposite mode. When the main key is minor, the trio will probably be in the tonic major. Mozart uses the dominant and subdominant relationships more than Haydn, but not third relationship as Haydn does.

finales

Mozart finales are either sonatas or rondos and only occasionally theme and variation form. Two important theme-and-variation finales are String Quartet, K. 421, IV, and Piano Concerto, K. 491, III. The latter is a splendid example of Mozart's orchestral genius. There are seven variations and a coda with the woodwinds participating equally and alternating with the piano. The variation technic goes beyond simply ornamental variation to freer character variations. Variation IV is in E♭ and VI is in C. The piano and orchestra take turns introducing successive variations in much the same way they alternate in the second movement.

The sonata finales usually have rondo-type themes like Haydn's. Usually the exposition is repeated and often there are the signs to repeat the development and recapitulation together. Finales in sonata form include:

Piano Sonata in C, K. 300h, III, has an episode in place of a development.
String Quartets:
K. 387, IV, fugal statement of themes.

K. 458, IV, has three themes in the first group, two themes in the second group and all return in the recapitulation.
K. 464, IV, terminal development.
K. 465, IV, has three themes in group two. The third is in third relationship: E♭ in the exposition and A♭ in the recapitulation. The coda is a terminal development.
K. 499, IV, terminal development.
K. 590, IV, based on one theme with long developmental transitions.
String Quintet, K. 593, IV and
Symphonies, K. 385 (Haffner), K. 425 (Linz), K. 504 (Prague), K. 543 (no. 39), K. 550 (no. 40) and K. 551 (Jupiter).

Mozart uses several variations on the basic rondo concept. Some are unclassifiable, as in the Violin Concertos, K. 216, 218 and 219, III, which involve free alternation of several tunes. The latter is a minuet with a Turkish rondo in duple time inserted as one of the sections of the larger rondo.

Mozart alters the conventional rondo and sonata-rondo patterns by frequently using an ABACBA design for rondos and ABA-Development-BA design for sonata-rondos. This design is sometimes called the Mozart rondo because of its characteristic use by him. In the rondo section C is a new theme or is transitional in nature as in:

Piano Quartet, K. 478, III. The C section is based on the closing phrase of transition from A. The B section opens in tonic, then modulates.
String Quintet, K. 516, IV. The long A theme has an aba cdc form. The C section is a new theme.
Piano Concerto, K. 488, III.

The sonata-rondo in this form has the effect of a reversed order for sections A and B after the development. The development may be based on the A theme or on transition material. Examples of the ABA-Development-BA forms are:

String Quartet, K. 575, IV. B is based on A, and C is a development of A.
String Quintet, K. 515, IV.
Piano Concerto, K. 466, III. The coda is based on B.
Piano Concerto, K. 595, III. The first B begins in tonic and modulates to dominant.
Piano Sonata in D, K. 576, III. This is a monothematic sonata-rondo. All sections are based on the same theme.

The conventional third rondo (ABACABA) is found in Piano Sonatas, K. 284c and K. 300d, III. The conventional sonata-rondo (ABA-Development-ABA) is found in Piano Concerto, K. 467, III, and String Quintet, K. 614, IV. The latter is a monothematic movement designed like the finale of Symphony, no. 103 by Haydn (Example 4).

In rondos and sonata-rondos it is not unusual for Mozart to start the first B section in tonic and then modulate to dominant in the course of it. Also the lyric nature of Mozart themes sometimes gives the B section a more independent form than in Haydn. See String Quartet, K. 428, IV, in which the B section is a double period repeated. Also it should be noted that where Haydn replaces the last A section with a coda based on A, Mozart nearly always brings in a full statement of the A theme before the coda or in the coda.

Two other variants of the rondo design are:

> Piano Sonata in A, K. 300i, III, with an ABCBAB design, and
> Piano Sonata in Bb, K. 498a, IV, with an ABAC-Development-A design.

The String Quartet, K. 428, IV, is a sonatina form with rondo-type themes and with a one-measure pause in place of a development, thus:

> Exposition ⌒ Recapitulation and Coda
> (based on the first theme).

Finales in sonata, rondo or sonata-rondo form usually have first themes or A themes in incipient three-part song form in which there is only a partial return of part a after part b, as in Example 14. Some themes are phrase groups or extended song forms.

Additional Examples to Be Noted or Analyzed for Various Stylistic Features

melodic structure

An analysis of Mozart themes will reveal the importance of appoggiaturas, auxiliary and double auxiliary notes in their construction. These effects are inherent even in the unison themes of String Quartets, K. 428, I, m. 1-4, and K. 499, IV, m. 1-11.

The measured trill is used to create energy and momentum in transitions and closing passages. It is ubiquitous in Mozart's works; the following are examples:

> String Quartet, K. 387, I, m. 39-42
> String Quartet, K. 465, IV, m. 388-390
> Piano Concerto, K. 595, III, m. 102-105
> Symphony, no. 36, K. 425, I, m. 204-207

> Symphony, no. 39, K. 543, IV, last 41 measures

The long, fast trill is used almost invariably in piano concertos over the dominant harmony at cadences which close a section of the sonata form.

Compare the first four notes of theme A in Example 15 to the four-note fugue subject (m. 1-4) of String Quartet, K. 387, IV. This movement incorporates fugal texture in sonata form. The return of the four-note subject of theme one in theme two results in a double fugue effect.

The second theme of String Quartet, K. 458, III, has an interesting harmonization involving mode changes and an unusual opening note for each phrase of the melody. See measures 14-20.

The development section of String Quartet, K. 465, I, is a good example of thematic transformation through interval expansion and rhythmic tightening of the principal motive.

A ragtime effect involving a three-note melodic figure cast in a four-note rhythmic figure occurs in String Quartet, K. 590, IV, in the development section. See m. 135-136, 140-142, 145-147 and so forth. The four-note rhythmic figure is common in sequential repetitions, as in m. 137-138, but the straight repetition is unusual.

Compare the melodic figure in Example 14, m. 3 and 7, with Piano Concerto, K. 595, I, m. 39-45.

for harmonic structure

Pedal points in Piano Sonata in a, K. 300d, I, and in String Quartet, K. 464, III, Variation VI and Coda.

Neapolitan sixths in Piano Concertos, K. 466, I, m. 49, and K. 488, II, m. 9-10. K. 466, I, also illustrates a sequence involving secondary dominants in m. 33-38 and other statements of that theme.

key relationships

The false, or sham recapitulation is a full statement of the first theme (or at least a phrase of it) in a key other than tonic at a point toward the close of the development section when the recapitulation might be expected. This is soon followed by the true recapitulation in the right key. An example of this is in Symphony, no. 38, I, at m. 189-195. See also Brahms, Symphony, no. 3, I, for an example of false recapitulation, m. 112-115.

Third relationships are not frequent in Mozart. Some examples are:

> Symphony, no. 40, K. 550, I is in g, II is in Eb.
> String Quintet, K. 516, I is in g, III is in Eb.

String Quartet, K. 465, IV, in C. The third theme of the second group is in E♭ and returns in A♭.

String Quartet, K. 499, I in D. The second section of group two is in F and returns in B♭.

String Quartet, K 589, IV in B♭. In the development section just before the retransition (m. 66-74) there is a section in D♭ reached by common-tone modulation. The retransition following this presents the theme in contrary motion. Note the resemblance of this theme to that of the Haydn Quartet, op. 33, no. 2, IV.

Symphony, no. 36, I, in C. The second theme opens in e and the repetition opens in a.

In String Quartet, K. 590, II, the development section closes on V of the relative minor, like some preclassic works.

SUGGESTED WRITTEN ASSIGNMENTS

1. Write a song form in the style of a Mozart finale theme.
2. Write a minuet involving extension and cadence avoidance.
3. Write a short development, about thirty measures, on a motive or phrase in the style of Mozart using sequences involving secondary dominants and/or a chain of dominants with roots descending by fifths.

BIBLIOGRAPHY

ABRAHAM, GERALD, et al., The Mozart Companion, New York: Oxford University Press, 1956.

BADURA-SKODA, EVA, Interpreting Mozart on the Keyboard, London: Barrie and Rockliff, 1962.

BIANCOLLI, LOUIS L., The Mozart Handbook, Cleveland: The World Publishing Company, 1954.

BLOM, ERIC, Mozart, London: J. M. Dent & Sons, Ltd., 1949.

BURK, JOHN N., Mozart and His Music, New York: Random House, Inc., 1959.

DAVENPORT, MARCIA, Mozart, New York: Charles Scribner's Sons, 1956.

DENT, EDWARD J., Mozart's Operas, London: Oxford University Press, 1947.

DEUTSCH, OTTO, Mozart and His World, New York: Bärenreiter, 1961.

DUNHILL, THOMAS F., Mozart's String Quartets, London: Oxford University Press, 1927.

EINSTEIN, ALFRED, Mozart, His Character, His Work, New York: Oxford University Press, 1962.

GIRDLESTONE, GUTHBERT M., Mozart's Piano Concertos, London: Cassel & Company, Ltd., 1948.

HUTCHINGS, ARTHUR, A Companion to Mozart's Piano Concertos, New York: Oxford University Press, 1950.

JAHN, OTTO, W. A. Mozart 6th ed. by Hermann Albert, 2 vols., Leipzig: Breitkopf and Hartel, 1923-1924.

LANG, PAUL HENRY, The Creative World of Mozart, New York: W. W. Norton & Company, Inc., 1963.

RICHNER, THOMAS, Orientation for Interpreting Mozart's Piano Sonatas, Bureau of Publications, Teachers College, Columbia University, 1953.

SAINT-FOIX, Georges, The Symphonies of Mozart, London: Dennis Dobson, 1947.

TURNER, W. J., Mozart, the Man and His Works, New York: Alfred A. Knopf, Inc., 1938.

EXAMPLE 5
MOZART
STRING QUARTET IN D MINOR, K 421
I
(First 8 Measures)

EXAMPLE 6
MOZART
STRING QUARTET IN D MINOR, K 421
I
(Measures 42-59)

EXAMPLE 7
Mozart
PIANO SONATA IN C MINOR, K 457
I
(First 107 Measures)

EXAMPLE 8
MOZART
STRING QUARTET IN C MAJOR, K 465
I
(Introduction, First 22 Measures)

EXAMPLE 9

Mozart
STRING QUARTET IN C MAJOR, K 465
III
(First 63 Measures)

EXAMPLE 10
Mozart
STRING QUARTET IN B♭ MAJOR, K 458
IV
(First 8 Measures)

EXAMPLE 11
Mozart
STRING QUARTET IN B♭ MAJOR, K 458
IV
(Measures 134-165)

EXAMPLE 12

Mozart

SYMPHONY NO. 39 IN Eb MAJOR, K 543

II

(Measures 87-108)

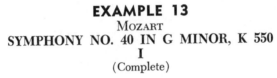

EXAMPLE 13
Mozart
SYMPHONY NO. 40 IN G MINOR, K 550
I
(Complete)

EXAMPLE 14
Mozart
SYMPHONY NO. 40 IN G MINOR, K 550
IV
(First 198 Measures)

D.C.

EXAMPLE 15
Mozart
SYMPHONY NO. 41 IN C MAJOR, K 551
IV
(Themes)

EXAMPLE 16
Mozart
SYMPHONY NO. 41 IN C MAJOR, K 551
IV
(Measures 216-253)

EXAMPLE 17

MOZART

SYMPHONY NO. 41 IN C MAJOR, K 551

IV

(Measures 384-389)

EXAMPLE 18

MOZART

PIANO SONATA IN D MAJOR, K 576

I

(Complete)

W. A. MOZART

LUDWIG VAN BEETHOVEN

1770-1827

With Beethoven the classical rhetoric becomes more dramatic, more personal, more introspective, more an expression of human aspiration and determination. Along with deep philosophical implications, there is also boisterous, uncomplicated humor. Themes are shorter and more epigrammatic, actually pregnant motives which generate longer, more expansive forms. Themes are important for what they become. The developmental process permeates the musical fabric to bring to life all the possibilities inherent in the germinal motive or theme.

Many of the formal and expressive elements closely associated with the musical romanticism of the nineteenth century are prefigured in the music of Beethoven. These elements which forecast styles to come include:

a. A shift of the weight of interest and climactic focus from the first to the last movement of three- and four-movement works;
b. Linking of movements by transition so they are formally connected;
c. Use of cyclic recall of themes to relate later movements to earlier movements;
d. Use of descriptive titles and descriptive musical effects;
e. Use of "motto" themes or germinal motives to provide greater unity;
f. Use of the introduction as an integral part of the form by referring to it later in the movement;
g. Injection of melodic ideas of operatic vocal character into instrumental works.

Dissonance, which has heretofore been used to provide piquancy, is now dwelt on, pointed up, dramatized. Beethoven's harmonic vocabulary is not greatly advanced over Mozart's, but Beethoven emphasizes harmonic effects which Mozart would have passed through in a more polite and casual manner. For example, minor dominant-ninth chords are common enough in Mozart, but would he have dramatized that chord the way Beethoven does in his Piano Sonata, op. 90, I, Example 24, m. 53-54 and 196-197?

In Beethoven, form is altered more and more to serve content. Form becomes the servant of the dramatic or lyric possibilities contained in themes or motives. Altered formal sections, cadence elision or avoidance, unexpected expansions, insertions or deletions of material, and strong contrasts of tonality, texture and dynamics contribute to a dynamic balance of form and content which reflects the vicissitudes of life itself.

His genius lies in his ability to draw from a germinal melodic or rhythmic motive those expressive possibilities which will produce the character desired, be it repose, humor, heroism, resignation or defiance. One melodic or rhythmic motive through repetition, sequence, tonal and textural manipulation may serve as the basis for an entire movement.

EXAMPLE 19 (pages 91-97)
Piano Sonata in D Minor, Op. 31, No. 2, I

The evolution of Beethoven's style can be traced through his piano sonatas and symphonies. The piano sonatas contain many formal innovations and seem to be his choice of form and medium when exploring new musical possibilities. This sonata was written in 1802 and contains several formal innovations.

1. There are several elements in the first-theme group:
   a. The dominant triad of m. 1-2;
   b. The eighth-note motive in m. 2-6 from which the second theme beginning at m. 42 is derived;
   c. The developmental restatement of the (a) idea combined with the answering turn in

m. 21-40. These measures of course act also as transition to the second theme.

2. The main theme contains several dramatic effects:

   a. The alternating slow and fast tempos;
   b. The rush to the high F in m. 13;
   c. The brooding effect of m. 17-18 leading to the resolution back to tonic;
   d. The progressive building of harmonic tension through m. 21-40.

3. The second theme is in dominant minor, a minor, and unusual because the relative major is heretofore the conventional second key for works in minor. The theme opens on V of the dominant which is fairly common in Beethoven.

4. The second theme consists of 2 four-measure phrases followed by a third which dissolves into the closing group at m. 55.

5. The closing area is in two sections:

   a. M. 55-74 in which the Neapolitan chord is emphasized;
   b. M. 75-87 in which a two measure idea is repeated. What is the relationship of the right and left hand parts in each repetition?

6. A short transition on open octaves leads to the development section and the motive of m. 1-2. The first section of the development (m. 99-121) is the same material as the transition (m. 21-41).

7. The remainder of the development (m. 121-142) is a retransition prolonging the dominant and building suspense.

8. The recapitulation begins at m. 143 with the dominant arpeggio. But here Beethoven extends the original A fermata of the second measure by injecting a recitative passage before the allegro eighth-note phrase. Here he borrows operatic drama to serve the instrumental sonata. The cadence at m. 152 is the same as at m. 6 and is followed by the C arpeggio as at first. The inserted recitative is in f ending on the tone A♭, which becomes G♯ in the V of f♯, at the beginning of the transition to the second theme. See Sonata, op. 110, IV, and Symphony, no. 9, IV, for other examples of instrumental recitative.

9. Notice that here he does not use the original transition material which also appeared as development, but instead uses a new way to get to the second theme (m. 159-171).

10. The second theme returns at m. 171 and the remainder of the recapitulation is regular.

11. Many opening themes in Beethoven consist of two statements or phrases with the second a free sequential repetition at an interval of a second or a third above or below the first. Here the first six measures form one statement in d and the seventh begins a second statement a third higher in F. For similar openings see Examples 21 and 24, and also Piano Sonatas, op. 2, no. 3, I and IV; op. 57, I; and Quartet, op. 59, no. 2, I.

12. In addition to the usual modulation technics of Mozart and Haydn, Beethoven also accomplishes key changes by reducing the texture to a single tone or octave, holding or repeating the single tone to obliterate its previous tonal function, and then using it as part of the new tonality or shifting up or down to other tones which will imply new tonality. When there is no shifting from the single tone, it is of course modulation by common tone. If it moves to another tone before new harmony is introduced it may have leading tone function. This manner of accomplishing modulation provides for both dramatic contrasts of texture and distant modulation. It is so frequent in Beethoven's music as to be a hallmark of his style. It is exemplified twice in this example:

   a. At m. 87-93 where A moves to G then to F♯ as part of the D chord;
   b. At m. 158-159 where A♭ is mediant in f becoming G♯ and supertonic of f♯.

13. Another characteristic of Beethoven is simply to assume a new key after a caesura such as a suspensive or conclusive cadence, or a pause. This is exemplified at m. 6-7 where, after a half cadence in d, the key of F is assumed.

14. Notice the following:

   a. In m. 6, F♯ in the turn is against F♮ in the d chord; F♮ is actually appoggiatura to E;
   b. The changing tone, or cambiata on the first beat of m. 9 and 10;
   c. The échappées and appoggiaturas in the second theme, m. 42-51;
   d. The Neapolitan chords, m. 55-68;
   e. The B♭ chord over the dominant A in m. 136;
   f. The E♭'s which imply a Neapolitan effect in m. 140-141;
   g. The use of VII$^{7♭}$ of V in m. 12, 38-40, and 169;
   h. The augmented sixth chords in m. 5 and implied in m. 120.

EXAMPLE 20 (pages 98-100)
Piano Sonata in Eb Major, Op. 31, No. 3, II

This sonata, also written in 1802, has no slow movement. The second movement is a scherzo in sonata form and displays Beethoven's robust humor, texture contrasts and modulations accomplished by reducing the harmony to one tone used as a pivot.

1. The first theme is three-part song form. Part a is a period (m. 1-8) with one measure of extension (m. 9), and Part b is a period (m. 10-19) with a two-measure extension leading to the repeat of Part a (m. 20-28). Following the repetition of Part a, a repetition of Part b begins (m. 29-34) but is suddenly interrupted by the transition to the second theme (m. 35-49).

2. The second theme is less significant than the first, being hardly a theme at all, and actually more in the nature of a closing passage confirming Eb. It is a phrase (m. 50-56) consisting of a two-measure idea constructed and extended as follows: 1 2 1 2 2 2 3. There are then six measures of transition: one version leading to a repeat of the exposition and one into the development.

3. The development, begins with a partial statement of the first theme in F. This leads to the transition material used in the exposition and another partial statement of the first theme in C followed by retransition and a regular recapitulation.

4. The staccato bass provides an energetic quality to the first theme. At m. 10 the texture is reduced to open octaves, allowing for a typical Beethoven modulation back to V^7 of Ab.

5. At m. 34 the sudden change of texture (octaves to full chords) and dynamics (pp to ff) is also typical.

6. Notice that m. 29-33 imply f, but instead we get F. Also m. 37-38 imply bb but at m. 39 we get Bb.

7. M. 42-48 are devoted to prolonging the VII^{7b} of Eb, the key of the approaching second theme.

8. In the recapitulation (not quoted) at m. 139, the octave C (as in m. 34), which implies the dominant of f, shifts up a half step to Db, becoming dominant of Gb, again the typical Beethoven modulation.

EXAMPLE 21 (pages 100-115)
Piano Sonata in C Major, Op. 53, "Waldstein", I

This sonata, written in 1804, illustrates in the first movement a work based on terse thematic material, the use of third relationship and expansion of form.

An examination of the broad formal outlines will reveal the balance and symmetry of this movement.

1. The main theme is a four-measure phrase (m. 1-4) repeated a step lower in Bb with extension and harmonic adjustment to lead back to the dominant of C (m. 5-13). The four-measure idea is repeated in C at m. 14-17 and repeated this time a step higher in d (m. 18-21). M. 22 is an extension, repeating the motive of m. 21 over an augmented sixth chord and leading to the transition.

2. M. 23-34 are a transition devoted to prolonging the B, the dominant of E, in which key the second theme enters.

3. The second theme is in the third-related key of E and is a period repeated (m. 35-50).

4. M. 50-65 are the closing extension of the second theme and lead to the codetta.

5. The codetta (m. 66-74) introduces a new motive which is also used in the transition back to C (for the repeat of the exposition) and to F for the opening of the development (m. 74-90).

6. The unusual length of this transition at the close of the exposition is necessitated by the need to modulate smoothly from E back to C (or F for the development). The introduction of a new motive for the codetta and transition (m. 66-67, 76-77 and 80-90) is to be expected in this style.

7. The development beginning at m. 90 is in three sections:

   a. M. 90-112 deal with the two figures in m. 3 and 4 of the first theme.
   b. M. 112-142 are devoted to the closing material following theme two. See m. 50-65.
   c. M. 142-155 are the retransition prolonging the dominant for the return of the first theme in the recapitulation.

8. The recapitulation of the first-theme section is regular except for a deception (Ab instead of G) in m. 168 which leads to an insertion of five extra measures (169-173) before the repetition of the first theme at 174.

9. M. 174-181 are the same as 14-21, but the next two measures (182-183) replace m. 22 of the exposition in order to throw the tonal center to A, a fifth below E, for the transition and second theme. Only one extra measure is required to make this adjustment.

10. The transition (m. 184-195) is the same as the exposition but on the dominant of A instead of E.

11. The second theme is in A for one phrase, then moves to C in the second phrase. Its repetition, the closing section, codetta and transition to the

coda (m. 200-249) are nearly identical to the respective sections of the exposition.

12. The coda is a terminal development beginning at m. 249. M. 249-283 are concerned with the first theme; m. 284-295 deal with the second theme; and the last eight measures constitute one of those sudden, brilliant, closing flourishes based on the first theme so frequent in the sonatas of Beethoven.

13. Beethoven's method of extending by cadence repetition is well exemplified in the closing section of the second theme, m. 50-60. The harmony is simply I and V^7 of E alternating, first at the rate of half notes (m. 50-57), then quarter notes (m. 58), then eighth notes (m. 59). This acceleration of the harmonic rhythm of a simple progression is typical of Beethoven's ability to create excitement with commonplace harmonic material.

14. The harmony of the second theme (m. 35-36) involves two consecutive V^7-VI progressions as noted. Of course the two measures are all in E with the $G\sharp^7$ acting as secondary dominant.

15. The change from f to F in m. 239-241 is unexpected. Why might Beethoven have done this instead of retaining the Ab's and Db's?

16. Notice that a terminal development so closely akin to the first development tends to give the movement a broad two-part form:

A
_____
Exposition   Development
B
_____
                  Terminal
Recapitulation   Development

This is sometimes the case with a long terminal development. Another example of this formal structure is Symphony, no. 8, IV.

17. M. 80-90 include five sequential repetitions of a two-measure pattern, each of which is made up of three sequential repetitions of a three-note pattern, very dangerously close to too much of a good thing. See Example 25 for another long sequential series.

18. Notice that immediately following m. 74, which closes the second-theme area in E, there is tonal movement to e on the way to reestablishing C. Likewise in the recapitulation there is the change of mode from A to a, only much earlier, at m. 200, in order to place the entire closing section of the second theme in C.

19. Augmented sixths are used at important modulatory points or cadences: m. 22, 111, 182 and 258.

20. Double auxiliary tones are used for the pattern of m. 278-279.

EXAMPLE 22 (page 116)
Symphony No. 3 in Eb Major, Op. 55, "Eroica", II

This slow movement is a funeral march cast in sonata form.

1. The principal theme is a three-part song form.

> Part a is a period repeated (m. 1-8).
> Part b is m. 9-22.
> Part a modified is m. 23-28.
> Parts b and a are then repeated though not quoted here.

2. Notice the use of the plagal progression I-IV-I to express somber dignity in m. 8 (both endings).

3. Notice the interrupting effect of m. 12 which seems to express grief uncontrolled. This effect is further exploited in the coda, Example 23.

4. The movement to the subdominant side for the reentry of Part a at m. 22-25 further emphasizes the gloomy emotion intended. The progression from the Neapolitan chord to the VII^{7b} is striking (m. 24-25).

5. Augmented sixths add color to this moving theme. Where are they?

EXAMPLE 23 (page 117)
Symphony No. 3 in Eb Major, Op. 55, "Eroica", II

These closing measures based on the principal theme of the funeral march are a superb expression of uncontrolled grief. Here the singer seems to be unable to control his emotion and cannot finish the melody without frequently breaking down. Or it is as if the speaker at the close of his eulogy is interrupted by his own sobs. In spite of these extramusical connotations this close is independently sound in musical terms.

This is an example in which romantic elements invade Beethoven's classical expression. Such elements, however, are never allowed to distort the purely musical focus of classical idealism.

EXAMPLE 24 (pages 117-125)
Piano Sonata in E Minor, Op. 90, I

This sonata was written in 1814 and exemplifies a movement based on a minimum of material but with strong contrasts of texture, mode, dynamics and emotion. The movement is based mostly on the two melodic figures of the first four measures.

1. The first theme extends to m. 24. What is its form?

2. The texture is reduced to octaves (m. 25-29) for a sudden shift into C (m. 29-32), a change to a (m. 33-36) and then to B♭ (m. 37-39).

3. The single B♭ at m. 39, acting as a pivot, becomes the leading tone, A♯, of b, the key of the second theme. Here again Beethoven uses dominant minor instead of relative major for the second-theme key.

4. The emotionally charged second theme covers m. 45-67 with a building of tension to the climax at m. 55 and a relaxation and falling of emotion to m. 67. Compare the right hand of m. 55-58 with 24-28.

5. The closing section (m. 67-84), emphasizing a suspension in the bass and the Neapolitan sixth, concludes with a single tone B as a tenuous connection to the development. Notice that the exposition is not repeated.

6. How is the thematic material manipulated in the development section (m. 85-144)? Two interesting effects to note are:

   a. the chromatic lines converging from G to G in m. 104-107;

   b. the retransition (m. 130-143) in which rhythmic augmentation and then diminution are combined with a gradual reduction of a five-note figure to the first three notes of the main theme. This has the effect of toying with notes, but is an unusual way to reintroduce the first theme.

7. The recapitulation is regular with tonal adjustments to place the second theme in tonic. Compare m. 168-171 with 25-28, and compare m. 182-187 with 39-44.

8. The closing section is extended by repetition of its last six measures (m. 223-228), plus the beginning of another repetition (m. 229-231) which leads into a statement of the first theme at m. 232.

9. The coda beginning at m. 232 consists of the first theme, concluding the work in a subdued manner.

10. A sense of momentum is created by the descending bass line in m. 85-100; by an ascending bass in m. 120-130.

11. Notice the E♯ appoggiatura against the E in the V_5^6 of b in m. 44. The same effect takes place in the key of e in m. 187.

12. The E on the downbeat of m. 51 has the effect of an appoggiatura even though it is not really nonharmonic. Why?

13. Analyze the first beat of m. 115, 117, 121, 123 and all of 125.

14. The use of the passing V_3^4 is well exemplified in m. 55-64 and 198-207.

15. Analyze the nonharmonic tones in m. 61-64 and 204-207.

16. The diminished third (inverted augmented sixth) appears in m. 65 and 208.

17. In m. 29-38 and 173-181 the scale passages include a variety of note values: sixteenths, sextuplets, quintuplets and eighth-note triplets. Such effects are frequent in piano music of Beethoven. In order to reach certain points at certain times the running passages are divided into groups of notes of various speeds. This is common in slow movements.

EXAMPLE 25 (pages 125-128)
Symphony No. 9 in D Minor, Op. 125, II

This unique movement is in the form of scherzo, trio, scherzo and coda. The scherzo, however, is a full-sonata form with extensive transitions to the trio and back to the scherzo.

1. The fast tempo of the scherzo makes the dotted half note the unit of time which identifies the beat. Thus each measure is one beat, and the main body of the scherzo falls into groups of four measures, each group like one measure of twelve-four meter. However, a section in the development section presents the thematic material altered to fall into groups of three measures, each group like one measure of nine-four meter. The latter is identified by *Ritmo di tre battute* and the return to four beats is identified by *Ritmo di quattro battute* (rhythm of four beats).

2. This example includes the development section and the first twenty-five measures of the recapitulation beginning at m. 272.

3. The exposition (not quoted) closes in the key of C, an unusual key for a movement in d. A progression of chords in root position from C to a to F to d brings us to the opening measure of the example. Here the long sequence involving alternating major and minor triads with roots successively descending minor and major thirds continues to m. 171. This is a sequence pattern consisting of a major triad to its relative minor triad, repeated a major third lower for a total of nine repetitions, as follows:

C a, F d, B♭ g, E♭ c, A♭ f, D♭ b♭, G♭ e♭, C♭ a♭, E c♯

The fast tempo saves it from seeming too long.

4. At m. 172-176 we see again the frequent device of reducing the texture to open octaves to effect a modulation: here to e. This passage is particularly reminiscent of similar effects in Symphony, no. 7, I.

5. The version of the theme cast in groups of three measures each (m. 177-233) should be com-

pared with the original version in four-beat rhythm beginning at m. 272.

6. How is the sudden modulation to F accomplished at m. 194-196?

7. The V⁷ of E♭ in m. 256-259 is used as an augmented sixth (A♭ treated as G♯) to establish the key of d at m. 260.

8. Analyze the key changes in the development section.

Examples and Suggestions for Further Study of the Music of Beethoven

Nearly every work of Beethoven contains its unique aspects of form, texture or tonal procedure, which attest to his imagination and wide range of expressive technics. The following references are simply illustrative of many interesting effects which may be found throughout his works.

first movements

A movement may be based on one theme, or rhythmic motive as in the Fifth Symphony, I, or it may have several distinct themes or motives as the Piano Sonata, op. 2, no. 3, I, and Symphony, no. 3, I. In some cases what appear to be contrasting themes have a subtle rhythmic or melodic relationship as in Sonata, op. 2, no. 1, I, in which the second theme is in contrary motion to the first theme; or in Sonata, op. 31, no. 1, I, in which the melodic figure of the first theme is given a new rhythm in the second theme. The most prominent examples of this are seen in the various themes in String Quartets, op. 130, 131, 132, and the Great Fugue, op. 133, which are derived from a four-note motive pervading these works.

The first theme or a motive may pervade a movement in such a way that it is present in transitions and closing sections, as in Quartet, op. 18, no. 1, I, and as accompaniment or countertheme to other themes, as in Piano Concerto, no. 4, I.

When the main key is minor, the second-theme area, unlike those of Mozart or Haydn, will often be in the dominant minor instead of relative major, as in Sonatas, op. 31, no. 2, I & III (Example 19), op. 90, I, (Example 24), the second movement of op. 109, and the finale of op. 57 (Appassionata). Occasionally the second theme is in a third-related key to the minor tonic, as in Quartet, op. 95, I, with the first

theme in f and the second in D♭ in both exposition and recapitulation; or in Sonata Pathétique, op. 13, I, in c minor with theme two in e♭ in the exposition.

Third relationship between themes is frequent in works in major keys as seen in Example 21. Other examples of this are:

Sonata, op. 31, no. 1, I, in G with second theme in B returning in E;

Piano Concerto, no. 4, I, in G with the second themes group entering in B♭ returning in E♭;

Trio, op. 97, I, in B♭ with the second theme in G;

Sonata, op. 106, I, in B♭ with the second theme in G;

Symphony, no. 8, I, in F with the second theme entering in D;

In the finale the second theme enters in A♭ in the exposition and D♭ in the recapitulation.

In these cases there is sooner or later a modulation to close the section in the proper key, that is, dominant for the exposition and tonic for the recapitulation.

Because Beethoven often introduces several themes in the second group and closing group it is not uncommon to find two or three keys used in these areas or to find one theme expressed in two consecutive keys. This is true in the third-relationship examples and also in the following:

Sonata, op. 2, no. 2, I
Sonata, op. 2, no. 3, I
Sonata, op. 10, no. 3, I
    Exposition keys: D, b, A
    Recapitulation keys: D, e, D
Quartet, op. 18, no. 2, I

In short, Beethoven expositions are likely to involve more keys and have a more developmental character than Mozart or Haydn expositions; yet, they open in tonic and close in dominant (or relative major). The closing theme often involves motives of the first theme.

Developments are seldom episodic, although a new theme is occasionally introduced along with previously stated material as in Symphony, no. 3, I; Sonata, op. 10, no. 1.

The *Leonora Overture*, no. 1 contains an episode or intermezzo in place of a development. Though the overtures are usually based on sonata form they involve some variants such as the repeat of the development before the coda in *Prometheus* and the return of the first theme in subdominant in *Coriolanus*.

The retransition leading to the recapitulation in sonata movements is highly intensified in the hands of Beethoven. This section at the close of the development becomes a moment of harmonic suspense heralding the return of the first theme. The contrapuntal-motivic manipulations of the thematic material moving through far-reaching modulations in the development focus toward a climax and creation of tension which is relieved with the entry of tonic at the recapitulation. This dramatic effect in tone takes on many shades of emotion. Compare the developments and retransitions of Examples 19, 21 and 24. Each approaches the concept of tension in a different way. The first movement of Symphony, no. 3 should be examined in this regard. The long dramatic development with the retransition containing a false entrance of the theme in tonic against the still-prevailing dominant (m. 394-395) is one of the best examples of this quality of drama which is the essence of the Beethoven style.

The tonal and rhythmic momentum or the constant generative quality of thematic manipulation required an expansion of form in the Beethoven sonata and rondo movements, whether first, slow movements or finales. This expansion is manifested in the Beethoven coda, which goes far beyond simple cadence extension. The coda becomes 1. a broad review of the previous drama; 2. a further development of thematic material; 3. an epilogue commenting on previous action or; 4. a bringing to repose of the previously conflicting motives. Though Haydn and Mozart occasionally wrote an extensive coda, it is Beethoven who makes the coda a regular functional section of the sonata or rondo form.

The first theme or motive is usually restated more or less completely in the coda, imparting a rondo quality to sonata forms. The subdominant or "flat" side of the tonic is emphasized in the first part of the coda, and dominant-tonic relationship closes it.

Often there is a gradual movement toward a quiet mood either of repose or of expectancy which is suddenly broken by a stormy, precipitous closing phrase based usually on a previous theme or motive.

Of what character are the codas of Examples 21 and 24?

Examine the codas of the following first movements to determine which of the above-named functions each serves:

Sonata, op. 2, no. 3
Sonata, op. 7
Sonatas, op. 31, no. 1 and no. 3
Sonata, op. 57

Quartet, op. 59, no. 1
Symphonies, nos. 3, 7 and 8
Piano Concerto, no. 4

slow movements

Like Mozart and Haydn, Beethoven sometimes places the slow movement third and the scherzo or minuet second as in:

Symphony, no. 9
Sonatas, op. 26; op. 27, no. 1; and op. 106
Quartets, op. 18, no. 5; op. 130; and op. 135

Why do you think a fast movement is second in the above works?

A variety of forms are used for slow movements with sonata form most frequent, especially in the quartets and symphonies, and theme and variations next. The following slow movements are in sonata form:

Sonata, op. 10, no. 3 in D, II in d, with episodic development and long coda
Sonata, op. 22 in B♭, II in E♭
Sonata, op. 106 in B♭, III in f♯ with the second theme in D (The coda is a terminal development.)
Quartet, op. 18, no. 1 in F, II in d
Quartet, op. 18, no. 4 in c, II in C
Quartet, op. 59, no. 1 in F, III in f
Quartet, op. 59, no. 2 in e, II in E
Quartet, op. 59, no. 3 in C, II in a
Quartet, op. 130 in B♭, III in D♭
Symphony, no. 1 in C, II in F
Symphony, no. 2 in D, II in A
Symphony, no. 6 in F, II in B♭

Theme and variation movements are in:

Sonata, op. 14, no. 2 in G, II in C
Sonata, op. 57 in f, II in D♭
Sonata, op. 109 in E, III (finale) in E (The theme is a two-part song form.)
Sonata, op. 111 in c, II (finale) in C
Quartet, op. 18, no. 5 in A, III in D
Quartet, op. 127 in E♭, II in A♭
Quartet, op. 131 in c♯, IV in A
Quartet, op. 135 in F, III in D♭
Violin Sonata, op. 47 in a, II in F
Violin Concerto in D, II in G
Symphony, no. 5 in c, II in A♭

Large ABA forms like first rondos are in:

Sonata, op. 7 in E♭, II in C, with long coda
Sonata, op. 31, no. 1 in G, II in C, with a

long coda (The B section is in c like Haydn
    movements of this type.)

Sonata, op. 79 in G, II in g (song form?)

Quartet, op. 18, no. 2 in G, II in C

Quartet, op. 95 in f, II Allegretto in D (The
    B section is a fugal treatment of ma-
    terial.)

Piano Concerto, no. 1 in C, II in A♭

Piano Concerto, no. 3 in c, II in E

The song form with trio design for slow movements is much like the ABA rondo (above) except
that the sections are more independent and are separated by double bars. The first two of the following
four examples are in allegretto tempo and could just
as well be considered in the category of minuet and
trio movements. All but the first of these has a coda:

Sonata, op. 10, no. 2 in F, II in f, trio in D♭

Sonata, op. 14, no. 1 in E. II in e, trio in C

Sonata, op. 26 in A♭, III in a♭

Sonata, op. 28 in D, II in d

The second rondo (ABACA) is used in:

Sonata, op. 2, no. 2 in A, II in D

Sonata, op. 13 in c, II in A♭

Quartet, op. 74 in E♭, II in A♭ with a long
    coda including themes from the A and B
    sections

Sonatinas are the slow movement forms in:

Sonata, op. 2, no. 1 in f, II in F

Sonata, op. 10, no. 1 in c, II in A♭ (The re-
    transition is one chord, V⁷ of A♭.)

Sonata, op. 31, no. 2 in d, II in B♭

Three-part song form constitutes the slow movements of:

Sonata, op. 27, no. 1 in E♭, III in A♭ (The a
    part returns in the coda of IV.)

Piano Concerto, no. 5 in E♭, II in B

An ABABA type of rondo is occasionally used. In
each case there are certain variants which need explanation:

Sonata, op. 2, no. 3 in C, II in E. The gen-
    eral design is:

section: A B A B A Coda

key: E e E E E

Quartet, op. 18, no..3 in D, II in B♭. The de-
    sign is:

section: A B A Development B A Coda

key: B♭ F B♭   B♭ ———

This is somewhat comparable to the
sonata-rondo form of Mozart.

Quartet, op. 132 in a, III in F. The design is:

section: A B A B A

key: F D F D F

In this case F stands for the Lydian
mode on F. The second B is extended.

Symphony, no. 3 in E♭, II in c. Here B is
like a trio:

section: A B A Development   A Coda

key: c C c   c ———

Symphony, no. 7 in A, II in a, is much the
same as the slow movement of Symphony
no. 3. The B section is like a trio, but
the return of both B and A themes in
the coda give it somewhat expanded dimensions like a sonata-rondo combined
with theme and variations:

section: A B A Development

key: a A a

section: A Coda with B and A

key: a   A   a

Symphony, no. 9 in d, III in B♭:

section: A B A B Development

key: B♭ D B♭ G

section: A Coda

key: B♭ ———

The development is like a retransition to
the A section. The coda is a terminal
development.

Symphony, no. 4 in B♭, II in E♭, is a sonata-
rondo with a short coda containing the
theme of A.

The technique of variation is applied throughout
all movements and forms. Sonata themes and rondo
themes are subjected to variation on successive returns. Even the repetition of a phrase or period is
seldom exact but more or less varied.

Slow movements are usually in keys nearly related to the key of the work, that is, keys whose
signature is not more than one accidental different,
or in tonic of the opposite mode. Occasionally a slow
movement is in a true third-related key. There are
nine in this category in the above lists. Which are
they? Notice that three of the five piano concertos
have slow movements in a third-related key.

scherzo or minuet movements

Beethoven expanded the traditional song form
and trio in three ways:

a. Internal expansion through motivic develop-
    ment of a short rhythmic, or melodic pattern;

b. By repetition of the trio and scherzo an extra time, producing an ABABA design;

c. By expanding the scherzo to a sonata form.

Most of the scherzos or minuets exemplify the first kind of expansion in some degree. Prominent examples are:

Sonata, op. 2, no. 2, III, with an extended Part b in the scherzo

Sonata, op. 106, II, with long transition to the return of the scherzo

Quartet, op. 18, no. 6, III, with much syncopation and Haydnesque humor

Quartet, op. 59, no. 2, III, with a trio consisting of two fugal expositions and a stretto on the Russian theme which Mussorgsky also uses in the coronation scene of the opera, Boris Godunov, Example 78

Quartet, op. 127, III, an excellent example of the use of a motive in every conceivable way resulting in a greatly extended movement with meter changes and a coda including both trio and scherzo motives.

The second method of expansion through an additional repetition of the trio and scherzo is illustrated in:

Quartet, op. 74, III

Quartet, op. 95, III. The return of the trio is in a different set of keys.

Quartet, op. 131, V

Symphonies, nos. 4 and 7, III

Sonata, op. 54, I. Here the first movement is in minuet style.

The third method is illustrated in the Symphony, no. 9, II, in which the scherzo is in sonata form and the trio is a five-part song form (abaca) with coda. The scherzo is repeated after the trio and is followed by a coda.

Beethoven is relatively conservative in his choice of key relationships between the scherzo (or minuet) and trio. In six of the nine symphonies and in five quartets the trio is in the main key of the work. The notable exception is in the Symphony, no. 7 in A, in which the scherzo is in F and the trio is in D. This situation is rare indeed. Quartet, op. 95 is another case of unusual key relationship in the scherzo movement.

Otherwise trio keys are usually 1. tonic of the opposite mode; 2. submediant major when main key is minor (usual in piano sonatas); 3. subdominant when the main key is major; and 4. occasionally relative minor in piano sonatas. A real third relationship in this regard is rare.

finales

Beethoven elevated the finale movement to a position of greater significance in the sonata cycle. In some cases it is the climactic movement as in sonatas, op. 27, no. 2 and op. 110, and Symphonies, nos. 5 and 9. In many cases it is at least equally as important in musical content as the first and slow movements with which it is associated. Finales are most frequently in sonata form, third rondo form and sonata-rondo form.

Those in sonata form frequently have a more or less complete statement of the principal theme in the coda which in turn may be of terminal development proportions. This complete or nearly complete statement of the first theme gives a rondo quality to the movement. The first theme of a finale in sonata form is likely to be less independent than was the case with Haydn and Mozart. Instead of a song form closing on a conclusive cadence, the first theme is likely to merge into the transition without a clear close as in Symphonies, nos. 1 and 4, IV.

The finales of the following works are in sonata form:

Sonatas:

op. 2, no. 1, IV (episode replaces development)

op. 10, no. 1, III (both first and second themes in the coda)

op. 10, no. 2, III (monothematic)

op. 27, no. 2, III (terminal development)

op. 31, no. 2, III (based on one prevailing rhythm; first theme in the coda)

op. 31, no. 3, IV (terminal development; closes with typical quick flourish)

op. 54, II (monothematic, Haydn-style humor)

op. 57, III (theme two in the dominant minor; long coda)

op. 81a, III

op. 101, IV (fugal development and a long coda)

Quartets:

op. 18, no. 2, IV

op. 18, no. 3, IV (long coda)

op. 18, no. 5, IV (first theme in the coda)

op. 59, no. 1, IV (first theme in the coda)

op. 59, no. 3, IV (a sonata in fugal texture)

op. 127, IV (a new theme enters in the coda)
op. 131, VII (based on three distinct themes)
op. 135, IV
Symphonies:
  no. 1, IV (theme one in the coda)
  no. 2, IV (theme one in the coda)
  no. 4, IV (theme one in the coda; ends with sudden flourish)
  no. 5, IV (A quotation from the third movement is unexpectedly interposed between the retransition and the return of theme one.)
  no. 7, IV
  no. 8, IV (has possibly the longest coda in Beethoven literature, 236 measures out of 502 for the entire movement, and is the epitome of brilliance, humor, wit and rhythmic drive)

The third rondo form appears somewhat more frequently than the sonata-rondo. Sometimes there is a full return of the A theme before the coda and sometimes, as in Haydn rondos, only a motivic reference to A in the coda replaces the fourth appearance of A. Some codas simply review previous themes (A and C) or are terminal developments in function. Analyze the following third rondo finales to determine the form of each theme, the key relationships and the function of the coda:

Sonatas:
  op. 2, no. 2, IV
  op. 2, no. 3, IV
  op. 7, IV
  op. 10, no. 3, IV
  op. 14, no. 1, IV (B returns in subdominant)
  op. 22, IV
  op. 26, IV
  op. 28, IV
  op. 53, III
Quartets:
  op. 18, no. 4, IV (sections separated by double bars)
  op. 132, V (Coda has new theme.)
Symphony, no. 6, V
Piano Concertos, nos. 1, 2, 3, III
Violin Concerto, op. 61, III

The following are sonata-rondo finales based on the design, ABA Dev. ABA Coda:
Sonatas:
  op. 27, no. 1, IV
  op. 31, no. 1, III
  op. 90, II

Quartet, op. 18, no. 1, IV
Piano Concertos, nos. 4 and 5, III

The Mozart-type sonata-rondo (ABA Dev. BA Coda) is used in Quartets, op. 59, no. 2, IV, and op. 95, IV. A new theme is introduced in the coda of the latter.

Finales of the following are theme and variation movements:

Sonatas, op. 109, III, and 111, II
Quartet, op. 74, IV
Symphony, no. 3, IV

Sonatina form is used for Sonata, op. 78, II, involving unusual key relationships between themes, and for Quartet, op. 18, no. 6, IV.

Second rondo is the design for Sonatas, op. 49, no. 2, II, and op. 79, III.

The following are unique designs for finales in the Beethoven literature:

Sonata, op. 14, no. 2, III (a type of rondo)
Sonata, op. 49, no. 1, II (a type of rondo)
Sonata, op. 106, V (a transcendental fugue in sonata design)
Sonata, op. 110, IV (arioso and fugue)

Large introductions and codas, introductions which recur later in the movement, the connecting of one movement to the next without pause or by transition, and the use of themes from earlier movements in subsequent movements (cyclic concept) are factors in the Beethoven style which affect style in the romantic period following Beethoven. The addition of a significantly large introduction or coda to the three-part sonata form creates a four-part sonata; the addition of both creates a five-part sonata.

The following works have significant introductions which recur later in the movement. Thus the introduction not only becomes an additional section in the form but is integrated into the movement by its reappearance.

Sonata, op. 13, Pathétique, I. The introduction theme appears not only between the exposition and development and in the coda, but it is also treated in the development itself.

Quartet, op. 18, no. 6, IV. The introduction theme reappears in the long coda. The form is introduction, exposition, recapitulation, coda. The coda fulfills the function of a terminal development.

Quartet, op. 127 in E♭, I. The slow introduction is short but reappears before and during the development. Note that the second-theme area, closely related to the first, is in g and that the closing material is related to the introduction. The long coda is developmental.

Quartet, op. 130, I. The introduction theme appears frequently throughout the movement and is used in allegro tempo in the closing sections.

Piano Concerto, no. 5, I. The first eleven measures of orchestra chords and piano cadenzas function as a broad I, IV, V, I cadence to introduce the movement. This same effect reappears to introduce the recapitulation (m. 362-382).

Long codas forming an obvious additional section are found in Sonatas, op. 27, no. 2, III, and op. 57, I and III; and Symphonies, nos. 8, IV, and 9, I.

The five-part sonata resulting from the addition of both long introduction and coda is illustrated by Symphony, no. 7, I, and Quartet, op. 74, I.

The cyclic effect is seen in the last quartets, op. 130 through 133, each of which uses the four-note motive shown on p. 84 in various ways. Other examples are:

Symphony, no. 5, in which a theme from III returns in IV.

Symphony, no. 9, in which themes from I, II and III are quoted in IV.

Sonata, op. 27, no. 1, in which the theme of III returns in the coda of IV.

Sonata, op. 101, in which the theme of I returns at the close of III.

These examples are but beginnings of the cyclic idea which is highly developed by later composers from Berlioz (*idée fixe*), Schumann, Liszt (thematic transformation), Wagner (leitmotifs), Franck and Tchaikovsky to Howard Hanson (Symphony, no. 2, *Romantic*, Examples 120, 121).

In the following works are instances where movements are connected by transitions or by indications to start the next movement without pause: Sonatas, op. 27, nos. 1 and 2, op. 101, and op. 106; Symphony, no. 5, and Quartets op. 95, op. 131.

The binding of movements together by the cyclic concept and by transitions leads to the one-movement symphony and symphonic poem of the later nineteenth and twentieth centuries.

Additional Examples to Be Noted or Analyzed for Various Stylistic Features

for modulation

Further illustrations of modulation through reduction of the texture to a single note are seen in the Piano Concerto, no. 3, III, m. 250-265, from the key of c to the key of E; in Piano Concerto, no. 4, III, m. 459-467, from the key of F♯ to the key of C; and in Quartet, op. 95, III, m. 40 (second ending), from F to G♭.

Occasionally a theme begins on a subdominant (IV or II) harmony as in Sonata, op. 31, no. 3, I (m. 1); Quartet, op. 127, I (m. 7); and Piano Concerto, no. 4, III (m. 1-5). In the following two quartets, however, the theme actually begins in a different key from tonic, and tonic is established only at the cadence:

Quartet, op. 59, no. 2, IV:

The theme begins in C and reaches the main key of e only in the last two measures of the nine-measure melody. It is like a harmonic effect of seven measures of VI, one of V, and one of I.

Quartet, op. 130, VI:

The theme starts in c, and B♭, the main key, is established only at the cadence.

In the Sonata, op. 101, III, m. 4, a modulation from a to C is started by changing the V chord (e) to a minor triad (III of C). This type of change of mode will be found frequently in Brahms' music also.

In Symphony, no. 7, III, in the transition from the trio back to the scherzo (m. 233-236), a modulation from D to F is accomplished by moving directly from V^7 of D (A^7) to V^7 of F (C^7) using the tones E and G as the common tones.

In Quartet, op. 135, II, the trio consists of three statements of the theme: the first in F, the second in G, the third in A, which is extended and leads through unison modulation back to the scherzo in F.

for other features

In the rondo, Sonata, op. 14, no. 1, III, the B section returns in subdominant instead of tonic.

In Sonata, op. 7, III, the first part (a) of the trio (minore) is repeated, but the second section (Parts b and a) is not. Why not?

Observe the variety of keys in which the seven movements of Quartet, op. 131, are written. Only the first and last are in c♯, the main key.

An example of an unusually high cello part is in Quartet, op. 132, V.

Beethoven, as we have seen, occasionally introduces a new theme in the coda or writes an episode in the development. In Symphony, no. 3, I, a new theme appears in the development section at m. 284 and again at m. 322 and returns in the coda at m. 581.

What is the form of the theme of the set of variations in Sonata, op. 109, III?

In some of the later works of Beethoven (after op. 59), the exposition of sonata forms is not repeated. Why?

The blending of a theme into transition and the anticipation of a coming theme by the preceding transition is clearly shown in Sonata, op. 49, no. 2, II. In m. 35-47 the transition from section B to the return of A blends the close of B into an anticipation of A. In m. 82-87 the transition out of C blends into the accompaniment figure of the coming return of A.

An interesting dissonance, resulting from simultaneous contrary motion (mirroring), occurs in Sonata, op. 90, II, m. 48-54. All lines in the left hand are moving in contrary motion to the respective right-hand lines so that the left is a mirror image of the right. Thus the measured trill of F♯-G♯ is expressed both ways simultaneously and results in a dissonance unusual for this time. Since the hands of the pianist are mirror images of each other, the fingering of the passage is the same for both hands.

The Sonata, op. 81a, I, contains another unusual dissonance in the coda (m. 230-235), where the overlapping statements of the *Lebewohl*, or coach horn motive result in I against V. Compare this entire passage (m. 223-243) with m. 130-145 of Sonata, op. 90, I, Example 24.

SUGGESTED WRITTEN ASSIGNMENTS

1. Write two or three eight-to-ten-measure examples illustrating modulation by reducing the texture to one tone and moving to the new key.
2. Reduce the exposition and development of the *Waldstein Sonata*, op. 53, I, to an outline of chord changes showing the harmonic rhythm.

BIBLIOGRAPHY

BERLIOZ, HECTOR, *A Critical Study of Beethoven's Nine Symphonies*, translated by Edwin Evans, London: W. Reeves, 1958.

BURK, JOHN N., *The Life and Works of Beethoven*, New York: Random House, Inc., 1943.

COCKSHOOT, JOHN V., *The Fugue in Beethoven's Piano Music*, London: Routledge and Kegan Paul, Ltd., 1959.

EVANS, EDWIN, SR., *Beethoven's Nine Symphonies* 2 vols., New York: Charles Scribner's Sons, 1923-1924.

FISCHER, EDWIN, *Beethoven's Pianoforte Sonatas*, London: Faber and Faber, Ltd., 1959.

MARLIAVE, JOSEPH DE, *Beethoven's Quartets*, New York: Dover Publications, Inc., 1961.

MIES, PAUL, *Beethoven's Sketches*, London: Oxford University Press, 1929.

JAMES, BURNETT, *Beethoven and Human Destiny*, London: Phoenix House, 1960.

KOMROFF, MANUEL, *Beethoven and the World of Music*, New York: Dodd, Mead & Company, 1961.

RIEZLER, WALTER, *Beethoven*, New York: E. P. Dutton & Co., Inc., 1938.

SCOTT, MARIAN M., *Beethoven*, London: J. M. Dent & Sons, Ltd., 1937.

SULLIVAN, JOHN W. N., *Beethoven: His Spiritual Development*, New York: Alfred A. Knopf, Inc., 1927.

THAYER, ALEXANDER W., *The Life of Ludwig van Beethoven*, Carbondale: Southern Illinois University Press, 1960.

TOVEY, DONALD FRANCIS, *Beethoven*, London: Oxford University Press, 1945.

—————, *A Companion to Beethoven's Pianoforte Sonatas*, London: Associated Board of the Royal Schools of Music, 1951.

EXAMPLE 19
BEETHOVEN
PIANO SONATA IN D MINOR, OP. 31, NO. 2
I
(First 175 Measures)

EXAMPLE 20
BEETHOVEN
PIANO SONATA IN Eb MAJOR, OP. 31, NO. 3
II
(First 63 Measures)

EXAMPLE 21
Beethoven
PIANO SONATA IN C MAJOR, OP. 53, "WALDSTEIN"
I
(Complete)

EXAMPLE 22
BEETHOVEN
SYMPHONY NO. 3 IN E♭ MAJOR, OP. 55, "EROICA"
II
(First 28 Measures)

EXAMPLE 23
BEETHOVEN
SYMPHONY NO. 3 IN E♭ MAJOR, OP. 55, "EROICA"
II
(Last 10 Measures)

EXAMPLE 24
BEETHOVEN
PIANO SONATA IN E MINOR, OP. 90
I
(Complete)

Mit Lebhaftigkeit und durchaus mit Empfindung und Ausdruck

EXAMPLE 25
BEETHOVEN
SYMPHONY NO. 9 IN D MINOR, OP. 125
II
(Measures 151-296)

ROBERT SCHUMANN

1810-1856

In Beethoven we find an objective, dynamic motive, which through the process of manipulation and development produces an expansive and extensive musical form, whereas in Schumann we find a self-contained, lyric theme woven into a fabric of frequently changing harmony expressed in a rhythmic pattern, unique and inseparable from the theme which it carries, the whole producing in small form a mood of poetic feeling and subjective imagery. Schumann's inherent lyricism expressed in an inseparable interrelationship of melody, harmony and rhythm produces effective works in small forms and larger works consisting mainly of a string of small enclosed forms.

MELODY: His melody is bound so closely to the harmony and rhythmic pattern which undergirds it that it is not usually suited for free flights of development. A Schumann theme is essentially a German lyric expression, a song expressing a single mood, not an independent motive that can be flexibly manipulated. In Example 27 how could the melody be separated from its harmonic and rhythmic surroundings?

HARMONY: Large forms usually involve augmented harmonic rhythm; their dimensions require broader planes of a single harmony, chord changes at less frequent intervals of time. Schumann's music, however, seems to show the influence of the frequently changing harmony of the Lutheran chorale, a new chord for each beat or half beat. This compression of harmonic change results in a compression of form, a unification of musical elements which cannot be easily broken apart. Notice the B section of Example 28, m. 19-24.

Abrupt modulation or sudden changes of key as in Example 28, m. 23, are common. Modulation resulting from sequential repetition is a favorite device for extension and development. These effects can be seen in Novelette in F, op. 21, no. 1, and nearly any other larger work.

RHYTHM: Pianistic figuration and syncopation are dominating influences on rhythm. Melodies often fall consistently on weak beats, on the weak half of beats, or all parts of the texture may be tied through the downbeat of the measure so there is no attack to define the strong beat. See the following piano works for this latter effect: *Whims*, from *Fantasy-Pieces*, op. 12, no. 4, m. 61-96; *Faschingschwank aus Wien*, I, second episode.

The syncopation figure (eighth, quarter, eighth) so common in Schumann persists throughout Examples 26 and 27.

The use of rhythmic hemiola is seen in two of the *Fantasy-Pieces*: op. 12, no. 1, *Des Abends* (throughout) and op. 12, no. 2, *Aufschwung* (m. 5-6 and 13-14); and also in the Piano Concerto in a, op. 54, III, m. 188-239 where two measures of three-four meter sound like one measure of three-two meter: ♩♪♩♩♪♩♩♪ sounds like ♩♪♩♩♪♩♩♪

FORM: Schumann is at his best in small forms and most consistently effective in slow lyric movements. Thus his short piano pieces and songs are best known along with a few larger works such as the piano concerto, the symphonies, the Piano Quintet in E♭, op. 44 (the first work for this medium), one or two piano sonatas, violin sonatas and string quartets.

He extended the cyclic concept and the connecting of movements to form a continuous whole in such works as Symphonies nos. 1 and 4 and the Piano Quintet.

Occasionally we find the form—exposition, development, recapitulation, development (repeated with variants), coda—as in the Piano Sonata in g, op. 22, III.

The nature of his themes results in developments which consist primarily of sequential repetition, a type of rhapsodic development.

There is a literary inspiration behind much of Schumann's music, and although many works have poetic or descriptive titles they are not programmatic in the sense of later romantic composers such as Liszt and Strauss. The music is imbued with intimate, subjective, poetic fancy in the true romantic sense, but its moods are a result of musical, not descriptive considerations. Even those works based on the notational equivalents of names such as ASCH, ABEGG, EBE, GADE and BACH are little colored by their source of theme.

EXAMPLE 26 (page 133)
Symphony No. 2 in C Major, Op. 61, III

This slow movement is probably the outstanding movement of this symphony, which is really his third, because the Symphony in d Minor, no. 4, was written earlier but later revised. The placement of the slow movement after the scherzo as in this work is also done in Symphony, no. 3, op. 97, in Eb.

1. The form of the movement is sonata with an episode in place of development. Theme one is embodied in this example. It is followed by six measures of transition.
2. The second theme in Eb begins at m. 26. The second part of this theme is a group of sequences based on the motive of the first two measures (m. 36-44).
3. The closing section in Eb (m. 48-62) is also based on the first theme.
4. The episode involving contrapuntal imitation and showing Schumann's interest in the music of J. S. Bach is m. 62-74.
5. The recapitulation with a shortened statement of theme one (m. 74-81) is followed immediately by theme two in C beginning at m. 82.
6. Example 27 consists of the last thirty-nine measures of the movement, including the second part of theme two, the closing section and coda.
7. The characteristic rhythmic pattern ♫♩ and ♪♩♪ is seen throughout the movement in both melody and accompaniment.
8. The expressive appoggiatura on beat one of m. 2 is emphasized, occurring in nearly every measure in the second half of the exposition and development. See Example 27.
9. In m. 5 the appoggiatura G in the melody resolves down a seventh to Ab instead of up a second. This octave displacement of the resolution contributes greatly to the expressive quality of the theme. Also observe that in the same measure the appoggiatura G in the left hand resolves

down to F in normal fashion. The rhythmic difference in these two resolutions of the G is interesting to consider. The process is repeated a step lower in m. 6 involving F to G and Eb.

10. Notice that the theme is a double period and that m. 8 serves as the close of the first period and the beginning of the second period, an elided cadence. The second period, m. 8-19, is extended. How?
11. Observe the suspension on D resolving upward (m. 18-19).
12. Chromatic changes as seen in the second half of m. 6 become more frequent with later romantic composers. Analyze the harmony of this measure.
13. There are seven secondary dominants in the example. Identify them.
14. M. 11 (in Eb) contains II_3^4 to VII_2^4 borrowed from eb.
15. This is a good example for the study of the subtleties of lyric melody construction involving:

   a. The balancing of the rising sixth and octave of m. 1, 3, 8 and 10 with the falling seventh and sixth of m. 5, 6, 12, 13, 16, and 17;
   b. The relationship of m. 7, 14 and 18 to the general contour;
   c. The relationship of motion between m. 2 and 11;
   d. The broad contour with the high point at m. 10 and the low point at 19.

16. Notice that the theme is an independent, closed form which is typical of Schumann.

EXAMPLE 27 (page 134, 135)
Symphony No. 2 in C Major, Op. 61, III

1. M. 1-2 are the repeated cadence closing the first part of the second-theme area. M. 3-14 form the second part.
2. M. 15-29 form the closing section, and the coda begins with m. 29.
3. Observe the secondary dominant of II over the pedal D in m. 1, or could E, C♯ and B on the first beat be considered appoggiaturas to the D^7 (V^7 of V in C)?
4. Beginning at m. 3-4 the motive of m. 1-2 of Example 26 is extensively used in overlapping sequential fashion. See the orchestra full score for part-writing detail showing this effect.
5. The tonic, C, is not stated until m. 6 and is followed by modulation to F, m. 7-13. Notice how the dominant of F is prolonged through two and and a half measures (7-9) with attendant appoggiaturas and passing tones. How would you analyze the second half of m. 7? Could m. 7-13 be

considered as remaining in C? Analyze them from that point.

6. M. 11-13 constitute a plagal effect on the F chord, the b♭ chord being IV borrowed from f.

7. The resolution from m. 14-15 has the effect of a kind of plagal moduation back to C, being II$_5^6$ from c to I$_4^6$ of C.

8. Both the exposition and recapitulation reach a climax in their closing sections. There are several factors contributing to this climax, including:

   a. The chromatically ascending bass (m. 15-23);

   b. The suspensions ornamentally resolved (m. 17 and 19);

   c. The converging lines of the soprano and bass, producing octaves at m. 17, 19 and 21, preceded by diminished thirds at 16 and 20 and the minor third at 18;

   d. The trills in m. 21-28;

   e. The tension produced through appoggiaturas and the diminished third chords (m. 16 and 20) and diminished seventh chords (m. 18 and 24).

9. The prolonged dominant (m. 25-28) followed by the coda produces a broad conclusive cadence to the movement.

10. The coda exemplifies a prolonged subdominant effect resolving finally to dominant and back to tonic in m. 29-32 and repeated in m. 32-35 with parts inverted and again a cadence elision at m. 32.

11. The Neapolitan chord is used in m. 30-31 and 33-34 for subdominant color.

12. The last chord in m. 31 (V^7 of C) is replaced in m. 34 by an augmented sixth resulting from the altered dominant of C.

13. The progression involving C♯ to D on the last eighth of m. 35-36 is a type found frequently in later nineteenth-century composers.

EXAMPLE 28 (page 136, 137)
"The Prophet-Bird," Op. 82, No. 7

Schumann's genius for poetic imagery, for portraying a mood is well illustrated here. It is an ABA form. Section A is a double period consisting of 4 four-measure phrases plus a two measure extension consisting of the first two measures of the piece. Section B is a short song in chorale texture interrupted by the return of A, which is repeated with only slight modification of m. 2-3.

1. One texture prevails in section A and the appogiatura followed by a quick ascending or descending arpeggio on its chord of resolution is the prevailing motive. The entire piece, including the B section, is an excellent study on the appoggiatura.

Every appoggiatura and its resolution should be identified in this example.

2. In the anacrusis before m. 1 and in the first beat of m. 1 the C♯ appoggiatura does go to D, but the rhythmic or psychological resolution could be construed to be the high D on beat 2 of m. 1. This effect gives the texture its ingenious character, but it cannot be used as a basis of analysis. Actually the D immediately following each C♯ constitutes a separate appoggiatura and its resolution, and the approach in analysis throughout the movement must be that the note immediately following each appoggiatura is its resolution.

3. Observe the stretto effect in m. 15.

4. The appoggiatura in a different texture is still a predominant element in section B. Except for the last beats of m. 18, 19, 22 and 23, we find single to quadruple appoggiaturas on every beat in section B. The analysis would be somewhat different if the G's, C's and E♭'s in the bass are interpreted strictly as pedal points.

5. Notice the small imitative effects in the tenor part of this section.

6. The sudden key change from G to E♭ in m. 23 is a typical Schumann effect. The common tone G is the relatively tenuous connection between the two keys. This third-related effect (G to E♭) through a common tone becomes more frequent throughout the century.

7. Observe that Schumann uses only nearly related keys including tonic major throughout this piece.

Additional Examples to Be Noted or Analyzed for Various Stylistic Features

Because of Schumann's relatively individual treatment of the formal design of each of the larger works, it is not feasible to categorize the various works under formal headings. Likewise, the various elements of style already discussed are illustrated in nearly any work one chooses to analyze. Therefore, the following paragraphs simply list some interesting additional points for consideration beyond those already cited.

The two albums of piano pieces for children, Scenes from Childhood, op. 15, and Album for the Young, op. 68, are recommended as splendid examples for analysis of small forms cast in relatively simple rhythmic and harmonic idioms.

Piano Concerto in a, op. 54:

I is essentially monothematic, the second theme being a major-mode version of the first theme. As in Mendelssohn the soloist and orchestra present the themes jointly in a single exposition. The traditional sonata design and key scheme is used.

II is an ABA form with a transition to III recalling the theme of I. This connecting of movements is also found in Beethoven and Mendelssohn.

III is a third rondo with a new theme (D) entering just before the coda: ABACABAD (Coda) AD.

Phantasie in C, op. 27, I:

A large movement designed somewhat along the lines of sonata form, opening with a great prolongation of the dominant.

Toccata, op. 7, illustrates rapid harmonic change in m. 35-39.

The compositions called Novelettes all vary in form, but are rondo types, being a string of self-contained strophes which exploit various rhythmic effects and pianistic techniques.

A scherzo with two different trios, ABACA, is found in Symphony, no. 1, III, and Symphony, no. 2, II. In Symphony, no. 4, III, the scherzo and trio are both repeated but IV follows the second trio without a break, so that the form of III is ABAB.

The Quintet for Piano and Strings in E♭, op. 44:

I is a sonata form.

II is a march in rondo form.

III is a scherzo with two trios: ABACA coda.

IV is a sonata-type movement of large proportions and distant keys and containing a fugal exposition on the first theme of I with a finale theme as countersubject. The movement opens in g then moves to E♭.

The finale of the String Quartet, op. 41, no. 3, is a rambling rondo form in an ABACAD, ABACAD

coda design. The use of a D section (third subordinate theme or third episode) is not infrequent in Schumann forms.

The same elements of harmony, melody and rhythm are found in the songs which are usually modified strophic forms or through-composed. The cyclic principle can be found throughout his works; and even a group of outwardly unrelated pieces such as *Papillons*, op. 2, seems to have a tenuous and unexplainable unity. Perhaps novelty of form and texture cannot break the thread of Germanic lyricism that goes through his music.

SUGGESTED WRITTEN ASSIGNMENTS

1. Write a short piece in three-four meter employing the hemiola as Schumann does in the finale of the Piano Concerto or the first movement of the Symphony, no. 3 in E♭, op. 97.
2. Write two short passages (about eight measures) in block-chord style demonstrating sudden key changes or changes through a common-tone relation.
3. Write a short lyric melody with the type of accompaniment figure in Examples 26 and 27.

BIBLIOGRAPHY

ABRAHAM, GERALD, *Schumann, A Symposium*, New York: Oxford University Press, 1952.

BOUCOURECHLIEV, ANDRE, *Schumann*, New York: Grove Press, Inc., 1959.

BRION, MARCEL, *Schumann and the Romantic Age*, New York: The Macmillan Company, 1956.

CHISSELL, JOAN, *Schumann*, London: J. M. Dent & Sons, Ltd., 1948.

EISMANN, GEORGE, *Schumann: A Biography in Word and Picture*, Leipzig: VEB Edition, 1964.

NIECKS, FREDERICK, *Robert Schumann*, New York: E. P. Dutton & Co., Inc., 1925.

SCHAUFFLER, ROBERT H., *Florestan*, New York: Holt, Rinehart and Winston, Inc., 1945.

EXAMPLE 26
SCHUMANN
SYMPHONY NO. 2 IN C MAJOR, OP. 61
III
(Opening Measures)

EXAMPLE 27

SCHUMANN
SYMPHONY NO. 2 IN C MAJOR, OP. 61
III
(Last 39 Measures)

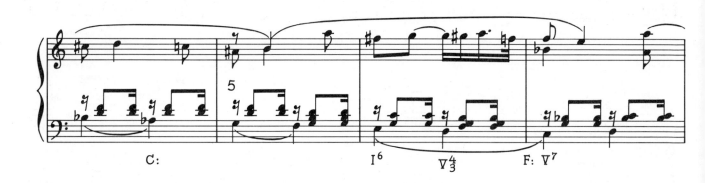

EXAMPLE 28

SCHUMANN
THE PROPHET—BIRD
(From "Forest Scenes," Op. 82, No. 7)
(Complete)

CHAPTER 6

FRÉDÉRIC CHOPIN

1810-1849

Chopin's wide-spaced sonorities, which exploit the resonance of the piano, his ingenious harmonic-rhythmic patterns and his suave melodies with their unique pianistic ornamentation, were unheard of before him. Though his considerable contribution to the evolution of western music was made solely through the medium of the piano, the influence of his handling of 1. harmonic resonance; 2. distribution of chord members for optimum sonority; 3. chromatic harmony in inventive rhythmic patterns affects later composers such as Liszt and Debussy in orchestral scoring as well as pianistic writing. He, along with Schumann, Mendelssohn and Brahms, is a composer of abstract, nonrepresentational romantic music. His style is more cosmopolitan than Schumann's. Because it does not express national origin in any way except in the mazurkas and polonaises, it has a natural and universal appeal.

The bulk of his compositions are single movement works in small part forms such as the mazurkas, preludes, etudes, waltzes, nocturnes and polonaises. Even the larger movements or cycles such as scherzi, ballades, sonatas and concertos are based on self-contained song forms strung together with elaborate transitions. Thus his music attracts us by its melodic, harmonic, rhythmic and resonant inventiveness which is effectively displayed in the forms in which he chose to cast it. In the sense that content and form are in balance, Chopin is a classicist.

Whereas Haydn, Mozart and Beethoven gain rhythmic variety through varying the length of phrases and contrasting contrapuntal and homophonic textures, Chopin and Schumann rely on the inner rhythmic interest within the four-bar phrases of homophonic texture.

The following examples are intended to illustrate Chopin's unique gifts in dealing with content of the four-bar phrase.

EXAMPLE 29 (pages 144, 145)
Nocturne in Bb Minor, Op. 9, No. 1

The form of this nocturne is a song form with trio. The A section (song form) encompassed in this example is a double period extended by two measures (18 measures).

The trio is an incipient three-part song form followed by an extended transition (m. 51-71) to the return of A.

1. The phrase structure in the example is 4 + 4 + 4 + 6 measures, the last phrase being extended by two measures, heightening the climax of m. 3, thus: 1 2 3 3 3 4.

2. The tonic pedal carrying at least through the first I-V-I progression is found in at least six of the nocturnes. This sets a mood of repose. Here the Bb pedal carries through the entire first and third phrases. The pedal point, or rhythmic pedal pattern is common throughout Chopin. Elaborate harmonic structures are often created above a pedal as in Examples 30, 40 and 41.

3. The roulades, or melodic ornamentations in m. 2, 3, 10, 11 and 14, which are a hallmark of Chopin, involve conjunct diatonic and chromatic motion combined with skips and arpeggio figures which color the harmony as well as the melodic element.

4. Some of the characteristic harmonic and melodic color in Chopin derives from the fact that, when in a major key, he frequently uses chords and melodic notes borrowed from the tonic minor and also the Neapolitan chord and the flat-second degree of the scale in both major and minor. Thus in major the melody will frequently contain a flat-sixth or flat-second degree, and the harmony will contain a IV, II^7 or V^9 with the flat-sixth degree, or a Neapolitan sixth chord. The flat-second degree melodically and the Neapolitan chord are common in minor keys.

M. 6 contains IV from the minor and flat-six in the melody. M. 17 contains the N[6] preceded by its own dominant G$\flat$[7] (V[7] of N).

5. M. 16 and 17, successively intensify the melodic motive of m. 15 with each measure starting at a higher pitch. This combined with a crescendo and the N[6] to V[7] in m. 17 replacing the I$^6_4$ to V[7] in m. 15 and 16 produces an effective close for section A.

6. The distribution of the chord in the left hand is a typical Chopin pattern and results in a resonant acoustical effect. The wide, open harmony of the left-hand pattern which follows the harmonic pattern of overtones is one of Chopin's most influential innovations, and will be seen throughout these examples.

EXAMPLE 30 (pages 145, 146)
Nocturne in C$\sharp$ Minor, Op. 27, No. 1

1. Here the left-hand pattern extends to two octaves and a third (m. 6, 13, 16).

2. This nocturne is an ABCA form. The A section after the two-measure introduction (vamp) consists of 6 four-measure phrases with the relationship of aabbaa.

3. Notice the eloquent rest in m. 10 which prolongs the function of m. 9 so that phrase 3 (m. 11) will begin in the tonic.

4. The harmony of the last beat of the third measure of each phrase (m. 5, 9, 13 and 17) is dominant with flat-second degree of the scale, clear enough in m. 13 and 17, but more ambiguous in m. 5 and 9 because of the C$\sharp$ pedal and the A which makes the chord VII[7] (B$\sharp$ D$\natural$ F$\sharp$ A). The predominance of the A in the left hand and flat-second degree makes it possible to consider the harmony of m. 5 and 9 as Neapolitan or subdominant in effect. Which do you think it is?

5. The tonic pedal is again present through the first twelve and a half measures except for the V[7]-I in E (m. 6-7).

6. Note the unusual effect of the V[7] of IV in the first measure of the melody.

7. Again the flat-second degree is an important melodic and harmonic element.

EXAMPLE 31 (pages 146-148)
Nocturne in B Major, Op. 32, No. 1

This nocturne is a large ABB design plus a striking coda.

The A section is a three-part (aba) song form as shown, and the B section is a phrase group closing each time with a reference to the closing measures of A. This example encompasses AB.

1. A characteristic of both the A and B sections is the effect of suspense at m. 6, 18 and 35 created by the crescendo and stretto followed by the pause before the two cadence measures.

2. Compare m. 8-11 with 31-34 and m. 6-8 with 35-37. These show the relationship of the last part of B with A material.

3. Notice the deceptive progression into m. 37 to avoid the cadence and extend the phrase to a close at m. 41.

4. The appoggiatura D$\sharp$ in the arpeggio pattern of the left hand at m. 39 is rare in this piece though a common element in the harmonic-rhythmic patterns of other Chopin works and likewise in the music of Liszt and Rachmaninov.

5. Analyze the chords above the dominant pedal of B in m. 8-10 and above the dominant pedal of g$\sharp$ in bars 31-34.

6. There are several double appoggiaturas (in thirds) to be located.

7. Notice in m. 16 the diminution of the ornamentation in m. 4.

8. The progression in m. 5 is an unusual one for this time.

EXAMPLE 32 (pages 149, 150)
Nocturne in G Major, Op. 37, No. 2

This example is interesting for its constantly modulating character and rapid harmonic rhythm. The form is ABAB[1]A with both A and B sections involving frequent key changes and the return of B in a new set of keys. This example encompasses the first A section.

1. Notice that the phrase structure involves elision so that the fourth measure is the last of phrase one but also the first measure of phrase two, and so on. Beginning with m. 2, m. 1 being introduction and anacrusis, the phrase-period structure could be interpreted as follows:

	Keys
M. 1—Introduction	
M. 2-7—Period 1 (3 + 3)	G a G
M. 8-13—Period 2 (3 + 3)	(B$\flat$) D$\flat$ e$\flat$ D$\flat$
M. 14-21—Period 3 (4 + 2 + 2)	b$\flat$ F a
M. 22-28—Period 4 (3 + 2 + 2)	G f→C

2. What would you call the nonharmonic tones in the first melodic figure? In the sixteenth-note passages the double notes in the right hand form with the bass a new chord on each sixteenth or form simply nonharmonic tones. Each sixteenth should be analyzed to understand the nature of this material.

3. What is the fourth eighth note in the left hand of m. 7, 8, 10 and 11? What is the fourth eighth note in the left hand of m. 16, 18, 20 and 24?

4. How is modulation accomplished in m. 25-28? Such involved modulatory passages are not at all uncommon in Chopin.

EXAMPLE 33 (page 151)
Etude in G♭ Major, Op. 10, No. 5

These next four examples illustrate further the types of patterns Chopin employed to exploit the resources of the piano and to produce simultaneously brilliant and spontaneous works of high musical value. This example shows the kind of glittering display he can conjure from an arpeggio pattern.

Here are 2 four-measure phrases, the first half of a double period, closing on V of VI (m. 8) but leading back to I in m. 9.

EXAMPLE 34 (page 152)
Etude in F Minor, Op. 25, No. 2

This etude is in three-part song form. Part a is a double period with the second eight measures extended to eleven. M. 9 is the beginning of the eleven-measure second part of the period.

1. The strange rhythmic pattern results in an effect of $\frac{6}{4}$ meter: two notes in the right hand to one in the left hand. The contour of the right-hand line demands that a phrasing according to triplets be maintained.

2. This is an interesting exercise in identification of nonharmonic tones in the right hand. Identify all nonharmonic tones in the example.

3. Write a block-harmony reduction of the chord progressions in this example.

EXAMPLE 35 (page 153)
Etude in A Minor, Op. 25, No. 11

1. Chopin seldom resorted to the writing of plain scales. Usually scale-type passages are combined with arpeggios and turns to give them a more individual character. This amazing work which epitomizes pianistic pyrotechnics is based on two types of figuration:

 a. the chromatic scale combined with arpeggio, m. 5-8;

 b. a pattern of four sixteenth notes, consisting of an appoggiatura followed by three chord tones, stated three times as a hemiola in a rhythmic pattern of two groups of six sixteenth notes each. Thus three statements of the pattern appear against two beats as in m. 9-12.

2. The form is like a monothematic sonata as follows:

Introduction, m. 1-4;

Section A, double period, theme in tonic (a) closing in C, 18 measures (5-22);

Section B, double period, theme in dominant (e) closing in C, 18 measures (23-40);

Section C, phrase group, development and retransition, 28 measures (41-68);

Section A, double period, recapitulation of theme in tonic, 21 measures (69-89);

Coda, 8 measures (89-96).

3. This example includes the introduction and the first period (8 bars) of the double period constituting section A of the exposition.

4. In the right-hand pattern of m. 5-8 there is an alternation of chromatic scale tones and tones of the a minor triad. The last note in m. 8 is an F implying an upper auxiliary to the E two notes before and the E opening m. 9. It should also be understood that the last F of m. 8 is the first note of the four-note pattern b (under paragraph 1 above) as bracketed in the music. The E (first note of m. 9) is in turn an appoggiatura resolving to D after an intervening chord tone B, an ornamental resolution of an appoggiatura. This pattern continues through m. 9-12.

EXAMPLE 36 (pages 154-155)
Etude in C Minor, Op. 25, No. 12

Here again is a brilliant work displaying a compactness and consistency in structure. It is a large three-part song form.

1. The lowest and highest notes of the right-hand arpeggios outline the melodic element. Compare the melody of the first four measures:

with the melody of m. 15-17:

for an example of melodic unity.

2. The tonic, C, carries throughout the first twelve measures as a pedal point. Notice the motion over C of the descending triads in m. 7-8 leading to the second phrase (m. 9).

3. M. 9-15 are the second phrase. M. 15 is also the beginning of the third phrase which is eight measures long.

4. M. 13 is a Neapolitan sixth. What is the harmony of m. 6?

EXAMPLE 37 (page 155)
Mazurka in B♭ Major, Op. 7, No. 1

Chopin exhibits in the mazurkas the widest possible range of moods, harmonic effects, modal qualities and rhythmic patterns within three-four meter. In form they range from short three-part song form (op. 6, no. 4) through five-part song form (op. 7, no. 1, present example) and group form (op. 6, no. 3), to song form with trio (op. 7, no. 2, Example 38).

1. This is a five-part (abaca) song form. Part a is a period repeated; parts b and c are each an eight-measure period.

2. This example covers the twelve-measure period of part a. It consists of a four-measure antecedent phrase and a four-measure consequent phrase repeated with melodic alterations for a total of twelve measures.

3. Notice the saucy character effected by the downward skip to the accented half note in m. 4-6 and 9-10, especially the appoggiatura, E, in m. 6 and 10.

4. Why do you think Chopin used a B♭ in the bass of m. 9?

EXAMPLE 38 (page 156)
Mazurka in A Minor, Op. 7, No. 2

This mazurka is a song form with trio and more restrained in mood than the preceding.

1. The example includes all but the return of part a of the aba song form. The missing part a is the same as m. 9-16.

2. Notice the opening on the IV chord; he established the return of part a (m. 25) through V⁷ of IV (m. 24), or in effect a modulation to d which in the course of the first phrase of part a returns to the key of a.

3. In m. 13-14 there is a V⁷-I progression in the Neapolitan key of B♭ followed by a pause at the same point in the phrase and having about the same effect as in the Nocturne, Example 31, m. 6.

4. The first four measures of part b constitute a melodic pattern of 1 2 1 2. Such patterns involving repeated measures in a four-measure phrase are common in folk music or music rooted in the folk idiom as the mazurkas and much of the music of Mussorgsky and Debussy (see Examples 77 through 94). The following illustrate other examples of this type of phrase construction in the mazurkas:

1 2 3 3, op. 7, no. 3, m. 41-44
1 2 1 3, op. 7, no. 4, m. 25-28
1 1 2 3, op. 7, no. 5, m. 5-8

5. The second of each pair of measures in this 1 2 1 2 pattern (m. 17-20) receives a different harmonic treatment. The augmented sixth chord of m. 17 resolves to V of c in m. 18; but the same chord in m. 19 resolves to V₂⁴ of E♭ in m. 20. The key of E♭ is of course not established because of the downward chromatic shift in the following four measures (21-24) to the return of part a.

6. M. 21-24 form a sequence in the right hand but not in the harmony of the left hand. Analyze these measures.

EXAMPLE 39 (page 157)
Mazurka in A♭ Major, Op. 59, No. 2

Here is an intensely concentrated dose of chromatic harmony constituting the extended closing phrase of part a of a three-part song form just preceding the coda.

1. M. 2-4 constitute an ascending sequence and 5-7, a descending sequence; but they are not exact sequences in all parts.

2. Though the example starts and ends in A♭, it is an interesting exercise to try to determine the intervening keys.

3. Every change of pitch in any voice of this four-voice texture forms a new chord. In other words, there is not a single nonharmonic tone in this example, with the possible exception of the high F in m. 8. Every chord should be identified.

EXAMPLE 40 (pages 157-159)
Ballade in G Minor, Op. 23

This ballade is designed along the lines of a sonata form with recapitulation of the themes in reverse order and introduction of an additional new theme in the development section, as follows:

Introduction

Exposition

    Theme 1, trans., theme 2, codetta and trans.
    g   E♭

Development

    Theme 1, theme 2, theme 3, retransition
    a   A   E♭

Recapitulation

    Theme 2, codetta, theme 1, coda
    E♭   g   g

This example includes:

1. Exposition of theme 2, m. 1-16;
2. Codetta of theme 2, m. 17-24;
3. Transition to development, m. 25-27;
4. (Development) theme 1 in a, m. 28-39;
5. (Development) beginning of theme 2 in A, m. 40-41.

Each of these sections of the example will be discussed separately.

1. (m. 2-16) Here is one of Chopin's most ingratiating melodies, a fifteen-measure double period. M. 4-5 are a sequential repetition of 2-3 a fifth higher in the dominant. M. 6 through 9 plus 10-11 (beginning the second period) constitute a six-measure sequence of eight seventh chords and two triads with roots descending by fifths. This is an excellent example of the use of diatonic sevenths combined with secondary dominants in a long sequence under an independent melodic line.

M. 2, 4, 10, 12 and 13 exemplify the V¹³ with the ninth present in all but m. 13.

2. (m. 17-24) This is simply a four-measure phrase repeated, reaffirming E♭ by a I-V⁷-I-(V¹³ of IV)-IV₄⁶ (from e♭)-I progression over a pedal E♭.

3. (m. 24-27) A transition to the d triad, IV of a, is accomplished by a succession of four triads, each a third above the preceding one: M. 24 (Eb), 25 (g), 26 (Bb), 27 (d).

4. (m. 28-39) This entire passage in the key of a, consisting of a partial statement of theme 1 plus transition to theme 2, is laid over a dominant pedal. Harmonic tension mounts throughout this passage as the sonorities over the pedal gradually expand and become more complex with the entry of the VII^7 of V which, with the appoggiatura G♯, is carried over three repeated measures (36-38) plus a fourth bar further tightening the suspense.

5. (m. 40-41) One of the most effective climaxes in romantic piano literature is achieved with the arrival of theme 2 in m. 40. Chopin's sense of piano resonance as well as his ability to build a climax is displayed in the expansive distribution of the chord members.

EXAMPLE 41 (page 160)
Ballade in G Minor, Op. 23

These ten measures are the beginning of the recapitulation with the return of theme 2 in Eb.

1. Notice the new accompaniment figure which is more animated, imparting a sense of commotion leading through theme 1 to the vigorous and furious climax of the coda.

2. M. 5-8, which are comparable to m. 6-9 of Example 40, are treated to a new ornamental figuration which includes one of Chopin's favorite appoggiatura effects, an appoggiatura on the tone one-half step above the seventh of a V^7 and struck against it then resolving upward, as seen in m. 5 with B♮ and Bb struck simultaneously over the C^7 chord and in m. 6 with A♮ against Ab in the Bb^7 chord. Two of the many other occurrences of this effect are seen in the Impromptu, op. 29, m. 4, and Impromptu, op. 51, m. 14. Such an effect is inherent in a style involving so much melodic ornamentation.

3. In m. 9 the sonority is further expanded by adding Bb above the original melody note F. Thus the thirteenth (G) of the V^{13} is placed below the Bb.

Additional Examples to Be Noted or Analyzed for Various Stylistic Features

preludes

The twenty-four preludes in op. 28, one in each of the twenty-four major and minor keys, contain the essence of Chopin's art. They are concise works in period or three-part song form, each vividly expressing the mood for which it is designed. No. 15 is a song form with trio and no. 17 is an abaca five-part song form. A modulation based on the enharmonic change of a single tone (Ab=G♯) is found in no. 17, m. 18-19.

mazurkas

Though these are idealizations of a dance in triple meter, there is a wide variety of musical resources imaginatively displayed in them. The frequently accented second or third beat typical of the dance gives Chopin room for additional rhythmic variety.

A typical melodic effect is the closing of a phrase on the second or last beat of the measure as in:

> op. 6, nos. 1 and 4
> op. 7, nos. 1 and 4
> op. 17, nos. 1, 2 and 3
> op. 50, no. 2
> op. 63, no. 2

Interesting modal effects occur in op. 24, nos. 2 and 4, and in part c of op. 7, no. 1. They include excellent examples of all types of song forms.

nocturnes

These works are in extended song forms, song form and trio and first rondo forms.

etudes

These are usually aba song forms. Part a is usually a period repeated or a double period and extended. Part b involves modulation and sequences. The return of part a is extended by a coda or codetta. Op. 25, no. 10, is a rondo design.

waltzes

These works are composed of a group of eight to sixteen measure tunes (periods) strung together in varying order. Various keys including third related are used. Op. 42 exploits the hemiola by putting the right hand in six-eight meter against the triple meter in the left hand.

scherzi

Contrary to the title these are large serious works. Whatever humor they imply could best be described as threatening, ironic or bitter; but the range of moods is from these to lyric, tranquil or joyful. The boisterous, good-natured humor of the Beethoven scherzo is not present here. These are precursors to the satanic type of scherzo of the twentieth century as found in the Walton Symphony 1937, II; the Vaughan Williams Symphony, no. 4, III; and the Hanson Symphony, no. 4, III.

Op. 20 in b is a song form with trio and coda. Beginning thirty-two measures from the end there is a six-measure passage of *fff* repeated chords consisting of E♯ G B D over an F♯ pedal which is reminiscent of Beethoven, Example 24, m. 53-54.

Op. 31 is really in D♭ even though it begins in b♭. It is designed along sonata lines but does not recapitulate the material of the second-theme area.

Op. 39 in c♯ is a sonata design as follows:

theme 1, theme 2, Development, theme 1,
c♯　　　　D♭　　　　　　　　　　c♯
theme 2, Coda
E　　　c♯

Compare the scale combined with triad-arpeggio in m. 159-163 (et seq.) with the right-hand figure in Example 35.

ballades

These works are more extended works like the scherzi. See Example 40 for the form of op. 23, which opens on an arpeggio of the Neapolitan sixth chord. The ballade in F, op. 38, contrasts a lyric and a fiery theme in an ABAB form and closes in a instead of F.

polonaises

These are song form and trio types. Op. 44 in f♯ is extended by the incorporation of a mazurka. Op. 53 includes a long transition from the trio to the return of A. The A section (song form) closes in A♭ and the trio is in E. The A♭=G♯ is the connecting thread in a third relationship. The Polonaise-Fantasy, op. 61, exemplifies complex chromatic harmony and rapid harmonic rhythm to a high degree.

impromptus

Op. 29, op. 51 and op. 66 (Fantasy-Impromptu) are song form and trio design. Op. 36 is more elaborate, having a design of ABCA(varied)B. See m. 58-61 for an unusually contrived modulation from G to F.

sonatas

Op. 35, I: Theme 1 is highly developed in the development section so that only theme 2 returns in recapitulation and theme 1 is referred to in the coda.

II: A furious scherzo in e♭ with a lyric trio in G♭.

III: The famous funeral march with the maudlin trio.

IV: A presto movement in octave triplets, a unique work.

Op. 58 is a virtuoso work of four movements designed along the same lines as op. 35.

concertos

The two concertos are early works, and both are in minor (e and f) as is typical of concertos of the romantic period. The conventional double exposition is used in both first movements. They are both in effect piano solos with only slight and usually insignificant orchestral accompaniment.

The second (slow) movements are ABA rondos. Concerto, no. 1 in e, III, is an ABAB form and no. 2 in f, III, is an ABA rondo.

Chromatic harmony, unusual modulation, melodic and harmonic ornamentation by nonharmonic tones so abound in the works of Chopin that almost any one work is likely to exemplify any or all of these aspects of his style. Therefore, a list of further specific examples is not provided, but it is suggested that any of the waltzes, preludes, mazurkas and etudes may be used for analysis of small forms and relatively less complicated harmonic texture, and that the larger works such as the scherzi, ballades, impromptus, sonatas, and polonaises be analyzed as examples of more complex tonal structures and expanded forms.

The *Berceuse*, op. 57, is one of the outstanding examples in all literature of variations over an ostinato and should be analyzed in detail.

SUGGESTED WRITTEN ASSIGNMENTS

1. Reduce two of the shorter works of Chopin to a block-harmony outline.
2. Write a short piece in the style of a Chopin nocturne.
3. Outline the harmony implicit in the last movement of the Sonata, op. 35, in b♭, or, as a shorter example involving the same problem, Prelude, op. 28, no. 14, in e♭.

BIBLIOGRAPHY

ABRAHAM, GERALD, *Chopin's Musical Style*, New York: Oxford University Press, 1946.

BOURNIQUEL, CAMILLE, *Chopin*, New York: Grove Press, Inc., 1960.

BROWN, MAURICE J. E., *Chopin: An Index of his Works*, New York: St. Martin's Press, Inc., 1960.

GIDE, ANDRÉ, *Notes on Chopin*, New York: Philosophical Library, Inc., 1949.

HEDLEY, ARTHUR, *Chopin*, London: J. M. Dent & Sons, Inc., 1947.

JONSON, GEORGE C. A., *A Handbook to Chopin's Works*, London: W. Reeves. [n. d.]

LISZT, FRANZ, *Frédéric Chopin*, New York: Collier-Macmillan, 1963.

PORTE, JOHN F., *Chopin the Composer and His Music*, London: W. Reeves. [n. d.]

WEINSTOCK, HERBERT, *Chopin*, New York: Alfred A. Knopf, Inc., 1949.

EXAMPLE 29

CHOPIN

NOCTURNE IN B♭ MINOR, OP. 9, NO. 1

(First 18 Measures)

EXAMPLE 30
CHOPIN
NOCTURNE IN C# MINOR, OP. 27, NO. 1
(First 18 Measures)

EXAMPLE 31
Chopin
NOCTURNE IN B MAJOR, OP. 32, NO. 1
(First 41 Measures)

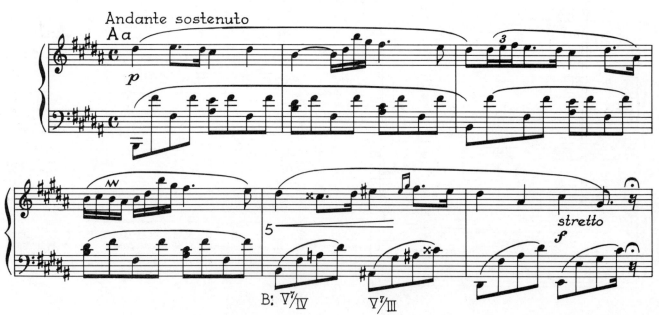

EXAMPLE 32
CHOPIN
NOCTURNE IN G MAJOR, OP. 37, NO. 2
(First 28 Measures)

EXAMPLE 33

CHOPIN

ETUDE IN G♭ MAJOR, OP. 10, NO. 5

(First 9 Measures)

EXAMPLE 34
CHOPIN
ETUDE IN F MINOR, OP. 25, NO. 2
(First 9 Measures)

EXAMPLE 35
CHOPIN
ETUDE IN A MINOR, OP. 25, NO. 11
(First 13 Measures)

EXAMPLE 36
CHOPIN
ETUDE IN C MINOR, OP. 25, NO. 12
(First 17 Measures)

EXAMPLE 37
CHOPIN
MAZURKA IN B♭ MAJOR, OP. 7, NO. 1
(First 12 Measures)

EXAMPLE 38
Chopin
MAZURKA IN A MINOR, OP. 7, NO. 2
(First 25 Measures)

EXAMPLE 39
CHOPIN
MAZURKA IN A♭ MAJOR, OP. 59, NO. 2
(Measures 81-89)

EXAMPLE 40
CHOPIN
BALLADE IN G MINOR, OP. 23
(Measures 67-107)

EXAMPLE 41

CHOPIN

BALLADE IN G MINOR, OP. 23

(Measures 166-175)

CHAPTER 7

JOHANNES BRAHMS

1833-1897

Brahms is the Beethoven of the romantic century. Though he used the harmonic materials common to other composers of the period, wrote a number of single movement works in small forms (piano pieces and songs), and though his use of minor to express somberness is typical of the time, he nevertheless remained faithful to the classical ideal of a carefully calculated balance of form with content. He was not impulsive but meticulous in his manipulation of material to make all the elements interrelate in a consistent and unified musical organism.

His objectivity and strict self-criticism result in a style and standard of quality which remains consistent throughout his music from earliest to latest.

His music has great emotional drive and vitality resulting from his ability to manipulate his material in strictly musical terms; literary ideas find no place as motivation for the emotional format of his music.

Any work of Brahms which one examines will reveal carefully contrived relationships of such small elements as intervals, melodic figures and rhythmic patterns with the larger aspects of themes, tonalities and formal sections.

He was a master of the large compound (symphonic and chamber music) forms as well as the single movement forms including songs and choral music.

EXAMPLE 42 (page 168)
Symphony No. 1 in C Minor, Op. 68, I

This and the two following examples illustrate the following general features:

a. Unification by some melodic figure, interval or rhythmic pattern; in this case the ascending and descending chromatic figure of three notes identified in brackets;

b. Relationship of the introduction to the rest of the movement; in this case the introduction previews nearly all the thematic material to follow;

c. Phrase structure, extension, prolongation of certain basic cadential progressions, as in m. 19-25 of Example 42;

d. Extensive use of change of mode to effect modulations or sequences, as in m. 16-36 of Example 44.

This example and Example 43 need to be closely compared to see the relationship of material. The introduction is thirty-seven measures of which the first twenty-five are quoted here. The first seventy-four measures of the exposition are quoted in Example 43 and include theme 1 and part of the transition to theme 2. Theme 2, not shown, begins almost exactly as theme 1 but in E♭, the relative major.

1. Compare the following passages from the two examples:

Example 42	Example 43
m. 1-2	with 1-3
m. 9-18	with 14-30
m. 21-25	with 5-6 and 33-36

There are of course many other comparisons to be made between the introduction and the exposition, and they can be more effectively sought out in the notes than discussed here.

2. The augmented sixth, A♭ to F♯, m. 8, is to be seen frequently throughout the movement.

3. The chromatically ascending effect in m. 11-12 and 15-18 should be analyzed carefully. These measures contain excellent examples of dominant (major-minor) seventh chords resolving chromatically instead of diatonically as V⁷ chords. Notice the triple suspension marked S.

4. Notice the importance of the diminished seventh chord in the Brahms' style. Identify the diminished seventh chords in Examples 42, 43, 44.

5. In m. 19-25 we see a prolonged cadential progression of N^6, I_4^6 to V, which is not unusual in the expansive movements of Brahms.

6. The basic figure of m. 1-3 appears also in the second movement (m. 4-5 et seq.).

EXAMPLE 43 (pages 169-171)
Symphony No. 1 in C Minor, Op. 68, I

1. Notice how closely the key of c or C is adhered to through the first fifty-two measures. Every phrase closes on I or V of c or C as identified by the mark √. The transition to theme 2 starts at m. 52. Analyze the form of the first-theme statement of fifty-two measures.

2. Observe the enharmonic changes involved in the harmonization of m. 26-29 in contrast to the harmonization of m. 22-26.

3. In m. 9-14 notice the change of mode from G to g (m. 9), the movement toward d and back to G as V of c (m. 14).

4. Observe the sequence in m. 52-56. The insistence on B♭ (m. 60-68), including the B♭ pedal (m. 64-68), are preparatory to the establishment of E♭ for theme 2. The descending bass from B♭ to F (m. 68-74) introduces a prolonged E♭ cadence beginning with F as V of V at m. 68.

EXAMPLE 44 (pages 172, 173)
Symphony No. 1 in C Minor, Op. 68, I

These measures from the development section deal with the motive first introduced in the closing section of the exposition. The rising chromatic figure is bracketed where it appears.

1. The constant modal shifts from major to parallel minor contribute largely to the great flexibility of Brahms' harmonic style. Such changes of mode can be seen in nearly any work, and they are especially obvious in m. 16-36, as follows:

C♭ and G♭ (m. 17-18) answered by b and f♯ (m. 19-20);

A and D (m. 23-24) answered by a and d (m. 25-26);

F (m. 31) answered by f (m. 33);

B♭ (m. 32) answered by b♭ (m. 35).

Identify the sequential pattern in this passage.

2. Notice in m. 37-49 the six statements of the basic three-note figure in the bass undergirding the five statements of the progression, N^6, VII^7 of V, V, plus one progression of IV^7, VII^7 of V, V (m. 47-49). These reiterations of the motive and progression to V serve to introduce a lengthy retransition on and around the dominant.

EXAMPLE 45 (pages 174, 175)
Symphony No. 1 in C Minor, Op. 68, II

This movement is a first rondo (ABA). The example includes all of section A. What is the form of section A?

1. Here again we see the alternation between tonic major and tonic minor. The key is E but the cadences at m. 4 and 16 are in e.

2. The bracket over m. 4-6 identifies the basic figure from the first movement.

3. The bracket under m. 22-23 identifies the motive of m. 1-2.

4. Notice the relationship of m. 3-4 to 15-16 to 24-25 to 26-27. What is the function within the form of these pairs of measures?

5. The last beat of m. 8 illustrates an ornamental resolution of an appoggiatura.

6. Observe the deceptive progressions of m. 6 to 7 and 11 to 12. Both are commonly found in Wagner, especially the latter involving the progression V of VI to IV with the double appoggiaturas B and D♯ on the downbeat of m. 12.

7. Observe the varying harmonic treatment given m. 9-11, each of which has the same melodic figure.

8. How do you explain the harmony of m. 19 and 21?

9. What factors contribute to the climax reached through m. 27-35?

10. Brahms' frequent use of an augmented sixth chord in approaching a cadence is seen again in m. 3, 24 and 37.

EXAMPLE 46 (page 176)
Symphony No. 2 in D Major, Op. 73, III

This movement is a song form with two trios, an ABACA form. Section A is a three-part song form of which the example includes parts a and b and one measure of the return of part a.

Here again we see Brahms' masterful ability to spin a theme out of a simple figure at any point in the form. Part a is a period of eight measures plus two measures (9 and 10) of extension repeating the cadence figure, E to D, of m. 8. One is led after m. 8-10 to expect a repetition of the first eight measures. A lesser composer would possibly have done this. Imagine a repeat sign at the end of m. 10 and play the example repeating the first ten measures to see what the effect would be. But this is not Brahms' way. He uses the E to D figure of m. 8-10 to generate the melody of part b (m. 11-22) harmonizing it a third way with V^7 of C. This flexible handling of small motives in a constantly shifting tonal design is the essence of the Brahm's style. Part b, because of this motivic relationship, seems almost like a twelve-measure extension of the cadence of part a.

EXAMPLE 47 (page 177)
Symphony No. 3 in F Major, Op. 90, I

Here, as in Symphonies, nos. 1 and 2, the first movement is infused with a basic three-note figure. In this case, it consists of the ascending three tones F to A♭ to F as bracketed in the example. This figure should not be confused with the actual first theme in any of these cases because it is an independent unifying factor which may occur at any point in the fabric. The first movement of the first three symphonies should be studied for a clear understanding of this procedure.

1. The change of mode feature is dramatically illustrated in the changes from A♮ in m. 1, to A♭ in m. 2, to A♮ in m. 3, to A♭ in m. 4, all accomplished through cross relationships.
2. It is typical of Brahms to move swiftly toward the subdominant side and back to tonic in the space of a few bars. We see this twice in this example:

   a. In m. 1-9, through change of mode, VI⁶ of f is introduced at m. 5 with a return to F at m. 9.
   b. In m. 9-13, the N⁶ chord at m. 11 is reached through V⁷ of IV to IV (m. 10-11) with a return to F at m. 13.
3. Phrase extension occurs within the course of the phrase as can be seen throughout these examples, and also by repetition of the penultimate measures as seen in m. 13-14 and in other examples such as Example 44.

EXAMPLE 48 (page 178)
Intermezzo, Op. 116, No. 6

This is Brahms in a chromatic mood resembling in m. 18-21 the chromaticism of César Franck. See Example 58. This example is section A of a first rondo form.

1. Interesting nonharmonic elements are:

   a. Triple appoggituras, m. 1, beat 1;
   b. Delayed resolution of appoggiatura A to G♯ in m. 5;
   c. Change of bass under the appoggiaturas and their resolutions as in m. 1, 5 and 7.
   d. Simultaneous E and E♯ as in Chopin (m. 3);
   e. Enharmonically spelled C chord resulting from passing between positions of the VII⁷ of III in m. 13-14.
2. Notice the shift of the eighth-note melodic figure between the inner and top voice in m. 1-6.
3. Observe the chromatic resolutions of dominant-type seventh chords in:

   a. Third beat of m. 6 to first beat of m. 7;
   b. Second to third beat of m. 12;

   c. Third beat of m. 19 and first two beats of m. 20. What is the harmony on beat two of m. 20?
4. How do you explain the enharmonically spelled D chord on beat one of m. 20?
5. Again we see the interchange of major and minor in:

   a. M. 9, third beat compared with m. 11, third beat;
   b. M. 21 compared with 22.
6. The harmony of the entire example should be carefully analyzed for an understanding of nonharmonic, enharmonic and chromatic effects.

Examples and Suggestions for Further Study of the Music of Brahms

As will have been seen from the preceding examples, the process of development permeates the Brahms' style. It is probably for this reason that he occasionally dispenses with an independent development section and instead incorporates development in the recapitulation. The result is like a sonatina with the recapitulation extended by development.

Following are examples:

Symphony, no. 1, IV. A large introduction which previews the thematic material of the allegro (as in the first movement) is then followed by a sonatina type of form in which the return of theme one is developed: introduction, theme 1, theme 2, theme 1 (developed), theme 2, coda. Here theme 2 returns in the tonic.

The same plan without the slow introduction is used for:

Piano Quintet, op. 34, IV
String Quartet, op. 51, no. 1, IV
Symphony, no. 3, IV
Symphony, no. 4, II (with short prologue and epilogue)

Though Brahms' music is nonrepresentational (nonprogrammatic) and is an expression of classical ideals of construction, it does not completely lend itself to analysis by the same methods which can be applied to the Viennese classicists. Problems in analysis arise from the following characteristics in his music:

1. Melodic ideas are seldom independent entities with a specific ending.

2. An exposition or other section may consist of several motives each in turn introduced, manipulated and merged into the next so it is difficult to identify one as more important than the other.
3. The constant process of motivic generation and transformation through a constantly shifting contrapuntal-harmonic fabric can make any point in the form sound like a development.
4. Elision of cadences, irregular phrase lengths and metrical shifts within the basic meter contribute to obscuring clear definition of classical formal divisions.

All this does not mean that Brahms' forms are vague. On the contrary, it is the attention to thematic detail, the greater harmonic and contrapuntal complexity and the concern for every musical relationship which results in a more integrated musical organism, but an organism whose joints are therefore less obvious. This process of complete control of every aspect of the musical process reaches its culmination in some serial and electronic music of the twentieth century. See Schoenberg and Křenek.

These characteristics apply equally to all forms from small piano pieces to large symphonic-type movements.

The insertion of a developmental passage as transition can be seen many places throughout the works, but a good illustration of this is in the Symphony, no. 2, II, a first rondo form, where the transition from section B to the return of section A is in effect a development section, so that the form becomes A B development A coda.

Nearly all codas of any length have the character of terminal developments.

first movements

Most sonata cycles are four-movement works. About half the sonatas and three of the four concertos are three movements, and in the String Quintet, op. 88 and the Violin Sonata, op. 100, the middle of three movements is a fusion of the slow and fast movements into one. First movements are sonata forms and the conventional repeat of the exposition is usually indicated; among the exceptions are Piano Sonata, op. 2, I, and Symphony, no. 4, I, where no repeat is written.

A slow (integrated) introduction which previews the thematic material of the movement appears in Symphony, no. 1, I (and IV) and Piano Sonata, op. 2, IV (introduction and postlude).

Conventional key relationships exist between themes in sonata forms and an occasional third relationship appears as in String Quintet, op. 88, I, and Symphony, no. 3, I, in F. In the latter the second theme is in A and returns in D.

slow movements

The slow movement is usually second but sometimes third as in Piano Quartet, op. 25, III; String Sextet, op. 36, III; Piano Concerto, no. 2, op. 83, III; and Piano Trio, op. 101, III.

The form of the slow movement is either first rondo (ABA) or a theme and variations. Exceptions are Symphony, no. 4, II, a sonatina, and the combined slow and scherzo movements as noted above.

When the main key of the work is minor the slow movement is most often the tonic major, the subdominant major or minor; less often is it the submediant or the relative major, and seldom a third relationship as in Symphony, no. 1, in c, II in E.

When the main key is major the slow movement is usually a third-related key or in the dominant but only occasionally in tonic minor, relative minor or mediant. A unique relationship exists in the Cello Sonata, op. 99 in F with II in F♯.

scherzi and intermezzi

Points of departure regarding Brahms' treatment of this movement are as follows:

1. The scherzo is often replaced by a more moderately paced intermezzo movement, usually allegretto, which is in a less boisterous mood. None of the symphonies contains a scherzo and the minuet is used only once, in String Quartet, op. 51, no. 2, III.
2. The scherzo or intermezzo movement is usually a song form with trio but is occasionally cast in a different form as follows:

Symphony, no. 1, III, second rondo

Symphony, no. 2, III, song form with two trios

Symphony, no. 4, III, sonata form

Piano Quartet, op. 26, III, and Piano Concerto, no. 2, II, scherzi in sonata form with contrasting trios

Violin Sonata, op. 108, III, a freely designed ABA rondo form

A one-movement scherzo for piano, op. 4, which has two trios

3. The key of this movement is frequently different from the first, slow or finale movements. Prior to this time the scherzo was nearly always in the key of the work, but in Brahms we frequently find the first three movements in three different keys as follows:

Symphony, no. 1, c, E, A♭, c
Symphony, no. 2, D, B, *G*, D
Symphony, no. 3, F, C, *c*, F
Symphony, no. 4, e, E, *C*, e
Piano Sonata, op. 1, C, c, *e*, C
Piano Sonata, op. 5, f, A♭, *f*, b♭, f
String Sextet, op. 18, B♭, d, *F*, B♭
String Sextet, op. 36, G, *g*, E, G
Piano Quartet, op. 25, g, *c*, E♭, g
Piano Quintet, op. 34, F, A♭, *c*, F
String Quartet, op. 51, no. 1, c, A♭, *f,* c
String Quartet, op. 67, B♭, F, *d*, B♭
Clarinet Quintet, op. 115, b, B, *D*, b
Cello Sonata, op. 99, F, F♯, *f*, F
Violin Sonata, op. 108, d, D, *f♯*, d

4. Both duple and triple meter are employed in these movements, sometimes both in one movement. Schumann and Mendelssohn began to break the dominance of triple meter by occasionally writing a trio in duple meter. Brahms uses duple meter as often as triple and sometimes places the song form in one meter, the trio in another. In Symphony, no. 2, III, which has two trios, the Allegretto song form is in $\frac{3}{4}$, Trio I in $\frac{2}{4}$ and Trio II in $\frac{3}{8}$.

The key relationships of trios to the movement proper are conventional. When the movement is in minor the trio is in tonic major or submediant major, seldom relative major, dominant, subdominant minor or third related. When the movement is in a major key the trio is usually in the same key, a third related key, or seldom in the subdominant.

The developmental character seen in the Beethoven scherzi is continued by Brahms. The song form is expanded by exploitation of motives replacing self-contained eight- or sixteen-measure melodies.

finales

1. Sonata form is frequently used, but the exposition is often not repeated. Finales in sonatina-type form in which the development is incorporated into the recapitulation are described on p. 163.

Works with finales in sonata form are:

Symphony, no. 2, IV
Piano Sonata, op. 2, IV
String Sextet, op. 36, IV
String Quintets, op. 88 and 111, IV
Piano Trios, op. 101 and 114, IV

2. Rondos are also frequently used for finales. The following are second (ABACA) rondos:

Piano Sonatas, op. 1 and 5, IV
Violin Sonatas, op. 78 and 100, III

String Sextet, op. 18, IV, and Cello Sonata, op. 99, IV are third rondos

The rondo form is treated in a manner which is individual and peculiar to each of the following instances. Each should be analyzed for its own particular formal treatment:

Piano Concertos, no. 1, III, and no. 2, IV
Piano Quartet, op. 25, IV
String Quartet, op. 51, no. 2, IV
Clarinet Sonata, op. 120, no. 1, IV

3. The sonata-rondo design is followed in a free manner in the following:

Piano Quartet, op. 26, IV
Piano Trio, op. 87, IV
Double Concerto, op. 102, III
Violin Concerto, op. 77, III
Violin Sonata, op. 108, IV

4. Theme and variations appear throughout Brahms' piano works as independent works and throughout the chamber and orchestral works as slow movements and finales. The Variations on a Theme of Haydn, op. 56a, is an independent orchestral work transcribed from two pianos. His entire output is imbued with the variation technic, and it is natural that he should have excelled in this form. His procedure is to develop in each successive variation some new rhythmic or melodic figure or harmonic feature extracted from the theme and by employment of a variety of textures to express a wide range of musical emotions.

The following finales are theme and variations:

String Quartet, op. 67, IV
Clarinet Quintet, op. 115, IV
Clarinet Sonata, op. 120, no. 2, IV

The finale of Symphony, no. 4 is the great chaconne movement consisting of continuous variations on an eight-measure theme.

cyclic effects

Brahms employs the cyclic concept in several works but not in an emphatic manner. In the following works a figure or motive from an earlier movement is recalled in a later one:

Symphony, no. 1, basic figure and harmony from I used in II and IV

Symphony, no. 3, the basic figure from I and motive of section B from II, appear in IV

Piano Sonata, op. 1, theme one of I used in modified version in IV

String Quartet, op. 51, no. 1, motive from I used in II and IV

String Quartet, op. 67, themes one and two from I appear in IV

Clarinet Quintet, op. 115, the opening basic motive or motto of I closes IV

single movement piano pieces

The sets of variations op. 9, 21, 24, 35 are the largest works in this category.

The three rhapsodies are in the following forms:

op. 79, no. 1, in b, is a third rondo plus coda dealing with B;

op. 79, no. 2, in g, is in sonata form;

op. 119, no. 4, in E♭, is a sectional form in ABCBA coda sequence and closes in e♭, a rare case of a work in major ending in minor.

The ballades are sectional pieces less extensive than the Chopin ballades.

The short piano pieces titled Capriccio and Intermezzo range in size from single song forms to song forms with trio and sectional designs. They are based on one or two piano figurations and rhythmic motives carried through complex harmonic and rhythmic elaborations. They are mature works which show his mastery of harmonic and contrapuntal elaboration. The Eleven Chorale Preludes for organ, op. 122, are further demonstration of his contrapuntal technic applied through the harmonic and melodic idiom of the romantic period.

Additional Examples to Be Noted or Analyzed for Various Stylistic Features

The following are only random samples of effects which appear in innumerable places throughout the literature.

for thematic derivations:

Symphony, no. 1, III, the melody of the first phrase (m. 1-5) is presented in contrary motion to form the second phrase (m. 6-10).

Compare the opening theme in e of intermezzo (for piano) op. 119, no. 2 with the trio theme in E.

for rhythmic effects:

The superimposition of a melodic-rhythmic pattern of a different meter on the existing meter is seen in:

Symphony, no. 2, IV, m. 130-134. A five-beat pattern is superimposed on 5 four-beat measures producing 4 five-beat metrical divisions. Also m. 135-137 contain a $\frac{3}{4}$ pattern expressed four times in three measures of $\frac{4}{4}$.

Piano Sonata, op. 1, IV, m. 5-8, a $\frac{6}{8}$ rhythmic pattern causes four measures of $\frac{9}{8}$ to sound like six measures of $\frac{6}{8}$.

The hemiola effect occurs frequently throughout the works. Actual changing of meter signaures in later works provides additional rhythmic variety. Also, rests on the strong beat of the measure or on the first half of the beat are found in passages in Brahms as well as in Schumann.

Can you identify some illustrations of both of these rhythmic effects?

Diminution and augmentation of the thematic material is of course an important rhythmic element in this style. Diminution is illustrated in:

Symphony, no. 1, IV, m. 81-84 are a diminution of the theme in m. 71-80.

String Quartet, op. 51, no. 2, IV, m. 334-338 are a free diminution of the first theme, m. 1-7.

Symphony, no. 4, II, m. 36-38 contain a diminution of the second theme which follows at m. 41.

Augmentation is illustrated in Symphony, no. 4, I. The recapitulation begins at m. 246 with the return of theme one in augmentation.

The Piano Variations, op. 21, no. 2, are based on a Hungarian song in seven-beat meter, alternating $\frac{3}{4}$ and $\frac{4}{4}$ measures.

contrapuntal devices

Piano Quartet, op. 26, III, has a canonic trio.

String Quintet, op. 88, III, opens with a fugal exposition.

Canonic imitation by contrary motion is seen in the Piano Trio, op. 114, IV, m. 47-57.

Free imitation by contrary motion is seen in Symphony, no. 3, I, m. 90-95.

Basso ostinato is illustrated in Symphony, no. 1, IV, m. 57-66.

tonal relationships

In view of the fluid, ever-shifting harmonic aspect of the style it is unusual to find the development section beginning with a nearly full statement of theme one in the tonic key as in Symphony, no. 2, IV, and in Symphony, no. 4, I and III. In Symphony, no. 4, III, the recapitulation opens in D♭ instead of tonic, C.

On the other hand the development section of the Cello Sonata, op. 99, I, in F, begins in f♯ and of the Trio, op. 101, I, in c begins in c♯.

The second movement of the Violin Concerto is a first rondo in F with the B section in f♯.

The Piano Sonata, op. 1, IV, is an ABACA rondo with each A statement opening in a different key.

the diminished seventh chord

This is a favorite chord of composers of the period (Liszt, Brahms and Wagner) and is sometimes overused. Emphasis on the diminished seventh is found in late piano pieces such as Capriccio, op. 116, no. 7, and Intermezzo, op. 118, no. 1.

SUGGESTED WRITTEN ASSIGNMENTS

1. Reduce a late piano work such as the Intermezzo, op. 116, no. 4, to block-harmony outline.
2. Write an eight- to sixteen-measure exercise in major, employing change of mode moving to the minor subdominant and submediant and returning to a cadence in tonic.

BIBLIOGRAPHY

EVANS, EDWIN, SR., *Handbook to the Works of Brahms* 4 vols.: vol. 1, *Vocal Works;* vols. 2 and 3, *Chamber and Orchestral Works;* vol. 4, *Pianoforte Works,* London: W. Reeves, 1912-1936.

GAL, HANS, *Johannes Brahms; His Work and Personality,* New York: Alfred A. Knopf, Inc., 1963.

GEIRINGER, KARL, *Brahms: His Life and Works,* New York: Oxford University Press, Inc., 1947.

NIEMANN, WALTER, *Brahms,* New York: Alfred A. Knopf, Inc., 1947.

MASON, DANIEL GREGORY, *The Chamber Music of Brahms,* New York: The Macmillan Company, 1933.

SIMROCH, N., *Thematic Catalog of the Collected Works of Brahms,* New York: Ars Music Press, 1956.

SPECHT, RICHARD, *Johannes Brahms,* New York: E. P. Dutton & Company, Inc., 1930.

EXAMPLE 42
BRAHMS
SYMPHONY NO. 1 IN C MINOR, OP. 68
I
(Introduction, First 25 Measures)

EXAMPLE 43
BRAHMS
SYMPHONY NO. 1 IN C MINOR, OP. 68
I
(Measures 38–111)

EXAMPLE 44
BRAHMS
SYMPHONY NO. 1 IN C MINOR, OP. 68
I
(Measures 225-273)

EXAMPLE 45
BRAHMS
SYMPHONY NO. 1 IN C MINOR, OP. 68
II
(First 38 Measures)

EXAMPLE 46

BRAHMS
SYMPHONY NO. 2 IN D MAJOR, OP. 73
III
(First 23 Measures)

EXAMPLE 47
BRAHMS
SYMPHONY NO. 3 IN F MAJOR, OP. 90
I
(First 15 Measures)

EXAMPLE 48
BRAHMS
INTERMEZZO FOR PIANO, OP. 116, NO. 6
(First 22 Measures)

CHAPTER 8

RICHARD WAGNER

Though nearly all Wagner's important music was written for the theatre (opera and music drama), still it has held an important place on the concert stage. This is because of his profound grasp of the process of symphonic development and the fact that the orchestra through the use of leading motives independently presents a satisfying dramatic and music experience.

Gone are the eight-measure periods set off with conclusive cadences of the classic and early romantic period. Instead there is a nonperiodic, continuous flow of musical sound consisting of a polyphonic texture woven with constantly developing motives, shifting tonalities and chromatic harmony kept in motion by cadence avoidance and deceptive progressions.

Form is achieved through the relationship of broad sections, each dealing with the development of a particular motive or group of motives.

This complex fabric of polyphony made up of constantly shifting key centers and chromatic harmony complicated by nonharmonic tones produces a sense of suspense and tension which was carried even further by Wagner's successors, Bruckner, Strauss, Berg, Schoenberg and Webern to a point of constant unresolved suspense.

Though Wagner used music in the service of drama and thereby is associated with the concept of programmatic music, he did not pictorialize so much as express abstract feeling in the orchestral parts. He relied on the declamatory vocal lines and words to carry the details of the story. And since most of his late operas deal with states of mind, the music of the orchestra is quite able to express their essence without words.

EXAMPLE 49 (page 183)
Tannhäuser Overture

Tannhäuser is an opera written before Wagner had developed his "continuous melody" concept, but certain elements of the later music drama are already present in its use of declamatory style, recurring motives, long transitional passages and the overture which previews events to come. The Pilgrims' Chorus melody quoted here appears in the body of the opera.

1. In this early style we have an example of three regular eight-measure periods. The first two are diatonic; the third chromatic.

2. Notice the cross relation between A$\sharp$ in m. 5 and A$\natural$ in m. 6.

3. The resolution of V^7 of III to I in m. 12-13 is a deceptive resolution as if it were V^7 to VI in g$\sharp$.

4. Analyze the harmony of the three-pattern sequence in m. 17-22.

5. Identify the augmented sixth chord on the second beat of m. 22.

6. Notice the importance of the appoggiaturas on the downbeat of m. 4, 8, 22, 23 and 24 as a characteristic melodic element.

EXAMPLE 50 (page 184)
Prelude to "Die Meistersinger"

Die Meistersinger was started before *Tristan and Isolde* and finished after it, but it is more diatonic (less chromatic) than *Tristan and Isolde*. The Prelude is a condensed version of the opera, treating several of the main motives of the opera and cast in sonata form.

The first-theme group consists of four themes:

The first (A) is the *Meistersinger* theme partially quoted in this example.

The second (B) is related to Walther's love.

The third (C) is the fanfare representing the singing contest.

The fourth (D) (Examples 51 and 52) from (A) m. 2 of this example.

The second theme which begins in E (m. 97 of Example 52) is derived from Walther's Prize Song.

The development treats themes A and D in diminution and in combination with new motives from the opera.

The recapitulation beginning at m. 158 in Example 53 presents themes A and C simultaneously with theme two in a contrapuntal fabric.

1. What is the effect of the C♯ in m. 2-3?

2. The II[11] in m. 7 and the long dominant passage over G in m. 8-13 illustrate the tendency of the time to build complex sonorities on the subdominant and dominant for increasing tension. Here the G is introduced in m. 8 as root of V[7] in C but resolves as fifth of V[7] of F. Notice the gradual shift to F by the introduction of B♭ in the chords in m. 12-13. Can G be considered a harmonic note throughout these measures? Notice how useful the diminished triad is in combination with the G in m. 12-13.

EXAMPLE 51 (page 185)
Prelude to "Die Meistersinger"

1. This and the next example illustrate the relatively diatonic style of Wagner.

2. Here is a four-measure phrase repeated except for the last beat of each fourth measure (62 and 66).

EXAMPLE 52 (pages 185,187)
Prelude to "Die Meistersinger"

1. Wagner's use of sequences and modified repetitions in extending and developing his material is illustrated here:

   a. M. 74-75 are the second and third repetitions of a stepwise ascending sequential pattern started the measure before.

   b. M. 76-79 are another stepwise ascending sequence in which the bass and upper melody participate. The harmony is not in the pattern.

   c. M. 82-84 constitute a three-pattern stepwise descending sequence modified in the third pattern and with harmonic modifications. Where is the pattern broken in inner voices or in the harmony?

   d. M. 91-92 are a modified repetition of 89-90, and m. 95-96 are a modified repetition of 93-94.

   e. In the same light, compare m. 105-106 with 109-110.

2. Notice how frequently the deceptive progression appears at points of important harmonic changes, such as, the close of one sequence to the beginning of another or the close of a phrase or section to the opening of another. These points are indicated by brackets below the staff. Analyze each progression which is bracketed. Each is a V-VI or V-IV progression except in m. 108-109. What is deceptive about it?

3. A greater amount of chromaticism is seen in the second-theme group and the transition to it (m. 89-110). Notice the increasing tension resulting from avoidance of a V-I progression in m. 88 to 97. M. 93-96 form a harmonic sequence to m. 89-92, that is, the harmony of m. 93-96 is nearly the same as m. 89-92, only a minor third higher. M. 93-95 are an exact transposition of 89-91; only 92 and 96 vary.

4. Observe that the establishment of the key of E at m. 97 is through a deceptive effect: M. 96 is V[7] of B so that the E chord in m. 97 sounds like IV[6] of B until its dominant is sounded on beat three of m. 97.

5. The chord vocabulary of m. 97-108 is relatively simple, but the complexity arises from the melodic lines highly ornamented with appoggiaturas and chromatic passing tones. The fluctuation between the half-diminished and diminished seventh chords serving as incomplete dominant ninths to I, V and II is a typical element of the Wagner harmonic-melodic idiom.

6. Again notice the use of repetition and sequence for expansion of the melodic idea:

   m. 102 is a repeat of 101
   m. 104 is a repeat of 103
   m. 109-110 are a transposition of m. 105-106

7. The downward resolving appoggiatura establishes the melodic character throughout this example. These appoggiaturas descend directly to the tone of resolution as in m. 100, beats one and three and four, or they resolve ornamentally by moving first to the lower auxiliary of the resolution tone as in m. 103 and 104 beat 3.

8. Every chord and every nonharmonic tone should be identified in this example.

EXAMPLE 53 (page 188)
Prelude to "Die Meistersinger"

1. Here the recapitulation is anticipated by a statement of A of theme one, m. 151-157. Notice the F♯, however, in m. 152.

2. The harmony of m. 150 functions as II $\frac{4}{3}$ from c resolving to a long dominant prolongation of V of C, m. 151-157. The G acts as a dominant pedal throughout these measures. Analyze the nonharmonic function of the right-hand sixteenth notes.

3. Notice that A of theme one and theme two are the important elements here. Theme C is essentially harmonic filler.

EXAMPLE 54 (pages 189, 190)
Tristan and Isolde, Prelude

The opera, *Tristan and Isolde*, is the ultimate example of Wagner's chromatic style. The predominant idea of the opera is endless longing. Wagner's style perfectly expresses this through its constantly shifting tonalities, cadence avoidance and deceptive progressions.

Throughout the romantic period we find the interval of the tritone being exploited for its ambiguity. From the time of Beethoven the diminished seventh chord (with two tritones) is used more and more as a pivot for modulation or deceptive progression. This leads to chromatic alterations of various other chords to produce tritones. In *Tristan and Isolde* we find a great use of the dominant seventh with lowered fifth, which is a chord with two tritones.

1. The lowered fifth is often treated by Wagner as a melodic raised fourth above the root resolving like an appoggiatura against V^7 to the fifth as the A♯ to B in m. 3. Or it may be used as a lowered fifth resolving downward as the F in m. 2 to E in m. 3.

2. The exploitation of the tritone produces a constantly shifting tonal center so that harmonic analysis reveals a series of "transient" modulations overlapping in such a way that a definitive key analysis which all ears could agree on is impossible.

3. Exact repetition and sequential repetition again play an important role in the unfolding of the music form. All these repetitions should be identified.

4. Considering the first three measures to be in the key of a, the first chord of m. 2 is VII $^4_2$ with D raised to D♯. On the last eighth note of the measure the chord becomes V $^4_3$ of B with lowered fifth (F). This resolves to V^7 with A♯ as appoggiatura to B instead of lowered fifth. Identify the tritones in m. 2-3.

5. M. 5-7 are a transposition of 1-3. M. 8-9 are like m. 1 expanded and extended; m. 10 is like m. 2 with harmonic substitution. The deceptive progression (V^7 to VI in a) at m. 16-17 closes a seventeen-measure section contructed as follows: 1, 2, 3 (3), 1, 2, 3 (3), 1, 2, 3, 2, 3, 3, 3, 3, 4.

6. Notice that the entire excerpt moves around the key center of A or a and that important points of climax emphasize A as at m. 16-17, 24 and 43-44.

7. M. 36-42 illustrate again the use of repetition and sequence combined with change of register to extend a motive. Here the appoggiatura one-half step below the fifth of the V^7 (as first seen in m. 3) appears again four times.

8. Observe the relationship of m. 16-17 to 43-44.

9. A careful harmonic and melodic analysis of this excerpt will reveal the essence of late nineteenth-century chromaticism.

EXAMPLE 55 (page 191)
Tristan and Isolde, Act II, Scene II

1. Compare the motive of the first two measures of this example with the extended and developed version of it in Example 56, m. 1-15.

2. It should be carefully observed that throughout this chromatic style, Wagner often introduces a chord in its chromatically altered form, then resolves the chromatic tone as a suspension or appoggiatura to the diatonic form of the same chord before resolving it. Thus the sequence of progression can be altered, unaltered, resolution as well as unaltered, altered, resolution. This is seen in m. 4 where A♭ in the tenor becomes the minor ninth of V^9 of C resolving on the third beat to A♮, the diatonic major ninth of C. Since m. 3-4 are a sequence of m. 1-2, it also occurs in m. 2 in relation to the key of C♭.

3. Observe that m. 8-10 are a harmonic sequence of 5-7. The movement in m. 11-22 is in pairs of measures.

4. In m. 17, the bass A♭ is a pedal and the upper voices (G B♭ D♭ F♭) act as a quadruple appoggiatura to the diminished seventh chord of m. 18.

5. The last eighth note of m. 20 is enharmonic V $^4_3$ of V with lowered fifth (F) of the key of A. The progression from m. 20 to 21 is exactly the same as Example 54, m. 2 to 3, but spelled enharmonically.

6. Notice that this entire excerpt is a gradual chromatic rise toward a climax.

EXAMPLE 56 (pages 192-193)
Tristan and Isolde, Act II, Scene II

1. This example with the voice parts indicated shows the relative importance of the accompaniment as compared to the voice line. It would appear that the orchestral accompaniment were written first and the voice lines dubbed in to fit what already existed.

2. Here the "Slumber Motive" is presented by the orchestra quite independent of the voices. The entire excerpt is based on the first four measures and is again a group of free sequential repetitions ascending toward a climax. Each climax leads to another tritone chord or deceptive resolution which continues the tension or longing instead of resolving or releasing it.

3. The first thirteen measures are in G♭. The chord on the third beat of m. 1 is the augmented sixth with doubly augmented fourth.

4. M. 3-8 are a highly chromatic prolongation of V^9 of G♭. Notice that the G♭ in m. 4 resolves ornamentally through D to E♭ and does not go to F, its expected resolution.

5. Compare the three seven-measure phrases: 9-15, 16-22 and 23-29. The last three measures of

each are the same kind of progression, but the first four measures of each vary harmonically and melodically from one phrase to another.

6. Compare the two four-measure phrases: 30-33 and 34-37. Notice that passages can be broken into phrases related to other phrases through sequence or repetition but that they are not independent by cadential definition.

EXAMPLE 57 (pages 194, 195)
Tristan and Isolde, Act III, Scene III

1. This famous passage which closes the opera finally resolves the longing, but not quite, because the final chord is in the position of the fifth.

2. Compare the predominant melodic motive (m. 1-4) of this example with the motives of the preceding examples from this work. Is there any relationship?

3. Analyze for repeated measures and sequences. Notice the prolongation over the dominant F♯ through m. 12-17 for the climax at 18 which involves the progression V^7 to IV, a common deceptive progression in Wagner. See Example 52, m. 23-24.

4. The extension of the final cadence from m. 18 to the end is a large plagal effect.

5. Observe the reference in m. 32-33 to the motive which opened the opera, Example 54, m. 1-3.

A thorough analysis of all aspects of these examples from Wagner will provide an understanding of his harmonic and melodic idiom plus an insight into the details of his formal procedures.

For an understanding of the large aspects of form in Wagner's music it is suggested that one or more of the following be analyzed:

> The Siegfried Idyll
> Rienzi Overture
> Prelude to Act III of Lohengrin
> Tannhäuser Overture
> Prelude to Act I of Parsifal

Suggested Written Assignments

1. In an exercise of about sixteen measures experiment with chromatic alteration of dominant sevenths and diminished sevenths. Include a V^7 to VI progression and V^7 to IV progression with accompanying appoggiaturas in the style seen in *Tristan and Isolde.*

2. Do a block-chord reduction of a section of about thirty-two measures from one of the "Ring" operas.

Bibliography

Newman, Ernest, *The Life of Richard Wagner* 4 vols., New York: Alfred A. Knopf, Inc., 1933-1946.

————, *The Wagner Operas*, New York: Alfred A. Knopf, Inc., 1949.

Stein, Jack M., *Richard Wagner and the Synthesis of the Arts*, Detroit: Wayne State University Press, 1960.

Truscott, Harold, "Wagner's Tristan and the Twentieth Century," *Music Review*, February, 1963. Pages 75-85.

Wagner, Richard, *Letters; the Burrill Collection*, ed. by John N. Burk, New York: The Macmillan Company, 1950.

————, *My Life*, New York: Dodd, Mead & Company, 1911.

EXAMPLE 49

WAGNER

TANNHÄUSER
OVERTURE

(First 25 Measures)

EXAMPLE 50
WAGNER
THE MASTERSINGERS OF NUREMBERG
PRELUDE
(Opening Measures)
(First Theme Group—Theme A)

EXAMPLE 51
WAGNER
THE MASTERSINGERS OF NUREMBERG
PRELUDE
(Measures 59-67)
(First Theme Group—Theme D)

EXAMPLE 52
WAGNER
THE MASTERSINGERS OF NUREMBERG
PRELUDE
(Measures 74-110)
(Close of First Theme Group [Theme D]—Transition—Opening
of Second Theme Group)

SECOND THEME GROUP

EXAMPLE 53

WAGNER
THE MASTERSINGERS OF NUREMBERG
PRELUDE
(Measures 150-165)
(Retransition and Beginning of Recapitulation)

EXAMPLE 54
WAGNER
TRISTAN AND ISOLDE
PRELUDE
(Opening Measures)

EXAMPLE 55

WAGNER
TRISTAN AND ISOLDE
ACT II, SCENE II
(Measures 630-652 of Accompaniment)

EXAMPLE 56
WAGNER
TRISTAN AND ISOLDE
ACT II, SCENE II
(Measures 714-750)

EXAMPLE 57
WAGNER

TRISTAN AND ISOLDE
ACT III, SCENE III
(Final 36 Measures of the Opera—Accompaniment)

(A = G✗)

CHAPTER 9

CÉSAR FRANCK

1822-1890

Franck, like Brahms, wrote in the idiom of romanticism but adapted that language to the classical forms by the use of thematic transformation and the cyclic concept. His music is highly chromatic but not in the Wagnerian sense. Whereas Wagner is nonperiodic, Franck's ideas are expressed in two-measure motives, four-measure phrases and eight-measure periods with regular cadences. Whereas Wagner prolongs a single harmony through chromatic alteration and ornamentation over a static bass, or stretches the bounds of tonality, Franck changes from one altered chord to another over a restless chromatic bass but remains basically tonal. Sequence and repetition, however, play a major role in the expansion of ideas in both styles.

In form Franck contributed certain individual solutions to the problem of combining romantic and classic elements. His melodies tend to revolve about a single tone, moving to and from it by a series of motive repetitions and expansions as in Symphony in d, I, m. 99-106 and 129-136 and Piano Quintet, I, m. 124-131. The flamboyant melodic lines and great climaxes of the Wagner and Strauss styles are not present in this more reserved introspective style. Franck nevertheless had great influence as a teacher of Ernest Chausson, Vincent d'Indy, Henri Duparc and Henri Pierné; and his school of French chromaticism led to the "conservatory" style which has existed into the twentieth century. Franck's mastery of counterpoint is displayed in all his works.

EXAMPLE 58 (page 199)
Prelude, Aria and Finale for Piano

The Prelude, Aria and Finale along with the Prelude, Chorale and Fugue and the Symphonic Variations comprise Franck's best-known piano works and all employ the cyclic approach.

Franck replaces the relationship of keys of the classic period with the relationship of themes in the cyclic form. The Prelude contains five themes, three of which appear in the later movements in combination with the new themes of those movements.

1. The work opens with a statement of the first theme which is an independent section of forty-two measures closing with a perfect authentic cadence in the tonic (E). This example consisting of the first fourteen measures illustrates:

   a. The simple two- and four-measure structure of phrases;
   b. Chord changes on each beat;
   c. Chromatic bass line and melody (m. 10-12);
   d. Chromatic alteration.

2. The first eight measures are constructed in four groups of two measures. M. 7-8 are a sequence of m. 5-6, a minor third higher. M. 9-12 form an unbroken four-measure phrase. M. 13-14 are the beginning of a varied restatement.

3. The movement directly to the III chord in m. 1 illustrates Franck's fondness for the mediant and submediant keys. Notice that he returns to E in m. 2 by a sequence of the first three chords of m. 1.

4. M. 3-4 are another movement to III and back to V of E.

5. M. 6, beats two and three, illustrates the dominant ninth and seventh with lowered fifth. On beat two the chord is B♯ D F♯ A, the incomplete dominant ninth of c♯ (VI) with lowered fifth, D. On beat three, the chord is V⁷ of VI, with lowered fifth, D. M. 8, a sequence of m. 6 contains the same progression.

6. Notice the parallel fifths between the outer voices in m. 6 to 7 and 8 to 9, and the parallel dominant seventh chords (C⁷ to B⁷) in m. 12, beats three to four. This parallelism becomes a salient feature of the impressionist style, and this along with the

altered dominants and regular phrase structure of Franck would indicate an influence by him and his students on Debussy and the impressionists.

7. Observe the various alterations of the submediant and subdominant in m. 10-12:

M. 10, beat 2 is VI $\frac{4}{3}$ with G♮ (F𝄪);
M. 10, beat 3 is VI $\frac{4}{3}$ diatonic to I⁶;
M. 10, beat 4 is IV from e;
M. 11, beat 1 & 3 is IV⁷ spelled as VII⁷ of V;
M. 11, beat 2 is IV from e;
M. 12, beat 1 is VI from e;
M. 12, beat 2 is V⁷ of VI from e;
M. 12, beat 3 is VI⁷ spelled as V⁷ of N.

Examples and Suggestions for Further Study of the Music of Franck

for individual treatment of form

The *Variations Symphoniques* for piano and orchestra is a work in one movement divided into three large, related sections comprising a fantasia, followed by a set of variations, and closing with a sonata form and coda.

The Symphony in d is a cyclic work which employs several unusual formal approaches. The first movement involves a first-theme group presented in both lento and allegro tempi and repeated in the mediant minor before the entrance of the second-theme group, thus forming a long exposition. The long development is full of contrapuntal display. The second movement combines elements of scherzo and slow movements. It is an allegretto in second rondo (ABACA) form. The B and C sections could be considered trios. The statements of A are ingeniously varied with only elements of the accompaniment figure or chord pattern present to remind the listener of the theme. The coda contains references to the B and C sections.

The finale is a sonata which uses the A theme of II in the development and in which the return of the second theme is replaced by a large coda which recapitulates themes from I and II.

Unusual key relationships abound in this work as in Franck's other works. However, second themes in movements in sonata form are usually introduced in the conventional keys, and the key relationships of middle to outer movements are typical of that time.

All Franck's important chamber works are in cyclic form. Often one theme or motive acting as a generating element reappears in various forms throughout the movements of the work, and entire themes are reviewed in later movements. The cyclic theme of the entire Piano Quintet in f is a re-employment of a theme he used in a trio many years earlier. Compare m. 124-131 of I with the Piano Trio, op. 1, no. 1, I, m. 9-16. This theme is the second theme of I, reappears in the development of II, and in the coda of the finale, III, in altered form. Each movement of this work is in sonata form.

The Sonata in A for violin and piano contains the following interesting formal characteristics:

I is a sonatina in allegretto tempo, more like a traditional second movement.

II is a sonata in allegro tempo more of a first-movement type.

III is a Recitative-Fantasia which reviews themes of I and II but in modified form.

IV is a unique rondo in which the A section is a canon between the violin and piano and C is a development section which employs thematic material from the preceding movements along with motives of the canon theme.

A	B	A	B	A	C	A
canon	from	canon	from	canon	Devel.	canon
in A	III	in C♯	III	in E		in A

The String Quartet in D is probably Franck's finest chamber work and as usual involves formal innovations.

I is a combination of two separate forms: a sonata form interpolated within an ABA rondo in such a way that each remains individual and complete and yet contributes to a unified movement:

⌈ A	Lento
Exposition ⌉	Allegro
⌊ B (based on A) ⌉	Poco lento
Development ⌋	Allegro
Recapitulation ⌋	Allegro
⌊ A	Lento

This form would appear to be the next logical step after the works with integrated introductions by Beethoven and Brahms.

II is a scherzo and trio containing a reference to A of I at m. 225 in the cello.

III is a second rondo.

IV is a remarkable movement which opens with an introduction which reviews themes from the previous three movements as in the Beethoven Symphony, no. 9, IV.

for harmonic and contrapuntal effects

Canons:

Symphony in d, I, m. 331-344

Symphony in d, III, m. 426-433

Sonata for Violin and Piano, IV

Ostinato:

Symphony in d, III, m. 350-380

Augmentation:

String Quartet, I, motive at m. 105-106 appears in IV in augmentation at m. 133 and double augmentation at m. 137

The augmented sixth chord with doubly augmented fourth is used in Symphony in d, III, m. 3-4, and the same chord appears inverted with a doubly diminished fifth in the Sonata for Violin and Piano, I, m. 57-58 and 94. Find it again in the recapitulation. The augmented sixth with augmented fourth moving to the augmented fifth appears in m. 70.

Unusual harmonic progressions can be found throughout the works of Franck, and it is suggested that they can be more readily identified in his organ and piano works.

SUGGESTED WRITTEN ASSIGNMENTS

1. Write a sixteen-measure exercise in four-voice harmony employing half-step motion in the various voices to produce the types of altered chords used by Franck.

BIBLIOGRAPHY

ANDRIESSEN, HENDRICK, *César Franck*, Stockholm: Continental Book Company. [194-]

DENMUTH, NORMAN, *César Franck*, London: Dennis Dobson, 1949.

GRACE, HARVEY, *The Organ Works of César Frank*, London: Novello, 1948.

INDY, VINCENT D', *César Franck*, London: John Lane, 1910.

VALLAS, LEON, *César Franck*, New York: Oxford University Press, Inc., 1951.

EXAMPLE 58

FRANCK

PRELUDE, ARIA, AND FINALE FOR PIANO
PRELUDE
(Opening Measures)

CHAPTER 10

RICHARD STRAUSS

1864-1949

Strauss applied a strong sense of formal logic to the symphonic poem and thus produced orchestral works with philosophical or descriptive programs which for the most part are consistent and unified from a musically abstract point of view. To be sure, he used such forms as sonata and rondo in a very free sense, but in a sense which was musically logical for his artistic goals.

He carries the Wagnerian harmonic idiom into a realm of greater dissonance, with polyharmonic and bitonal effects which, though they may seem commonplace today, were highly original and influenced the French impressionists and the German atonalists.

His influenecs are the romantic doctrine of programmatic music of Liszt and Berlioz, and the leitmotif, continuous melody, and the large orchestral sound from Wagner.

It should be understood that many of Strauss' works such as *Don Juan, Death and Transfiguration* and *Thus Spake Zarathustra* are expressions of abstract, philosophical ideas and emotions and in that sense are no more programmatic than Beethoven's Symphonies, nos. 3, 5 and 6.

On the other hand, works based on a program of more prosaic or narrative character such as *Till Eulenspiegel* and *Don Quixote* are nevertheless cast in forms which for the most part do not require an awareness of the program and result in an independent musical experience. *Till Eulenspiegel* is in free rondo form and *Don Quixote* is a theme and variations design.

In his operas, such as *Salome, Elektra* and *Der Rosenkavalier,* which were written after his most significant orchestral works, Strauss continues the development of his harmonic idiom into even greater complexity so that the next inevitable step is the overwrought style of Alban Berg.

Strauss' themes are great, sweeping gestures which soar over the entire orchestral range with a freedom made possible by his masterful orchestration

and counterpoint carried in a fluid and resourceful harmonic idiom.

EXAMPLE 59 (page 203)
Till Eulenspiegel's Merry Pranks

The two themes associated with *Till* are presented at the outset and exemplify Strauss' ability to delineate in music an idea or a person. These two ideas express the roguishness, ironic humor and wistfulness of *Till*. The work, as Strauss indicates in the full title, is in rondo form but not in the conventional sense. The sense of rondo is recognized in the alternation of the *Till* themes which express his feelings with the musical ideas which represent his mischievous pranks.

1. The first four notes form a motive which appears in many forms throughout the work to express *Till's* attitudes. The first five notes of the theme beginning at m. 6 also are transformed in similar manner.

2. The V^7 with raised fifth in m. 1 (F^7 with C$\sharp$) is a common alteration on the dominant seventh seen frequently in all works of this period and type. Here it is V^7 of IV in F.

3. The wide range of the theme beginning at m. 6 is typical of Strauss.

4. Observe the sixteenth-note rush of parallel triads in m. 12. This parallelism becomes a more frequent element in Strauss and composers influenced by him and Wagner.

EXAMPLE 60 (pages 203, 204)
Don Juan

This famous work was completed when the composer was only twenty-four. It is cast in the general lines of a sonata form, but the constant process of development and thematic transformation make the form less obvious. Yet, in spite of their harmonic complexity, the symphonic poems remain strongly tonal, key areas are well defined, as can be seen in these examples.

1. Though the opening harmony is VI from e, the main key, E, is strongly established at m. 3.

2. The first two measures imply e, and a cross relation reminiscent of Brahms occurs going from m. 2 to 3. The expanding effect of the bass descending and the upper parts ascending creates a brilliant opening statement.

3. The ornamented arpeggio in m. 5-6 is a device of Strauss to create commotion.

4. After the firm establishment of E at m. 7, a I in root position is then avoided even with the beginning of the theme at m. 9.

5. Notice that B is retained as a pedal at m. 10.

6. The progression from dominant of the dominant directly to tonic as seen in m. 8 to 9 and 10 to 11 is frequent in both Wagner and Strauss. This elision of the dominant in between V of V and I gives a bright effect to the harmonic motion by allowing the raised fourth of the scale in V of V to move directly to I. The last chord in m. 8 is V $\frac{4}{3}$ of B with lowered fifth (C).

7. From m. 13, beat two, to m. 15, beat three, the prevailing harmony is dominant of IV. The bass notes A, A♯ and C♯ are passing between G♯, B and D.

EXAMPLE 61 (pages 204, 205)
Death and Transfiguration

This work deals with the philosophical concept of the victory of the spirit over death or the transfiguration of the soul through suffering. The poem associated with it was written by Alexander Ritter after Strauss composed the music. In form it consists of a slow introductory section, a long development of thematic material and a majestic epilogue representing the transfiguration.

1. This excerpt is the first forty of the last seventy measures of the work which deals with the transfiguration theme in its fullest expression. Here we see the ability of Strauss to expand to greater dimensions what has previously appeared as only a motive.

2. Here again the D⁷, V⁷ of V, m. 2-3, is used without the intervening V chord.

3. The first five-measure phrase is a large plagal progression, I, IV, I. The bass F in m. 4 acts as a pedal under the VII⁷ of IV on beats one and two.

3. M. 6-9 are a long dominant phrase. The tonic C is maintained through the first twenty-two measures comprising a period of nine measures plus a period of thirteen measures.

4. A theme heard earlier in the work enters at m. 23. M. 26-29 are a sequence of m. 22-25 a step higher. A third statement of the sequence in E begins at m. 30 but is not carried through.

5. Notice the enharmonic resolution of the B⁷ in m. 33 to E♭ in m. 34. If the chord in m. 33 were spelled according to its resolution it would be an augmented sixth with doubly augmented fourth: C♭ E♭ F♯ A. Notice that Strauss resolves it freely with B going to G in the bass.

6. A careful analysis of nonharmonic tones will reveal much about the harmonic-melodic idiom of Strauss.

EXAMPLE 62 (page 206)
Ein Heldenleben (Theme)

The opening theme of this work is quoted to illustrate the extremely wide range (one-half step less than three octaves) and complex shape which Strauss employs in later works. The opening statement of this theme is played by horn and strings like a recitative with only an occasional accompanying chord. Its length and number of motives for manipulation imply that a work of large proportions is to follow.

EXAMPLE 63 (page 206)
Ein Heldenleben (Fanfare)

This fanfare is included as an example of the free use of triads in parallel or nontonal relationship which appears frequently in later Strauss works. Though the passage is in B♭, the non-B♭ chords are either quite remote like the F♭ (E) chord or result from parallelism as the C♭ and G♭ chords do. Here, as in the impressionist style of Debussy, chords are used for color without regard for tonal function.

The juxtaposition of chords whose roots are a tritone apart (b♭ to F♭ in m. 6-8) is not unusual in post-romantic music and is an effect also exploited by Stravinsky.

Examples and Suggestions for Further Study of the Music of Strauss

An important element in this style is the prolongation of harmonies with dominant function for building suspense and expanding the form. Some of these long dominant preparations have the same effect as the retransitions of late classical sonata forms. Also, long pedal or ostinato passages contribute to the large dimensions of late romantic forms. Both of these elements which can be found throughout the work of Strauss are illustrated in *Death and Transfiguration*:

   a. M. 49-66.

   b. M. 164-179. The dominant (B♭) preparation for E♭ resolves at m. 180 by deceptive progression to dominant (D) of G, and m. 180-186 are the dominant (D) preparation for a section in G.

c. In m. 310-320 the dominant preparation for
   A♭ involves a two-measure ostinato figure in
   the bass (m. 310-335).
d. M. 382-395 form a large I $\begin{smallmatrix}6\\4\end{smallmatrix}$ to V effect over a
   pedal G in preparation for the long epilogue
   in C representing the transfiguration. This
   epilogue begins at m. 396 with an ostinato on
   a C-G pattern which lasts until m. 426.

It should be kept in mind that Strauss' most significant symphonic poems were written before 1900
and that his important operas were written after 1900.
Since his harmonic style in the operas included increased use of nonfunctional color chords, dissonance
and bitonal effects, a study of the operas, *Salome,*
Elektra and *Der Rosenkavalier* is suggested. The
"rose" motive of *Der Rosenkavalier* played by the
celesta illustrates the use of chords usually associated
with impressionism.

Suggested Written Assignments

Write an example of about twenty-four measures
comprising a sustained eight-measure dominant ornamented with nonharmonic effects resolving to a tonic
pedal or ostinato passage with a variety of altered
chords, introduced through suspensions and appoggiaturas, above it.

Bibliography

Berlioz, Hector, *Treatise on Instrumentation,* enl. and
   rev. by Richard Strauss, New York: Edwin F. Kalmus,
   1948.

Del Mar, Norman, *Richard Strauss: A Critical Com-
   mentary on his Life and Works,* London: Barrie &
   Rockliff, 1962.

Finck, Henry T., *Richard Strauss,* Boston: Little, Brown
   & Company, 1917.

Krause, Ernst, *Richard Strauss: Gestalt und Werk,* Leipzig: Breitkopf and Härtel, 1955.

Newman, Ernst, *Richard Strauss,* London: John Lane,
   1908.

Strauss, Richard, *Correspondence Between Richard
   Strauss and Hugo von Hofmannsthal,* New York:
   Alfred A. Knopf, Inc., 1927. Translated by Paul
   England.

————, *Recollections and Reflections,* New York: Boosey
   & Hawkes, 1953.

EXAMPLE 59
Strauss
TILL EULENSPIEGEL'S MERRY PRANKS
(Opening Measures)

EXAMPLE 60
Strauss
DON JUAN
(Opening Measures)

EXAMPLE 61
STRAUSS

DEATH AND TRANSFIGURATION
(Measures 431-470)

EXAMPLE 62
Strauss

EIN HELDENLEBEN (THEME)
(Opening Measures)

EXAMPLE 63
Strauss

EIN HELDENLEBEN (FANFARE)
(Measures 361-370)

CHAPTER 11

PETER I. TCHAIKOVSKY

1840-1893

The criticism leveled by twentieth-century musical essayists at romantic composers in general and at Tchaikovsky in particular is more a result of today's bias against nineteenth-century romantic expression than of objective weighing of intrinsic musical values. It is fashionable in a neoclassic period to consider recently popular romantic music as morbid, unrestrained, hysterical or theatrical. As a composer in the German romantic tradition, Tchaikovsky did not develop his thematic material in the way that Brahms did, but he needs no apology. He was a first-rate melodist, was rarely surpassed in his ability to manipulate rhythmic material; and though his treatment of symphonic form is less taut and more rambling than some of his contemporaries, it suited his themes and artistic goals.

He wrote effectively in nearly every area of composition: opera, symphony, ballet, piano, chamber music, concerto and symphonic poem.

His works in sonata form are characterized by an energetic first theme contrasted by a lyric, usually meloncholy, second theme. He parlays small melodic or rhythmic motives into intense climaxes through a combination of repetition, sequence and rhythmic crowding by successive shortening of the motive or pattern.

Though his music is intensely emotional in effect there is little difference in form and content between his abstract and descriptive works. In this sense he expresses emotion unrelated to programmatic detail but arising from musical requirements.

EXAMPLE 64 (page 211)
Symphony No. 4 in F Minor, I

This illustrates his ability to spin a soaring melodic line from a single motive (bracketed). This is the opening statement of the first theme (first period) following a twenty-six measure slow introduction.

1. The descending nature of the motive brings the melodic line through rhythmic repetition plus modified melodic sequence to a low point at m. 4 where the melodic direction is inverted and a rise to the half cadence at m. 8 is accomplished by the same process.

2. Intensity and momentum for the climax at m. 8 are provided by shortening the motive to two notes (♩ ♪) stated three times in rising sequence (m. 7, beats 2-3, and m. 8, beat 1) followed by the cadence chords (m. 8, beats 2 and 3). This method of building a climax is typical.

3. The rhythmic nature of the melody against the punctuating chords produces a syncopated and self-propelling flow to the theme.

4. The entire passage can be analyzed in f, but a transient modulation to b♭ is indicated by the chord symbols.

5. The second theme (m. 136-160) and the closing theme and codetta (m. 161-192) are all derived from this theme.

EXAMPLE 65 (page 211)
Symphony No. 6 in B Minor, I

Symphonies, nos. 4, 5 and 6 each open with a slow introduction which presents motives to be developed in the course of the movement and/or reappears later to introduce the development section and/or coda. This and the next example illustrate the manner in which the introduction previews the first theme.

1. The descending bass line along with the appoggiaturas and minor mode set a mood of gloom.

2. The four-note motive which constitutes the head of the first theme (Example 66) is subjected to a series of sequences comprising the material of the introduction.

EXAMPLE 66 (page 212)
Symphony No. 6 in B Minor, I

These first five measures of theme one show how the four-note motive is repeated with the first two notes elaborated into a figure of four sixteenths. This four-note motive and its elaborated echo are later crowded together and repeated sequentially in building a climactic transition to the second part of the first-theme group (m. 34-38).

The continuous sixteenth-note passage (m. 3-4) acts as a balancing factor to the disconnected character of the first two measures.

EXAMPLE 67 (page 212)
Symphony No. 6 in B Minor, I

Here is exemplified the extended melodic second-theme contrasting sharply with the energetic, fitful, first-theme material. It will be seen that the downward resolving appoggiatura effect (in brackets) is an important element in this theme as in the preceding themes of this movement (Examples 65 and 66).

The entire second theme and closing sections of this movement taken together form an independent extended three-part song form with coda (m. 89-160), and therein lies the rambling quality of Tchaikovsky's symphonic form. His concern with a lovely self-contained melody tends to destroy the continuity. It is like taking time out for a lovely aria in the midst of a seething conflict. Yet this contrast of mood is part of the style's unique attractiveness.

EXAMPLE 68 (page 212)
Symphony No. 6 in B Minor, II

Here is one of the suave, graceful, refined melodies for which Tchaikovsky is especially noted and which is characteristic of his ballet music. This elegant movement replaces a slow movement at this point because the finale is the slow (adagio) movement. The meter so common today was a rarity in his time.

The form of the movement is a song form with trio with the return of the song form written out and a coda based on the themes of both sections. The trio is in b and D but presented over a D pedal that continues throughout its entirety like the old musette. A pedal D extends throughout the coda also. Compare this trio to the trio of Schumann's Symphony, no. 3, II, m. 33-48.

Part a of the song form is a double period. The example includes the first period and two measures of the second period, showing the manner in which the original melodic voice moves under the repetition of the theme as a countermelody.

EXAMPLE 69 (page 213)
Symphony No. 6 in B Minor, IV

The finale is an adagio in sonatina form. The first theme is an expression of despair only momentarily relieved by the lyric second theme. The example comprises the second part of the first-theme statement leading to V_3^4 of D in preparation for the entrance of the second theme.

1. The first four measures are written with voice crossing in the four string parts, for which it is scored. The orchestral score should be consulted for this effect.

2. The sequence of seventh chords all with tritones is an especially intense effect at the slow tempo. Parallel diminished seventh passages in fast tempo appear frequently in the works of Liszt, where they have a wind-machine effect.

3. The appoggiatura on the downbeat of every measure from five through fourteen is reminiscent of the downward appoggiaturas in I.

4. There are two sequential repetitions of m. 5 6 in 7-8 and 9-10. The sequences are exact except for one note. Which note is not in sequence?

Examples and Suggestions for Further Study of the Music of Tchaikovsky

Though he occasionally used a Russian folk-song theme as in the Symphony, no. 4, IV, theme 2, and wrote an occasional work on a Russian subject such as *March Slav* or the opera, *Eugene Onegin*, he cannot be considered a nationalist composer. He is essentially a cosmopolitan composer of great melodic eloquence, who writes in abstract forms filled with the emotional content of romanticism.

Following are some of the broad formal characteristics of a group of his orchestral works:

The fantasy overture, *Romeo and Juliet*, is a sonata form with slow introduction and coda. The keys of themes 1 and 2 in the exposition are b and D♭; they return in b and D. The agitated first theme is contrasted by an eloquent, lyric second theme.

The *Capriccio Italien*, op. 45, is a potpourri of Italian-type melodies and dances in an ABCADBD coda design.

Symphony, no. 4, op. 36, in *f*:

I has a slow introduction, the material of which reappears to open the development section and the coda. The keys of themes 1 and 2 are f and a♭ returning in a and d modulating to F for the closing section and f for the coda.

II is a first rondo (ABA) with A in b♭ and B, derived from theme one of I, in F.

III is a scherzo in F and trio in A and D♭. The scherzo theme appears in the trio. The repeat of the scherzo is written out and closes with a long coda which reviews all the themes of the movement.

IV is a sonatina in F. The first theme, however, is a closed form with a conclusive cadence in tonic (F) followed immediately without transition by theme 2 in b♭, a quotation of a Russian folk song. After a short transition, theme one returns in shortened form followed without transition by theme 2 in d. The introduction of I returns to open the long, bombastic coda which is based on themes 1 and 2 in F.

Symphony, no. 5, op. 64, in e, employs the cyclic principle much more extensively than Symphonies, nos. 4 or 6. The introduction theme of I returns abruptly in II twice, appears at the close of III, and, changed to major (E), becomes the introduction of IV, serves as closing theme and is the main theme of the grandiose coda which closes with a reference to theme 1 of I.

In I, theme 1 in e is connected to theme 2 in D by a transition which has the effect of an independent theme in b. The closing section includes the theme 1 motive. The development deals with both themes 1 and 2. Theme 2 returns in E. The coda closes with theme 1 repeated over an ostinato bass figure (m. 507-534).

II is a first rondo form as follows:

A is an extended three-part song form in D preceded by a short introductory chord sequence.

B is a phrase group modulating through sequences from f♯ to c♯. An episode based on the introduction of I is inserted.

A returns in shortened form. A second episode based on the introduction of I is inserted before the coda.

III is a waltz in song form and trio design closing with a reference to the introduction of I.

IV opens with the introduction theme of I in major and greatly expanded. Theme 1 in e involves canonic imitation in m. 98-114 and is followed by theme 2 in D. The introduction theme of I closes the exposition in C. Theme 2 returns in E. The coda is devoted to the introduction theme of I, first in e then in E. The closing measures quote the first motive of theme 1 of I.

Symphony, no. 6, op. 74, in b, I, II and IV are discussed in connection with Examples 65-69. III in

G is a sonatina form in scherzo-march style in which the lead motive of theme 2 appears in the theme 1 statement and becomes the predominant idea of the movement. Theme 2 is first in E and returns in G.

It will be seen from the foregoing works that even though theme 2 often appears first in an unusual key, it returns in the recapitulation in tonic. The exposition is not repeated in any of the sonata movements of these three symphonies.

The second String Quartet, op. 22, in F, employs the strings in full sonorous fashion. The full texture produces a symphonic sound. A slow introduction opens I which is regular in form with theme two in the dominant and returning in tonic.

II is a scherzo in D♭ and trio in A based on a Russian-type theme. The meter of the scherzo is a seven-beat pattern consisting of two measures of $\frac{6}{8}$ plus one measure of $\frac{9}{8}$.

III is an ABA rondo with a particularly sonorous B section. The A section is in f; B is in E.

IV is a highly rhythmic allegro-finale involving two alternating themes but with a single rhythmic background throughout. The design is:

A in F
B in D♭
A in F
B in A
A in the form of a fugato in F
B in F
Coda based on A

The Piano Trio, op. 50, in A, consists of two large movements. The first is a sonata with four themes extended to symphonic proportions. The second is a theme with eleven variations, an extended finale and a coda. Each variation is in the character of a different type of dance or other form.

The finale develops the theme at great length and a theme from I is quoted at the close.

Certain of the themes of the Piano Concerto, no. 1, in b♭, op. 23, have a folk song character. In I the soaring introduction (almost an independent form) is in D♭. Theme 1 is in b♭, theme 2 is in A♭ and returns in B♭. The solo piano and orchestra share the single exposition. The cadenza before the closing theme begins on VI of b♭.

II is a first rondo with section A in D♭ and B in F.

III is a typical Tchaikovsky rondo in ABABAB design with each appearance of B in a new key: D♭, E♭ and B♭, respectively.

The Violin Concerto in D, op. 35, exhibits somewhat the same design as the one above.

The first movement has a single exposition shared by soloist and orchestra. The key relationships are regular but an unusual feature of the movement is the placing of the cadenza at the close of the development before the recapitulation in the position of a retransition.

II in Bb is a three-part song form framed by a short prelude and a postlude. The latter extends into a transition to III.

III has a Russian dance (trepak) character. It is an ABABA rondo with the B sections in A and G, dominant and subdominant.

Generally speaking, Tchaikovsky relegated his less significant musical conceptions to the piano. Like Schumann he wrote many piano pieces in small forms including a *Children's Album* of twenty-four pieces, op. 39.

His *Scherzo a la Russe*, op. 1, *Doumka*, op. 59 and *Invitation a la Trepak*, op. 72, no. 18, are excellent works in the form of the Russian-Oriental dance, consisting of a tune repeated over and over with changing harmonies and increasing excitement to a point of frenzy. This kind of endless repetition being typical of a vigorous Russian dance is, of course, a major element in the style of Mussorgsky and some of the music of Bartók. See Examples 79, 80, 83, 148 and 149.

The Sonata in G, op. 37a, is a work for piano of symphonic proportions.

The collection of piano pieces called *The Months*, op. 37b, the *Children's Album*, op. 39, and eighteen *Pieces*, op. 72, are recommended for analysis of small forms and relatively uncomplicated harmonic analysis.

The last movement of the Violin Concerto contains good examples of both single and double rhythmic pedal points. Also m. 122-126 of I illustrate an augmented sixth chord, II $^{6\sharp}_{5}$ in A, extended over five measures to a climax at m. 127. This is, of course, repeated in D in the recapitulation.

As an examination of his works reveals, Tchaikovsky's popularity lies in his eloquent melodies presented in a direct way with appealing harmony, exciting climaxes and effective handling of the medium.

SUGGESTED WRITTEN ASSIGNMENTS

1. Invent a two-measure motive typical of the style and build it to a climax through direct and sequential repetition combined with shortening of the motive to create a stretto effect.

2. Select a section from a larger work of Tchaikovsky and do a phrase analysis by numbering each measure according to the thematic motive or figure it contains. This will illustrate the role of repetition and sequence in the style. See Example 2 (1) for an exemplification of this process of analysis.

BIBLIOGRAPHY

ABRAHAM, GERALD (ed.), *The Music of Tchaikovsky*, New York: W. W. Norton & Company, Inc., 1946.

BOWEN, CATHERINE DRINKER, *Beloved Friend*, New York: Random House, Inc., 1937.

EVANS, EDWIN, *Tchaikovsky*, London: J. M. Dent & Sons, Ltd., 1957.

SHOSTAKOVICH, DMITRI, *et al.*, *Russian Symphony; Thoughts About Tchaikovsky*, New York: The Philosophical Library, 1947.

TCHAIKOVSKY, MODESTE, *The Life and Letters of Peter Ilich Tchaikovsky*, ed. by Rosa Newmarch, New York: Dodd, Mead & Company, 1924.

WEINSTOCK, HERBERT, *Tchaikovsky*, New York: Alfred A. Knopf, Inc., 1943.

EXAMPLE 64
TCHAIKOVSKY
SYMPHONY NO. 4 IN F MINOR
I
(Measures 28-35)

EXAMPLE 65
TCHAIKOVSKY
SYMPHONY NO. 6 IN B MINOR
I
(Opening Measures)

EXAMPLE 66
TCHAIKOVSKY
SYMPHONY NO. 6 IN B MINOR
I
(Measures 20-24)

EXAMPLE 67
TCHAIKOVSKY
SYMPHONY NO. 6 IN B MINOR
I
(Measures 90-97)

EXAMPLE 68
TCHAIKOVSKY
SYMPHONY NO. 6 IN B MINOR
II
(Opening Measures)

EXAMPLE 69

TCHAIKOVSKY

SYMPHONY NO. 6 IN B MINOR

IV

(Measures 20-36)

CHAPTER 12

N. A. RIMSKY-KORSAKOV

1844-1908

Musical fantasy infused with appealing lyricism and garbed in brilliant orchestral colors characterizes Rimsky-Korsakov's style. Though he is probably the best-trained musician of the Russian nationalist group known as "The Five," he does not show the originality or dramatic power of Mussorgsky or the sense of formal organization of Borodin, but his knowledge and technique of orchestration and understanding of the capabilities of the instruments probably exceed that of most of his contemporaries. In fact, the orchestral settings of Rimsky-Korsakov's ideas are integral to those ideas. His music, based as it is on a rather conventional harmonic idiom and formal design involving much repetition and sequence, depends on a brilliant orchestral garb of constantly changing instrumental colors for its effectiveness.

His most important works are symphonic poems or suites and operas based on Russian legends and fairy tales plus the *Capriccio Espagnol,* a symphonic suite exploiting the musical idioms of Spain.

Antar and *Scheherazade,* both symphonic suites in four movements, are programmatic works employing themes which appear in each movement in the manner of the *idée fixe* of Berlioz.

EXAMPLE 70 (page 216)
Scheherazade I

The formal design of the four movements of this work is as follows:

I in E is a two-part form in sonatina design with introduction and coda.

II in b is an ABA form with introduction and coda. A is a two-part song form extended by several repetitions. B is a free fantasy or sectional form. In m. 132-154 the tritone, C to F♯, is treated alternately as part of the D⁷ chord and as part of the A♭⁷ chord (C to G♭) just as Mussorgsky does in Example

77. This exploiting of the ambiguity of the tritone is seen in the introduction of Hanson's Symphony, no. 2, Example 120. See also m. 12-13, 15-16, 17-19 of this example. See number 7 below.

III in G is again a two-part, sonatina design with coda. Theme 2 appears in B♭ and returns in G. Neither I nor III can be considered true sonatina forms because each theme comprises a self-contained melody spun out by direct and sequential repetitions of motives and then repeated as a whole. The key relationships of the sonatina are present but not the spirit.

IV beginning in e, closing in E, is a sectional form designed along sonata lines containing themes from the previous three movements and closing with a long coda on the opening theme of I. It is remarkable that a work involving so much repetition of short motives and conventional harmonies can yet sustain so much musical drive and interest.

1. The theme representing the Sultan, Sharier, and that representing Scheherazade are stated as the introduction to I. They both appear throughout the work; the former is the basis of I as seen in this example. Both themes act as introductions or intrude as episodes, cadenzas or countermelodies in other movements.

2. This example comprises one statement of the theme based on the Sultan motive from the introduction. It is immediately repeated with harmonic adjustment to lead into the key of C for the second theme which is derived from it. The repetition is exactly the same number of measures as the first statement and constructed in the same manner.

3. The sequential structure is revealed through phrase analysis as follows:

Phrase 1 (5 meas.) 1 2 3 4 4
Phrase 2 (5 meas.) 1 2 3 4 4
Phrase 3 (9 meas.) 1 2 3 1 2 3 $\overline{1\ 2}$ $\overline{3\ 1}$ $\overline{2\ 3}$
Phrase 4 (5 meas.) 1 2 3 4 4

4. Rimsky-Korsakov is fond of the type of chord in m. 2. This chord contains two tritones, E to A♯ and D to G♯, and like the French sixth (augmented $\frac{6}{4}$♯) with which it is enharmonic and like the diminished seventh chord it has many possibilities for resolution. If D to G♯ were considered the diatonic tritone then the chord would be a dominant seventh, E⁷, with A♯ displacing B, the fifth. If E to A♯ is the diatonic tritone then the chord is a half-diminished seventh on A♯ or the incomplete dominant ninth with F♯ as the missing root and D displacing C♯, the fifth.

The chord in m. 2 is used in the latter function.

Inasmuch as the first four measures modulate to B the harmony of m. 2 would be VII $\frac{4}{3}$ of B (with D as appoggiatura to C♯) resolving deceptively to II $\frac{6}{5}$ from b in m. 3, the latter acting as a delay to the normal resolution to B which comes in m. 4.

5. M. 1-5 constitute a modulation from E to B, and m. 6-10 constitute a modulation from B to F♯. The progression in m. 6-8 is the same as in m. 1-3 except that the chords are in different inversions. Where II $\frac{6}{5}$ in m. 3 resolved to I⁶ in m. 4, the comparable resolution does not take place in m. 8 to 9. The II $\frac{4}{3}$ in m. 8 resolves to V⁷ of F♯ instead of I in m. 9.

6. M. 11-13 form a sequence pattern which is repeated a whole step higher in m. 14-16 and twice more, each a whole step higher, in m. 17-19 by rhythmic diminution so that the pattern is shortened from three to one and a half measures for the third and fourth repetitions as bracketed.

7. The harmonic relationship of the second to the third chord of this sequence pattern is that of two dominant sevenths enharmonically sharing the same tritone. The E⁷ chord in m. 12 resolves chromatically to B♭⁷ in m. 13; both are dominant seventh chords having the common tritone D to G♯ (A♭). See m. 15-16 and 17-19.

8. M. 20-24 are an exact transposition of m. 6-10, bringing the tonal center back to E with a half cadence on V⁷.

9. The tonal pattern of the example is:

m. 1-5, E to B
m. 6-10, B to F♯
m. 11-19, C♯, E♭, F, G
m. 20-24, A to E

For an example of what the art of orchestration can do for music of simple harmonic, melodic and formal design one should study the *Capriccio Espagnol* of Rimsky-Korsakov. Here the simplest musical rhetoric is elevated to eloquence by brilliantly executed orchestral scoring.

The *Russian Easter* overture based on Russian liturgical themes exemplifies Rimsky-Korsakov's handling of the modal idiom, an idiom which is probably more effectively manifested in Mussorgsky's music.

Rimsky-Korsakov's interest in oriental fantasy is shown not only in *Scheherazade* but also in the opera, *Le Coq d'Or*, as well as other works. The oriental sound comes from application of west European harmonies to themes involving the chromatic scale and augmented second skips.

SUGGESTED WRITTEN ASSIGNMENTS

1. Write an exercise in four-voice harmony employing dominant sevenths with altered fifth (raised or lowered or replaced by raised fourth or lowered sixth) and involving the connecting of chords having enharmonically a common tritone.
2. Write a four-measure theme in major using the progression I, V⁷ with lowered fifth in second inversion, I, V⁷ of IV, IV from minor, V⁷, I.

By repetition, sequence and harmonic variation expand this four-measure idea to about thirty-two measures.

BIBLIOGRAPHY

ABRAHAM, GERALD, *Rimsky-Korsakov*, London: Gerald Duckworth & Co., Ltd., 1949.
————, *Studies in Russian Music* (chapters on Rimsky-Korsakov, Tchaikovsky and Mussorgsky), London: W. Reeves, 1939.
RIMSKY-KORSAKOV, NICOLAY, *My Musical Life*, New York: Alfred A. Knopf, Inc., 1942.
SCROFF, VICTOR, *The Mighty Five*, New York: Allen, Towne, & Heath, 1948.
ZETLIN, MIKHAIL, *The Five*, New York: International Universities Press, 1959.

EXAMPLE 70

RIMSKY-KORSAKOV

SCHEHERAZADE
I
(Measures 20-43)

CHAPTER 13

SERGEI RACHMANINOV

1873-1943

The sensuous, soaring melodic line is a hallmark of Rachmaninov's style. His music has its roots in the style of Tchaikovsky, his teacher, but his melodic eloquence and ability to sustain and expand certain moods surpasses that of the latter. Though Tchaikovsky was capable of a much wider range of expressive moods, Rachmaninov's limited variety of moods are portrayed with more conviction than the comparable moods of Tchaikovsky.

Much of his music is inspired by poetry or pictures, but it is not programmatic in the descriptive or narrative sense. Having been a great pianist, his best known and possibly most effective works are for piano, the short pieces and the works with orchestra.

Though he is a twentieth-century composer his tonal idiom is of the nineteenth. Thus his music does not contribute to any stylistic evolution except that it is a truer and deeper extension of elements of the Tchaikovsky approach, and as such has achieved the same popular appeal.

His works have a vitality and urgency which result from two types of long-breathed, expressive melodies in a flowing rhythmic continuum.

One type rises to a great climax and slowly through a series of descending sequences subsides to a point of repose. This type is seen in Examples 71 and 73. Also theme 2 of the finale of Piano Concerto, no. 3, and the introduction to Symphony, no. 2, illustrate this type.

The other type of melody revolves about a central tone and through sequential repetition rises to a climax. The general curve, the rise and fall, of both types is about the same except that there is more conjunct motion, less skipping, in the second type. Example 72 illustrates this type. The first themes of the first movements of both Piano Concertos, nos. 1 and 3 and the theme in E♭ in *Isle of the Dead* as well as the 2nd, 4th and 11th of the Thirteen Preludes, op. 32, exemplify this melodic type.

Much of the thematic material of larger works is derived from a motto theme or germ motive leading to employment of the cyclic principle in a sometimes subtle, sometimes more obvious, manner.

Examples 71, 72 and 73, all from the Piano Concerto, no. 2 in c, op. 18, illustrate Rachmaninov's melodic construction and his harmonic idiom involving textural complexities expressed in essentially diatonic and conventional tonal language.

A mood of gloomy melancholy or fatalism pervades much of his music. This possibly is emphasized by his predilection for the minor mode. All his piano concertos, symphonies, the *Rhapsody on a Theme of Paganini* and *Isle of the Dead* are in minor keys. Also, in major passages he frequently borrows chords from the tonic minor.

EXAMPLE 71 (page 221-223)
Piano Concerto No. 2 in C Minor, Op 18, I

The first movement opens with introductory chords in the solo piano. The orchestra states the first theme (in c) with piano accompanying, and the piano states the second theme in E♭ with the orchestra accompanying.

1. The thirty-one measures of this example include three of the four periods which comprise the opening statement of theme 2. Period one is m. 1-11, period two is m. 11-21 and period three is m. 22-31. Period four begins with m. 31. The periods overlap at m. 11 and 31, each of these measures serving as the last measure of one period and the first of the next period. In fact the lack of a strong definition of phrase endings within the periods makes each period sound somewhat like one extended phrase, especially m. 22-31. This avoidance of caesura contributes to the breathless, restless, urgent quality so prevalent in Rachmaninov's music. The same quality

in the late Wagner style (see Examples 54-57) is due not only to cadence elison, but also to constant shifting of the tonal center, which is not so much a factor in Rachmaninov's music.

If the downbeats of m. 1, 11 and 31 are considered closing beats of the preceding phrase and beats two, three and four of each of these measures are considered an anacrusis to the next phrase, then there is no overlap and each period is ten measures. This is actually the effect of m. 21; the downbeat is the close of period two and the next three quarters form an anacrusis to period three. The phrasing, however, and the entrance of the piano tend to prevent this interpretation.

2. The tonality remains E♭, but there are some interesting harmonic progressions involving engaging nonharmonic elements. The first three measures appear to be a I-V⁷ of VI-I progression, but they are perhaps better interpreted as I-VII⁷-I with G as appoggiatura and B♮ really C♭ in m. 2. This interpretation is more obvious in the return of this theme in the key of A♭ in the recapitulation. Compare to Example 72, m. 11-12.

3. M. 4 involves appoggiaturas and échappées in relation to II⁷ with raised root and third going to VII $\frac{4}{3}$. The first chord (altered II⁷) could be considered V $_9^0$ of V by spelling F♯ as G♭, but this proves hardly valid when the supposed missing root, F, is placed in the bass.

4. M. 25-26 have a subdominant function as augmented sixth chords. In both measures the G♭ is really F♯ in function, resolving to G in I $_4^6$ in m. 27. Both chords in these measures are enharmonic to dominant (major-minor) seventh chords, A♭⁷ in m. 26 to C♭⁷ in m. 27, but they function as indicated.

5. Notice that the harmonies of m. 26 and 28 are enharmonic but function quite differently. The chord in m. 26 is an augmented sixth with subdominant function. The chord in m. 28 is a secondary dominant, V⁹ of the Neapolitan chord, resolving as such. It is really a C♭⁹ resolving to F♭ in m. 29, but Rachmaninov spelled it as B⁹ to E for easier reading.

6. Notice the great amount of ornamentation especially in the left-hand patterns and in the right hand in m. 30-31. This musical filigree is a prevalent texture in Rachmaninov's piano music and is seen also in passages such as m. 29-40 of Symphony, no. 2 in e, op. 27, III.

7. What kind of nonharmonic tones are the fourth eighth-notes in m. 9 and 19?

EXAMPLE 72 (pages 223-227)
Piano Concerto No. 2 in C Minor, Op. 18, II

The second movement is an ABA form on one theme with introduction. The first four measures serve as a transition from c, the key of I, to E, the key of II. M. 5-8 serve as a sort of "vamp" in the piano, setting the scene for the entrance of the theme which is stated twice and closes in the key of B.

The B section opens with a partial statement of the theme in the dominant and then it evolves into a development section dealing with the theme in various keys. This section closes with a cadenza with orchestral accompaniment, m. 105-128, leading to the return of A which is covered by this example.

1. The first measure is the close of the cadenza referred to. M. 2-5 are the "vamp" phrase which appeared at the beginning.

2. A sense of deep repose is imparted by the tonic pedal through the first sixteen measures and through m. 27-33.

3. The statement of the theme covers m. 6-21, and m. 21 to the end constitutes a closing extension or coda.

4. The phrase structure in keeping with the mood is less taut than in Example 71. Analyze the phrase structure of this example.

5. Observe the following interesting harmonic features:

   a. The harmonic progression of m. 11-12 is the same as Example 71, m. 1-3, except that here the middle chord is V⁷ of VI because of the strong presence of G♯, the root.

   b. The last chords in m. 14 and 15 are augmented sixths, the first in c♯ and the second in E. Notice that the one in m. 15 retains G♯ forming an augmented fifth with C♮.

   c. The second chords in m. 28 and in m. 30 are altered dominants of E. The one in m. 28 is the incomplete minor dominant ninth with raised fifth, F♯ raised to F𝄪 but spelled here as G♮. Notice that this G♮ resolves upward to G♯ the same as the F𝄪 in m. 30.

6. What is A in m. 17, the thirteenth of the chord or an échappée? What is G♯ in m. 18?

EXAMPLE 73 (pages 227, 228)
Piano Concerto No. 2 in C Minor, Op. 18, III

The second movement and finale were written before the first movement of this work. The resemblance of theme 2 (B) (Example 73) of the finale to theme 2 (Example 71) of I indicates that the latter was derived from the former rather than the contrary.

The form of the finale is:

An introduction serving as a transition from II in E to III in c;

Section A in c;

Section B in Bb, first by orchestra and second by piano;

Section A in c developed and extended;

Section B in Db, an exact restatement of the first B transposed to Db; first by orchestra then by piano;

Section A in c and C;

Section B in C plus coda. Theme in orchestra, decoration in piano.

This might be considered a sonatina form with the last sections in the key of C as the coda.

1. The second, or B theme in Bb (one of Rachmaninov's most famous themes) is stated first in the orchestra. It is a seventeen measure melody consisting of four phrases of $4 + 4 + 4 + 5$ measures. The repetition of the theme in the piano covered in this example is twenty-nine measures, of which the first thirteen measures are an exact repetition and the remainder is an extension based on the last phrase of the opening statement. The second statement closes on a deceptive cadence, V^7 to IV^6_4, m. 28-29.

2. M. 1-3 express the Phrygian mode through the Ab and Cb of m. 2. These three measures sound like V-II^7-V of eb over a Bb pedal, a typical Phrygian progression.

3. Notice the Bb pedal through m. 1-8.

4. M. 17 is the augmented sixth $IV^{6\sharp}_{5\flat}$ spelled enharmonically in sharps, resolving irregularly to II^7 from bb in m. 18.

5. M. 25-27 are a prolongation of the I^6_4 resolving to V^7 in m. 28.

6. Locate and identify the several secondary dominants in this example.

Examples and Suggestions for Further Study of the Music of Rachmaninov

The opening notes of the old plainsong sequence *Dies Irae* (Day of Wrath) are frequently employed by Rachmaninov as a theme in his later works. Its appearance in *Isle of the Dead*, a symphonic poem inspired by Alexander Böcklin's painting, is impressive and natural for this subject.

In the *Rhapsody on a Theme of Paganini* he introduces it as a countersubject to the Paganini theme, where it has no extramusical connotations.

This theme also appears in his Symphonic Dances, op. 45. It was also used by Tchaikovsky, Liszt, Berlioz, Mussorgsky and Saint-Saëns.

In comparing early with late works one will find that he tends to abandon the complex overladen texture seen in the Piano Concerto, no. 2 and tends to employ a clearer, less involved texture as illustrated by the *Rhapsody on a Theme of Paganini*.

Because of the difficulty of fitting long melodies into sonata forms Rachmaninov is especially effective in theme and variation forms. The *Rhapsody on a Theme of Paganini,* op. 43, for piano and orchestra is a theme with twenty-four variations and coda and is one of Rachmaninov's finest works. He uses the same theme used by both Schumann and Brahms before him. It is a particularly happy work and contains in Variation 18 one of his finest melodic inspirations. After a short introduction, the first variation appears preceding the statement of the theme. After the theme the other twenty-three variations and coda follow in order from relatively simple to more and more complex treatment. The main key is a, but variations toward the middle are in d, F, bb and Db. Variation 22 involves the Phrygian mode. Piano Concerto, no. 3 in d, op. 30, II; Variations on a Theme by Chopin, op. 22; and Variations on a Theme by Corelli for piano are other good examples of works in this form.

The Piano Concerto, no. 1 in f♯, op. 1, employs conventional forms and key relationships, but the Piano Concerto, no. 3 is an unusually effective example of cyclic form. The rhythmic motive, ♩ ♪♩ ♪ , pervades the entire work, and the thematic material which appears from movement to movement grows and develops as it reappears and is not simply a series of quotations from previous movements. This represents the cyclic principle used in its best sense.

In I, theme 2 appears first in Bb and returns in Eb. The cadenza at the close of a long and effective development continues the process of development with orchestral reference to theme 1. Theme 2 in Eb is included in the latter part of this long cadenza, which leads to a short recapitulation of theme 1 and only a short reference to theme 2. The involvement of the cadenza as an integral part of the musical form which is seen in the Mendelssohn Violin Concerto in e, I, is here extended and deepened by Rachmaninov.

II is a theme and variations movement with the contour of a gradual rise to a climax and slow fall found in single melodies of Rachmaninov.

III is connected to II by a transition, again in the tradition of Mendelssohn, and has a long development involving modified versions of themes 1 and 2 of I. Theme 2 of III involves two ideas, one in C and one in G. These return in B♭ and F. The long coda includes a long climactic melodic line developed from elements of the second themes of both I and III.

Symphony, no. 2 in e, op. 27, is also cyclic. The opening three measures state a motto theme or germ motive from which much of the material of the symphony is subtly developed.

I is preceded by a long introduction which constitutes almost an independent movement. Themes 1 and 2 return in reverse order in the recapitulation. The form is introduction, 1 in e, 2 in G, development, 2 in E, 1 in e, coda.

II is the scherzo movement in ABACA form.

A (in a) is a three-part song form (aaba).

B (in C) is a typical soaring Rachmaninov melody.

A (in a) is a statement of only the final part a.

C (in e) is labeled, Trio, and is a fugato.

A (in a) leads to a long coda containing subtle references to material of I.

III is an ABA form.

A is in the key of A.

B is derived from theme 1 of I and is in e.

A returns in A and is stated along with the theme of section B.

IV in E has the typical long, soaring melody for theme 2 and is in D returning in E. The development contains references from I, II and III, and acts as a fusion of the thematic material of the entire work. Augmentation and diminution are exemplified in his treatment of the descending scale toward the close of the development.

Similar passages are found in the coda of the Piano Concerto, no. 4 in g, op. 40, III, and in the *Rhapsody on a Theme of Paganini*, Variation 22, and in the *Moments Musicaux*, op. 16.

Rachmaninov often presents the second theme in a key a second above or below the main key as shown in the works discussed here.

Many of his songs (of which he wrote nearly seventy) and piano pieces exemplify him at his very best. His twenty-four preludes (1 in op. 3, 10 in op. 23, and 13 in op. 32) like the Chopin preludes represent every major and minor key, and the last four of op. 32 should be studied as examples of his best writing for piano. In his songs he shows the influence of Schumann and comes close to equalling Mussorgsky as an important Russian song composer.

SUGGESTED WRITTEN ASSIGNMENTS

1. Analyze carefully Rachmaninov's melodic idiom and write a short piece for violin and piano employing a long, lyric melodic line in this idiom.
2. Write an eight-measure exercise in four-voice harmony, employing some of the chromatically altered chords found in Examples 71, 72 and 73.

BIBLIOGRAPHY

BERTENSSON, SERGEI and JAY LEYDA, *Sergei Rachmaninov*, New York: New York University Press, 1956.

CULSHAW, JOHN, *Sergei Rachmaninov*, London: Dennis Dobson, 1949.

GRONOWICZ, ANTONI, *Sergei Rachmaninov*, New York: E. P. Dutton & Co., Inc., 1946.

EXAMPLE 71
RACHMANINOV
PIANO CONCERTO NO. 2 IN C MINOR, OP. 18
I
(Measures 83-113)

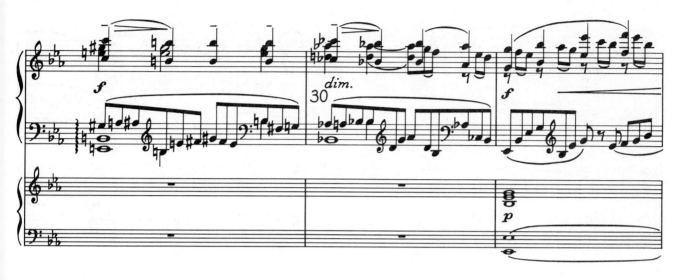

EXAMPLE 72
RACHMANINOV
PIANO CONCERTO NO. 2 IN C MINOR, OP. 18
II
(Last 35 Measures)

EXAMPLE 73
Rachmaninov
PIANO CONCERTO NO. 2 IN C MINOR, OP. 18
III
(Measures 122-150)

CHAPTER 14

GIACOMO PUCCINI

1858-1924

Melodic appeal is the dominant element in Puccini's music. The Italian opera of his time demanded direct, uncomplicated melodic expression and this is what Puccini provided. His music is homophonic in the extreme. The melody in the voice part is often doubled in the bass with the harmony being defined in afterbeat chords in between. Thus, there is no real bass part in such passages.

His harmonic idiom contains modal elements resulting from emphasis on the secondary triads, II, III and VI, and shows some influence of impressionism in his use of chords in parallel motion to express color rather than tonal function. These elements stem indirectly from Mussorgsky, whose style is discussed in Chapter 16.

Here again is the romantic tradition of lyric sentiment carried well into the twentieth century. Though Puccini relies on the appeal of his melodies, they are not the long, sweeping lines seen in Rachmaninov. They consist of shorter motives, expressed in a flexible tempo, with frequent climaxes on high, held notes. In short, they are constructed to provide direct appeal as "good theatre."

EXAMPLE 74 (page 230)
La Bohème, Act I, Mimi's Aria

This is a quotation from Mimi's aria in Act I, and is arranged as a composite of the voice line and accompaniment to illustrate the simplicity of texture. In this one example are illustrated many of the features of the style such as:

1. The doubling of the voice line in the bass in m. 1-2 and 7-8.
2. The shallow texture in all but m. 5-6 and 9-11.
3. The emphasis on the II, III and VI which imparts the touching effect of f♯, natural minor, in m. 3-8.
4. The large number of chords in second inversion resulting from the melodic doubling in the bass.

5. The avoidance of a V⁷ except in m. 9.
6. The fermata at m. 9.

Other illustrations of these stylistic elements which appear throughout the same opera are:

1. The free use of parallel diatonic triads in Act I, m. 475-500, the opening 121 measures of Act II, and the beginning of Act III.
2. The emphasis on secondary triads and sevenths and frequent second inversions in Rudolph's aria preceding Mimi's aria in Act I.
3. The duet at the close of Act I illustrates the many instances where the melody is doubled even in a duet.

Formal coherence is achieved by repeating and modifying various striking melodic motives throughout the opera. The duet theme at the close of Act I is an example of an idea which appears later.

SUGGESTED WRITTEN ASSIGNMENTS

1. Write a short song or solo for clarinet or other woodwind or string instrument illustrating your grasp of the harmonic and textural idiom of Puccini.
2. Write an exercise in four-voice harmony using only diatonic triads and sevenths involving the following key sequence: C, a (natural minor), e (natural minor), G, C.

BIBLIOGRAPHY

CARNER, MOSCO, *Puccini: A Critical Biography*, New York: Alfred A. Knopf, Inc., 1959.

MAREK, GEORGE R., *Puccini: A Biography*, New York: Simon and Schuster, Inc., 1951.

SPECHT, RICHARD, *Giacomo Puccini; The Man, His Life, His Work*, New York: Alfred A. Knopf, Inc., 1933.

EXAMPLE 74
PUCCINI

LA BOHÈME, ACT I
MIMI'S ARIA
(Last 11 Measures)

CHAPTER 15

VAN DENMAN THOMPSON

1890-

Here we find the nineteenth-century harmonic idiom of tonal chromatic harmony turned to effective use in the writing of twentieth-century church anthems. This style is characterized by much use of appoggiaturas and chromatic voice lines and chords reminiscent of the style of Franck. These are mostly shorter works involving the frequent use of sequences for development of the form which is usually an extended song form. The various diatonic and altered seventh and thirteenth chords and melodic lines involving expressive appoggiaturas and added sixths are presented in a simple four-voice texture which has the same direct kind of unsophisticated sentimental appeal found in the Puccini style.

EXAMPLE 75 (page 232)
"A Sweeter Song"

This work is a three-part song form (aaba). The opening part a, a period, is quoted here.

1. Note the dominant thirteenth chords at m. 2, 3, 4 (last chord) and the augmented sixth built on the raised fourth degree in third instead of the conventional second inversion, m. 9.

2. The chord on beat two of m. 2 is analyzed as I with added sixth instead of VI_5^6 because of its position (with G in the bass) following the V^{13}, which gives it definite tonic function. This effect is frequently seen in this style. See Example 76, m. 1.

3. M. 5 is analyzed as three chords. Could some of the motion be considered nonharmonic?

4. Notice the chromatic bass line in m. 5-9.

5. In this style certain chord formations appear to be the result of nonharmonic motion which is set up by the melodic pattern but they also serve a harmonic function. Thus, there is a question of how to identify these formations. Examples of such cases are the first chords of m. 3, 5 and 7.

6. The melodic sequence in the soprano of m. 6-7 is not carried out in the other voices nor is the repeated figure in the soprano of m. 8-9 carried out as repetition in the other voices.

EXAMPLE 76 (page 232)
"O Love Divine"

This work is an extended song (group) form with an abca coda design. The first six measures of part c are quoted here.

1. The first chord in m. 1 has been analyzed as the diminished seventh on raised II of the scale with A as an appoggiatura resolving to G with the change of chord on the fourth beat. This could also be analyzed as the A triad, V of III, over a Bb pedal, or all three upper voices could be considered appoggiaturas to the I^{+6} on beat four.

2. Relevant to point five in Example 75 the formations on beats one and three of m. 2, beat one of m. 3, and on beats one and three of m. 4 and 5 are chord sounds which can be considered the result of nonharmonic motion or functional harmonies. Do you agree with the interpretation indicated?

There are many works by Thompson which clearly illustrate harmonic language of this type. A similar kind of harmonic idiom but with different rhythmic setting can be found in American popular music of about 1930 to 1950. Though such music is not so important in the mainstream of musical styles evolved by the master composers, it provides clear and uncomplicated illustrations of harmonic procedures necessary to musical understanding.

SUGGESTED WRITTEN ASSIGNMENTS

As a way of arriving at an imitation of the preceding examples first write a sixteen-measure exercise in four-voice harmony using only diatonic chords. Then write a variation on it by introducing chromatic alteration in the harmonies and by injecting nonharmonic motion, especially appoggiaturas, in the upper voices.

EXAMPLE 75
Thompson
A SWEETER SONG
(Opening Measures)

EXAMPLE 76
Thompson
O LOVE DIVINE
(Measures 28-34)

CHAPTER 16

MODEST MUSSORGSKY

The examples with which we have been concerned up to this point are drawn from a line of composers whose styles have evolved directly or indirectly from the eighteenth-century Viennese classical approach to harmony, form and tonality. This line of composers forms a musical geneology grounded in the Germanic academic tradition which has lasted well into the twentieth century and to which we will return with the study of Schoenberg and Krenek.

With Mussorgsky we move back chronologically to 1874 to pick up a line of styles based on somewhat different tonal, formal, melodic and harmonic resources and procedures. This line of composers descending from Mussorgsky includes Debussy, Stravinsky, Prokofiev, Shostakovich and Milhaud, and their styles involve greater use of modal scales and harmony, new approaches to part writing and harmonic relationship, thematic ideas evolved from or based on folk-music forms, new formal designs and expressive goals of a different type.

Mussorgsky as a member of the Russian nationalist group known as "The Five" was the least well-equipped in the academic technics of composition but was the greatest of the group by virtue of his great originality, his highly individual style, and revolutionary impetus which he injected into the European musical milieu. His lack of formal training may have been an asset because it forced him to develop an original musical language to express himself. On the other hand, this lack caused him to compose slowly and that coupled with too many "lost weekends" (he died of acute alcoholism) may have deprived us of many more works by him.

His music, which is a faithful depiction of Russian life and culture, has had a great influence on a later group of composers.

His vocabulary of chord formations is not as advanced as what we have already seen, but his chord relationships and progressions which result from modal thinking and tonal imagination display a highly individual harmonic idiom. This idiom is relatively simple and direct but difficult to analyze in the traditional terms of major-minor tonality.

Though his style is strongly rooted in Russian folk melody, he quotes only occasionally an actual folk tune. His method of formal expansion closely follows the structure implicit in much folk music. Typical folk tunes are modal, in irregular meter, and consist of one or two motives repeated over and over either directly or in sequence with a solid cadence every two or four measures. Mussorgsky's musical forms grow from this formal seed. Whole sections are based on a single idea which is repeated over and over with harmonic variations and textural accumulation.

Various elements of his style are illustrated in the following excerpts from his greatest single work, the opera, *Boris Godunov*. Examples 79, 82, 83 and 84 are quoted from the original version and Examples 77, 78, 80 and 81 are quoted from the Rimsky-Korsakov revised version.

EXAMPLE 77 (page 237)
Boris Godunov, Prologue, Scene II

Alternation of the two dominant seventh chords, D^7 and $A\flat^7$, having the common tritone, C to F$\sharp$ (G$\flat$), is a predominant element in this scene. This is in effect a simulation of church bells and with chorus produces a scene of solemn pomp. See Examples 81 and 120 for other instances of this type of harmonic effect.

EXAMPLE 78 (page 238-240)
Boris Godunov, Prologue, Scene II

The other predominant element of this scene is the old Russian traditional melody, m. 2-8, which Beethoven employed in his String Quartet, op. 59, no. 2, III.

1. Though this is only the first forty-one measures of a section of one hundred nine measures based on this theme (later combined with the alternating chords of Example 77) the importance of repetition and sequence in building the effect is obvious.

2. By m. 35 the melody of m. 2-8 has been repeated directly or sequentially six times.

3. M. 35-41 are also based on the tune. Notice the modal effect (Dorian on a) of the alternating D and a triads of m. 35-37.

4. Compare the harmonization of m. 2-7 with their repetition, m. 8-13. Notice the emphasis on secondary triads in the latter measures.

5. Notice the effective climax resulting from the modulating repetitions of the melody over the pedal G, m. 14-33.

6. There is a quick movement to the a triad in m. 33-34. Notice the V $\frac{4}{2}$ to III progression here.

7. Make a harmonic analysis of this entire example.

EXAMPLE 79 (page 241)
Boris Godunov, Act I, Scene I

This illustrates construction of a passage based on two one-measure figures, stated in m. 1 and 2.

1. Notice the unusual harmonic effect of m. 2. M. 1-4 appear to be in a (Aeolian) with cadences in m. 2 and 4 on III.

2. M. 5-6 have a quality of Mixolydian on C. The D♭ to A♭ in m. 5 could be interpreted as implying the Neapolitan chord.

3. M. 7-12 imply a tonal center of e: e Phrygian in m. 7-9, and e minor in m. 10-12. Notice the dissonant connection from beat four of m. 11 to m. 12. Perhaps such a passage was considered too crude by Rimsky-Korsakov who left it out of his version.

4. This repetition of a figure (m. 1) with various modal inflections as seen here is an important feature of Mussorgsky's style.

EXAMPLE 80 (pages 241-243)
Boris Godunov, Act I, Scene II

Mussorgsky frequently moves from one key or tonal center to another without modulation, simply by assuming the new key. This is illustrated in the introduction measures of this example.

1. M. 1-3 imply c♯ Phrygian.
M. 4-10 are in d modulating to C.
M. 11-14 are in c♯ Phrygian.
M. 15-25 are in A.

Notice that there is no modulatory connection from m. 10 to m. 11.

2. M. 17-21 show a typical Mussorgsky melodic figure. A similar idea, for example, plays an important part in the opera, *Khovanshchina*.

3. Ostinato figures as seen in the introduction are another important ingredient of the style.

4. The entire *Hostess' Song*, of which the opening measures are quoted here, is based on the three-beat motive (1), repeated in m. 35-37, and on the motive (2) of m. 38-39. The song consists of repetitions of the seven-measure melody first stated in m. 35-41 with each repetition having a varied harmonic treatment. Even the seven-measure melody consists of a three-beat motive (1) repeated (m. 35-37) followed by a four-beat motive (2) repeated (m. 38-41).

This type of melodic construction is characteristic of Russian as well as other folk melody, and its use as a theme repeated with harmonic and rhythmic variation is a central formal characteristic of Mussorgsky's style and the style of those whom he influenced.

1. M. 27-32 are based on motive 1.

2. The C♮ in m. 39, 41, 46 and 48 again illustrates modal inflection. The minor V is a chord frequently found. The cadence on the III in the same measures also points up the modal quality of the style.

EXAMPLE 81 (pages 243-246)
Boris Godunov, Act II, Song of Feodor

This song is quoted in its entirety because it is an excellent example of Mussorgsky's formal design on a single motive repeated with variation. It is a light-hearted song but with the usual Russian touch of minor.

1. The harmonic setting changes every four measures and there are 2 two-measure phrases (m. 21-22 and 35-36) inserted preceding the returns to f♯. The design is as follows:

    (a) M. 1-4 in f♯
    (b) M. 5-8 in A
    (c) M. 9-12 in F
    (d) M. 13-16 in f
    (e) M. 17-20 in F
    (f) M. 21-22 in F♯
    (g) M. 23-26 in f♯ to A
    (h) M. 27-30 in D♭
    (i) M. 31-34 in F
    (j) M. 35-36 in F♯
    (k) M. 37-40 in f♯ to A
    (l) M. 41-43 in A (epilogue)

2. The connection of two dominant seventh chords with a common tritone is illustrated in (e), (h)

and (i). The first of the two chords in each case is the augmented sixth on the raised subdominant IV$\frac{6\sharp}{5\flat}$, but it resolves to V^7 of V.
3. Notice the delayed resolution of the G$\sharp$ in the final chord.

EXAMPLE 82 (pages 247, 248)
Boris Godunov, Act III, Scene II

This orchestral excerpt illustrates both modal effects and sudden modulations.

1. This is an aba song form with a varied harmonization of the return of (a) as follows:

M. 1-4 are introduction

Part (a) ⌐M. 4-8 in C Lydian
    M. 9-12 in E Lydian
    M. 13 is a repetition of the cadence pattern of m. 12 closing part (a) suddenly back in C instead of E

Part (b)   M. 14-25 (see paragraphs below)
Part (a)   └M. 26-29 in C Lydian to c
    M. 30-33 in E$\flat$ Lydian instead of E as before
    M. 34 is a repetition of the cadence pattern of m. 33 bringing the tonality back to C for the close.

2. A type of shift of tonal center found later in Prokofiev, Shostakovich and Milhaud is seen here. This consists of changing one note in a passage (usually an unharmonized scale) a half step too high or too low to effect an unexpected modulation or to throw the expected modulation a half step off key center. This device appears in three cases as follows.

In m. 8-9 there is a modulation from C to E. In m. 29-30 (comparable to 8-9) an E$\flat$ is substituted for E in the second beat, throwing the next four measures a half step lower into the key of E$\flat$ instead of E as originally.

Since both the passage in E (m. 9-12) and the comparable passage in E$\flat$ (m. 30-33) move to a closing measure in C (m. 13 and 34) an adjustment is necessary. In m. 12 to 13 the modulation is from E to C with a half step, F$\sharp$ to G, over the bar line; whereas, in m. 33-34 the modulation is from E$\flat$ to C with a whole step, F to G, over the bar line.

The unison passage of m. 14-17 shows the key of E implied by measure 16, but in m. 17 the last two eighth notes are raised a half step so that the last four eighths sound like 5, 4, 3, 2 of the A$\flat$ scale. Thus, a modulation from E to A$\flat$ is accomplished by

substituting a C instead of an expected B after D$\sharp$-C$\sharp$ and continuing down the A$\flat$ scale. D$\sharp$ to C$\sharp$ enter as 7 to 6 of E but become enharmonically 5 to 4 of A$\flat$.

3. The last beats of m. 2 and 4 illustrate interesting dominant effects.

4. Notice how often the III appears.

5. Part b is based on two ideas: the one in m. 14 and the one in m. 16. M. 14 is repeated in 15. M. 17 is freely sequential to 16. M. 19 is a repetition of 18. M. 20-21 are repeated in tonic minor (a$\flat$) in m. 22-23.

6. M. 24-25 illustrate the progression involving two dominant sevenths with a common tritone. How would you define the harmony of m. 24 in relation to the key of C?

7. How would you define the E and F (sixteenths) in the left hand of m. 18 and 19? Could each be considered a free anticipation to the harmony that follows it?

8. Do you think that m. 5-8 and 26-29 are over a pedal on C, m. 9-11 are over a pedal on B, and m. 30-32 are over a pedal on B$\flat$? The low bass notes seem to indicate this.

9. In m. 13 and 34 the C (tonic) is retained throughout the measure almost as if the E chord of m. 12 and the E$\flat$ of m. 33 were the penultimate chords in the cadence.

EXAMPLE 83 (page 249)
Boris Godunov, Act IV, Prelude

1. Here the natural, harmonic and a touch of Dorian forms of e$\flat$ and a$\flat$ are used.

2. Notice the frequency of II, III, VI and the major VII on subtonic.

3. The Dorian quality is seen in the major IV chord in e$\flat$, m. 2, and in the I with added major sixth in a$\flat$, m. 12-13. The latter is the pivot to E$\flat$, being II$\frac{6}{5}$ of e$\flat$.

4. Notice the changes of mode in m. 13-20.

5. Again there is a tonic pedal figure in m. 14-17.

EXAMPLE 84 (pages 250, 251)
Boris Godunov, Act IV, Scene II

1. Here is a lively Russian dance based on a three-measure tune which is wildly tossed about from octave to octave, key to key, and with changing harmonies.

2. The harmonic scheme of the three-measure tune is tonic-subdominant (IV or II)-tonic. In m. 30-36, however, it is tonic-dominant (VII^7)-tonic, and in m. 40-42 a key change takes place within the three-measure pattern.

3. Each three measures is a separate unit and may be followed by a unit in a new key.

4. Interesting effects to be noted are as follows:

a. The G⁷ chords in third inversion in m. 21 and 24 are unresolved so that m. 19-24 sound like G Mixolydian.

b. M. 25-30 contain an E♭ throughout so that the I of G is augmented, E♭=D♯.

c. The C♭'s and D♭'s in 31-36 are modal alterations in E♭. What modes are implied?

d. The II⁷ built on the raised second degree of the scale of A♭ is used in m. 50. Here the C♭ is really B (raised supertonic) forming an augmented sixth above D♭ and resolving upward to C in I.

e. The chord in m. 53, 55 and 56 is IV⁷ built on the raised fourth degree of the f♯ scale. The diminished third, B♯-D, is retained instead of being inverted to form an augmented sixth. Notice its resolution to I $^6_4$ in f♯ in m. 57.

Examples and Suggestions for Further Study of the Music of Mussorgsky

In studying Mussorgsky's music it is important to distinguish between the original music of Mussorgsky and that which was revised by Rimsky-Korsakov. The strength and originality of Mussorgsky is usually diluted by Rimsky-Korsakov's "corrected" versions.

It is interesting to compare the original version of *Boris Godunov* with the Rimsky-Korsakov version to see the real individuality of Mussorgsky.

Since the orchestral piece, *Night on the Bare Mountain*, is a composite of both Mussorgsky's and Rimsky-Korsakov's thinking it is less valuable for stylistic study than the songs, for instance.

Mussorgsky's songs, of which he wrote about seventy, place him as Russia's greatest songwriter. The songs like the operas allow him to display his dramatic genius. His vocal lines tend to follow natural speech inflection, which results in irregular rhythms and phrases and few long melodic lines.

The original piano version of *Pictures at an Exhibition* along with the songs are excellent for stylistic study.

Maurice Ravel's interest in the music of Mussorgsky is shown in his brilliant orhcestration of *Pictures at an Exhibition.*

SUGGESTED WRITTEN ASSIGNMENTS

1. Write a dance in the style of Example 84, employing various modal inflections of a basic melodic motive which is repeated over and over in various keys and harmonies.

2. Experiment with a passage in slow tempo in which dominant sevenths with common tritones are employed.

3. Write a short song in the formal style of Example 81.

BIBLIOGRAPHY

ABRAHAM, GERALD, *Studies in Russian Music*, London: W. Reeves, 1939.

CALVOCORESSI, M. D. and G. ABRAHAM, *Masters of Russian Music*, New York: Alfred A. Knopf, Inc., 1936.

————, *Modest Mussorgsky*, Fair Lawn: Essential Books, 1956.

LEYDA, J. and S. BARTENSEN (ed.), *The Mussorgsky Reader*, New York: W. W. Norton & Company, Inc., 1947.

NEWMARCH, ROSA, *The Russian Opera*, New York: Oxford University Press, Inc., 1914.

RIESEMANN, OSKAR VON, *Mussorgsky*, New York: Alfred A. Knopf, Inc., 1929.

EXAMPLE 77
Mussorgsky
BORIS GODUNOV
PROLOGUE, SCENE II, THE CORONATION SCENE
(First 22 Measures)

EXAMPLE 78
MUSSORGSKY
BORIS GODUNOV
PROLOGUE, SCENE II, THE CORONATION SCENE
(Measures 51-91)

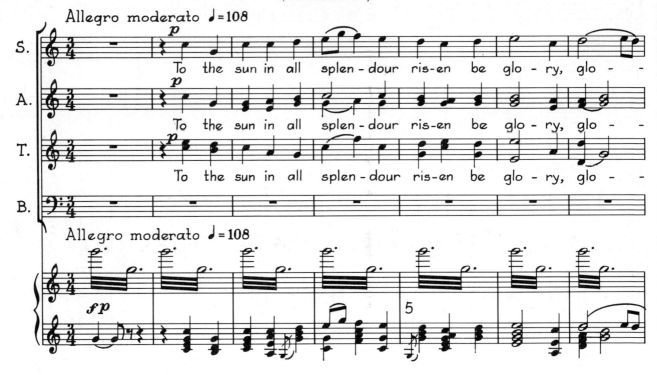

Tsar, our fa - ther, long life__ long life__ and glo-ry!

Tsar._____ Tsar, our fa - ther, long life__ long life and glo-ry!

Tsar, our fa - ther, our gra - cious Tsar, long life__ and glo-ry!

all__ hail! Hail our gra - cious Tsar, long life__ and glo - rie!

cresc. 30

I V$^4_2$ III VI

Sing, re - joice ye, peo-ple!

Sing, re - joice ye,__ Rus-sian peo-ple!

Sing, re - joice ye, peo-ple!

Sing, re - joice ye, Rus-sian peo-ple!

mf 35 40

EXAMPLE 79

MUSSORGSKY
BORIS GODUNOV
ACT I, SCENE I
(Measures 252-263)

EXAMPLE 80

MUSSORGSKY
BORIS GODUNOV
ACT I, SCENE II, INTRODUCTION AND
BEGINNING OF THE HOSTESS'S SONG
(First 48 Measures)

Once I caught a drake with feathers green and blue.

O thou my darling drake, come again, my mate so true! Where the pond shines clear, I will

take thee dear, There to float and swim at ease 'Neath the shade of flow'ring trees.

EXAMPLE 81
MUSSORGSKY
BORIS GODUNOV
ACT II, SONG OF FEODOR
(Complete)

Andantino ♩ = 84
molto cantabile

Po - pin-ka, our old par-ra-keet set the maids laughing Chat-t'ring without a

pause, Oh he was so fun-ny! Bend-ing his lit-tle head and asking them to scratch it,

Pocchissimo più mosso

Yes, ev'-ry one in turn, he made them all car-ess him. On - ly nurse Nas -

tas - ia would not pet or scratch him. Po - pin-ka in a rage used some shocking lan-guage

Then she grew ve - ry cross, seized his poor neck rough - ly. Po - pin-ka scream'd and

swore ruf-fling out his feathers. Well, ev'-ry-bod-y tried with kind words to soothe his temper

Soon, all the wait-ing-maids were gather'd round a-bout him. But

ritard. poco   Tempo I

no, Pop-ka was furious! Sul - ky and cross he sat, with his beak beneath his wing.

Pocchissimo più mosso

Would not look up, but still swore at old Nas-tas - ia. All of a sud-den

then, with-out— an-y warning, straight in her face he flew, In her fright she fell right o - ver.

EXAMPLE 82
Mussorgsky
BORIS GODUNOV
ACT III, SCENE II, POLONAISE
(First 34 Measures)

Alla polacca, ma non troppo allegro

EXAMPLE 83
Mussorgsky
BORIS GODUNOV
ACT IV, PRELUDE
(First 20 Measures)

EXAMPLE 84
MUSSORGSKY
BORIS GODUNOV
ACT IV, SCENE II
(Measures 240-296)

CHAPTER 17

CLAUDE DEBUSSY

1862-1918

Though he is a romantic composer, Debussy's language and intent are entirely different from his predecessors and contemporaries. Whereas European romanticism before his time was concerned with the passions, philosophies and exploits of men and with detailed descriptions of nature, Debussy's art is devoted to the objective sensuousness of nature, to moods instead of feelings and to suggestive gestures rather than literal illustration.

This music, like impressionist paintings and symbolist poetry of the time, expresses through subtle allusions and characteristic inflections the sights and sounds of nature. The goal of this art is to pique our imagination, invoking nebulous dreamlike visions and intuitions.

For this intent Debussy developed a new harmonic vocabulary and usage. In addition to traditional chord structures (triads, sevenths, ninths, etc), he uses chords with added tones (seconds and sixths) and chords built in fourths or fifths instead of thirds, and chords derived from the whole-tone scale (dominant sevenths and ninths with raised and/or lowered fifths). His harmonies are used nonfunctionally, for their intrinsic colors and independent effect, rather than for their tendencies in the tonal scheme.

Though this music remains tonal it involves many other departures from the then-conventional methods.

In its concern for passing impressions the dynamics of form in the classic sense are replaced by a unity achieved from diverse colors and ideas in a fluid, rhapsodic organism. Though new orchestral, harmonic and scale colors are used, the range of musical emotion is narrower. This results from the premise of this art which is to convey an impression by nuance, inflection and understatement rather than to overwhelm the listener by extravagant detail and sonority.

The texture is essentially homophonic, and thematic material is subjected to extension and development by repetition, sequence and intervallic and rhythmic modification though seldom by contrapuntal manipulation.

Modal, artificial, pentatonic and whole-tone scales are used for tonal organization, and the tonal center is maintained, despite the free use of harmony, by frequent pedal figures and periodic return to the tonic note or chord.

The influences on Debussy's style include:

a. The artistic goals and reaction to romantic opulence and overexaggeration from the impressionist painters and symbolist poets.
b. The cyclic concept and chromatic harmony from Franck.
c. In opera, the declamatory vocal line with expression of the inner meaning of the plot relegated to the orchestra from Wagner. Aside from this, Debussy's opera subjects, artistic objectives, and the means employed to achieve them are anti-Wagnerian.
d. Modal concepts, folk-music elements and rhapsodic forms developed through varied repetitions from Mussorgsky and Russian gypsies.
e. Orchestral colors from Javanese and Balinese gamelans.
f. Pianistic textures from Ravel, Chopin, Liszt.
g. Interest in Spanish music from Chabrier and Ravel.
h. Musical caricature from Satie.

In turn, nearly every composer of the early twentieth century has been influenced, if not by the impressionistic aspect of Debussy's music, certainly by the harmonic, melodic and rhythmic approach and materials of his language.

It is interesting to note that Ravel was greatly influenced by Debussy's harmonic language though not his artistic objectives, and Debussy was in turn influenced by Ravel's employment of this language in piano music.

Thus Debussy's style functions as a transition from the eighteenth-century concept of tonality to the twentieth-century concepts of tonal organization. It is music concerned with the poetry of sound, harmonic colors and sonorities, the evanescent and tenuous rather than the definite and clear cut, emphasizing mood and sensation rather than design.

The following examples illustrate these qualities in specific musical terms.

EXAMPLE 85 (page 262)
String Quartet, Themes from I, II, IV

Being an early work, this, his only quartet, does not depart from tradition as much as later works. The movements are based on conventional formal designs. Development principles including rhythmic transformation, cyclic treatment, repetition, sequence and some contrapuntal manipulation are present. In its general design and feeling it has much in common with the string quartet of Edvard Grieg with which an interesting comparison can be made. Yet its harmonic colors, use of modes, textures and melodic ideas give it an air of individuality unheard before.

I is in sonata form and opens with the first theme shown below which is the generating theme of the entire quartet. Elements to note about this theme are:

a. It is in Phrygian mode.
b. The element of repetition so characteristic of Debussy, Mussorgsky and Tchaikovsky and which will be seen in Ravel and Stravinsky is dominant in the construction of this theme. Exact repetition as seen in m. 3 and 4 appears in pairs of measures throughout the work. Sometimes the second measure of the two is in a different octave. Notice this element of exact repetition in the other themes of this example. Modified repetition by shortening of the theme to one figure is seen in m. 5-12. Compare this with Tchaikovsky, Example 64, and Ravel, Example 103. Thus this entire statement of theme 1 of I is based on two motives, m. 1-2 and m. 3.

The other theme from I is the first of two ideas in the second group. The second idea (not quoted) is developed in close relationship with theme 1 and returns with rhythmic transformations in the recapitulation. The theme quoted here appears only once in the exposition. It is a four-measure phrase repeated. It illustrates the folk-tune design seen in Mussorgsky themes. The repetition of the first measure makes a 1123, 1123 design. This idea is in e♭, Aeolian in character.

Elements of theme 1 and the second theme of group two appear in free augmentation in the recapitulation.

II is a scherzo type of movement in ABAB coda design. It is based on one theme, m. 3-4 of the second movement example below, which is obviously derived from theme 1 of I. This two-measure motive dominates the entire movement. It is the theme of section A and is continuously repeated like an ostinato throughout the first statement of A. In augmentation it serves as the theme of section B and appears in the coda highly modified. It is given a variety of harmonic treatments throughout.

III is a lyric movement in ABA form. The B section is independent like a trio. The thematic material contains allusions to theme 1 of I. There is much use of pentatonic and whole-tone scale effects and many pairs of repeated measures.

IV is based on theme 1 of I almost entirely. The quotation below from IV appears in the introduction and is from 1 of I. The main theme of the movement, derived from 1 of I, is later combined with 1 of I in augmentation, and the coda includes the version of the generating theme used in II. There is much use of one-measure and two-measure motives repeated.

EXAMPLE 86 (pages 263-265)
Pelléas and Mélisande, Act II, Scene I

Pelléas and Mélisande is the only successful impressionistic opera based on an impressionistic libretto. It is interesting to compare it to Wagner's setting of *Tristan and Isolde* because the subject matter of each is comparable but the treatment entirely different. Both operas are symbolic, representing an unfulfillable love between two who are not supposed to love one another. Both heroes die from stabbing, and both heroines suffer from less tangible causes. Both are operas of "states of mind," and the inner meaning is carried mostly by the orchestra with little action on the stage, and the voice parts are declamatory in style with little thematic significance. Both operas are highly successful in their objectives, in their intended effect on the listener. Yet the musical means employed to achieve the effect epitomize the contrast between German romanticism and French impressionism.

Over the range of three long acts Tristan and Isolde insist on their love for one another, constantly supported by a large, lush, orchestral fabric expressing overwhelming musical passion and longing. The listener is captured and inundated by the emotional impact.

On the other hand, the subtleties of the music of Debussy and the poetry of Maeterlinck beckon to the listener, and by veiled implication and gesture make it absolutely clear from the first that Pelléas and Mélisande love each other even though they do not say so until the fourth act; and even then it is expressed with a quiet intensity and without the orchestra. Throughout the work the orchestral fabric is refined and subdued, seldom full and forte.

These contrasting approaches are equally valid and demonstrate the versatility of the musical expression.

In this excerpt Mélisande implies her childlike unconcern for her marriage to Golaud, comparable to Isolde's attitude toward King Mark.

The following features are to be noted:

1. The great number of triplets in the voice parts in this and Example 89 and, of course, throughout the opera are a result of the rhythm of French speech.

2. The harmony of m. 1-2 consists of triads of c or B♭ with contrary motion between the outer voices. Compare this to the harmonization of the same melodic figure in m. 4-5. Here the harmony is a variety of dominant forms over a generating root of C♯ with the tritone E♯-B.

This illustrates two types of harmonic color used by Debussy: one, a play on nondominant triads, sevenths and chords with added notes for a quasimodal effect as in m. 1-3; the other, a play on dominant-sounding chords with tritones as in m. 4-7.

3. The left hand of m. 4-5 is a three-beat pattern and the dominant chord formations of the two measures based on the root C♯ are:

> Beat 1, incomplete dominant ninth (major) (D♯);
> Beat 2, incomplete dominant ninth (minor) (D♮) with major thirteenth, A♯;
> Beat 3, dominant seventh;
> Etc.

4. The roots of the dominant chords of m. 6-7 are indicated.

5. The arpeggio of m. 7 is a bit of literal description, the ring falling.

6. A third type of harmonic color akin to the play on dominant formations is the use of formations derived from the whole-tone scale illustrated in m. 13-14. The six tones of the whole-tone scale when distributed by thirds form an augmented dominant eleventh chord with raised fifth. Any of the six notes may be the root of this chord by enharmonically changing the spelling since the whole step relationship exists among all of the chord members.

The spelling here implies the root G, although Debussy seldom resolves such chords according to the root function. Thus the chord spelled in thirds from G is:

$$G \quad B \quad D\sharp \quad F \quad A \quad C\sharp$$

With B as root it is:

$$B \quad D\sharp \quad F\times(G) \quad A \quad C\sharp \quad E\sharp(F)$$

and the other chord notes as roots produce:

E♭(D♯)	G	B		D♭(C♯)	F	A
F	A	C♯		E♭(D♯)	G	B
A	C♯	E♯(F)		G	B	D♯
D♭(C♯)	F	A		C♭(B)	E♭(D♯)	G

Though such a structure has many possible implications it is a very limited sound, and Debussy seldom maintains it for very long. (See Prelude II, *Voiles,* from Book I for an exception.) This is one of those chameleon chords like the diminished seventh and the augmented triad, any tone of which can function as the root, according to the spelling.

7. Nondominant harmonies producing a neutral tonal effect prevail throughout the remainder of the example (m. 15-24) except for the arpeggio in m. 18 and the D⁷ chords in m. 22.

8. Notice the contrary motion between the upper voices and the bass in m. 16-17 and 20-24. This is a common voice-leading procedure in the style.

9. The succession of unrelated triads in m. 23-24 is an effect commonly seen in this style.

EXAMPLE 87 (page 265)
Pelléas and Mélisande, Act I, Scene I

This passage occurs near the end of the scene.

1. M. 1-2 constitute a motive which has appeared throughout the scene in various harmonizations. Here it is in nondominant harmonization. Other appearances of this motive in Act I, Scene 1, are:

> m. 5-6, whole-tone scale harmonization
> m. 12-13, nondominant harmonization
> m. 18-20, dominant harmonization
> m. 146-147, dominant and whole-tone harmonizations

2. Seemingly unrelated chords appear again in m. 3-4 as in Example 86, m. 23. The progression, however, from the D⁹ (beat 1) to the augmented triad (beat 2) sounds like V⁹ to I (aug.) in G with the E♭ considered a D♯.

3. Also the "progression" from beat two to three sounds like V (aug.) to I in A♭. Yet the lack of any attempt to connect the chords of these two measures by any semblance of voice leading would indicate that Debussy's interest was more in isolated chord color than in chord progressions in spite of the tonal relationships which are present.

4. A Phrygian-type of progression exists in m. 5-6 with the downward motion into A through B♭.

EXAMPLE 88 (page 265)
Pelléas and Mélisande, Act II, Scene I

1. These measures from the interlude at the close of Act II, Scene 1, illustrate a chromatic passage with all the chords except the first two derived from the whole-tone scale.

2. The first two chords are half-diminished sevenths (incomplete dominant ninths) on G and B♭.

3. From the third chord onward the combination of descending chromatic figures in free sequence and the whole-tone chords produce a mood of dark vagueness. Notice that each whole-tone chord by enharmonic spelling can be considered one or more forms of altered dominant-type chords as in Example 86, m. 13-14. For example, is the chord on beat four of m. 2 a dominant ninth on the root G with the fifth raised (D♯) or is it a dominant ninth on the root A with the fifth lowered (D♯ being E♭)? This possibility of vagueness gives the passage its color, but again, one which is limited.

4. The third to the fourth chord in m. 1 can be considered a dominant to tonic progression in G. What is the third chord in this case?

EXAMPLE 89 (pages 266, 267)
Pelléas and Mélisande, Act IV, Scene IV

In this passage of emotional intensity the harmonies are of the dominant type, that is, chords with tritones. Nondominant and whole-tone chords are relatively noncommittal or tonally neutral and would be less effective in a decisive passage such as this where **Pelléas** and **Mélisande** first profess in words their love for each other. Both Debussy and Wagner found the use of unresolved dominants, though handled differently by each, to be especially effective in such situations as this.

1. The dominant of F is implied in m. 1.

2. M. 2-3 imply dominants on E and A reached through appoggiaturas on beats one and three, respectively.

3. The dominant on A remains through the first two beats of m. 4, then changes on beats three and four to the dominant on C (key of F) which carries through m. 5-7.

4. Notice that the unaccompanied line in m. 5-7 is diatonic in F, and that "I love you" is sung at a lower pitch by Mélisande than by Pelléas. This exemplifies impressionist understatement. Of course, the sonorities and rhythmic motion increase as the scene progresses but the dynamics seldom rise above forte.

5. The distribution of tones in the dominant ninth chords in m. 8-9 and 11-12 with the ninth below the third and seventh form a structure commonly found throughout the impressionist styles.

6. From the last half of m. 12 through m. 15 the prevailing root is E. This extension of dominant sound through several measures, as in m. 4-7 as well, is also common in Wagner and Strauss. Can the C♯ in m. 15 be considered the thirteenth over the root E?

7. M. 16-17 function as a cadence (subdominant-dominant-tonic) in F♯.

EXAMPLE 90 (page 268)
Feux d'Artifice (Fireworks), Prelude No. 12

The two books of preludes (twelve in each book), the first published in 1910 and the second in 1913, are an important segment of Debussy's piano music. Both Ravel and Debussy developed through the impressionist language a new style of piano writing which represented the most significant advancement of the tonal possibilities of the instrument since the style of Chopin. The titles of the preludes form a catalog of the favorite subjects of impressionism:

Scenes and sensations from nature (*The Wind in the Plain, The Sounds and Perfumes Swirl in the Evening Air, What the West Wind Saw*);

Poetic allusions to legend or mythology (*The Sunken Cathedral, Ondine, The Delphic Dancers*);

Gentle Caricatures (*Minstrels, General Lavine— eccentric, Homage to S. Pickwick, Esq.*);

Exotic places (*The Gate of Wine, The Hills of Anacapri*).

1. This and Example 91 illustrate respectively the use of unrelated triads in root position and the use of diatonic triads in parallel motion.

2. The tritone is melodically emphasized in this prelude. In these measures we see it employed both harmonically and melodically. In m. 1-2 the C triad is followed by the F♯ triad and the outer notes of the chords in the second half of the measure spell the F♯ seventh (F♯,E,B♭(A♯) in m. 1) and the F♯ ninth (F♯,E,B♭(A♯),G in m. 2). A comparable situation exists in m. 3-4.

3. The glissandos along with tremolos (shakes) and harplike arpeggios are prominent elements in the impressionist styles, providing subtle animation, bursts

of brilliance and whisps or swirls of sound appropriate to the subjects.

4. The predominance of major triads gives a bright but neutral quality to these measures.

EXAMPLE 91 (page 268)
Canope, Prelude No. 10

1. Though this excerpt is comparable to Example 90 in the use of triads in root position and in parallel motion the effect is quite different because of the
   a. modal quality of the melody;
   b. steady rhythm;
   c. predominance of minor triads.

2. The tonal quality is d Aeolian in m. 1-3, but the last three chords of m. 4 give the effect of d Phrygian. This roundabout approach to the tonic seen in m. 3-4 is a quasimodal cadential effect typical of Ravel and developed in a somewhat different manner by Hindemith. See Ravel, Examples 101 and 104, and Hindemith, Examples 140 and 141.

3. This example illustrates the neutral-type harmonic color in Debussy.

EXAMPLE 92 (page 269)
La Puerta del Vino, Prelude No. 3

Like Rimsky-Korsakov and Ravel, Debussy was fond of Spanish musical idioms: dances, rhythms and the Phrygian quality of flamenco style. This prelude, *The Evening in Granada*, and the orchestral suite *Iberia* are works based on Spanish color and are highly effective even though Debussy was never in Spain.

1. This prelude is based on the rhythm of the habañera and is a free ABA form. The left-hand ostinato pattern prevails throughout the A sections. The B section is based on a B♭-F ostinato pattern.

2. The characteristic rhythm is present most of the time.

3. The melodic movement to D♭ from D or E♭♭ as in m. 2 and 7 is characteristic of Phrygian.

4. An appoggiatura chord is exemplified by the C dominant ninth chord over the ostinato in m. 5-6.

5. Notice the clustered arrangement of the C and D dominant ninth chords in m. 5-6 and 9-10, and also the veiled, evanescent effect implied by the notation, especially in the left hand of m. 9-10. This reliance on and imaginative use of the damper pedal is another outstanding characteristic of impressionist piano style.

6. The unresolved E♭ in the last six measures produces a D♭ triad with added second. Why cannot this last chord be considered a I^9 instead of a I^{+2}? Chords with added sixths, seconds and fourths

become a common ingredient of twentieth-century popular style. See Example 93.

EXAMPLE 93 (page 270)
Feuilles Morte, (Dead Leaves) Prelude No. 2

This prelude explores complex dominant-type sonorities. It is cast in free ABA form in that the material of the opening measures returns toward the end.

1. The chord in m. 1 sounds like a minor dominant ninth on F♯, but with its return in m. 3 the added D♯ in the left hand makes it a minor dominant ninth with F♯ an appoggiatura to the ninth, E, but unresolved. In m. 2 the same chord structure appears on C♯ as a root. Here E is an appoggiatura to the ninth, D, and resolves to it ornamentally through C♯. The chord structures in m. 2-3 are like a V^9 chord with both a major and minor third, considering the appoggiaturas as the minor thirds of the two chords. See page 280 on Ravel's style.

2. M. 6-7 illustrate triads with added seconds. The sound here is of a dominant ninth chord on A moving to a B^7 chord in third inversion. The C♯ is an added second or the ninth of the chord. The B♭ chord is taken like a lower auxilliary chord to the B chord.

3. M. 8-9 illustrate triads with added fourths. The sound has the predominant effect of a dominant cluster of tones on the root A, resolving on the third beat of m. 9 to D with added sixth and second.

It can be seen from such passages as this that it is not possible to make a definitive analysis of these complex clusters on a conventional tonal basis. It is difficult to ascertain whether a tone in a cluster is a functioning member of the chord or whether it is an "added" tone.

4. The tonal definition of m. 10-14 is clearer, being a dominant complex on G as a root. The last eighth-note chord of m. 10 and 11 has the effect of I^6_4 preceded by appoggiaturas on beat three. M. 12-14 are good examples of the dominant thirteenth chord on G.

5. The harmony of m. 15 is the same as m. 2. Notice that E is the minor third and F (E♯) the major third of a C♯ dominant seventh chord.

EXAMPLE 94 (page 271)
Feuilles Morte, Prelude No. 2

1. Here is a true polytonal effect. The chord in the lower staff has been introduced in the preceding two measures like IV^7 on A♯ in the key of E, but its maintenance through these four measures destroys this kind of implication.

2. It appears that in these four measures there are three distinct tonal ideas running simultaneously

at three pitch levels. The lower staff implies one tonal center. The center staff carries a melodic idea, the key of which cannot be defined because of the effects the chords above and below have on it. The upper staff consists of an ostinato of four major triads, abstrusely spelled, with a tritone between the first two (A to D♯) and the second two (F♯ to B♯).

3. Simpler examples of duotonality are found in the piano pieces, *Saudades do Brazil,* by Milhaud. In these Latin American dances the left hand is clearly in one key and the right hand in another. Milhaud's style shows the influence of passages such as this example.

EXAMPLE 95 (pages 271-279)
Reflets dans l'Eau from Images

There are two sets of three piano pieces called *Images,* which were published in 1904 and 1907. This is the first number of the first set, and one of Debussy's best works for piano.

1. The thematic material consists of two ideas: a. the first four measures and b. the motive in the left hand of m. 24-27. Varied statements based on these two ideas alternate in an ABABA design:

        A, m. 1-15
        Transition, m. 16-23
        B, m. 24-34 (over A♭ pedal)
        A, m. 35-42
        Transition, m. 43-49
        B, m. 50-70
        A, m. 71-94

The theme associated with A always appears in D♭ and is a more specific tonal entity, while the motive associated with B is more tenuous in nature and appears in a variety of ways.

The descriptive possibilities implied by the title are thoroughly explored.

2. The first eight measures constitute a repeated phrase with a broad V-I-V-I progression over the double pedal, D♭-A♭. The right-hand chords include the sevenths, ninths and elevenths of the basic harmonies or added tones to the basic chords, or freely resolved nonharmonic tones of various types. Which is your interpretation?

3. M. 9-10 contain a chromatic sequence of dominant thirteenth and seventh chords. The second chord in m. 9 is an altered dominant seventh on A. Notice that in m. 10 the pattern is repeated and extended by two more chords.

4. The D♭^{13} in m. 11 resolves to its own tonic G♭ with added sixths at the end of the measure.

5. The thirteenth is placed below the ninth in the A♭^{13} of m. 12.

6. The minor seventh chord in m. 13 comes as an unusual color after so many chords with tritones.

7. The second half of m. 14 is a sequential repetition, a perfect fourth lower, of the first half. What are the chords in this measure?

8. M. 15 sounds like V^7 of D♭ with D♭ and B♭♭ as appoggiaturas, and there is a free resolution of this harmony in m. 16 with the D♭ in the bass.

9. The open fifths and wide spacing between hands in m. 16 followed by the bare seconds in m. 17 seem to imply the hollow resonance of deep water. Debussy uses the same type of effect in *The Sunken Cathedral* (Prelude, no. 10, Book I).

10. The effect of m. 17-19 seems to be a drop of water falling into a pool, followed by the rippling or shimmering caused on the surface of the water. At any rate, the rippling pattern of m. 18-19 is carried through a two octave sequence of half-diminished seventh chords in m. 20-21, and m. 22-23 establish the arpeggio pattern for the entrance of the B motive in m. 24.

11. The B section beginning at m. 24 contains an elaborate series of chords over the dominant pedal, A♭. The B motive is stated in the whole-tone scale in m. 24-26; and after the shift to the V^9 (of D♭) chord at m. 27 the motive returns in m. 29-30 against the V^9.

12. The four chords in the second half of m. 30-31 are somewhat the reverse of the pattern in m. 9-10. The descending arpeggios in the first half of m. 31-32 are simply a continuation of the minor dominant ninth chord on C immediately preceding. Notice the location of the minor ninth, D♭, in this chord.

13. The conflicting C harmony is gradually eliminated through m. 32-34, preparing for the return of the A theme in D♭.

14. It is important to notice that the principal melodic line of m. 29-34 is entirely diatonic but the chords used to harmonize it are various dominant sounds generally having no relation to the tonal implication of that melodic line.

   Chords used independently for their intrinsic color to harmonize essentially simple and direct diatonic melodies is an important feature of the style.

15. M. 35-42 are a repetition of the first eight measures with the right-hand chords broken into an arpeggio pattern.

16. M. 43-49 exploit the whole-tone scale and at m. 50-51 the B motive returns in a whole-tone version.

17. Compare m. 50-55 with m. 24-30.

18. The resolution of the G♯⁹ to E♭ in m. 55 to 56 will be better understood if G♯, B♯, D♯ are spelled A♭, C, E♭. How can you relate this progression to conventional chromatic harmony?

19. In m. 56-64 motive B is given a different rhythmic treatment (m. 57) and expanded by an additional connecting motive (m. 60, 62, 63). The tonality is E♭ Mixolydian dissolving into a whole-tone scale at m. 63-64. Notice that there is a digression into the whole-tone scale in m. 60 also but a return to E♭ in m. 61.

20. Assuming E♭ to be the key center, the last half of m. 58 is VII⁷ of E♭; and the tonic chord, because of the Mixolydian flat seventh, D♭, is a dominant type of formation, but does not act as dominant of A♭.

21. The B motive is stated still differently in m. 65-66 in the key of A Lydian.

22. The movement from A in m. 66 to c in m. 67 and back to A in 68 is another effective progression of unrelated triads. The c in m. 67 acts as a digression, an "aside," inserted between m. 66 and its repetition in m. 68.

23. The progression from A to the A♭⁹, V⁹ of the main key D♭, in m. 68 to 69, is simply a conventional VI from d♭ to V⁹ progression.

24. Notice that the melodic material of m. 68-70 consists of three notes from the B motive.

25. A full eight measure return of A appears in m. 71-78. Analyze the difference between m. 71-74 and m. 1-4.

26. The whole-tone motive of m. 60, 62-63 returns in m. 79-80 as a digression before the coda based on A.

27. M. 81-90 function as a prolonged subdominant involving various versions of the II and IV chords resolving to tonic at m. 91 with resolution of the extended appogiaturas B♭ to A♭ and E♭ to F finally in m. 93.

28. One of Debussy's ways of introducing a whole-tone scale effect into a predominantly major tonality is to substitute 4, 5, 6 and 7 of the major scale with ♯4, ♭6 and ♭7 to form a whole-tone scale with 1, 2, 3. The chord which he usually introduces to accomplish this is IV⁷ with raised 4 and lowered 6 of the scale. This chord implies four of the six tones of the whole-tone scale. The inclusion of ♭7 and 2 of the scale provides the possibility for a whole-tone dominant chord as discussed in Example 86, Paragraph 6. The scale of D♭ is altered in this fashion in m. 43-47, and the scale of E♭ is likewise altered in m. 60 and 63. Thus, throughout the style ♯4 of the scale forming a tritone with the tonic along with ♭6 and ♭7 are common altered tones. The ♯4 and ♭7 also provide the melodic inflection for the Lydian and Mixolydian modes which appear regularly in Debussy's music.

The whole-tone scale is also evolved by substituting 1, 2, 3 of the scale with ♯1 and ♯2. This involves the chord VII⁷ with ♯2 of the scale.

Examples and Suggestions for Further Study of the Music of Debussy

Insight into the style of Debussy can be pretty thoroughly gained through study of his piano music, though an understanding of his technique in handling timbres can be gotten only from his orchestral and vocal music.

Generally the early piano pieces, prior to 1900, are formally less rhapsodic and more direct, with clearly defined sections and cadences; and they are tonally more conventional, with long diatonic passages interspersed occasionally with the harmonic and tonal effects that predominate in his later works. The melodic ideas are longer and of more definite shape in the early works as compared to the short, suggestive motives that fulfill the melodic function in later works. The following five early piano pieces in this category are suggested for beginning analysis in this style and for tracing the developing of Debussy's technic of composition from its earliest influences.

Arabesque, no. 1 (1880) is a song form with trio design, the trio in the subdominant key (A). It is almost entirely diatonic. Its flavor comes from his use of nonharmonic tones and some parallel diatonic triads.

Arabesque, no. 2 (1888) is in the same form with the middle section (trio) in the subdominant key (C) also. The diatonic nature and use of parallel diatonic chords (especially triads in first inversion) also prevail.

Danse (1890) is an ABACA form making great use of the hemiola. The melody of A is diatonic. The transitions and themes of B and C involve more of a play on unresolved dominants so common in late works.

Clair de lune, the third number from Suite Bergamesque (1890) is a well-proportioned ABA form with a long dominant preparation for the return of A comparable to the one in Reflections in the Water (Example 95). Again the work is quite diatonic, relying on diatonic seventh and ninth chords in resonant formations and on the Mixolydian (♭7) and the Lydian (♯4) modes for color, especially in section B. Modulation back to D♭ (the main key) from E is accomplished through II^7 of E which is IV^7 of c♯ (d♭). See Example 95, m. 68-69, for a comparable modulation.

Prelude in a from the suite, *Pour Le Piano* (1891) exploits almost excessively augmented triads, passages based on the whole-tone scale and tritones. It is a large work but seems to lack the poetry which is the best part of Debussy.

The piano music of Debussy which is most truly representative of impressionism is that written after 1900 and influenced technically by Ravel's piano music, much of which was written before 1910, the year Debussy's first book of preludes appeared.

A collection of three piano pieces under the title *Estampes* (Prints) appeared in 1903. The first, *Pagodes* (Pagodas), makes use of the pentatonic and whole-tone scales. The second, *La soirée dans Grenade* (The evening in Granada), is the forerunner of *La Puerta del Vino* (Example 92) being in the same mood as the latter and employing the habañera rhythm and flamenco color (Phrygian mode) but on a broader scale. Here again a diatonic Phrygian melody is harmonized by parallel dominant seventh chords (m. 17-20, 27-30) and by parallel triads (m. 31-34). The rhythmic pattern ♪♫ ♫♪ runs through like an ostinato and is sometimes employed as a pedal pattern (m. 1-14, 21-28, etc.). It is in a free ABA design and in texture consists of a series of harmonic and melodic patterns over ostinato or pedal effects. The third, *Jardins sous la pluie* (Gardens in the Rain), includes the quotation of two French folk tunes in a texture of arpeggiated chords and trills. A good example of whole-tone dominants employed in conjunction with two chromatic lines expanding and contracting in contrary motion appears in m. 64-70.

L'Isle joyeuse (1904) is one of Debussy's most unrestrainedly happy works and perhaps his best work for piano up to that time. It is broadly conceived, a large ABAB design, and of complex texture and technic. The main melodies, one a lighthearted, rhythmic and scalewise line and the other a soaring, eloquent, lyric expression are in the Lydian with occasional touches of Mixolydian. This combination of these two modes—a major scale with ♯4 and ♭7—is common throughout Debussy's music. The free use of diatonic sevenths, ninths and elevenths, or added tones in the presentation of the second theme results in a pandiatonic effect. Actually complex diatonic chord formations resulting partly from melodic appoggiaturas are sounded over a tonic ostinato pattern. See m. 67-94.

Debussy's late style is represented in the two books of preludes. The second book contains more and more abstract, precious and remote examples of the types of moods created in the first book and other earlier works.

BOOK I (1910)

No. 1, *The Delphic Dancers,* is mainly a diatonic line harmonized by whole-tone dominants and parallel triads.

No. 2, *Voiles* (Veils or Sails), is based, except for five measures, entirely on the whole-tone scale.

No. 3, *The Wind in the Plain,* employs a pentatonic motive.

No. 4, *The Sounds and Perfumes Swirl in the Evening Air,* exploits complex dominant sonorities plus parallel triads and dominant sevenths.

No. 5, *The Hills of Anacapri,* includes a pentatonic theme. It is essentially a diatonic work with tonic and dominant pedal effects.

No. 6, *Steps in the Snow,* is based on a one-measure ostinato figure.

No. 7, *What the West Wind Saw,* is a complex texture of arpeggios, tremolos and trills against various chord formations, including bare major seconds as in Example 95, m. 18-19.

No. 8, *The Girl with the Flaxen Hair,* is one of Debussy's best-known lyric expressions. It is a simple diatonic song with pentatonic emphasis in the melody.

No. 9, *The Interrupted Serenade,* is a gently humorous piece inspired by the Spanish idiom. The melodic fragments and contrasting accompaniment patterns juxtaposed one after another are typical of Debussy's modus operandi, especially his "caricature" style. Here this kind of writing is perfect for the title it is illustrating. This same approach is used and the same mood evoked in *Minstrels,* in *General Lavine—eccentric,* and in *The Golliwog's Cakewalk* from the *Children's Corner* suite.

No. 10, *The Sunken Cathedral,* exploits piano resonance through bell-like effects of chords in open fourths and fifths, widely spaced chords between left hand and right hand, and triads doubled in both hands over low octave pedal points. The work is essentially a diatonic exploration of sonority.

No. 11, *The Dance of Puck,* consists of a sprightly diatonic melody with contrasting transitions or interludes.

No. 12, *Minstrels,* is a mild caricature or parody on the instruments and certain melodic idioms of the minstrel show.

Book II (1913)

The technic involving the alternation of contrasting chords or arpeggios in the same pitch range by one hand playing directly over the other was developed by Ravel and is employed in Preludes, nos. 1, 2, 4, 7, 11 and 12.

No. 1, *Brouillards* (Mists), emphasizes the diminished triad and tritone much as in *Nuages* (Clouds). Much of the texture consists of chords on the white keys alternating with scale figures or arpeggios on the black keys.

No. 2, See Examples 93 and 94.

No. 3, See Example 92.

No. 4, *The Fairies are Exquisite Dancers,* consists of elusive bits of melody fleeting among arpeggio patterns and trills involving chords of dominant and whole-tone formations. It is a free ABA design.

No. 5, *Heather,* is a counterpart of *The Girl with the Flaxen Hair.* It evokes the same mood with the same kind of tonal language.

No. 6, *General Lavine—eccentric,* is in the disconnected style of the *Interrupted Serenade* which displays Debussy's technic of juxtaposing flashes of short, contrasting ideas. There is a recurring pentatonic tune reminiscent of other preludes.

No. 7, *La terrasse des audiences du clair de lune,* is similar in mood and harmonic content to no. 2, *Dead Leaves.*

No. 8, *Ondine,* is based harmonically on formations of the dominant thirteenth chord and melodically on the Lydian mode. The chord cluster consisting of the seventh, root and ninth of V^9 chords (m. 1-10) and the formation of a perfect fourth above an augmented fourth derived from the seventh, third and thirteenth of V^{13} chords (m. 1-10, 43-52) are two predominant harmonic elements.

No. 9, *Homage to S. Pickwick, Esq.,* is a caricature which employs the tune of "God Save the King." It is essentially diatonic with some whole-tone touches.

No. 10, *Canope,* exploits the appoggiatura a half-step below the root of V^7 contrasted to parallel triads as seen in Example 91. It closes on a major triad with added second.

No. 11, *Alternating Thirds,* as the title states consists of thirds alternating above and below re-

peated thirds in the Ravel cross-hand style. It is somewhat in the nature of a perpetual motion.

No. 12, *Fireworks,* in addition to the material of Example 90, employs two-hand patterns of rapid scale figures and tremolos and emphasizes pairs of notes forming a major second tossed about like sparks in the whole-tone scale tonality.

The following works should be examined for the features indicated as well as for the many other points of style which each work in its entirety will of course display.

Prelude to the Afternoon of a Faun:

1. The use of $\sharp 4$ of the scale as referred to above is an important harmonic factor in this work. The IV^7 on $\sharp 4$ (like VII^7 of V) is important in the opening and closing sections in E, m. 1-20 and 100 to the end. The IV^7 on $\sharp 4$ with $\flat 6$ of the scale to form the whole-tone scale is used in the section in D$\flat$, m. 55-78.
2. A half-step shift between half-diminished seventh chords occurs in m. 27.
3. Since this work is earlier than the examples of piano music here included it will be interesting to note that it is more clearly tonal than are many of the preludes for piano.

Nocturnes for Orchestra:

1. The cyclic principle is employed in this set of three pieces though not as obviously as in the string quartet.
2. The first piece, *Nuages* (Clouds), involves an emphasis on the tritone both melodically and harmonically and closes with the tritone B to F predominating.
3. In the second of the three pieces, *Fêtes* (Festivals), the following are of interest:
   a. parallel dominant ninth chords in m. 9-14;
   b. parallel triads, forming a melodic line reminiscent of the opening motive of *Nuages,* in m. 27-38;
   c. whole-tone scale evolved by altering 1, 2, 3 of the D$\flat$ scale, m. 44-46;
   d. the use of repeated figures, measures or pairs of measures as an important structural element in the work recognizable throughout;
   e. the A$\flat$ pedal throughout the middle section in $\frac{2}{4}$ meter functions as part of two enharmonic tritones: A$\flat$-D and G$\sharp$-D.
4. The third number, *Sirènes,* is unusual in its use of women's voices without words employed for their

timbre per se as part of the orchestra. This use of the vocal sound is now a common ingredient of background music for movies and television.

The orchestral works employ the same harmonic vocabulary as seen in the piano pieces but usually in a broader formal design. Repetition of figures, measures and pairs of measures as well as pedal and ostinato effects likewise play an important part in these works.

Suggested Written Assignments

1. Write three exercises of eight to sixteen measures: (a) one based on predominantly neutral harmony (chords without tritones) in diatonic and nontonal relationships, (b) one based on dominant chord formations (chords with tritones) involving parallel motion and chromatic alterations, and (c) one based on the whole-tone scale using whole-tone dominant formations.
2. Write a short piece with a predominantly pentatonic melody interrupted by passages involving the whole-tone scale, parallel chord formations, and/or open fourth, fifth and second chord structures.
3. Experiment with resolutions of the following chords in the key of C:

   IV^7 with ♯4 and ♭6—F♯ A♭ C E—and
   VII^7 with ♯2—B D♯ F A

Bibliography

DEBUSSY, CLAUDE A., *Monsieur Croche: The Dilettante Hater*, New York: Lear, 1948.

LIEBICH, MRS. FRANZ, *Claude Achille Debussy*, London: John Lane, 1908.

LOCKSPEISER, EDWARD, *Debussy, His Life and Mind*, New York: The Macmillan Company, 1962.

MYERS, ROLLO, *Debussy*, London: Dobson, 1948.

SEROFF, VICTOR, *Debussy, Musician of France*, New York: G. P. Putnam's Sons, 1956.

SHERA, FRANK HENRY, *Debussy and Ravel*, London: Oxford University Press, 1925.

THOMPSON, OSCAR, *Debussy, Man and Artist*, New York: Dodd, Mead & Company, 1937.

VALLAS, LEON, *Claude Debussy*, Paris: Michel, 1958.

————, *The Theories of Claude Debussy*, London: Oxford University Press, 1929.

EXAMPLE 85
Debussy
STRING QUARTET
Themes from I, II, and IV

I (Theme 1)

Animé et très décidé

I (From second theme group)

II (Opening Measures)

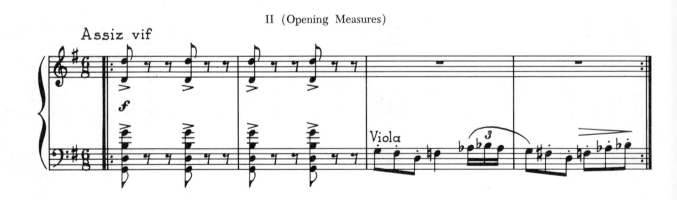

Assiz vif

IV (Measures 15-16)

EXAMPLE 86
Debussy
PELLÉAS AND MÉLISANDE
ACT II, SCENE I
(Measures 77-100)

lost   'tis lost___   nought but a cir-cle of wa-ter re-mains.

EXAMPLE 87
Debussy
PELLÉAS AND MÉLISANDE
ACT I, SCENE I
(Measures 177-182)

Trés modéré   Plus lent

EXAMPLE 88
Debussy
PELLÉAS AND MÉLISANDE
ACT II, SCENE I
(Measures 137-139)

Lent

EXAMPLE 89

DEBUSSY
PELLÉAS AND MÉLISANDE
ACT IV, SCENE IV
(Measures 86-102)

EXAMPLE 90

DEBUSSY

FEUX D'ARTIFICE (FIREWORKS)

Prelude No. 12, Second Book

(Measures 61-64)

EXAMPLE 91

DEBUSSY

CANOPE

Prelude No. 10, Second Book

(First 5 Measures)

Permission for reprint granted by Durand & Cie of Paris, France, copyright owners; Elkan-Vogel Co., Inc. of Philadelphia, Pa. sole agents.

EXAMPLE 92
Debussy
LA PUERTA DEL VINO
Prelude No. 3, Second Book
(Last 16 Measures)

EXAMPLE 93
Debussy
FEUILLES MORTES (DEAD LEAVES)
Prelude No. 2, Second Book
(First 15 Measures)

EXAMPLE 94
DEBUSSY
FEUILLES MORTES
Prelude No. 2, Second Book
(Measures 25-28)

Permission for reprint granted by Durand & Cie of Paris, France, copyright owners; Elkan-Vogel Co., Inc. of Philadelphia, Pa. sole agents.

EXAMPLE 95
DEBUSSY
REFLETS DANS L'EAU (REFLECTIONS IN THE WATER)
From Images (First Suite) for Piano
(Complete)

Roots: A♭ A♮ B♭ C♭ C D♭

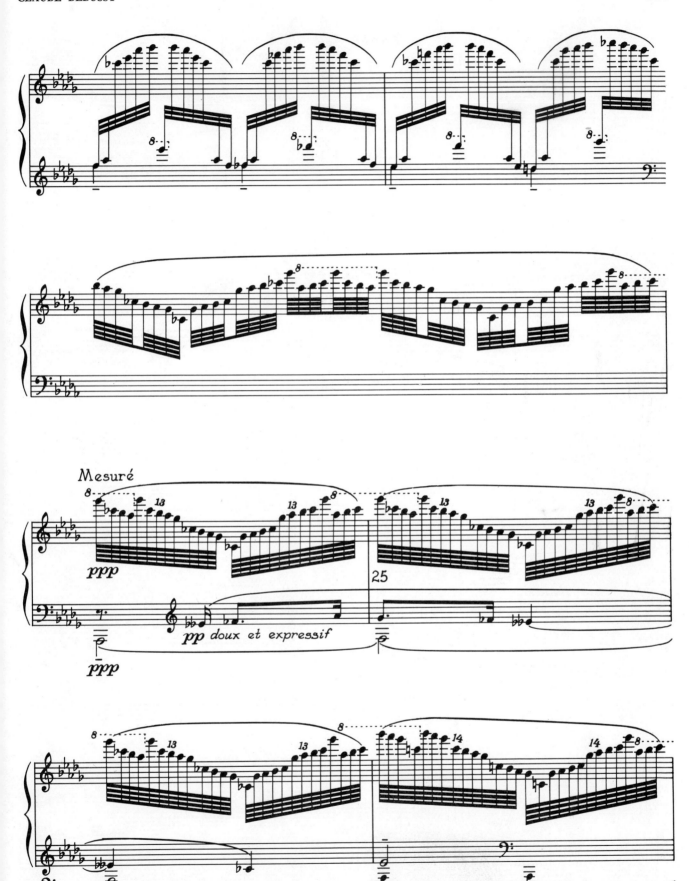

harmonieuse et lointaine)

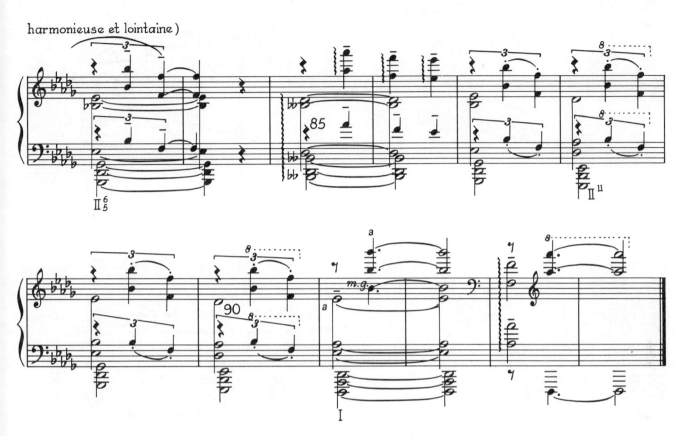

CHAPTER 18

MAURICE RAVEL

1875-1937

The harmonies, textures and timbres of impressionism are applied by Ravel to classical forms. He uses his complex and sophisticated harmonic vocabulary in a functional manner in works of classical formal clarity.

Though both Debussy and Ravel are considered impressionists and employed comparable materials their formal approaches and artistic goals differ considerably.

Debussy's music is rhapsodic, impulsive and sensuous, and its goal is a romantic one in the sense that it expresses mood, atmosphere and feeling. Debussy is a romantic impressionist.

Ravel is a classic impressionist. His works are cast in carefully delineated forms with clearly defined themes, cadences, harmonic organization and sections. His music is more detached from the emotional aspect of the picture it reflects and is governed more by purely musical requirements than by extra musical associations. Ravel tends to keep content and form in more equal balance; his goal is to charm by using technical perfection.

Debussy's style is highly original and imaginative but its very individuality placed limits on it. The possibilities inherent in such a personal mode of expression were pretty much exhausted by Debussy himself.

On the other hand, Ravel is more of an eclectic. Many influences besides the materials of impressionism are present in his music. Works by Chopin and Liszt had some influence in his piano music; Rimsky-Korsakov and Strauss influenced his orchestral writing; the idioms of the Viennese waltz, Spanish music, jazz, and of folk music of Russia and other countries appear in various works.

Yet the two composers did influence one another, and the descriptive titles they chose for their music bear a close resemblance. The organization of the

musical material under similar titles is quite different in each case, however.

The whole-tone scale rarely appears in Ravel's music. The Dorian and Phrygian modes are used more than Lydian and Mixolydian. The Aeolian form of minor (natural minor) is common but not harmonic minor. The unresolved appoggiatura to the ninth of V^9 (V^7 with both major and minor thirds) and the

augmented eleventh as well as various types of thirteenth chords appear frequently. Because of his frequent use of the Dorian scale, a dominant seventh or ninth formation on IV is common. In f Dorian this chord would be Bb D F Ab (C). See Examples 104 and 105.

Also many other types of unresolved appoggiaturas or added tones are used with functional harmonies in unusual formations to produce both the luxuriant and acid flavors in his music.

Much of the chromatic alteration in his harmony is a result of his free mixing of the modes, including oscillation between major and minor.

EXAMPLE 96 (page 287)
Daphnis and Chloé, Suite No. 2, Part I

In his writing for ballet Ravel's classical attitude required that the music should have its own form as music and not be subservient to the dancing. He therefore called *Daphnis and Chloé* a choreographic symphony, and based it on a strict key plan and a small number of themes. This work is probably Ravel's most important orchestral work. It is best known in the second orchestral suite which he extracted from the full ballet version.

1. The excerpt here illustrates the importance of the intervals of the perfect fourth and fifth in his

melodies. Compare this with the other Ravel examples. The prevalence of these intervals is probably related to the diatonic, tonal quality of his music.

2. Notice the diatonic modal quality and the symmetry.

EXAMPLES 97, 98, 99, 100 (page 287)
Le Tombeau de Couperin

Ravel made highly original contributions toward expanding the technical and aesthetic possibilities of the piano, which influenced many twentieth-century composers besides Debussy. Thus his piano music is important and displays his artistic growth and the full range of his style (except for orchestration). Though he was one of the greatest masters of the art of orchestration, many of his orchestra works were first conceived for piano.

This suite, *The Tomb of Couperin* (1917), is Ravel's last work for solo piano and is intended as homage to eighteenth-century clavecin composers and their music. The six movements each in a specific form are:

I. PRELUDE. Comparable in form to the binary form of the eighteenth-century dance suite. Uses Aeolian and Dorian modes. Material presented mostly in groups of two measures and occasionally three.

II. FUGUE. The only fugue in Ravel's published works. Ingeniously constructed with modal flavor.

III. FORLANE. (See Example 101.) In second rondo form, A B A C A plus coda. Sections A B and C are all three-part song forms. Eight- and occasionally nine-measure periods prevail throughout with some overlapping cadences. The long coda consists of four periods, each closing on I, and a final six measure extension.

IV. RIGAUDON. An A B A form. The A section is a lively dance and B is like a contrasting trio and involves a drone bass. The A sections open and close each time with the cadential figure of Example 97. This is a good illustration of a Ravelian treatment of a II-V-I cadence in C major.

V. MINUET. In traditional song form and trio design plus coda. The melody of part a of the minuet is quoted in Example 98. It is a regular eight-measure period. The trio is a musette over a tonic-dominant drone bass. Example 99 is the melody of the opening eight-measure period of the musette. What mode is it? This musette melody in a change of mode is combined with the minuet on its return. The movement closes on a I^9 chord.

VI. TOCCATA. A brilliant rhapsodic form with chords alternating between hands and often overlapping. The rhythmic and melodic ideas are stated in two-, three- and four-measure groups. The three-measure Phrygian melody of Example 100 occurs in m. 57-62. It appears first an octave higher and is repeated in the octave shown.

EXAMPLE 101 (pages 288, 289)
Le Tombeau de Couperin, Part III—Forlane

This includes the last phrase of the A melody and the first two and a half periods of the coda.

1. The bass of the first five measures outlines the harmonic function as shown. These phrases illustrate Ravel's method of piling up complex chord structures over fundamental bass movement.

2. In m. 1, chord 1 is a minor-major seventh, chord 2 an augmented-major seventh which becomes the top of a IV^{11} in the first half of m. 2. Chord 2 of m. 2 is a IV^9 and becomes a II^{11} in m. 3. Notice the parallel structure in the upper four chord notes from the last eighth of m. 3 to m. 4. These are typical Ravel chord structures as illustrated on p. 280. Chord 1 in m. 4 could be considered a chord appoggiatura to chord 2, which is the real V formation.

3. The next period consists of 2 four-measure phrases (m. 6-9 and 10-13) each cadencing on I. The fundamental harmony is similar to the first five measures. The basic idea here is the piling up of sonorities in thirds.

4. Notice that the entire period is completely diatonic and closes with a perfect authentic cadence in E.

5. The harmony is much more abstruse in the next period, m. 14-21, but filters out to another authentic cadence.

6. The simple G triad in m. 13 by addition of tones below becomes a thirteenth chord on A in m. 14 and resolves to the complex sound over D in m. 15. This latter chord, because of the wide distance between hands, sounds like a C♯ triad with added sixth over D; but Ravel because of the spelling must have had in mind a complex thirteenth resulting from the voice leading B-B♭-A and G-G♯-A, the A being in the second chord of m. 15. The process is repeated a step lower leading to the E triad over C in m. 17. Notice how Ravel meticulously changes A♭ to G♯ and G to F𝄪 to maintain a subtle (perhaps imaginary) integrity in the voice leading.

7. The B♯'s in m. 19 are appoggiaturas to C♯ (the added sixth in I^6_4) but the chord changes with the arrival of the C♯ in m. 20.

8. The harmony in the last five measures is even more recondite but again returns to cadence on I in m. 25.

9. The second chord in m. 21 is probably an eleventh on D♯, a highly altered VII¹¹ with the real root, B, missing. By the time a chord is this highly altered, its true definition disappears.

10. The first chord in m. 22 is a V¹³ of V on F♯. A major thirteenth with minor ninth is typical.

11. Thus this last phrase seems to consist basically of an alternation between V, and V of V resolving to I in m. 24 with the tones F♯, A, C♯ in m. 24 acting as nonharmonic tones finally resolving at m. 25.

12. Thus we see that Ravel by maintaining fundamental bass movement is able to pile up complex eleventh and thirteenth chords with altered tones above that bass without destroying tonal direction. Notice also that the cadence usually clears up any remoteness in the harmony of a phrase, and the free use of modal changes provides much latitude for harmonic and melodic color within the fundamental tonal framework.

EXAMPLE 102 (pages 289-292)
Jeux D'Eau (The Fountain)

Ravel indicated that *Jeux d'Eau* (Play of Water, or The Fountain) (1901) was at the origin of his innovations in pianistic style. He also compared it to a sonata first movement with two themes but without conforming to the classical key relations.

1. It vaguely resembles sonata form, the first theme group being the first eighteen measures and the second theme group beginning at m. 19. After a section of more rapidly shifting tonality, a development, there is a return of both theme groups.

2. Notice the frequent repetition of half-measure motives as in m. 1, 3, 5, 7, 9 and 14 and of full-measure motives as in m. 19-21 and 24-25. Also notice the expansion of the motive of m. 22 in m. 23.

3. The basic harmonies marked in the score indicate how closely the music follows fundamental tonal progressions. Each harmony should be identified in detail as to whether it is a seventh, ninth, eleventh or thirteenth chord and what tones are altered.

4. Beginning with beat 2 of m. 4 there is a series of augmented dominant eleventh chords in root position carrying through beat two of m. 6.

   a. Compare the augmented eleventh on D, beat 2, m. 4, with the altered chord in m. 3.

   b. How does the last chord in m. 4 differ from the other eleventh chords on either side of it?

c. Compare the first chord of m. 5 with the IV⁷ with ♯4 and ♭7 used by Debussy.

5. The last three eighths of m. 6 show Ravel's rare use of the whole-tone scale. What alterations are involved in the last three chords of this measure?

6. Notice that the first six measures form a period which returns by a V⁷-I progression to the opening idea, m. 7-8.

7. M. 9-10 are analyzed as I and IV with added sixths rather than VI⁷ and II⁷. If you agree, why? If not, why?

8. M. 11-18 constitute a Phrygian effect involving the D triad and b triad on either side of the c♯ triad, VI.

9. M. 19-21 are a prolonged dominant with the tone E as an internal tonic pedal resolving finally to D♯ on the last eighth of m. 21. The melodic line in these measures taken alone has a modal quality but the harmony that accompanies it belies this quality.

10. M. 22-23 are simply the IV over a descending bass.

11. M. 24-25 consist of the alternation of a dominant ninth on D♯ with a dominant thirteenth on G. Measure twenty-six introduces a three-measure passage on the E♭ major seventh chord.

12. Notice the importance of the interval of a perfect fourth in the melodic ideas.

13. Identify all nonharmonic as opposed to chord elements in this example.

EXAMPLE 103 (pages 292-297)
Sonatine for Piano, I

Much of Ravel's music has an archaic flavor which is a result of modal melody and nondominant harmony combined with simple repetition of motives and phrases. This quality is particularly evident in the *Sonatine* (1905).

1. The first movement is a sonatina form in f♯ with the second-theme group in A (m. 13-26) returning in F♯ (m. 68-84) and with a repeated exposition.

2. The first five measures consist of diatonic triads in parallel motion. The melody then remains diatonic throughout m. 6-12, but it is harmonized by parallel dominant formations instead of triads.

3. Note that the melodic line is diatonic throughout the entire exposition and that chromaticism exists only in the underlying harmonies.

4. Notice how the motive of m. 7 is progressively shortened to a three-note figure, stated four times in m. 11-12.

5. The first phrase of theme 2, m. 13-19, is expanded from four to seven measures by repetition as follows: 1 1 2 3 2 3 4.

6. Repetition plays an important part likewise in m. 20-31.

7. The development or transition section is in b modulating to D as indicated, m. 26-39.

8. M. 40-48 illustrate a Ravel version of a dominant sequence based on the circle of fifths. Over a triple pedal, E A D, appears a sequence of dominant formations on roots A, D, G, C resolving to F, m. 49.

9. M. 49-51 seem to be in the key of C over an E pedal.

10. The function of the harmony of m. 52-55 is V⁷ of V in f♯. C is really B♯ making the chord of these measures G♯, B♯, D (lowered 5th of the chord), F♯. This resolves to V of f♯ in m. 56.

11. The recapitulation is the same as the exposition except for measures 66-67, which serve to place the second-theme group in F♯, and the final four cadence measures.

12. The German sixth chord appears on beat two of m. 81. Its resolution is a bit free, however.

13. The a minor triad in m. 82-83 spelled with a B♯ for voice-leading niceties produces a modal-colored cadence. Such effects are common in Ravel and much imitated by later composers.

14. A careful analysis of this movement for the purpose of deciding which notes are nonharmonic and which are chord elements (7ths, 9ths, 11ths, etc.) is recommended.

EXAMPLE 104 (pages 297-300)
Sonatine for Piano, II

1. This movement in minuet style is also a sonatine design but based on one melodic idea as follows:

Theme 1 is an extended period repeated, m. 1-12, D♭ closing in f.

Theme 2 is based on the same melody as theme 1. It begins at m. 13 and dissolves into a short transition at m. 39.

Measures 39-52 constitute a transition.

Theme 1 returns in D♭ and closes in D♭, m. 53-64.

Theme 2 returns in c♯ (tonic minor), m. 65-78, but closes in D♭ with the same motive with which the exposition closed, m. 79-82.

2. The second theme section begins in f, m. 13, and the melodic line is diatonic in f until m. 22 where the G♭ implies a return to D♭ (or b♭). The chords in m. 15-25 imply the key of e♭ but the insistence on F and C in the melody denies e♭. How would you interpret the tonality of these thirteen measures (13-

25)? Be sure to take into account Ravel's frequent use of Dorian and Phrygian and the pedal on F in m. 13-15, and compare m. 13-22 with m. 65-75 for clues.

3. Notice the grace notes with no following note in m. 16 and the F tied by an implied damper pedal in m. 15.

4. The transition, m. 39-52, is a play on the tones C♯ to G♯ (D♭ to A♭) preparing for the return of theme 1 which opens on D♭ to A♭.

5. In m. 39-45 the melodic line consists of the C♯ minor triad which is harmonized by two dominant structures containing it, E¹³ and A♯⁷(F♯⁹).

6. E¹³ is maintained throughout m. 45-49, and chromatic alteration of the inner voices in m. 50-52 leads to F and A♭, the minor third in m. 53, beat one. At the same time the ostinati in the outer voices continue from m. 49 through m. 54.

7. The return of theme 1 is modified to make it end in D♭ instead of f. Analyze the modification.

8. The theme 2 area is somewhat altered on its return. The F♯-C♯ pedal in m. 69-78 indicates a subdominant prolongation. The A and B♯ in m. 70 and 72 are lower auxiliaries to A♯ and C♯ in m. 71 and 73, respectively. But in m. 76-78, as part of the augmented sixth chord, VII⁷ of c♯ with ♭2 of the scale (C E♭♭ G♭ B♭♭), the A and B♯ (B♭♭ and C) resolve to A♭ and D♭ respectively in the I at m. 79.

The difficulty in notation arises from the enharmonic shift from tonic minor, c♯, back to tonic major, D♭.

9. How do you explain the G♮ in m. 80 as well as 34?

EXAMPLE 105 (pages 300, 301)
Sonatine for Piano, III

1. The last movement shows the Sonatine to be a cyclic work because much of its thematic material is based on ideas from I and II.

2. III is a sonata form. The first theme group and transition (the first 36 measures of the movement) contain two ideas, the second of which does not reappear in the recapitulation.

3. This second idea (m. 12-17) involves a device common in Ravel (see Example 104, m. 49-54 and 69-78) and exemplified by Griffes also in Example 106. This device consists of a diatonic melody in the upper voice over a pedal or ostinato bass with the inner voices moving parallel chromatically up and/or down in a pattern of thirds or some triad or seventh pattern. In this case, the inner voices move in a pattern of half-diminished sevenths in parallel motion.

4. This example includes the first ten measures of the second theme group, m. 37-46 of the move-

ment. Theme 2, derived from theme 1 of I (Example 103), opens in a Dorian for three measures, moves to e Dorian for three measures, then to c♯ Dorian. Measures 47-53 of the movement (not quoted) consist of a transition back to A (quasi-Mixolydian) for six measures (54-59), which close the exposition. At measure fifty-three Ravel employs the V of A with simultaneous augmented and diminished fifth—♯2 and ♭2 of the scale—resolving to 3 and 1 of the tonic of A.

5. The development section deals with themes 1 and 2 and employs the same ostinato figure from m. 49-54 of II.

6. In the recapitulation, theme 1 returns in F♯ Mixolydian, compared to f♯ Dorian in the exposition, and, without a return of the second idea, moves soon to the theme 2 group which is practically a literal transposition down a minor third to f♯ (F♯) of the exposition version. Compare m. 37-59 with 140-162. A ten-measure cadence extension serves as a codetta.

7. Notice in the example the importance again of the interval of a perfect fourth in the melodic structure and the amount of repetition of melodic and harmonic patterns.

8. How do you explain the harmony in the third beat of m. 1-6?

9. Analysis of the entire last movement is recommended.

Examples and Suggestions for Further Study of the Music of Ravel

Pavane pour une Infante défunte (for a Dead Princess), an earlier piano work (1899), is an extended five-part song form (abaca). It illustrates diatonic seventh and ninth chords in circle-of-fifths sequences and parallel dominant ninths.

Alborada del Gracioso (1905) is a tempestuous, brilliantly colorful work in Ravel's Spanish manner. It should be studied for his ingenious use of:

a. Spanish dance rhythms including the hemiola;
b. minor dominant ninth chords and major dominant thirteenth chords with the minor ninth;
c. various complex harmonic formations over pedal patterns;
d. full chord appoggiaturas;
e. Phrygian mode;
f. IV⁷ on ♯4 and VII⁷ with ♭2;
g. IV¹¹ on ♯4;
h. glissandi in thirds and fourths;
i. various other diatonic and chromatically altered ninth, eleventh and thirteenth chords.

This work, the fourth in a set of five piano pieces under the title *Miroirs* (Mirrors), was orchestrated by Ravel.

The suite *Gaspard de la Nuit* (Satan) (1908) is a monumental piano work of transcendent difficulty.

The set of *Valses Nobles et Sentimentales* (1911) represents the epitome of Ravel's music, containing all the salient harmonic elements of his style. He orchestrated this music for ballet.

A more simplified type of writing is exemplified in the suite, *Ma Mère l'Oye* (Mother Goose) (1908). This consists of five short pieces for children written for piano duet. Ravel orchestrated them for ballet.

His last piano works are the two concertos for piano and orchestra written in 1931. The Concerto in G involves acrid, dissonant harmonies, jazz influence including the "blues" scale and harmonies, energetic rhythms and brittle textures.

I is a sonatina design having an exposition and a recapitulation of equal length and no development section.

II is based throughout on the hemiola and is a lyric expression unusually subjective for Ravel.

III is a free sonata design. It is a brilliant, rhythmic, toccata-like texture with jazz elements and duotonality.

The Concerto in D is an astonishing one-movement work for left hand alone.

A comparison of these last works with his early works for piano show the wide range of development which Ravel's style underwent in forty years of composing.

Ravel's chamber music generally has an unusually resonant, symphonic sound. His use of widely spread chords, tremolos, shakes, arpeggios, harmonics and multiple stops results in a rich, colorful texture and a fullness of sound unexpected from a few instruments.

The String Quartet in F (1903) exemplifies this brilliant texture, the characteristic repetition of short phrases and motives and the use of ninth and eleventh chords in unusual formations.

I is a sonata form. Theme 2 is introduced in d and returns in F, but the melody is not transposed in the recapitulation. Instead the harmony is altered to conform to F, mainly by raising the bass a minor third. For example, the opening chord of theme 2 in the exposition is I⁹ in d (D F A C E); in the recapitulation it is I⁷ of F (F A C E).

A study of Ravel's music will reveal that he frequently uses a third-related key for his second themes.

II is a scherzo in free sonata design. Nearly all Ravel's sonata cycles show a relationship of themes among movements. Sometimes the relationship is obvious as an intended employment of the cyclic principle, but often it is only a subtle relationship resulting from emphasis on a certain interval, rhythm or harmony. Compare theme 2 of I with theme 1 of II. The hemiola rhythmic effect prevails throughout most of II.

III is a rhapsodic movement based on three themes. Compare theme 2, m. 19 with theme 1 of I.

IV is a rondo on three themes in the sequence: A B C, A B A, C B C, A coda. Themes B and C are derived from the themes of I.

Introduction and Allegro (1906) for harp, string quartet, flute and clarinet is an ingratiating rhapsodic work in Ravel's opulent, romantic style. It is one movement based on three thematic ideas.

The *Trio in e* (1914) for piano, violin and cello is one of his finest works.

I is a short sonata design. The prevailing rhythm is 8/8 meter grouped into 3 + 2 + 3 eighth notes. Ravel identified this movement as Basque in character.

II is a lively movement titled *Pantoum* (a poetic form). It features much use of harmonics and pizzicato alternating with arco in the strings and a duometric section with the strings in 3/4 against the piano in 4/2 followed by the reverse.

III is a passacaglia in which the nine-measure theme is stated first by piano, then cello, then violin and in reverse order at the close.

IV is a brilliant technical display consisting of a theme in 5/4 (3+2) alternating with a theme in 7/4 (3+4).

This trio is intermediate in style between the opulent, more subjective early style and the later sardonic, spare, dissonant works such as the *Sonata for Violin and Cello* (1922) and the *Sonata for Violin and Piano* (1927).

These latter two works are characterized by economy of texture, emphasis on melody rather than lush harmony. The *Sonata for Violin and Cello* in four movements contains bitonal passages in II and borders on atonality in IV.

The *Sonata for Violin and Piano* emphasizes the incompatibility of the tone of the violin as opposed to the piano and treats the two instruments in an independent contrasting fashion. II is a blues and III is a perpetual motion. The three movements have a cyclic relationship.

The works for voice (songs) and the orchestra, ballet and operatic works are equal in importance to the piano and chamber works.

His many (about 50) songs show his excellent taste in texts and his interest in the folk music and idioms of other countries (Greek, Hebrew, Spanish, Madagascan, Russian). The following sets of songs will provide insight in the range of Ravel's vocal style.

Histoires naturelles (1906) (Stories of Nature) is a set of five songs for voice and piano ranging in expression from mocking humor to tenderness and perfectly interpreting the ironic poems of Jules Renard.

Three Poems of Stéphane Mallarmé (1913) for voice with piano, two flutes and two clarinets was influenced by Schoenberg's *Pierrot Lunaire* in external aspects of instrumental and vocal texture and color but not in internal tonal organization. Debussy set two of these poems for voice in the same year. A comparison of the two composers' treatment of the same two poems is an interesting study.

Ravel considered the *Three Madagascan Songs* (1926) to be one of his finest works. They are difficult songs in his later style.

The three songs titled *Don Quichotte á Dulcinée* (1932) are Ravel's last work and are Basque and Spanish in character.

Of the orchestral works the *Rapsodie espagnole* (1907) should be compared to Rimsky-Korsakov's *Capriccio Espagnol* and to Debussy's *Iberia*.

The *Bolero* (1928) is a unique work based on a rhythmic and tonal ostinato and displays the composer's brilliant technic of orchestration.

La Valse and *Daphnis and Chloé* and his and other composers' piano works which he scored for orchestra are important not only for the study of his style but also for the study of the art of orchestration.

L'Heure espagnole (The Spanish Hour) (1907), a one act comedy-opera and *L'Enfant et les Sortilèges* (The Child and the Sorceries) (1925), a one act fantasy, are important contributions of Ravel to the musical stage. The latter makes use of some jazz idioms including the fox trot.

Suggested Written Assignments

1. Write a short piece (about 32 measures) having a melody in the Dorian or Aeolian mode harmonized by diatonic ninth, eleventh and thirteenth chords.

2. Write an exercise (12 measures) in block harmony in the key of C using at least one each of the following chord formations:

   a. IV^{11} on ♯4 from c minor;
   b. V^{13} with a minor ninth;
   c. II^7 on ♯2;
   d. a dominant seventh formation with both major and minor thirds;
   e. I^9;
   f. VII^7 with ♭2 and ♮6 of the scale.

3. Analyze the *Rigaudon* from *Le Tombeau de Couperin* (piano solo version).

4. As an advanced analysis project compare Ravel's setting of *Soupir*, the first of the *Three Poems of* *Stéphane Mallarmé* with Debussy's setting of the same poem for voice and piano.

BIBLIOGRAPHY

DENMUTH, NORMAN, *Ravel*, New York: Farrar, Strauss & Giroux, Inc., 1949.

GOSS, MADELEINE, *Bolero. The Life of Maurice Ravel*, New York: Tudor Publishing Co., 1940.

JANKELEVITCH, VLADIMIR, *Ravel*, New York: Grove Press, Inc., 1959.

MANUEL, ROLAND, *Maurice Ravel*, London: Dobson, 1947.

MYERS, ROLLO H., *Ravel, Life and Works*, London: Gerald Duckworth & Co., Ltd., 1960.

SEROFF, VICTOR, *Maurice Ravel*, New York: Holt, Rinehart & Winston, Inc., 1953.

EXAMPLE 96
RAVEL
DAPHNIS AND CHLOÉ, SUITE NO. 2 FROM THE BALLET
PART I, DAYBREAK
(Theme)

EXAMPLE 97
RAVEL
LE TOMBEAU DE COUPERIN (THE TOMB OF COUPERIN)
SUITE FOR PIANO, PART IV—RIGAUDON
(First 2 Measures)

EXAMPLE 98
RAVEL
LE TOMBEAU DE COUPERIN
PART V—MINUET
(Theme of First 8 Measures)

EXAMPLE 99
RAVEL
LE TOMBEAU DE COUPERIN
PART V—MINUET
(Theme of First 8 Measures of the Musette)

EXAMPLE 100
RAVEL
LE TOMBEAU DE COUPERIN
PART VI—TOCCATA
(Measures 60-62, Theme)

EXAMPLE 101
RAVEL
LE TOMBEAU DE COUPERIN
PART III—FORLANE
(Measures 117-141)

EXAMPLE 102
RAVEL
JEUX D'EAU (THE FOUNTAIN)
For Piano
(First 26 Measures)

EXAMPLE 103
RAVEL
SONATINE FOR PIANO
I
(Complete)

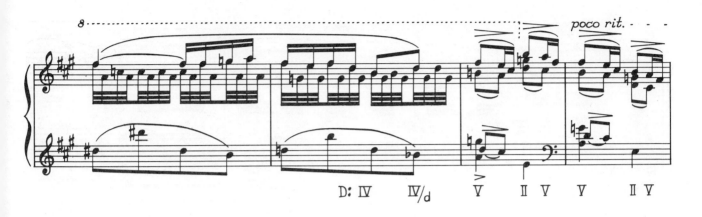

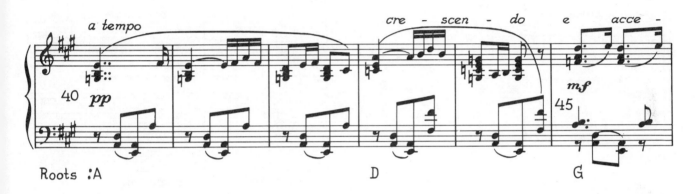

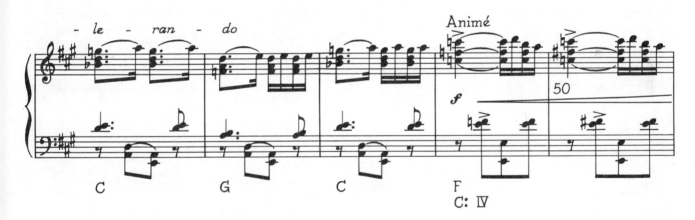

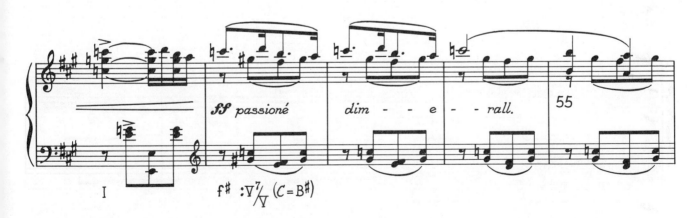

EXAMPLE 104

RAVEL

SONATINE FOR PIANO

II

(Complete)

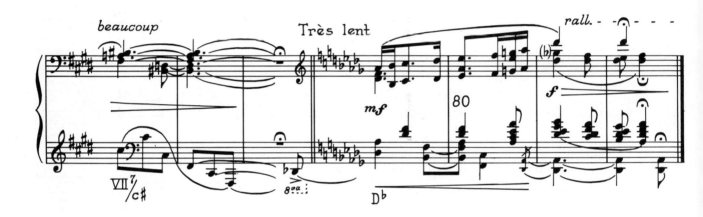

EXAMPLE 105

RAVEL

SONATINE FOR PIANO

III

(Measures 37-46)

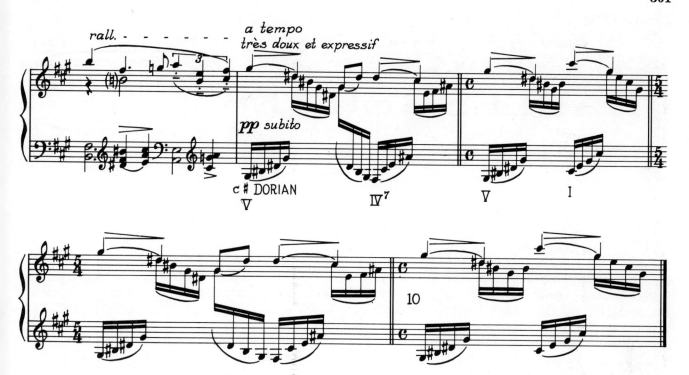

CHAPTER 19

CHARLES GRIFFES

1884-1920

The American branch of impressionism is represented by such composers as Charles Griffes and Charles Martin Loeffler, though the latter was a native Alsatian.

Griffes' influences are Debussy, Mussorgsky, Scriabin (in later works) and oriental idioms.

Like Ravel, Griffes transcribed some of his piano works for orchestra, including the *White Peacock* (1917) and *The Pleasure Dome of Kubla Khan* (1912).

EXAMPLE 106 (page 303)
The White Peacock, Part I, Op. 7

This is the first of four piano pieces in a set titled *Roman Sketches*. It is in a freely designed ABA pattern. The key signature is four sharps, but it opens and closes on a motive which outlines a dominant seventh on F♯ with both augmented and diminished fifths (C𝄪 and C♮) or II⁷ with ♯2 and ♭2 of the scale.

This exerpt from the middle section involves:

1. An ostinato, m. 1-4, in which all voices but the upper voice (melody) participate. The harmony is I on the first three beats and V on beats four and five. The lower voices of the RH in major thirds form a turn pattern around A-C♯.

2. D♯ on beats one and two of m. 1-2 is a long appoggiatura as is G♯ in m. 3.

3. The last two beats of each of measures 1-4 are a V⁷ with augmented 5th (B♯) plus some form of the ninth.

4. M. 5 is a V of IV formation including the major 9th (beat 1), the minor thirteenth (beat 2) which is an appoggiatura to E, and the diminished 5th, E♭ (beats 3, 4, 5).

Griffes' interest in orientalism is apparent in his chromatic lines and use of artificial scales a la Scriabin. These elements are present in the *Poem for Flute and Orchestra* (1918) and the *Sonata* for piano (1918). The *Sonata* is a large, complex and very original work in three movements and exemplifies romantic expression through exotic scale formations.

Suggested Written Assignment

1. Write a short piece (approximately 32 measures) with a chromatic melodic line harmonized by I, II, IV, V (sevenths, ninths, elevenths, thirteenths) in various altered forms. Invent an ostinato similar to that in Example 106 to be included for at least four measures.

Bibliography

Maisel, Edward M., *Charles T. Griffes: The Life of an American Composer*, New York: Alfred A. Knopf, Inc., 1943.

See general reference works on contemporary composers, especially American composers.

EXAMPLE 106
Griffes
THE WHITE PEACOCK
Part I from Roman Sketches, Op. 7
(Measures 28-32)

CHAPTER 20

CYRIL SCOTT

1879-

The English form of impressionism is expressed in the music of Frederick Delius, Arnold Bax and Cyril Scott. The latter's musical moods tend toward the nostalgic or exotic. Both he and Griffes studied in Germany but developed a style based on Debussy impressionism. Many of his piano works are quite popular salon music and his Suite for Piano, op. 75, is a large work which closes with a fugue.

EXAMPLE 107 (page 305)
Tallahassee Suite, Part I, Bygone Memories

The *Tallahassee Suite* for violin and piano (1911) is in three parts, the titles of which give a clue to the type of expression which is typical of much of his music: a. Bygone Memories; b. After Sundown; c. Negro Air and Dance.

1. This work with its emphasis on "juicy" block harmonies in the piano is rather static, depending on chord colors rather than rhythmic vitality for interest, and in this sense is akin to the style of Delius.

2. These opening eleven measures establish the mood of the movement, which is a small ABA rondo and in which the return of A is an exact restatement of the first twenty measures.

3. The harmonic content of the movement consists mainly of various dominant-type formations (ninths, thirteenths), the I^7, I^{+6}, I^{+2} and the traditional augmented sixth, IV^7 on $\sharp 4$ (the German sixth chord) spelled as a dominant seventh on $\sharp 5$ of the scale and resolving as a chord of the doubly augmented fourth. See m. 7 and 9 (beat 1), and also see m. 1 (beat 2), m. 2 (last eighth) and m. 3 (beat 3) where the E is replaced by the F (the thirteenth?) which is present throughout m. 1-3 like an inner pedal.

4. What is the B♭ in m. 3?

5. The dominant ninth on G with augmented fifth, m. 10, beat two, functions as an appoggiatura chord to the V^9 with augmented fifth on beat three.

6. What is the harmony of m. 5?

7. The chord on beat one, m. 6, is a VI^7 with $\sharp 6$ and $\sharp 1$ of the scale resolving to V^7.

SUGGESTED WRITTEN ASSIGNMENTS

1. Write a short piece (32 measures) for violin and piano using chord formations typical of this example.
2. Analyze a piano work of Scott.
3. Compare *Tallahassee* to a work like *Summer Night on the River* by Delius.

BIBLIOGRAPHY

FRANK, ALAN, *Modern British Composers*, Chester Springs, Pa.: Dufour Editions, Inc., 1955.

WALKER, ERNEST, *History of Music in England*, Oxford: Clarendon Press, 1952.

See general historical works and references such as *Grove's Dictionary of Music*.

EXAMPLE 107
TALLAHASSEE SUITE FOR VIOLIN AND PIANO
PART I—BYGONE MEMORIES
(First 11 Measures)

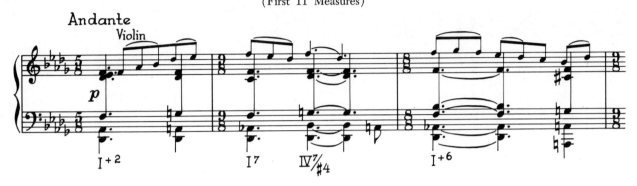

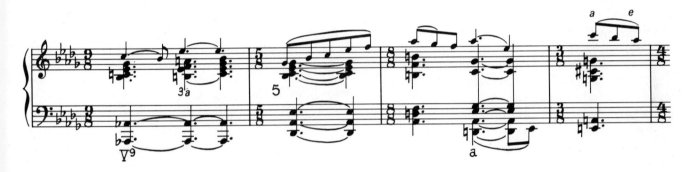

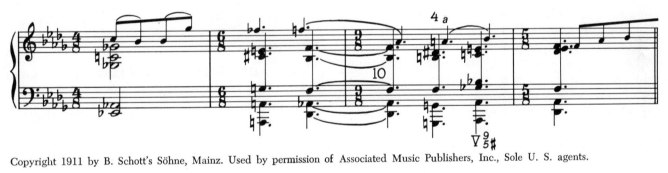

CHAPTER 21

JEAN SIBELIUS

1865-1957

Here we return to the line of late nineteenth-century symphonists. Sibelius stems from the group of composers such as Schumann, Franck and Tchaikovsky, who were concerned with cyclic treatment, thematic transformation and fusion of movements.

Though Sibelius' tonal resources are relatively conservative and though there are precedents for many of his formal approaches, yet his individual treatment of already existing harmonic and formal procedures sets him apart as a composer of importance. His originality lies in the nature of his thematic materials, the way he manipulated them and the resulting overall formal treatment.

In general his approach is to introduce thematic fragments, then combine and recombine them into longer melodic ideas, and often later to reduce them to fragments again. Many of these fragmentary ideas first occur in subordinate situations—as accompaniment motives or transitory passages—but reappear expanded, combined with other ideas and intensified. This juxtaposition of seemingly unrelated fragments which are later combined produces what seems to be a paradox: On the surface the effect seems spasmodic, impulsive and disconnected with ejaculatory outbursts, pauses, long harmonically static passages and animated effects following one another in various order, but the total effect is one of cohesiveness and unity through constant flow and growth because of the subtle combination and manipulation of material.

His method of orchestration is akin to Tchaikovsky's, and his earlier style is romantic in the Tchaikovskian sense; but he gradually moves to a more objectively controlled expression. He could be considered a nationalist composer only because a certain emotional quality in his music seems to reflect Finland and because his melodic ideas have a vague rhythmic affinity with the Finnish language. He does not quote national folk melody.

His most important works are his seven symphonies, a few symphonic poems based on Finnish legend and his *Violin Concerto*.

EXAMPLE 108 (pages 310, 311)
Symphony No. 2 in D Major, Op. 43, I

This symphony, completed in 1902, contains the seeds of formal procedures which come to fruition more and more in later works. Such procedures include:

a. Presentation of fragments which are combined to form complete melodic statements as illustrated in this example;

b. fusion of movements seen in the connection of III to IV without pause;

c. condensing of form illustrated by the return of themes 1 and 2 simultaneously in the recapitulation of I.

1. I illustrates Sibelius' individual treatment of sonata form. The four excerpts of this example illustrate the progressive expansion of a theme by gradually combining more motives with it in successive statements.

   a. The first theme group extends from the opening through m. 56 and contains all the motives which are in number 4.

   b. The second theme group opens at m. 57 in the dominant A. The first statement of the theme of this example which appears to be a closing motive is heard at m. 82-86 (number 1). It is again heard at m. 88-91 and a third time slightly extended at m. 100-103 (number 2).

   c. The exposition closes at m. 117 in A with the motive bracketed in 1 and another from theme group 1.

2. The development opens with the version of the theme shown in 3. Here the melodic line shifts from the top to a lower voice in m. 4 and is a

more complete statement with the addition of the motive from the first theme group (m. 5-8).

3. Points to note which are typical of Sibelius are:

   a. The long initial note of the theme. Long held notes or repeated notes are typical melodic elements. See theme 2 of III.

   b. single harmonies sustained over a long period as in 1, m. 1-3 and in 3, m. 4-7, and throughout 4.

   c. the ostinato-like pattern of thirds in 3, m. 4-8.

4. The development section closes with the version illustrated in number 4. Here the theme is expanded to its fullest extent and serves as the climax of the movement. It extends by cadence avoidance actually beyond the example to m. 259 and the recapitulation.

5. The recapitulation contains the thematic elements somewhat dispersed as they first appeared and presented simultaneously with the second theme motives.

6. Versions 1 and 2 appear as in the exposition but transposed a fifth lower for the close in tonic. The movement ends with the same motive as used to close the exposition. Though the movement is complete in itself it closes in such a way that the listener is led to expect the next movement. This tends to focus toward the last movement which is the climactic movement of the work.

7. A thorough formal analysis of this movement with attention to motivic relationships is recommended.

EXAMPLE 109 (pages 311, 312)
Symphony No. 2 in D Major, Op. 43, II

II is a large binary form with introduction and coda as follows:

> Introduction (m. 1-39)—pizzicato strings.
>
> First half (m. 40-118)—in three sections with three themes (A B C). This half opens in d and closes in F♯.
>
> Second half (119-221)—in three sections with the same three themes (A B C), but B and C are extended. A appears with a modification of the introduction theme. This half opens in f♯ and closes in d.
>
> Coda (m. 222-240)—based on A and C motives. Closes in d.

This might be interpreted as a sonatina except for the key relationships. The first half moves from tonic to the third-related key of F♯, and the second half moves from f♯ back to d. Though the three sections

return in the same order, they do not return in the same keys. The themes of A and C are closely related.

1. This example quotes the last sixteen measures of the return of B. This same material appears a half step higher in tonality in the first half of the movement. The B material has a transitional quality because of its sequential nature and indefinite beginning and ending.

2. Note the ejaculatory quality of the short melodic figures separated by rests.

3. The typical Sibelius swell effect is seen in m. 5 and 10 when there is a fortissimo attack followed by a diminuendo and then a crescendo on a long, sustained chord.

4. The entire passage is based on two melodic figures. What are they?

5. The F in m. 2 and B♮ in m. 4 have the melodic character of escape tones but are harmonic.

6. The last chord in the example is a pivot between c♯ and d, the key of the next section. Can you explain it further?

7. Do a harmonic analysis of this example.

The third movement of this symphony is a scherzo in B♭ and a trio in G♭. After the return of the scherzo, which contains an anticipation of theme 1 of IV, the trio theme returns as a transition to IV. The closing motive of the trio melody is closely related to theme 1 of IV, and Sibelius uses this motive for a smooth and effective progression into the finale.

IV is a sonata form in D. Theme 2 is first in f♯ and returns in d. It is stated over a one-measure, scalewise ostinato figure. In the recapitulation theme 2 is greatly extended and the ostinato is stated in the upper instruments also. The coda is based on theme 1 in triumphant chorale style in D.

Examples and Suggestions for Further Study of the Music of Sibelius

Symphony, no. 1 in e (1899) is a mature work for a first symphony. This work is op. 39 and shows that he, like Brahms, had many works and years behind him before essaying a symphony. All seven symphonies were written between 1899 and 1925.

I is sonata form which is regular except for recapitulation of theme 1, which begins in the middle of it. The introduction theme is used to introduce the finale also. Compare part two of the first theme (a three-part form) with Example 108.

II is a second rondo (ABACA) in E♭. The C section is a development of A material making the form comparable to Beethoven, Symphony, no. 3, II, and Piano Sonata, op. 31, no. 1, III. The B section is in A♭ and the middle A section is in C♭. M. 29-30 contain a reference to theme 1 of I.

III is a scherzo in sonata form with a rather long development which closes with an episode involving new material.

IV is a sonata form with an introduction related to that of I. Theme 2 is in C and returns in B. The development is highly contrapuntal and deals entirely with theme 1. Theme 2 is derived from theme 1. Transitional material is reminiscent of II.

Symphony, no. 3 in C (1907) shows a continuation in the direction of tight formal organization and economy of means. III is a combination of scherzo and finale.

I is a sonata characterized by the combining and recombining of motives to transform thematic ideas.

II is a sonata in which only theme 1 is recapitulated.

III is in two parts: The scherzo-like first part presents the motivic material, and the second part (finale) is a full-blown statement of the theme, resulting from the expansion and combination of motives. The interval of a diminished fourth emphasized in the first part becomes a major third in the second. A two-measure rhythmic ostinato pattern in the melody over various pedal patterns pervades the last part, which is in the style of a march.

Symphony, no. 4 in a (1911) is strongly based on the whole-tone scale. It is cyclic in form with the tritone C-F♯ appearing as an important interval in the related themes of the various movements.

I is a slow movement in compressed sonata form.

II is the scherzo-type of movement in which the tritone predominates in the thematic material. String tremolos and pedals are typically present.

III illustrates the gradual expansion of a theme from a motive. It is based essentially on one theme and the motives which contribute to it.

IV opens in A but closes in a. It is an A B A rondo greatly expanded by development in each section.

The combining of two movements into one continuum is again seen in Symphony, no. 5 in E♭ (1916-1919).

Here the I (slow) and II (allegro) are connected and related by thematic derivation. The thematic material of I, an introductory movement, is dealt with in II in a rhapsodic developmental fashion.

III (in G) is a theme and variations. The melody involves a one-measure rhythmic pattern frequently repeated much like the two-measure rhythmic pattern in Symphony, no. 3, III, part 2.

IV is a sonata form. Theme 2 is a nine-measure idea, and at one point where it is first introduced in tonic, E♭, the horns state this idea four times while the lower basses state it once in triple augmentation, m. 117-152. Theme 2 is extended into a coda of large proportions to conclude the work with an air of grandeur.

The Dorian mode is a predominant tonal element in the Symphony, no. 6 in d (1923). Since this mode is common in Finnish folk song, the symphony is considered to reflect some national color even though Sibelius does not quote folk themes. Basic motives which appear in the opening permeate the entire work in a subtle employment of the cyclic approach.

I is in sonata form. The second theme group appears in C, which tends to emphasize the character of Dorian on d. Woodwind passages in thirds, ostinatos in the strings playing tremolos and sustained bass pedals, so common in Sibelius, are abundant here.

II in g closes with a cadence which emphasizes the raised sixth degree of the Dorian scale though it is not actually a Dorian cadence. It is a lyric movement involving two themes alternating and varied on each appearance in an A B A B A B coda design.

III is a scherzo on three themes each in the Dorian mode. The design is as follows:

Eight introductory measures based on the theme of section C;
A—in d Dorian;
B—in a Dorian;
The eight introductory measures in a used as an epilogue to A B;
C in g Dorian and could be considered the trio;
A repeated in d;
B repeated in d;
Epilogue (as before) in d;

C repeated in d;
Coda on the theme of A.

What is the design here in its broadest aspects? This is an excellent movement to analyze for Sibelius' use of the Dorian mode, the basic motive of the entire symphony and ostinato character of the C section.

The design of IV is as follows:

A—a lyric section in d Dorian consisting primarily of four-measure phrases alternating between the woodwinds and strings in call and response style;

B—a section consisting of three statements (each differing somewhat) of a rhythmic theme made up of a variety of terse motives;

A—the melodic ideas are here modified and extended;

Coda—an epilogue to the entire symphony involving a sort of apotheosis of the basic motive.

Symphony, no. 7 in C (1924) is a one-movement work having the proportions of a symphony but not the traditional formal design. In fact, Sibelius originally called it *Fantasia sinfonica*. It is, of course, an entirely unique formal design and sets the precedent for later one-movement orchestral works to be called symphonies, for example, Roy Harris' Symphony, no. 3 (1936) and Samuel Barber's Symphony, no. 1 (1936) among others.

Space does not allow inclusion of an analysis of this work here, but a study of its form in light of the controversial opinions regarding its structure is recommended. Authors listed in the bibliography on Sibelius should be consulted for the divergent opinions regarding the form of this work. Actually such works which cannot be categorized must be examined in detail for any insight into their formal design. Suffice it to say that in the Symphony, no. 7 Sibelius applies his technic of motivic accumulation, thematic transformation and cyclic organization to a one-movement work.

Several of Sibelius' symphonic works other than symphonies and the Violin Concerto in d (1905) have become part of the standard repertoire. In fact, the chorale-type melody from *Finlandia* has been used widely as the tune for various hymns so that it has actually become what might be called a traditional melody in our culture.

SUGGESTED WRITTEN ASSIGNMENTS

1. Write two passages about sixteen measures each, using each of the following textures:

   a. An ostinato in middle range on alternating notes of a third (a measured tremolo) with related melodic phrases alternating above and below the ostinato;

   b. a running bass pattern with slow-moving chords above.

2. Analyze one of the following orchestral works of Sibelius:

   a. *The Swan of Tuonela;*

   b. *Finlandia;*

   c. the Violin Concerto in d, I;

   d. Symphony, no. 5, I or the Finale;

   e. *Tapiola.*

BIBLIOGRAPHY

ABRAHAM, GERALD, *The Music of Sibelius*, New York: W. W. Norton & Company, Inc., 1947.
————, *Sibelius; a Symposium*, London: L. Drummond, 1952.
EKMAN, CARL, *Jean Sibelius, His Life and Personality*, New York: Alfred A. Knopf, Inc., 1938.
GRAY, CECIL, *Sibelius*, London: Oxford University Press, 1935.
————, *Sibelius: The Symphonies*, London: Oxford University Press, 1935.
HANNIKAINEN, ILMARI, *Sibelius and the Development of Finnish Music*, London: Hinrichsen, 1948.
JOHNSON, HAROLD E., *Jean Sibelius*, New York: Alfred A. Knopf, Inc., 1959.
PARMET, SIMON, *The Symphonies of Sibelius*, London: Cassell & Company, Ltd., 1959.
RINGBOM, NILS ERIC, *Jean Sibelius, A Master and His Work*, Norman: Oklahoma University Press, 1954.

EXAMPLE 108
SIBELIUS
SYMPHONY NO. 2 IN D MAJOR, OP. 43
I
Four Exerpts Showing Thematic Expansion

(1) Measures 82-86

(2) Measures 100-103

(3) Measures 118-125

(4) Measures 210-241

EXAMPLE 109
SIBELIUS
SYMPHONY NO. 2 IN D MAJOR, OP. 43
II
(Measures 163-178)

CHAPTER 22

SERGEI PROKOFIEV

1891-1953

Russian (Soviet) music of middle twentieth century contains, in general, certain elements which are reflected in the music of Prokofiev, Shostakovich, Kabalevsky, Khachaturian and early Stravinsky. These elements are:

a. Russian nationalistic subjects, politically required if not artistically chosen;

b. Classical forms or designs based on a classical approach to form;

c. rhythmic drive and variety;

d. generally sparse, transparent texture;

e. traditional melodic and harmonic concepts spiced by deceptive progressions and modulations, unexpected humorous or grotesque turns of melody, mixture of modes and piquant dissonance;

f. a retention of tonality;

g. thematic material influenced by folk or popular melody;

h. a general aura of objectivity, vitality and freshness in contrast to the introverted, excessively complex and hyperemotional music stemming from late German romanticism.

This music of Prokofiev and Shostakovich has its roots in the styles of the Russian "Five," Tchaikovsky, and in the impetus that a revolutionary social change can bring to the arts. The term *neoclassicism* has been applied to this music and much of twentieth-century French music after Debussy as well as to the music of any other composer who adopts classical formal procedures and avoids melodic elegance or emotional extremes in favor of objective design.

Prokofiev's music in particular is characterized by:

a. Rhythmic momentum like a perpetual motion or toccata;

b. deliberate dissonance injected into what otherwise seems to be unsophisticated tonal organization, see Example 110;

c. sudden, apparently arbitrary, distortions of traditional-sounding melodies;

d. key relationships of a tritone or a second, see Example 110;

e. unexpected shifts of tonality a half step away, see Example 111;

f. expressive qualities ranging from sarcastic humor and mock sentiment to unrestrained exuberance and barbarism.

Because of Prokofiev's travels and long period away from his homeland, his music is perhaps somewhat less nationalistic in flavor and subject matter than others in this group. His fondness for stage and film music colors his works with a marked degree of the descriptive elements and results in a very free application of traditional formal designs.

EXAMPLE 110 (page 318)
Marche, Op. 12, No. 1

Because Prokofiev was a piano virtuoso his music, which encompasses many works, including nine sonatas and five concertos, is highly representative of his style.

In addition, some of his stage and orchestral works, his two violin concertos and flute sonata show him at his best.

This example is from one of ten pieces for piano written in 1906 and revised in 1913.

1. This little *Marche* well illustrates Prokofiev's treatment of a simple form and diatonic melody with dissonant, ironic harmony.

2. It also illustrates the shift to keys a half step away through deceptive progression.

3. The form consists of regular eight-measure periods throughout with a four-measure extension, a

repetition of the last phrase, at the end. The design using a letter for each period is:

period: a a b a, c c b a, c c a
key: f f f f♯ D♭ e♭ f f♯ D♭ e♭ f

The example includes the first three periods and the first measure of the fourth period in f♯.

4. The D♭ added to the I (as + 6) and to the V⁷ (as the ninth) in m. 1, 7, 8, 9 is characteristic of the a period. Notice that in m. 17 the D in the bass produces a VI⁷ instead of I + 6.

5. M. 2, beat one, the expected chord is II⁷ but instead there is the e♭ triad. Beat two appears to be a V⁹ with A♭ as appoggiatura but the F♭ (E♮) to E♭ changes it to a minor seventh on V.

6. The chromatic bass line in m. 3-4 produces a phrase ending on VI in m. 4. This deceptive progression at the cadence is typical.

7. It is difficult to analyze the function of the chords of m. 2-3 and 5-6 because they are formations chosen for their color rather than key relationship. In spite of the wayward quality of these chords the tonal center remains clear because of the diatonic melody (C♯ in the melody of m. 6-7 is diatonic D♭) and V to I cadences. Notice the whole-tone dominant quality of the chords in m. 3, beat two, and m. 7, beat one. Each of the chords in m. 3, 5-7 are dominant-type formations used in a free association. In m. 6 the progression is from a dominant seventh on E♭ to one on A, both sharing the same tritone. The A♭ in the tenor is an appoggiatura resolving to G with the change of chord.

8. The third period is primarily an ostinato on V⁶ to VI⁶. In m. 15-16 the F-E-E♭ in the lower voice leads to the interval E♭-D♭ in the second chord of m. 16 which is then resolved like an augmented sixth, E♭-C♯, into the VI of f♯ at m. 17, with each of the four voices moving a half step into the chord of resolution. This is an unusual augmented sixth formation and application.

EXAMPLE 111 (pages 319, 320)
Classical Symphony, Op. 25, III

The Classical Symphony in D, op. 25 (1917) was written after two youthful symphonies and before the Symphony, no. 2 in d, op. 40 (1924). This is Prokofiev's idea of how Haydn might have written if he had lived in the twentieth century.

I is in regular sonata form with theme 2 in the dominant A and returning in tonic. Most modulations are accomplished through the deceptive progression V to VI. The VI in most cases is the form from the tonic minor (a major triad on ♭6 of the major scale) as in this example.

II in A is a small ABACA rondo. Each return of A is in a cleverly devious manner, through VI of a the first time and through V of V the second. An introductory phrase serves also as a short coda.

III is a miniature song form with trio and illustrates unexpected modulations by four means:

1. Free modal association of triads, m. 1-2.
2. The deceptive V-VI progression, m. 3-4, 5-6, 7-8.
3. The V⁷ used as an augmented sixth chord (German sixth), m. 9-10. (AC♯EG = A C♯ E F𝄪)
4. The half-step displacement of a melody note to throw the tonality into an unexpected key a half step away, m. 11-12. Here the tonality implied in m. 10 and the first two beats of measure 11 is C♯. The expected melodic notes on beats three and four of m. 11 and beat one of m. 12 are B followed by B♯ to C♯, a V-I cadence in C♯. Instead Prokofiev substitutes B♯ for B on beat three of m. 11, which throws the cadence a half step higher into D, the tonic key.

Part b in the subdominant has the tonic-dominant drone bass of a musette. For other examples of musettes, see J. S. Bach, English Suites, nos. 3 and 6; Mozart's opera, *Bastien and Bastienne;* and Ravel's *Le Tombeau de Couperin* (Example 99).

The finale of the Classical Symphony is also a regular sonata form involving modulations based on the same devices seen in Example 111.

Examples and Suggestions for Further Study of the Music of Prokofiev

A study of the following works of Prokofiev will provide a comprehensive view of his style:

FOR PIANO:
  The Sonatas
  Suggestion Diabolique (op. 4)
  Fugitive Visions, op. 22
  Tales of the Old Grandmother, op. 31
  Concerto, no. 3 in C, op. 26

FOR ORCHESTRA:
  Scythian Suite, op. 20
  Overture on Hebrew Themes, op. 34
  Lieutenant Kije, Suite, op. 60
  Romeo and Juliet Ballet, Suite, op. 64A
  Peter and the Wolf, op. 67
  Symphony, no. 5, op. 100

OPERAS:
  The Gambler, op. 24
  The Love for Three Oranges, op. 33

Bethrothal in a Convent, or The Duenna, op. 86

OTHERS:

Concertos for Violin, nos. 1 and 2, op. 19 and 63

Sonata for Flute and Piano, op. 94

The Piano Concerto, no. 1 in Db, op. 10 (1912) is a one-movement work involving the characteristics of first-movement form infused with a scherzo theme and a lyric episode in the character of a slow movement. There are long passages based on ostinatos in which rhythmic drive predominates over melody or in which melody is nonexistent. This texture based on a constantly recurring idea allows for the free injection of arbitrary dissonance.

Free association of triads, mixing of modes and tonal shifts of a half step, for example, Db to C, are commonly seen. The design is introduction theme in Db, cadenza, theme 1 in Db, theme 2 in e (two ideas), introduction theme in Db, lyric episode in g♯ (dominant minor), scherzo-like development of theme 2 and cadenza, return of theme 1 in C (piano alone, quasi cadenza), return of theme 2 in c♯, return of introduction theme in Db.

The Piano Concerto, no. 2 in g, op. 16 (1913) is a four-movement work emphasizing the elements (especially in II and III) of primitive rhythmic momentum, sharp dissonance including polychords, a virtuoso piano texture and a minimum of sustained lyric material.

I is the slowest of the four movements (andantino) with a lyric first theme and is designed as follows:

Introductory motive;

Theme 1 in g stated first by the piano then by the orchestra;

Theme 2 in a stated first by the piano then by the orchestra;

Transition;

Return of theme 1 in g and development of both segments of theme 1 simultaneously played by piano alone like a cadenza;

Coda based on augmentation of the introductory motive and return of theme 1.

II is a scherzo in which the solo piano part consists of both hands playing the same single line of continuous fast sixteenths an octave apart from beginning to end without a break. This perpetuum mobile in the piano is like the Chopin,

Prelude, no. 14 and Sonata in bb, IV, in texture and technic. The form of this movement follows the scherzo and trio design. The keys of the scherzo part are d-c♯-d. The middle or trio section is an aba design involving vaguely the tonal centers of Bb-Ab(f) and C. The scherzo is only partially recapitulated, and the coda restates the trio idea.

The orchestra, of course, carries the harmonic, rhythmic and most of the thematic material under the running sixteenths of the piano. The harmony of the first section (scherzo) is characterized by the open primitive-sounding fifths. The second section (trio) consists of a texture of thirds and open octaves.

III is an intermezzo contrasting to the scherzo in its emphasis on bizarre harmonic color and full texture but equally barbaric in character.

IV is an A B C A B design. The C section is a set of variations on a theme suggestive of a Russian folk song and includes cadenza-like passages for the piano. The savage A and B sections are shorter and form a contrasting frame for the long lyric C section. An example of the use of two separate harmonies simultaneously (polychords) is in the coda where the piano plays the G triad against the orchestra's A triad (m. 8-7 before the end).

The Piano Concerto, no. 3 in C (1921) though full of calculated eccentricity is less savage and distorted than the Second Concerto. Here simple diatonic passages in C are contrasted with complex chromatic harmonies and simple melodic lines with grotesque bravura episodes.

I again involves an important introductory theme in a sonata design as follows:

Introduction, lyric in style;

Exposition of themes 1 and 2;

Short development based on the introduction theme in canonic treatment;

Recapitulation and coda.

II is a theme with five variations and coda. It is one of Prokofiev's best-known melodies and exemplifies his brilliant handling of variation technics.

III is an A B C B A design. The A material is an energetic, rhythmic theme which undergoes much development with each appearance. The B material consists of an ironically turned lyric theme like theme 2 of I. The C section is an episode of veiled diabolical nature typical of Prokofiev in his *Fugitive Visions* for piano.

The Violin Concerto, no. 2 in g, op. 63 (1935) is less dissonant and complex and more restrained and avowedly lyrical in style, which is typical of his later writing after his return to Russia in 1933.

I is a rather regular sonata on two lyric themes. The second enters in B♭ and returns in G in conventional key pattern. The development involves the interweaving of both themes and the coda involves a short canon on theme 1.

II involves two themes in an ABA design as follows:

A—Theme 1 in E♭
    Theme 1 repeated in B
    Transition
    Theme 1 in C closing in E♭
    Transition (use of parallel major triads over a pedal)
B—Theme 2, a three-part song form in D
    Transition
A—Theme 1 in E♭
    Transition (same material as the transition before B)
    Theme 1 in E♭ (only the first four measures used as the closing phrase)

III is a brilliant third rondo form (ABACABA) with the return of B in tonic. A long, tumultuous coda involving new material closes the movement.

Symphony, no. 5 (in B♭), op. 100 (1944) is an epic work showing further progress toward a lyric-romantic quality and away from grotesquerie and tonal experimentation but retaining the dynamic rhythmic quality.

I is andante and in sonata form with climactic development section and coda.

II is in scherzo style with a constrasting trio. The scherzo section includes a sinister, roguish theme carried through various keys and stated in augmentation. A sarcastic bridge theme occurs before, in the middle of and at the close of the trio. The scherzo on its return is developed and intensified. The technic of octave displacement in which adjacent melodic tones are tossed into another octave (higher or lower) is applied throughout to the themes. This free exchange of octaves in a thematic statement is a device much used by other twentieth-century composers such as Schoenberg, Stravinsky, Bartók and Copland and is part of the technic of the melodic pointil-

lism of serial music in which single tones or figures are tossed from octave to octave over a wide range.

III is adagio in a large ABA design. The B section is a tragic, funeral expression. The themes include melodic motives emphasizing small intervals such as diminished thirds contrasted with motives having wide skips. See the theme of Section B. Such melodic writing is also typical of Bartók. Half-step relationships between keys are prominent.

IV opens with an introduction which quotes theme 1 of I in cyclic fashion. It is in sonata form with theme 2 in the dominant (F) returning in the subdominant (E♭). The closing theme is based on theme 1. The development section opens with an episode devoted to several statements of a new, diatonic lyric theme of Russian folk character. This is followed by a retransition to the recapitulation. A long energetic coda builds to a triumphant ending.

With the Symphony, no. 7 (in c♯) op. 131 (1952) Prokofiev seems to have returned, full circle, to the spirit of the Classical Symphony (no. 1). This work is relatively free of strong dissonance and the expression of conflict or cynicism. Perhaps this is because it was originally planned as a symphony for young people, or perhaps its aura results from the official definition of music for the people.

I is a sonata with three themes, short development section and shortened recapitulation.

II is a waltz in A B A B A design. The main key is F and the first B section is in E showing the half-step relationship so frequent in Prokofiev.

III is in a lyric A B A form in relatively conventional tonal style. The B section uses the same harmonic sequence as the first three chords of Example 111, the Classical Symphony, III. See m. 31-42.

IV is in D♭, tonic major of c♯, in ABA coda design including quotation, cyclic style, from I. Theme 1 (A section) is carried through several keys before the entrance of theme 2 (Section B) in C (half-step relationship again). The coda recalls themes 2 and 3 of I in expanded form and closes with a last, quick statement from theme 1 of IV.

The elements which typify Prokofiev's music are present throughout his works but the dissonant, polytonal and more extreme elements become tempered after the late 1930s with more emphasis on the lyrical, less-complex textures. The opera, *The Duenna,* op. 86 (1940) and the ballet, *Romeo and Juliet,* with the two orchestral suites from it, represent the lyric, humorous, objective style of later Prokofiev which has such a generally universal appeal and so typifies twentieth-century Russian music.

Suggested Written Assignments

1. Analyze a section from a pre-1935 work in Prokofiev's more dissonant, savage style (for example, the Scythian Suite, or Piano Concerto, no. 2) and compare it with a movement from the ballet *Romeo and Juliet* or scene 6 or 8 from *The Duenna.*
2. Write a forty-eight measure piece which involves:

   a. A simple march- or waltz-like accompaniment pattern;

   b. A melody which through unexpected skips and enharmonic procedure produces modulations in and out of keys a half step or tritone away;

   c. Modulation by deceptive harmonic resolutions.

3. Write an exercise in block harmony using only triads and modulate as follows:

   C to D♭ to A to E♭ to C

Bibliography

Abraham, Gerald, *Eight Soviet Composers,* New York: Oxford University Press, Inc., 1943.

Nestyev, Israel V., *Prokofiev,* Stanford: Stanford University Press, 1960.

Prokofiev, Sergei, *Autobiography, Articles, Reminiscences,* Moscow: Foreign Languge Publishing House, [n. d.]

EXAMPLE 110
PROKOFIEV
MARCHE, OP. 12, NO. 1
(First 17 Measures)

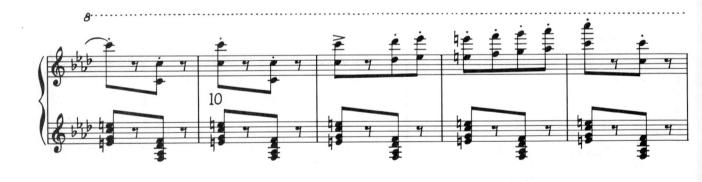

EXAMPLE 111
PROKOFIEV
CLASSICAL SYMPHONY, OP. 25
III—GAVOTTE
(Complete)

CHAPTER 23

DMITRI SHOSTAKOVICH

1906-

Like Prokofiev, by whom he is strongly influenced, Shostakovich has a gift for parody and caricature, especially of dance styles and rhythms as in Example 116. The elements of style outlined in the previous chapter apply likewise to Shostakovich though his humor is less ironic and more straightforward and his lyric themes more extended than is the case in Prokofiev's music. Integrated introductions, the cyclic principle and the grand symphonic style of Tchaikovsky and Mahler are characteristics of Shostakovich.

EXAMPLE 112 (page 325)
Symphony No. 5, Op. 47, I

The Symphony, no. 5, op. 47 (1937) shows the influence of Mahler in the broadly conceived themes of I and III, the influence of Prokofiev and folk melody in the humor and surprise of II and the influence of Tchaikovsky in the excitement of I and IV. This is perhaps Shostakovich's best-known work and contains nearly all the elements which make up his style.

I is a large sonata design with an elaborate development which deals with all the thematic material in various transformations, including augmentation, diminution and various contrapuntal imitations.

1. Theme 1 is a broad, discursive theme which contains several ideas, some of which are immediately elaborated and extended and all of which are later developed. The tonality of this theme is essentially d, but contrapuntal lines associated with it form generally nonfunctional harmonic formations which result from melodic coincidence and which are neutral or nontendential in effect.

This type of nonfunctional or neutral counterpoint (with emphasis on seconds, fourths, fifths and sevenths, and on thirds and sixths only in nondiatonic sequences) has sometimes been referred to by the absurd and syntactically redundant term of *linear counterpoint,* presumably to distinguish it from tonal or harmonically controlled counterpoint.

2. This example is that part of theme 1 with which the recapitulation begins. It is a three-voice passage illustrating nonfunctional counterpoint.

3. The upper (main) line is quite diatonic, making some free use of modal inflections and in m. 3-4 and 8-10 the melodic contour has an eighteenth-century classic quality.

4. The lower voices gain a neutral quality from the a. parallel minor thirds in m. 1-2, b. parallel perfect fourths in m. 3, c. the parallel minor sixths in m. 7 (beats 3-4) and 8 (beat 1). A careful analysis of the intervals between voices and the harmonic implications of the three-voice harmonic formations is recommended. For example, note that the climax of the passage on the downbeat of m. 12 is achieved in part by the tonal focus in the previous measure. In other words, the impulse of tonal relationship in the voices in m. 11 makes the climax more effective, more inevitable sounding after the casual harmonic content of the earlier measures.

5. Are there any other instances in this example where melodic direction is combined with a particularly obvious harmonic function? What seems to be the tonal implication of measures 4-6; of measures 12-13?

6. See Example 122 for a form of nonfunctional counterpoint which might be called pandiatonic counterpoint inasmuch as it is in one scale.

EXAMPLE 113 (page 326)
Symphony No. 5, Op. 47, I

1. The motive which formed m. 6-9 of theme 1 appears here in the upper staff in augmentation at the beginning of the development section.

2. The anapestic rhythmic pattern in the lower staff (♫ ♩) acts as a rhythmic ostinato through-

out the first thirty-five measures of the development section. The dactylic pattern (♩ ♫) serves as a rhythmic ostinato for theme 2 in its appearances. See Example 115. It first appears in m. 4 as part of theme 1.

This dactylic motive appears in diminution (♫ ♫) against the theme of this example later in the development. It is a popular rhythmic motive with both Prokofiev and Shostakovich as well as other Russian composers.

EXAMPLE 114 (page 326)
Symphony No. 5, Op. 47, I

1. After development of other aspects of theme 1, the motive of Example 113 reappears in march style as shown here.

2. This all-too-facile device of presenting parallel triads over an ostinato bass has been given rather heavy workouts in the music of Prokofiev, Shostakovich, Vaughan Williams, Copland and others of the last seventy years. This is an easy way to harmonize any melodic line. It is colorful for awhile and saves the composer from having to come to grips with any tonal problems. Anything goes in this texture. It makes good "filler" and is akin to the often meaningless scale passages which were used as padding to fill out transition passages in mideighteenth-century styles.

EXAMPLE 115 (page 327)
Symphony No. 5, Op. 47, I

1. This example includes the recapitulation of theme 2 which opens in D here compared to e♭ in the exposition. Notice the half-step relationship again.

2. The dactylic ostinato from m. 4 of the movement here again serves as accompaniment.

3. The flute states the theme followed by the horn in canon a fifth lower for a distance. Where is the canon broken?

4. Analyze the harmony of this passage. Are there any eleventh or thirteenth chords?

EXAMPLE 116 (pages 328, 329)
Symphony No. 5, Op. 47, II

II is a parody on the old German dance, the Ländler. It is a scherzo-trio-scherzo form. Each section is a two-part song form with each part repeated (aa bb).

1. This example includes part b of the scherzo (repeated) through part a of the trio.

2. Here we see that arbitrary distortion of an essentially simple diatonic tune which has been labeled the "wrong note" style. This free mixing of the various modal forms of a scale, the occasional weak intervallic relationship between melody and bass (m. 28-29), the over-simplified character and the element of banality are calculated for the effects of

humor, surprise and deception. It is a form of musical slapstick, a mild form of "Spike" Jones, which is none the less entertaining in carefully measured doses.

3. Usually such a passage begins diatonically and conventionally in a well-defined tonality, then begins to fall apart at the seams as it progresses, again "Spike" Jones style. It must seem perfectly normal at first to set the stage for the later humorous injection of unexpected "wrong notes." The first two measures are conventional enough, c minor with middle C retained in beat three as a pedal.

4. Beginning with m. 3 the descending use of B♮ and A♮ produces a mild distortion. M. 4 is back in convention, but beginning with m. 5 through 9 the free exchange between forms of c minor and C major with peculiar harmonic formations and a measure with an extra beat produce an effect of simple crudity but also of certain freshness.

5. The element of banality handled with sophisticated irony appears in m. 12-18. Again the first four measures (12-15) are firmly and simply in F. But with m. 16-17 the crude sonorities on the downbeats and the ambiguity of the thirds in m. 17 sound like a comical falling apart.

6. The simple V⁷-I cadence in A♭ in the first ending leads in conventional fashion back to c. But the second ending represents a distorted form of "modulation" to C of the trio (19-23).

7. Again, the trio opens as a simple tune in C, but with m. 28-29 the formation of the dominant with the exposed tritone—the VII chord in root position with no third—is a crudity which no beginning harmony student working in the "common practice period" would be allowed to perpetrate.

8. The shift to A at m. 34-35 is a clever maneuver prepared for in m. 32-33.

9. The free association of modal colors is seen in m. 36-39. Lydian over G is seen in m. 36. A form of f is in m. 37. The cadence of 38-39 is Mixolydian in sound.

The third movement of the Symphony, no. 5 is a largo of great breadth and intensity. It consists of long melodic lines evolved with relatively simple but moving harmonies to a great climax and gradual subsidence to a peaceful close.

IV is in the nature of a rondo and consists of the gradual transformation of an energetic march theme in d into a grand closing chorale in D. Much of the subordinate thematic material is reminiscent of the latter part of theme 1 of I. The closing section is a good example of a widely dispersed orchestral double pedal on D and A. The influence of Tchaikovsky and Rimsky-Korsakov is heard in this writing.

Examples and Suggestions for Further Study of the Music of Shostakovich

Shostakovich has shown more interest than Prokofiev in specifically contrapuntal textures as evidenced by his several string quartets, his excellent *Quintet for Piano and Strings*, op. 57 (1940), and *Twenty Four Preludes and Fugues*, op. 87, for piano (1951).

The best known of his twelve symphonies are the first, fifth, seventh and ninth.

The Symphony, no. 1 (in f), op. 10 (1925) is quite original and spontaneous, relatively free from arbitrary dissonance but containing an air of humor and impertinence.

I is a sonata with an introduction theme which reappears in the development and concludes the movement. Themes 1 and 2 in f and A♭ respectively return in reverse order in the recapitulation, theme 2 in F then theme 1 in f.

II (in a) is a scherzo and trio (in e) design. In the coda the trio and scherzo themes are presented simultaneously.

III (in D♭) is an ABA form with both themes presented simultaneously in the coda as in II.

IV is connected to III by a snare drum roll. There is a slow introduction, material from which is brought back at the close of the development. The shortened recapitulation again includes both themes simultaneously, but with theme 2 in augmentation, and closes in F.

Symphonies, no. 2, op. 14 (1927) and no. 3, op. 20 (1931) were written to celebrate historical occasions. The latter is a one-movement work with chorus.

Apparently for political reasons the Symphony, no. 4, op. 43 (1936) was withdrawn during rehearsals and never published. It is a large three-movement work, gloomy in character and with a dramatic finale.

Symphony, no. 6, op. 53 (1939) is dedicated to Lenin and is three movements in slow, scherzo, finale sequence. The character of its themes relates it somewhat to the Fifth Symphony.

Symphony, no. 7, op. 60 (1941) is a large four-movement work recalling the seige of Leningrad. The march episode with the dactylic rhythm so frequently seen in Shotakovich's music is expanded to great proportions in the long first movement. II is the light scherzo-type movement; III, the slow movement; and IV, an allegro-finale.

The Symphony, no. 8, op. 65 (1943) deals further with the subject of war. It is in five movements. II and III are marches; IV is a passacaglia; I and V are related thematically; and the whole work is pervaded by military color.

The Symphony, no. 9, op. 70 (1945) is a short work which in mood is quite the antithesis of the previous two works. It is in five movements which range in expression from buffoonery to despair. The comedy element is predominant, however.

Symphony, no. 10, op. 93 (1953) includes in I (in d) an integrated introduction, a formal element frequent in the works of Shostakovich. Here material from the introduction reappears in the coda.

II (in b♭) is usually the scherzo movement in Shostakovich symphonies, and here it is an ominous march involving much use of pedal point.

III (in c) points up the frequent use of the cyclic approach by Shostakovich in the reference to the introduction of I, m. 271-280. It closes on the C triad with added A♮ held against a last statement of the basic motive of the movement in c minor. This basic motive, D E♭ C B, is D S(es) C H in German notation, and, as such, forms the initial of his first name and the first three letters of the German spelling of his last name. This theme, its spelling and its important position in both III and IV would tend to imply some autobiographical connotation in this work.

At any rate, IV involves both the integrated introduction and the cyclic process. The basic motive (DSCH) of III is stated at the climactic close of the development. It is followed by a return of the slow introductory material. Then the DSCH motive is combined with themes of IV in their recapitulation. The work closes in E.

The Symphonies, no. 11, op. 103 (1957) and no. 12, op. 112 (1962) are both written to celebrate a historic occasion. The former is titled *1905*, and each of the four movements has a programmatic title. The latter is a work of four-connected movements to be played without pause and is titled *The Year 1917*.

SUGGESTED WRITTEN ASSIGNMENTS

1. Analyze a short piano piece of Shostakovich, such as the piano version of the *Polka* from the ballet *The Golden Age*. Such a work illustrates humor achieved from application of the "wrong note" technic.

2. Analyze the harmony of a slow movement such as Symphony, no. 5, III, or Symphony, no. 6, I, for an insight into Shostakovich's use of sustained so-

norities, especially simple chord structures, for dramatic effect.

3. Analyze the Violin Concerto, op. 99, III, or the Symphony, no. 8, IV, for Shostakovich's handling of passacaglia.

4. Analyze the *Quintet for Piano and Strings,* op. 57, II, or one of the fugues in op. 87 for his approach to fugue writing. Compare one of these to a Bartók fugue.

BIBLIOGRAPHY

BROCKHAUS, HEINZ A., *Dmitri Schostakowitsch,* Leipzig: Breitkopf and Härtel, 1962.

MARTYNOV, IVAN, *Dmitri Shostakovich, the Man and His Work,* New York: The Philosophical Library, 1947.

RABINOVICH, D., *Dmitry Shostakovich,* Composer, Moscow: Foreign Languge Publishing House, 1959.

SEROFF, VICTOR, *Dmitri Shostakovich: The Life and Background of a Soviet Composer,* New York: Alfred A. Knopf, Inc., 1943.

EXAMPLE 112
SHOSTAKOVICH
SYMPHONY NO. 5, OP. 47
I
(Measures 18-32)

EXAMPLE 113
SHOSTAKOVICH
SYMPHONY NO. 5, OP. 47
I
(Measures 120-129)

EXAMPLE 114
SHOSTAKOVICH
SYMPHONY NO. 5, OP. 47
I
(Measures 188-194)

EXAMPLE 115
Shostakovich
SYMPHONY NO. 5, OP. 47
I
(Measures 259-276)

EXAMPLE 116
SHOSTAKOVICH
SYMPHONY NO. 5, OP. 47
II
(Measures 45-102)

CHAPTER 24

RALPH VAUGHAN WILLIAMS

1872-1958

Vaughan Williams' music is a blend of the following influences:

a. English folk song and hymnody (the spirit of the melody and rhythm rather than specific quotation);
b. the modal and rhythmic freedom and character of seventeenth-century Elizabethan music;
c. impressionism and mysticism as seen in certain devices such as streams of parallel triads, in orchestral coloring learned partly from Ravel, in interest in biblical subjects.

His melodies are often:

a. pentatonic as in *A London Symphony*, I, theme 2 and the *Pastoral Symphony*, IV;
b. modal as in the *Pastoral Symphony*, III, and Example 117; he is especially fond of Mixolydian inflection;
c. based on "blues" inflections as in Symphony, no. 4, IV, and Symphony, no. 6, I, theme 2 and closing theme;
d. exotic in influence as in *Hodie* for chorus and orchestra and *Flos campi* for viola, wordless chorus and orchestra.

Though his style is conservative when compared to his contemporaries' styles, it is not reactionary in any sense. Though he employs a wide range of tonal resources and expresses himself in both the intimate and grand manner, he is never obscure. He believed that music should be an expression of the life of the community. By being faithful in his reflection of English life, by remaining an individual, he has written music which through its freshness, lyricism and strength has universal appeal.

Though he wrote in all forms and media his contributions to choral and orchestral literature are particularly important. He restored choral music to an important position in the world of music and wrote many important works for chorus both accompanied and unaccompanied.

EXAMPLE 117 (pages 333-336)
Te Deum in G

This work for double chorus and organ (orchestra) was written in 1928 for the occasion of the enthronment of the Archbishop of Canterbury.

1. The form is a free, through-composed setting of the *Te Deum* poem. However, the pattern of the first measure and its inversion, which is predominant throughout this excerpt, reappears in both the accompaniment and voices throughout the work as a basic rhythmic-melodic motive and unifying factor.
2. Also, the approach through minor to a major tonic chord at the cadence, as in m. 6-8, 13-15 and 35-38, is characteristic throughout. The final cadence is this type.
3. The choral part writing in this work is fairly characteristic of much of the choral writing of Vaughan Williams. The features to be noted here follow in 4, 5 and 6.
4. There is a predominance of scalewise (conjunct) motion with an occasional leap of a perfect fourth or fifth, or a third.
5. Observe the frequent divergence and convergence of pairs of voices from a small to a large interval and back or vice versa, for example:
   a. In m. 13 the S and A (doubled by the T and B an octave lower) move by contrary motion from a unison to a fifth and back.
   b. In m. 29-31 the upper voices in thirds move in contrary motion to the lower voices in thirds.
   c. In m. 34-36 and 38-46 a wider expansion by contrary motion takes place.

6. Notice the free mingling of four-part texture, two parts doubled at the octave and octave writing.

7. The above characteristics of part writing combined with modal harmony, bare-fifth sonorities, nondominant harmony, the absence of tritones and the frequent parallel fifths and octaves between voices impart a rough, archaic quality, but at the same time, a quality of strength and vigor to this music.

8. The characteristics of the choral part writing appear likewise in the accompaniment, as in m. 6-7, 8-13, 19-22.

9. Notice that all the chords with dominant function are:

   a. open fifths (m. 23, beat 4);
   b. simple triads (m. 16, beat 4);
   c. minor seventh chords (m. 35, beats 2 and 4).

   There is not a single chord with a tritone except in m. 46, beat two. All the seventh chords are major or minor, for example, m. 6-7, beat three and m. 14, beats two and three. There are some ninth chords but without tritones. These occur in m. 39-43 and preceding the cadence chord in m. 14 and 37, beat four. How would you describe the cadential progression from each of these latter chords to the chord that follows (m. 15 and 38, beat 1)?

10. An interesting drone effect is produced by the overlapping of the two choruses and the accompaniment in m. 30-36. The entire g♯ minor triad is the drone. The same effect, but less pronounced, takes place in m. 40-44 with regard to the tones C and E♭.

11. The entire work should be analyzed for an understanding of this type of modal writing.

Examples and Suggestions for Further Study of the Music of Vaughan Williams

Vaughan Williams seldom quotes a folk melody or preexisting theme, but two works which should be studied for his treatment of such material are his "Fantasia on Greensleeves" from the opera *Sir John in Love* (1929) and *Fantasia on a Theme by Thomas Tallis* (1919). The latter work for strings involves harmonization of the melody by parallel triads and large blocks of triadic harmony moving in contrary motion and parallel motion.

Important choral works to be studied are:

Five Mystical Songs (1910)
Lord, Thou Hast Been Our Refuge (1921)

Mass in G Minor (1922)
Sancta Civitas (1925)
The Hundreth Psalm (1929)
Five Tudor Portraits (1935)
Dona nobis pacem (1936)
Hodie (1954)

His Symphony, no. 1, A Sea Symphony (1909) is also for chorus with soloists and orchestra and is set to poetry of Walt Whitman. I is *A Song for All Seas, All Ships.* II is *On the Beach at Night Alone,* the slow movement. III is the scherzo, titled *The Waves,* and cast in sonata design. Theme 1 is in g; theme 2 is in B♭, returning in G in the orchestra; augmented triads and the whole-tone scale are employed in passing. IV is *The Explorers* and has tenuous thematic relationships to I.

Symphony, no. 2, A London Symphony (1914), revised in 1920 and 1936, is one of Vaughan Williams' best-known symphonies and employs some of the effects usually associated with the impressionists. I is a sonata with slow introduction which is referred to in the epilogue at the close of IV. The slow movement is II in ABA form and as with III is somewhat descriptive in its use of London street cries and other sounds of the city. III is a scherzo subtitled *Nocturne,* representing London at night. IV contains an additional final section labeled epilogue, which brings the work to a contemplative close. The epilogue is an important formal element in several of Vaughan Williams' works. The third, fourth, fifth, sixth and seventh symphonies close with an epilogue.

The Pastoral Symphony (1922) is the third and is contemplative and quiet throughout, suggestive of the title, with no allegro in the four movements. The prologue (at the opening of IV) and the related epilogue (at the close of IV) appear in the unusual form of a wordless soprano voice intoning a pentatonic plainsong melisma. A subtle sense of the cyclic process results from motivic relationships among the movements.

Symphony, no. 4 in f (1935) is a contrast to the preceding three symphonies. It is more intense, vigorous, dissonant and formally distinct in comparison to the previous, more-rhapsodic works. Three basic motives pervade the work, but one in particular is prominent in I, III and IV, appears in II, and forms the basis of the great fugal epilogue at the close of IV. This four-note motive is FEG♭F which appears in many transpositions and rhythmic variants. It also appears expanded to coincide with the famous BACH (B♭ A C B♮) form.

I is a sonata form in which theme 1 (in f) exploits the interval of a minor ninth and the basic four-note motive. Theme 2 is a soaring, rhapsodic theme of changing modal character. Another element prominent in each movement is a motive involving a fluctuation between the major and minor third in the descending pattern C A A♭ F. The A A♭ F imparts a "blues" quality in places.

II involves the polyphonic interweaving of long-breathed melodic lines in a free ABA design. It closes with the two motives just described in combination.

III is a scherzo and trio. The scherzo in diabolical mood involves the basic motive stated and answered in two successive forms of diminution. The trio in boistrous canonic mood involves a wide-ranging theme of ascending and descending perfect fourths and fifths in which the tuba predominates. Vaughan Williams' fondness for the tuba is shown by many such passages in his works and by his Concerto in f for Tuba (1954).

IV, which is connected to III by transition, is a sonata of a rather jazzy yet devilish character. At its close, before the epilogue, the fluctuation between f and F is emphasized.

The epilogue is a grand fugal movement involving contrapuntal manipulation of the basic motives combined with the themes of IV. The various contrapuntal devices such as canon, augmentation, diminution and contrary motion appear throughout.

This is an outstanding example of a symphony in which the basic motive and cyclic principles are employed to provide a formal structure of clarity, inevitability, unity and variety.

Symphony, no. 5 in D (1943, revised 1955) in contrast to the fourth is a return to modal and pentatonic characteristics and a more leisurely formal structure. The finale (IV) consists of a set of variations on a ground bass, a thematic development and a coda (epilogue style).

Symphony, no. 6 in e (1947, revised 1950) is in four-connected movements, the fourth being an epilogue which is an eery, mysterious pianissimo movement involving contrapuntal manipulation of a theme with the tritone as the prominent interval. This work is like the Fourth Symphony in its dissonance, bitonality, jazzy themes and diabolical scherzo based on the tritone.

Symphony, no. 7, Sinfonia Antarctica (1952) was derived from his music for the film, Scott of the Antarctic (1948). Each of the five movements is labeled with a text relating to Scott's journey. V is again an epilogue. The "motto theme" or basic motive is also employed as a unifying factor in this programmatic symphony.

Symphony, no. 8 in d (1956) makes much use of percussion instruments in I and IV (the finale). I is titled Fantasia—Variations Without a Theme and is in eight sections involving the manipulation of two motives. II is a humorous scherzo, and III is titled Cavatina. The finale is titled Toccata and is a rondo which is fantastic in mood.

Vaughan Williams wrote his Symphony, no. 9 (1958) at the age of eighty-five. It is an expansive work with an abundance of thematic material. Saxophones and percussion occupy a prominent place in the orchestration especially in the humorous scherzo (III). A cyclic application of thematic material is seen in the reference to I at the close of IV in epilogue style.

SUGGESTED WRITTEN ASSIGNMENTS

1. Analyze a smaller choral work or part of a larger work (such as Shepherds of the Delectable Mountains from the opera Pilgrim's Progress) for understanding of modal melody and harmony.
2. Write five short exercises (about 16 measures) in four-voice texture each in one of the following modes: Dorian, Phrygian, Lydian, Mixolydian, Aeolian.
3. Choose a short text and write a work for mixed voices (SATB), with or without accompaniment, using the stylistic features seen in Example 117.
4. Analyze the epilogue of Symphony, no. 4.

BIBLIOGRAPHY

DAY, JAMES, Vaughan Williams, New York: Farrar, Straus and Cudahy, 1961.

DICKINSON, A. E. F., Vaughan Williams, London: Faber and Faber, Ltd., 1963.

FOSS, HUBERT, Ralph Vaughan Williams: A Study, London: Oxford University Press, 1950.

HOWES, FRANK, The Music of Ralph Vaughan Williams, London: Oxford University Press, 1954.

KENNEDY, MICHAEL, The Works of Ralph Vaughan Williams, New York: Oxford University Press, Inc., 1964.

PARKENHAM, SIMONA, Ralph Vaughan Williams: A Discovery of His Music, London: Macmillan Company, Ltd., 1957.

VAUGHAN WILLIAMS, RALPH, The Making of Music, Ithaca: Cornell University Press, 1955.

————, National Music and Other Essays, London: Oxford University Press, 1963.

YOUNG, PERCY, Vaughan Williams, London: Dennis Dobson, 1953.

EXAMPLE 117
Vaughan Williams
TE DEUM IN G
(First 51 Measures)

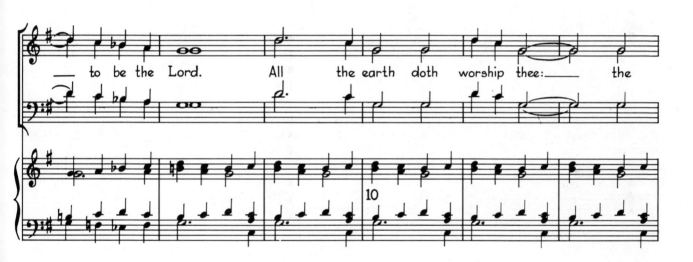

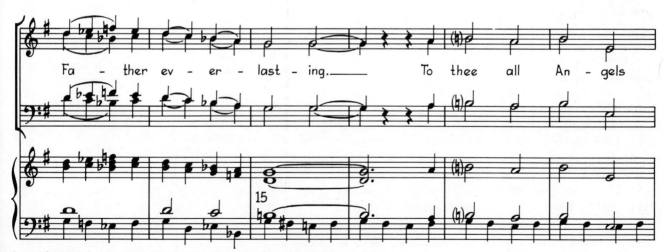

Ho - - - ly, Ho - - - - - - - - - -

- - - ly, Ho - - - ly, Ho - - - - -

- - ly,_____ Lord God of Sa - ba - oth;

- - ly,_____ Lord God of Sa - ba - oth;

CHAPTER 25

WILLIAM WALTON

1902-

The three outstanding composers of the twentieth-century renaissance of English music are Vaughan Williams, William Walton and Benjamin Britten. Sir William Walton is recognized through a few highly respected works as a leading exponent of a style which is a fusion of both neoclassic and romantic elements. The general features and influences that mark his music are:

a. Long, lyric melodies and the grand symphonic gesture from Sibelius;

b. rhythmic vitality and vivid orchestration from Stravinsky;

c. humor and satire from jazz;

d. choral technic and melodic invention influenced by national tradition;

e. tonal organization based on an approach comparable to Hindemith.

His music is essentially tonal, but it involves complex harmonic formations with all kinds of chromatic alteration and nonharmonic involvement. A very romantic quality in his music results from eloquent melody, brilliant orchestration, expressive harmony and contrasting moods and thrilling climaxes. The theatrical quality in his art is seen in nearly every work in his ability to intensify any mood whether tragic, humorous, diabolic or triumphant.

EXAMPLE 118 (pages 341-343)
Symphony (1937), III

The Symphony (1937) is a large scale work of great, dramatic effect. Its characteristics are:

a. Great reliance on pedal points for breadth of style and complex sonority;

b. free use of the twelve notes of the chromatic scale in a tonal framework based on modal scales (especially Dorian, Phrygian and Aeolian), the eight-tone symmetrical scale (see below) and other artifical scales as well as major and minor;

c. a complex texture resulting from extensive use of nonharmonic tones, especially appoggiaturas, against altered chords, and often placed over a pedal bass;

d. a rhythmic complexity resulting from the interplay of polyphonic lines against background rhythmic patterns;

e. long, lyric lines with wide leaps involving octave displacement;

f. slow harmonic rhythm resulting from several consecutive alterations of a single harmonic function often undergirded by a pedal.

These characteristics are not exclusive of one another but naturally are interdependent aspects of a total effect.

I is a sonata form of broad dimensions. Theme 1 opens in b♭ Dorian and is spun out over an ostinato. After a transition involving the eight-tone symmetrical scale and a greatly expanded II-V (of F) progression, theme 2 opens in F colored by various modal inflections especially Phrygian. Both themes are extensively developed and return with B♭ as tonic.

II is one of those scherzi which have a malicious sound, a devilish spirit. The key center is e with modal inflections. There are three or four trenchant little themes which are tossed about and extended through various keys.

III is a lyric-tragic expression which is one of the most moving in twentieth-century orchestral literature.

1. It is an A B A B form based on two lyric themes. The first (A) m. 3-34 is a long, expressive melody and the second (B) m. 35-38 is a basic four-

measure phrase which undergoes various modifications.

2. The tonal organization of the entire movement is as follows:

Introductory measures, 1-2.

Section A (m. 3-34). The tonal center is c♯ (sometimes Phrygian, sometimes Aeolian). The theme is stated over a tonic pedal (m. 1-12), followed by progression toward prolongation of the dominant (m. 13-16), a dominant pedal (m. 17-26), and then a transition to section B over a D♯ pedal (dominant of g♯) (m. 27-34).

Section B (m. 35-75). The tonality shifts more in this section as the theme phrase is developed. The section opens with g (Dorian and minor) as tonal center over a subdominant pedal. The eight-note symmetrical scale (C C♯ D♯ E F♯ G A B♭) is employed in m. 53-64.

Section A (m. 76-107). The long A melody is fully restated but with certain intervallic adjustments at key points to place it and then keep it in the orbit of f♯. The relationships between the first and second statements of A are thus:

1st A   m. 3-10, c♯ | m. 11-26, c♯ | m. 27-32, g♯
2nd A   m. 76-83, f | m. 84-99, f♯ | m. 100-105, f♯

(Example 119 begins at m. 104)

The B theme appears in counterpoint to that part of the A melody which is in m. 84-87.

Section B (m. 108-131). The key center remains f♯ over a dominant pedal (C♯) which began at m. 90. The tonality, remaining over the C♯ pedal to the end, changes to b at m. 113-117, then to the eight-note symmetrical scale (C♯ D E F G A♭ B♭ B♮) in m. 117-124 and back to the c♯ tonal center at m. 125. See example 119.

The last seven measures form a short coda based on the first theme (A). A careful study of the entire movement is recommended.

3. Notice that m. 3 is here the opening of A and also acts as the closing measure of B (m. 131) and the beginning of the coda. See Example 119.

4. The tonality of the first twenty-six measures fluctuates between c♯ Phrygian and various inflections of minor.

5. The chord indications do not identify what might be considered alterations because the fluctuations in mode in this style result in most chord tones being momentarily diatonic. What is alteration and what is diatonic depend on the specific definition of mode and the limitation on the number of tones considered diatonic in a scale. Therefore, this aspect of the analysis is left to the individual to decide according to the premises from which he works.

6. M. 15 illustrates two simultaneous inflections of V, B♯-D♯ against B♮-D♮, the latter functioning as appoggiaturas.

7. M. 17-26 function as a prolonged expression of the dominant. The middle voices in parallel major thirds serve as fluctuating colors of V over the static G♯ root or pedal. The minor dominant ninth is emphasized by the constant return to A in the top voice, the theme.

8. The shift to g♯ as tonic is reached at m. 27. Here the minor dominant ninth chord of g♯ is prolonged for six measures (27-32), and parallel minor thirds in the inner voices act as harmonic color.

9. Notice that m. 31-32 are a repetition of 27-28 with octave adjustments. Also the transitional nature of these measures is seen in the four statements of the two-measure motive in m. 27-28, 29-30, 31-32, 33-34. This indicates that the A theme has been completed about m. 26 and that the next eight measures are connecting in function to section B beginning at m. 35.

10. What is the harmony of m. 33-34?

11. Section B opens with a marked shift in tonality. The mode is a fluctuation between g Dorian and minor.

12. The B theme in the second staff has been anticipated by the parallel thirds in m. 19-20. Notice that this theme is a four-measure idea which is then restated in modified fashion a number of times and then extended and developed. The triplet figure in m. 37, beats three and four, is an unusually dramatic inflection with its drop of a diminished octave to F♯ in m. 38. How would you identify the nonharmonic tones involved in it?

EXAMPLE 119 (pages 344-346)
Symphony (1937), III

1. This excerpt begins with the last four measures of the transition connecting the return of A to the return of B. The transition between the first statements of A and B consisted of m. 27-34 (8 measures). This transition is also eight measures (100-107) with the same melodic content in the first six measures. M. 100-105 in f♯ are comparable to 27-32 in g♯. M. 106-107 differ in content from 33-34.

2. Here the B section opens at m. 108 introduced by the triplet figure of B used as an anacrusis.

3. With the exception of m. 115-116 the C♯ pedal which entered at m. 90 continues to the end. Here the C♯ is dominant of f♯ through m. 112. In m. 113-116 the b minor scale prevails. Then beginning in m. 117, beats three and four through m. 124, the tonality is based on the eight-tone symmetrical scale.

The eight-tone symmetrical scale is one built on alternating half steps and whole steps. The scale used here is C♯ D E F G A♭ B♭ B♮. Because of its symmetry any tone can be used as the tonal center. Because of the C♯ pedal, it is logical to assume that it is tonic.

In this scale alternate notes spell two diminished seventh chords: C♯ E G B♭ and D F A♭ C♭ (B♮). Using the tones of the first diminished seventh as roots various diatonic chords can be spelled. Thus a major triad, a minor triad, a dominant (major-minor) seventh chord, a minor seventh chord, a half-diminished seventh chord, a diminished seventh chord and a minor dominant ninth chord can be spelled diatonically on C♯, on E, on G and on B♭. Enharmonic changes are necessary to change diminished fourths to major thirds, for example, C♯ to F = D♭ to F, etc.

On the second diminished seventh fewer chord possibilities prevail since only minor thirds are available. Obviously the composer using this scale must be careful not to fall into a diminished seventh emphasis.

4. Here (m. 117-124) Walton combines the various chords available on the roots C♯, E, G, B♭ in a polychordal texture over the C♯ pedal. The seventh chords used in combination are shown but the kinds of seventh chords are not indicated. Identify the kinds of seventh chords used.

5. Compare m. 116-120 with m. 53-57 in the first B statement; in the first B section these measures (53-57) are comparable to m. 116-120 in thematic material, but they are based on the eight-tone symmetrical scale: F♯ G A B♭ C D♭ E♭ E♮.

6. At m. 125 there is the return to the opening tonality of the movement, c♯ minor and Phrygian, with the V⁹ of c♯ minor still over the C♯ pedal which now functions as a tonic pedal.

7. Notice throughout this movement the emphasis on the interval of the minor ninth which appears immediately in the first measure of the theme (m. 3, Example 118) and is highly pointed in m. 128-131 to close the movement.

Examples and Suggestions for Further Study of the Music of Walton

Walton's ability for parody is demonstrated in the *Façade Suite* (1936), which is based on a set of pieces written in 1923 to accompany the recitation of some satirical poems by Edith Sitwell. This work consists of an orchestral burlesque of five dances: polka, waltz, Swiss yodeling song, tango pasodoblé, tarantella Sevillana.

Bright, rhythmic melodies and a neoclassic harmonic vein characterize the overtures, *Portsmouth Point* (1925) and *Johannesburg Festival* (1958).

The *Viola Concerto* (1929) and the *Violin Concerto* (1939) are important works in the repertoires of these instruments and show Walton's lyric qualities and ability to exploit the technical possibilities of the instruments.

The *Sinfonia Concertante* in D (1943) for piano and orchestra is a short three-movement work in neoclassic spirit.

The formal design of I is as follows:

Introduction (Maestoso)
Sonatina form (Allegro spiritoso)
    Exposition:
        Theme 1 in D restated in D♭
        Theme group 2, first theme in a, transition, second theme in e repeated and varied
    Transition, same material as the transition in theme group 2
    Recapitulation:
        Theme 1 in D with rhythimc modification
        Theme Group 2, all return in d but in contrapuntal combination
Coda, theme 1 in its original form in D

II is a slow movement in modal character involving contrapuntal treatment of motives and repetition of rhythmic patterns.

III is a scherzo in F in ABA rondo form. It closes with an extended coda in D which includes a return of the theme of the introduction of I, the theme of II and a final, quick statement of the scherzo theme (III). In this regard III is somewhat like the viola, violin and cello concertos in which themes of preceding movements are recalled at the close of the finale. The scherzo is reminiscent rhythmically of I, and the harmonic treatment is strongly pandiatonic, that is, the diatonic chords in F are used without regard to their traditional tonal function but for free rhythmic or contrapuntal effect. See Stravinsky examples for further discussion of pandiatonicism.

The *Cello Concerto* (1956) requires great technical virtuosity of the soloist. The spirit of the work is neoclassical and the texture is lucid but dissonant, involving bitonal effects, chord clusters and extensive chromaticism. The finale (III) includes an epilogue recalling themes from I.

It is interesting to note that the *Sinfonia Concertante, Viola Concerto, Violin Concerto* and *Cello Concerto* are all cyclic works in which thematic material from earlier movements is recalled in the closing section of the finale. Also in all but the *Sinfonia Concertante* the slower movement is I, and II is a scherzo movement.

Belshazzar's Feast (1931) for chorus and orchestra is perhaps Walton's best-known work, and possibly the outstanding one in its form in the twentieth-century repertoire. Though it is a relatively early composition it represents the spirit and style of the composer as well as any one work. It is a highly dramatic work of many moods and a study of it is strongly recommended.

Suggested Written Assignments

1. Compare the *Sinfonia Concertante,* III, with Stravinsky, *Serenade* (1925), or Paulenc, *Suite* (1920), or with a piano piece by Satie such as *Embryons desseches* in regard to pandiatonic texture.
2. Analyze the last movement of the Symphony (1937).
3. Write a short piece (32 measures) based on the eight-tone symmetrical scale C♯ D♯ E F♯ G A B♭ C. Use only tones in the scale. Notice that D♯ F♯ A C are the roots which will provide the greater number of chord structures based on superimposed thirds.
4. Compare the melodic designs of the Walton, Symphony, no. 2 (1960), first movement, with the melodic designs in his Symphony (1937), III. Compare intervals emphasized, rhythmic stresses and so forth.
5. Analyze the last movement (III) of the Walton, Symphony, no. 2. It is in three sections: passacaglia, fugato, and scherzando-coda. Note the character of the passacaglia theme.

Bibliography

Howes, Frank, *The Music of William Walton* 2 vols., London: Oxford University Press, 1942.
See general reference works on contemporary composers, especially British composers.

EXAMPLE 118

WALTON
SYMPHONY (1937)
III
(First 42 Measures)
(Piano Duet Arrangement)

EXAMPLE 119
WALTON
SYMPHONY (1937)
III
(Last 34 Measures, 104-137)

Arranged by Herbert Murrill. Copyright 1937 by the Oxford University Press, London.

CHAPTER 26

HOWARD HANSON

1896-

Though Hanson employs a wide range of technics in his compositions, the predominant qualities are lyric beauty and emotional force associated with romantic expression. His work grows from the conviction that music must appeal to the sense of beauty and should not disgust in any way.

His style could be considered a personal fusion of several elements which would include the symphonic gesture of Sibelius, the harmonic colors reminiscent of Grieg and Ravel, a neoclassic approach to counterpoint and tonality as seen in his use of nonfunctional, dissonant or pandiatonic counterpoint (Example 122) and the eight-tone symmetrical scale (Examples 120 and 123) and the cyclic formal organization and brilliant orchestral writing of the neoromantic line of composers stemming from Liszt and Franck as seen in his Symphony, no. 2, *Romantic*, Examples 120 and 121.

EXAMPLE 120 (pages 350, 351)
Symphony No. 2, "Romantic," Op 30, I

The Symphony, no. 2, *Romantic* (1930) is perhaps the best known of his five symphonies. Cyclic recall is prominent in the formal organization of the three movements.

1. Both the introductory motive (measure 1) and the thematic material shown in Example 121 appear in II, and all the themes of I and II are recalled in III in original or modified form.

2. I is a sonata design with an introduction which states basic motives reappearing throughout the work. This example includes the introduction (m. 1-23) and the first eight measures of theme 1 (m. 24-31).

3. The second theme is quoted in Example 121 and is preceded by an intermediate or transitional theme which appears between it and theme 1.

4. The development consists of a quiet treatment of theme 1 building to a climax in the retransition to the recapitulation.

5. The recapitulation includes a transition based on the introduction motive (m. 1) placed between the two themes of the second-theme group.

6. The figure ♫♪ first appearing in m. 23 plays an important part throughout the work. It not only accompanies the entrance of theme 1, but it also is the closing inflection of each period of the theme of Example 121, m. 7 and 14; it closes the first movement and is the introductory flourish accompanying the opening theme of III.

7. The general outline of tonal centers for I would be:

Introduction and theme 1, D♭ center, based primarily on the eight-tone symmetrical scale, D♭ D♮ E F G A♭ B♭ B♮
Intermediate or transitional theme, B♭
Theme 2, E♭
Development
Theme 1, D♭, as before
Transitional theme, B♭
Introduction motive, eight-tone symmetrical scale one-half step lower on C D♭ E♭ E♮ F♯ G A B♭
Theme 2, D♭.

8. Note that the first eighteen measures consist of eighteen repetitions of the one-measure motive developed to a climax at m. 13 through expanding texture and brought back to a state of quietness in m. 14-18. Compare m. 1 with Example 78.

9. The introduction of E♭'s and C's in m. 6-10 and 13 destroys the pure effect of the symmetrical scale.

10. M. 19-21 form a momentary bitonal effect of C against D♭ and a point of suspense for resolution into the chord of m. 22 which is a return to the opening motive (m. 22-25) in the lower staves.

11. The triplet figure of two perfect fourths in m. 27-29 is exploited in the development section. Here

also chords of superimposed perfect fourths are emphasized. Note such chords in m. 27-29 and the superimposed perfect fifths in m. 30-31.

12. Compare the scale and chordal material of this example to m. 117-124 of Example 119. Notice that the prevailing harmonic quality in this example (120) is the superimposition of two triads a tritone apart, G and Db, which are also diatonic in the symmetrical scale. This effect is found earlier in the closing measures of *The Firebird* by Stravinsky.

13. Compare m. 1-18 with m. 24-31.

EXAMPLE 121 (page 352)
Symphony No. 2, "Romantic," Op. 30, I

1. This initial presentation of the second theme consists of three periods of seven measures each, the third period being a repetition with expanded orchestration of the second period. The first two periods are quoted here.

2. There are two melodic elements: the upper staff line and the countermelody in the center staff. The latter reappears without the former in II and both elements are recalled in III.

3. The tonality of this example is Eb and each harmony and nonharmonic tone should be identified.

4. A formal analysis of each of the three movements of this symphony is recommended for an understanding of its cyclic and tonal organization.

EXAMPLE 122 (page 353)
The Cherubic Hymn, Op. 37

The *Cherubic Hymn* (1949) is one of several effective works for chorus and orchestra by Hanson.
1. The tonal ingredients include:
    a. Pandiatonic counterpoint as in this example;
    b. eight-tone symmetrical scale as in Example 123;
    c. parallel unrelated triads as in Example 123;
    d. artificial scales such as G A B C D D♯ E♯ F♯ in m. 44-59;
    e. modal effects as in the closing measures.
2. Notice in this example the emphasis on the intervals of perfect fourths and fifths and sevenths and seconds (including ninths). Such emphasis produces an archaic, nontonal quality. The voices move in a natural scalewise fashion but most thirds and sixths fall on the weak part of the beat while the other intervals are accented.
3. In m. 1-4 the tonal center is f♯.
4. In m. 5-11 the tonal center is e.
5. The texture in m. 5-10 is two parts doubled at the octave.

EXAMPLE 123 (pages 354-357)
The Cherubic Hymn, Op. 37

1. Here is illustrated the building of a climax through an ascending eight-tone symmetrical scale and a repeated rhythmic pattern.

2. The eight-tone scale, E F♯ G A Bb C C♯ D♯, is used in m. 1-8.

3. At m. 9 the scale changes to D♯ E♯ F♯ G♯ A B C D through m. 23. How is it related to the scale of m. 1-8?

4. In m. 24-27 the unrelated triads and the augmented seconds in the eight-note figures produce an exotic quality.

5. Notice that in m. 1-23 the music is diatonic in the sense that there are no tones used outside the prevailing eight-tone symmetrical scale.

6. In m. 11-23 three of the four major triads available in the scale are used: G♯, B, D. What is the fourth major triad which is diatonic in the scale?

7. Notice in m. 20-23 the polychords resulting from the chords in the middle staff ascending against the ostinato pattern of three chords in the upper staff. The hemiola is expressed in the rhythm.

8. As the climax builds Hanson puts the voices in octaves so they will carry well through the accompaniment and moves them back into chords at the height of the climax in m. 24.

Examples and Suggestions for Further Study of the Music of Hanson

Each of Hanson's five symphonies as well as his Piano Concerto in G, op. 36 (1949) involves the cyclic principle. Symphony, no. 1 in e, op. 21, "Nordic" (1922) and Symphony, no. 2 are three movement works; Symphony, no. 3 in a, op. 33 (1941) and Symphony, no. 4, op. 34, "Requiem" (1943) are four-movement works. In each of these four symphonies and the concerto, the finale recalls themes from previous movements, particularly the first movement. The Symphony, no. 5 is in one movement, but the cyclic idea is present in the final section which recalls themes from the opening sections.

In Symphony, no. 1, I, the opening theme, later recalled in the closing section of III, is a Dorian melody. The use of modes and artificial scales both melodically and harmonically is frequent in the style.

I is a modified sonata form.

II, in F, is an ABA form in which elements of section B are present in the return of A. Compare this movement to the Chopin, Nocturne in c♯, op. 27, no. 1.

III recalls motives from II rhythmically and tonally modified and introduces theme 1 of I in a long, closing section in which various themes are combined.

The third movements of symphonies nos. 3 and 4 are scherzi of the satiric or diabolical type. Each movement of Symphony, no. 4 bears the name of a section of the requiem mass: Kyrie, Requiescat, Dies Irae, Lux Aeterna.

Symphony, no. 5 in one movement is subtitled *Sinfonia Sacra* and is inspired by the story of the resurrection according to the Gospel of John.

The *Piano Concerto* is in four movements. I is in the following form of eight sections:

Introduction, A, B, C, A extended, B extended, C shortened, epilogue recalling the introduction material.

II is a scherzo type of movement involving themes derived from I.

III is a meditative movement based primarily on one idea.

IV recalls the themes of A and B of I in the coda.

The *Lament for Beowulf*, op. 25 (1925), for chorus and orchestra involves extensive use of quartal harmonies, chords built in fourths.

SUGGESTED WRITTEN ASSIGNMENTS

1. Write three short (8 measures) exercises in two-voice counterpoint, exploiting the intervals of seconds, sevenths and perfect fourths and fifths on the beat as in Example 122.

2. Write a short exercise (24 measures) in the following eight-tone artificial (nonsymmetrical) scale: C D E♭ F F♯ G A B.

3. Do a harmonic analysis of the entire *Cherubic Hymn*.

BIBLIOGRAPHY

HANSON, HOWARD, *Music in Contemporary American Life*, Lincoln: University of Nebraska, 1951.

————, *The Harmonic Materials of Modern Music*, New York: Appleton-Century-Crofts, 1960.

TUTHILL, BURNET C., "Howard Hanson," *Musical Quarterly*, April, 1936.

See general reference works on contemporary composers, especially American composers.

EXAMPLE 120
HANSON
SYMPHONY NO. 2, "ROMANTIC," OP. 30
I
(First 31 Measures)

EXAMPLE 121

Hanson
SYMPHONY NO. 2, "ROMANTIC," OP. 30
I
(Measures 99-112)

EXAMPLE 122
HANSON
THE CHERUBIC HYMN, OP. 37
For Chorus and Orchestra
(Measures 144-154)

EXAMPLE 123

HANSON
THE CHERUBIC HYMN, OP. 37
For Chorus and Orchestra
(Measures 178-204)

CHAPTER 27

ROY HARRIS

1898-

The unique style of Harris owes little to traditional influences and yet it is music which is essentially diatonic and consonant. His music focuses on the broad structure rather than on sensuous details, and he is thus most effective in large abstract instrumental forms. The various elements of his style may be outlined as follows.

FORM: It is related to the motivic-generative process of baroque style but without the repetition and sequence. There is an autogenetic unfolding of expansive melodic ideas in a harmonic-contrapuntal texture. Canon and imitative development of motives are combined in free fugal design. Literal recapitulation of ideas is seldom present. Passacaglia is used in the Piano Quintet (1936). The continuously evolving nature of the music, the use of asymmetrical rhythms whose accents are independent of melodic emphases and avoidance of cadences produce a sectionless kind of form, or form in which sections are not clearly defined.

HARMONY: Major and minor triads and sevenths and polychords of a nondominant nature (without tritones) are used in tonally unrelated connection. The harmonic style is essentially consonant but nontonal, sometimes modal. Chord connections result from common tone relationships rather than functional or tonal tendencies. See the Harris examples.

Nonharmonic tones are unimportant in the style. There are few appoggiaturas.

No use is made of dominant-type chord structures, augmented or diminished triads, whole-tone scales or twelve-tone technic. There is little use of melodic or harmonic sequences or repetition.

MELODY: Long-breathed phrases expand from a diatonic motive. There is an interchange of major and minor seconds and thirds from the same tone. Melodic lines consisting of a stream of equal note values in asymmetrical rhythmic and intervallic patterns are common. Little use is made of chromatic melodic inflections such as chromatic passing tones and appoggiaturas. Though augmented and diminished triads may be outlined in the melody they are not harmonized by those triads.

RHYTHM: Polymetric rhythmic effects abound. There is motion of equal note values in the predominant melodic line with contrasting rhythmic complexity in the background or subordinate voices.

The texture is contrapuntal but evolved from diatonic and consonant harmonic considerations. Most of the harmonic features of Harris' style are illustrated in the examples which follow. An understanding of the personal formal style of Harris requires the study of entire movements or works. This is true also for a revelation of the interrelationships of rhythm and melody in the unfolding of Harris' forms. The independence or noncoincidence of metrical pattern with melodic pattern in Harris' music is somewhat akin to the independence of the bar line found in Brahms' style. In general, Harris freely uses the contrapuntal devices of imitation to extend the characteristics of a motive or theme autogenetically into melodic designs of varying lengths and shapes.

EXAMPLE 124 (page 362)
Little Suite, III

The *Little Suite* for piano (1938) consists of four short character pieces for children titled:

I BELLS. Exploits chords in fourths (quartal harmony) in the upper octaves over sustained chords in the low octaves.

II SAD NEWS. Uses nonrelated minor triads and quartal harmonies over a plaintive tune in alto-tenor range.

III CHILDREN AT PLAY. The first eight measures quoted here illustrate the character of this short (17 measures) piece.

IV SLUMBER. See Example 125.

1. In this example asymmetrical rhythmic figures and the connection of triads related only by common tone are illustrated.
2. Note that D is the common tone in the LH ostinato figure.
3. The RH melody involves:
   a. A returning to D;
   b. A repetition of certain motives (m. 2 and 4) and a rhythmic modification of the same motives; compare m. 2-3 with 4-5 with 5-6.
4. The interchange of major and minor thirds from D to F♯ and F in the LH of m. 7 and from D♭ to F to D♮ in the LH of m. 8 is a melodic idiom of the style.
5. The RH is essentially a D major melody while the LH alternates between D and B♭. Thus the last three eighths of each measure contain a bitonal effect of D and B♭ sounding simultaneously, and the piece ends on this bitonal relationship.

EXAMPLE 125 (page 362)
Little Suite, IV

1. This little piece (10 measures long) is based on tonally unrelated major and minor triads and sevenths with an occasional complex nondominant sound such as the F^9 in m. 5. The final chord (not quoted) is a thirteenth containing the seven tones of the F scale distributed above a low B♭.
2. The cross relationships resulting from these chord progressions are inherent in this harmonic style. Locate all the cross relationships in this example.
3. What is the chord in the first half of m. 3?

EXAMPLE 126 (page 363)
Symphony No. 3

Symphony, no. 3 (1937) in one movement is probably Harris' best-known and one of his most effective works. It is a short work but is a highly original, profound and compelling expression with qualities of epic expansiveness and healthy optimism. The work is in five sections described by the composer as follows:

I Tragic—low string sonorities (m. 1-91)

II Lyric—strings, horns, woodwinds (m. 92-208)

III Pastoral—woodwinds with a polytonal string background (m. 209-415)

IV Fugue—dramatic (m. 416-566)

   a. Brass and percussion predominating (m. 416-504)
   b. Canonic development of materials from Section II constituting background for further development of fugue (m. 505-566)

V Dramatic—tragic (m. 567-703)

   a. Restatement of violin theme of Section I: tutti strings in canon with tutti woodwinds against brass and percussion developing rhythmic motif from climax of Section IV (m. 567-634)
   b. Coda—development of materials from sections I and II over pedal tympani (m. 634-703)

1. This example (m. 60-72) includes the first thirteen measures of the violin theme (Section I) which is restated in canon form between string and woodwinds in Section V(a). The entire melodic line is thirty-two measures long in Section I (m. 60-91). The canonic version in Section V is in rhythmic augmentation and occupies sixty-eight measures (m. 567-634).
2. Notice that nearly all the chords are major or minor triads or seventh chords. Occasionally, because of voice-leading requirements, these chords are spelled enharmonically as the E major seventh chord in m. 65, the d♭ minor seventh chord moving to a D♭ major seventh chord in m. 67 and the A major seventh chord in m. 68.
3. The shift between major and minor in m. 65 and m. 71-72 is often found in the style.
4. Notice the D♭^{11} in m. 63; the polychord, B (E♭=D♯) against D, on the second beat of m. 66 and 70; the C^9 in m. 69; and the D^{11} (A♭=G♯) on the first beat of m. 70.
5. Observe that the violin line, the upper voice, is diatonic but is harmonized by consonant chords not in the scale implied by the upper voice. *This is the essence of the Harris tonal style.*

EXAMPLE 127 (page 363)
Symphony No. 3

1. These are the first nine measures of Section V(b) (m. 634-642). The repeated D's are the tympani pedal.
2. Here the three minor triads which include the tone D are exploited, b to g to D^7 to d.
3. The melodic idea in m. 640-642 is from Section II.
4. The work which opened in G closes in g. The free interweaving of contrasting ideas in a fluid, contrapuntal fabric gives this work a soaring, multidimensional architecture which is both well integrated and yet unbounded.

Examples and Suggestions for Further Study of the Music of Harris

Harris has written two works he calls symphonies but are choral works.

The Symphony for Voices (1936) is a three-part work for unaccompanied chorus and is set to words of Walt Whitman.

I is "Song for All Seas, All Ships," the same text used by Vaughan Williams in *A Sea Symphony*, I. In the first half of the movement Harris employs an ostinato pattern that alternates between the tenor and alto voices and in the second half there is a declamation of the words in the tenor against ascending and descending patterns in the other voices vocalizing on vowel sounds. These effects are descriptive of the motions associated with the sea.

II is "Tears" also from "Sea Drift." Here there is simultaneous use of words sung, words spoken and vocalization of vowel sounds in a realistic portrayal of the text.

III is "Inscription" and involves the separate presentation of three musical ideas which are then combined in a contrapuntal treatment.

The Folk Song (fourth) Symphony (1939) is a sort of fantasy for chorus and orchestra on American folk and popular tunes. It consists of seven sections including two orchestral interludes based on traditional and original dance tunes as follows: choral, choral, orchestral, choral, orchestral, choral, choral.

The Symphony, no. 5 (1942) includes a triple fugue in the finale. The Symphony, no. 6 (1944) is in four movements inspired by Lincoln's Gettysburg Address and titled "Awakening, Conflict, Dedication, Affirmation." The finale again is in fugue style.

Symphonies, no. 7 (1952) and no. 8 (1961) are both one-movement works. The former includes a long section in 11/8 meter: 3 + 3 + 3 + 2. Each section of the work exploits a specific orchestral sound, or rhythmic character, and/or melodic contour somewhat like the Third Symphony.

The Symphony, no. 8 includes a prominent part for the piano which is amplified by loud speakers. In fact, the piano part predominates in such a way as to give the work a concerto character.

In the five-movement work for chorus and piano titled *Folk Fantasy for Festivals* the piano has a similarly prominent role. Here the amplified piano furnishes a resonant chordal background for the voices. The work deals with various aspects of American life and folklore.

  I. "My Praise Shall Never End," is Harris' treatment of the idioms of New England psalm tunes and camp revival songs.

 II. "The Weeping Willow," is a free adaptation of southern mountaineer love songs.

III. "David Slew Goliath," includes a narration (the preacher) telling the story of David against choral and piano background.

IV. "The Working Man's Pride," is a free treatment of working heroes of song and legend.

 V. "Fun and Nonsense Parody," is clever handling of game songs and nursery rhymes.

In I and IV there is much use of quartal harmonies in the piano.

Contemplation, Variations on an Irish Theme for piano (1938) is a treatment of the old traditional Irish tune *Slane*. Here this diatonic melody is harmonized by quartal harmonies, unrelated triads and sevenths and some polychordal structures. It is an excellent study of Harris' harmonic idiom.

The Piano Quintet (1930) exemplifies Harris' interest in contrapuntal textures. I is titled Passacaglia. II is titled Cadenza and involves a free rhapsodic treatment of the passacaglia theme. III is a triple fugue on the same theme.

The String Quartet, no. 3 (1938) consists of four preludes and fugues exploiting the various modes.

Harris has expressed the theory that the emotional quality or musical color of the modes results from the intervals from the tonic (or final) tone up to each of the scale tones. Thus Locrian, Phrygian and Aeolian (minor) are the darkest (most subjective) because of the small intervals up from tonic:

LOCRIAN
(darkest)

PHRYGIAN

AEOLIAN

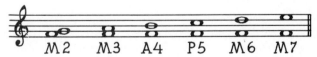

Lydian, Ionian (major) and Mixolydian are the brightest (most objective) because of the large intervals up from tonic:

LYDIAN
(brightest)

IONIAN

$$M2 \quad M3 \quad P4 \quad P5 \quad M6 \quad M7$$

MIXOLYDIAN

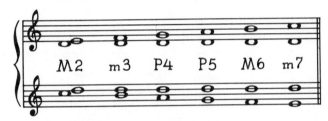

$$M2 \quad M3 \quad P4 \quad P5 \quad M6 \quad m7$$

The Dorian mode being invertible represents perfect equilibrium:

DORIAN

$$M2 \quad m3 \quad P4 \quad P5 \quad M6 \quad m7$$

SUGGESTED WRITTEN ASSIGNMENTS

1. Analyze the passacaglia from the Piano Quintet. Notice the form of the passacaglia theme and the number of different tones used in it.

2. William Schuman was a student of Harris and much influenced by him. Schuman's Symphony, no. 3 opens with what he calls a passacaglia. Compare this with Harris' treatment of the passacaglia idea in the Piano Quintet.

3. The choral work *Requiescat* (1942) by William Schuman is based on a free association of minor triads typical of passages in Harris' music. Analyze this and works by Harris such as the *Soliloquy and Dance* (1938) for viola and piano or a *Song for Occupations* (1934) for chorus, and write a short piece (32 measures) for solo instrument and piano, using only major and minor triads and seventh chords in nontonal relationships as in the Harris examples.

4. Write a short (16 measures) exercise in block chords using quartal harmonies and polychords in the style of Harris.

BIBLIOGRAPHY

SLONIMSKY, NICOLAS, "Roy Harris," *Musical Quarterly*, January, 1947.
See general reference works on contemporary composers, especially American composers.

EXAMPLE 124
HARRIS
LITTLE SUITE FOR PIANO
III CHILDREN AT PLAY
(First 8 Measures)

EXAMPLE 125
HARRIS
LITTLE SUITE FOR PIANO
IV SLUMBER
(First 5 Measures)

EXAMPLE 126
HARRIS
SYMPHONY NO. 3
In One Movement
(Measures 60-72)

EXAMPLE 127
HARRIS
SYMPHONY NO. 3
In One Movement
(Measures 634-642)

CHAPTER 28

AARON COPLAND

1900-

Taken as a whole Copland's music shows a clearly individual style with characteristic features evident throughout his output; yet his works fall into four generally recognized and fairly distinct stylistic periods as a result of changing influences and shifts in artistic emphases and purposes.

Works of the first period, up to 1929, show the influence of Ravel, the neoclassic French style and jazz. Representative works of this period are:

Passacaglia for piano (1922)
Symphony, no. 1 (1928)
Music for the Theater (1925), see Examples 128 and 129
Concerto for Piano (1926)
Vitebsk (A Study on Jewish Themes) for violin, cello and piano (1928)
Symphonic Ode (1929)

A shift of emphasis from jazz to abstract, neoclassic, dissonant, austere and intellectually conceived works marks the second period, 1929-1937. Here the influence of Stravinsky and concentration on the organization of characteristic intervals or motives are found in such works as:

Piano Variations (1930), see Example 130
Statements for orchestra (1934)
Sextet for string quartet, clarinet and piano (1937)
Piano Sonata (1941, started in 1935)

A complete change in emphasis takes place around 1936, and the music of the third period, 1936 to 1944, is characterized by simplicity, directness of appeal, use of folk idioms, programmatic elements and nationalism.

Music for ballet, radio, films, student performance and generally for mass appeal is typical of this period. Works based on folk idioms of the United States or Latin America include the following.

El Salón México (1936), see Example 131, Lincoln Portrait (1942) and Danzón Cubano (1942) for orchestra; and the ballets, Billy the Kid (1938), Rodeo (1942) and Appalachian Spring (1944).

A return to a nonprogrammatic and more abstract style takes place during the early forties. The works of this (the fourth) period range from the diatonic, declamatory style of third period works as seen in Symphony, no. 3 (1946) and the clarinet Concerto (1948) to involvement with serial procedures as found in the Piano Quartet (1950) and the Piano Fantasy (1958).

The purpose of the following outline is to point out those features or elements in the music of Copland which apply more or less generally to all his work regardless of any style period.

MELODY: Predominantly diatonic. Melodic ideas composed of motivic fragments or figures such as the outline of a triad or one or two characteristic intervals (3rd, 4th or 5th) reiterated with rhythmic changes in a declamatory fashion. See Examples 128-131. Folk tune or jazz idioms, including the interchangable major-minor third of the "blues" scale, Example 128.

HARMONY: Polychords as in Example 128 and 130 (coda). Nonfunctional use of triads. Pandiatonicism. Major and minor triad simultaneously as in Example 130, Variation 4. Superimposed V over I, forming I^9 as in Appalachian Spring. Chords in fourths and fifths. Open fifth sonorities, third omitted. Music is sometimes polytonal, modal or nontonal but not atonal.

RHYTHM: Much rhythmic variety and vitality through syncopation, changing meters (Examples 128 and 131), asymmetrical patterns and simple rhythms contrasted to complex rhythms.

TEXTURE: Spare, little unnecessary doubling, much unison, two- and three-part writing; contrapuntal effects include canon (Sonata for Violin and Piano and *Statements*) and canon by contrary motion (*Appalachian Spring* and *In the Beginning*). Texture is predominantly homophonic in nature rather than contrapuntal. Assimilation of the serial technic into his already-existing, individual style.

FORM: Most effective in forms based on theatrical requirements such as ballets and suites. The cyclic principle in *Music for the Theatre*, Symphony, no. 3 and other works. Adaptations of the sonata and other classical formal designs appear in Symphony, no. 3, Sextet, and Piano Sonata. The Symphony, no. 1, the Piano Sonata and the Piano Quartet all close with a slow movement.

Copland applies a lyric and essentially romantic musical temperament to neoclassic forms and textures. Thus he imbues contemplative moods, boisterous folk scenes and wistful recollection with freshness, vitality and clarity.

EXAMPLE 128 (page 370)
Music for the Theatre, I

This suite for small orchestra represents "theatrical type" music and is not written for a specific production. It is strongly based on jazz and blues elements as well as music hall types, the latter especially in II and IV. The five movements are related in such a way as to create the effect of an arch form:

    I Prologue, Slow
   II Dance, Fast
  III Interlude, Slow
   IV Burlesque, Fast
    V Epilogue, Slow

V consists of a shortened return of the material of I, and III is the keystone of the arch being the central slow movement with themes derived from I and V. The two lively movements are II and IV.

1. I opens with a trumpet fanfare introduction. It is followed by a slow, lyric section including the measures quoted in this example. A contrasting middle section consists of a fast, asymmetrical rhythmic treatment of the same thematic material. The fanfare and slow lyric material then return in shortened form to complete an ABA design.

2. Notice the reiteration of both the accompanying chord figure and the motives which make up the upper melodic line.

3. The chords which underlie the melody exemplify a bitonal and polychordal effect. The fifths in the bass staff imply one tonality and the parallel triads in the upper staff which move in contrary motion to the bass fifths imply another tonal center.

4. In a polytonal texture such as this the upper, middle and lower tonal bands or strata are kept separate one from the other. There is little overlapping of ranges, which might confuse the individual tonal color of each stratum.

5. The descending three-tone pattern (mi, re, do) is the basic melodic figure in the chords and melody of the upper staff. This is balanced by the ascending three-tone pattern in the lower staff.

6. In m. 10-13 the melodic idea is a return of the fanfare theme used to connect with the fast middle section.

The ingredients of II are the blues scale, syncopation and a parody on the "corny" jazz style of the twenties. There are two ideas: one in 5/8 meter and one in 4/4 involving an unsophisticated blues melody over a square, "oom-pah" accompaniment.

EXAMPLE 129 (page 371)
Music for the Theatre, III

III is a slow blues-type movement which includes an ingenious ostinato and a contemplative melody congenerous to the themes of I and V. In fact, the trumpet fanfare theme and the theme of Example 128 are recalled in m. 25-31 and serve to connect the two sections devoted to the main melodic idea shown in this example. The form is as follows:

A

M. 1-11 in C. Arioso introduction of thematic idea by English horn unaccompanied.

M. 12-24 in G. Lyric theme over ostinato figure similar to Example 128.

M. 25-31 in B♭. Recall of trumpet fanfare of I and three-note melodic figure of Example 128, leading to

B

M. 31-35 in B♭. Arioso theme by English horn.

M. 36-64. The second and extended statement of lyric theme over ostinato figure, opening in B♭ (this example), interrupted by a short reference to the trumpet fanfare motive of I, and continuing in G as in the first section (A).

M. 65-72 in C. Arioso theme by the English horn as an epilogue.

1. This example quotes the first nine measures (36-44) of the lyric theme over the ostinato on its reappearance in B♭.

2. Notice that 4/4 is broken into 3 + 3 + 2 eighth notes.

3. The elaborate ostinato involves all three lower staves.

4. What is the effect of the tone E in this ostinato pattern?

5. What is the modal quality of the melodic line in the upper staff? What is the modal quality of the melody in the tenor range of the lower staff beginning at m. 4?

EXAMPLE 130 (pages 372, 373)
Piano Variations

1. Much of the astringent dissonance of this work results from the major sevenths and minor ninths which are produced when the first two notes of the theme, E-C, are sounded against the third and fourth tones, D♯-C♯ as a pair. This manipulation of the melodic figure E-C-D♯-C♯ simultaneously against D♯-C♯-E-C, as in Variation 2, is a characteristic device exploited with ingenious variety throughout the work.

2. The theme itself exemplifies Copland's method of developing an idea through a reiteration of characteristic intervals or figures. Compare m. 1-2 with 3-4 and with m. 8-10. The four-note figure involving E-C-D♯-C♯ appears three times. Do not be confused by the octave transpositions of melodic tones. Such octave displacements are a feature of the work and produce a jagged melodic effect from an otherwise unspectacular theme in c♯.

3. What is the form of the theme? Of how many phrases does it consist?

4. Notice the harmonics produced at m. 2 and 5. Can you explain their production? What string and what pitch actually sounds in the production of these harmonics?

5. In Variation 2, m. 1-2, lower staff, we see the first four notes of the theme, the basic motive, stated in the two lines simultaneously—$\frac{1\ 2\ 3\ 4}{3\ 4\ 1\ 2}$—a device which is much used throughout the work.

In m. 3-4 the lower voice is a retrograde version of the voice above it in the lower staff. Note the arrows.

The brackets in m. 5-7 enclose a passage in contrary motion between the hands.

Compare m. 8-11 of Variation 2 with m. 7-10 of the theme. Notice the relationship of the thirds in each hand in m. 10 of Variation 2.

How do you explain the upper-staff notes in m. 1-2 and 4-5?

6. In Variation 4 the basic motive is reiterated as an ostinato over which the elements of phrase three of the theme are stated in varied form. Notice the compressed effect of this variation by the superimposition of thematic motives.

The triad on A with both C♯ and C♮ as well as the other chord forms are a result of melodic considerations involved in the motivic manipulation.

7. The chords in the measures quoted from the coda are a result of the accumulation of dissonance and of the need to intensify further an already dissonant texture toward the close of the work.

What is your analysis of these polychords?

8. This entire work consists of theme, twenty variations and coda. A careful analysis of it is highly recommended.

9. What is the tonal center of the theme? Could C in the four-note figure which dominates the theme be better spelled B♯?

EXAMPLE 131 (page 373)
El Salón México

This composition is of that same genre of works which includes Rimsky-Korsakov's *Capriccio Espagnol*, Tchaikovsky's *Capriccio Italien* and Chabrier's *España*. It is an entertaining fantasy on Mexican local color based on Mexican tunes such as *El Mosco*, *El Palo Verde* and *La Jesucita*.

1. The first sixteen measures of the piece quoted here illustrate:

   a. The typical declamatory opening found in many of Copland's work;
   b. the typical emphasis on a triad pattern, reiterated in various asymmetrical rhythmic versions;
   c. the "skinny" unison texture so prevalent in such passages;
   d. changing meter to produce all sorts of rhythmic syncopation.

2. M. 2-3 are shown in some editions as one measure of 10/8 like m. 6.
3. How do you explain the tonal content of the cadence measures, 13-16? What is the F♯ in m. 16?
4. The motivic material of these first sixteen measures reappears in a variety of treatments throughout the work somewhat in the form of connecting or transitional passages and also appears at the close to form the coda.
5. Typical of the work are changing meters, use of hemiola, use of melodies in thirds to parody Mexican folk song and bitonality, for example, G in the upper register against B♭ in the lower register.

Examples and Suggestions for Further Study of the Music of Copland

The *Passacaglia* for piano, an early work, is an interesting study of the kind of motivic treatment intensified later in the *Piano Variations*. The passacaglia theme is stated in diminution, and the first four tones developed separately in the course of the work.

The Sextet for clarinet, string quartet and piano is in three movements. I has much in common with *El Salón México* in its emphasis on:

a. Polymetric rhythmic effects;
b. changing meters;
c. spare texture, much unison work;
d. triadic motives;
e. declamatory style.

There is much use of octave transposition or displacement of tones and canonic imitation. The major seventh chord in third inversion is emphasized.

II, Lento, is somewhat in the character of I of *Music for the Theatre,* employing a descending four-note motive, B♭AGF. It is connected to the Finale, III, which has the same frenzied rhythmic and thematic character as I and involves motives related to both I and II. Simultaneous major and minor thirds on the same root are a prominent harmonic effect in III, and triadic motives, spare texture and changing meters are typical.

The *Dance Symphony* (1929) is in three connected but contrasting movements. Copland's characteristic use of the piano in the orchestra to provide bright, percussive color and the elements of jazz and syncopation are present.

The Piano Sonata is typical of Copland's second period.

I, Molto moderato, emphasizes such elements as the conflict between the major and minor triad on the same root, thirds in each hand forming bitonal effects, and spare texture except for the return of the first idea at the close stated in declamatory style with sonorous doublings and octave transpositions. The second-theme motive is used at the opening of the finale, III.

II is devoted to manipulation of a six-note motive in 5/8, 6/8 and 7/8 meters with an accompanying major sixth pattern forming a bitonal relationship. The six-note motive is also intervallically altered and treated in contrary motion. This motive and the rhythmic and textural character of the entire movement are quite similar to Variations 15, 16 and 17 of the *Piano Variations.* Key signatures are used in both I and II.

The finale, III, is a slow movement of contemplative character involving a contrast of simple triadic to complex polychordal sonorities. Wide skips, repetition of short figures and polytonal effects are prominent. Compare this movement with the Lento finale of the Piano Quartet. The mood of this kind of movement is found also in the opening of *Appalachian Spring,* of *Lincoln Portrait* and in other works.

The *Lincoln Portrait* for speaker and orchestra combines lines regarding Lincoln as a man with quotes from the Gettysburg Address, and the music includes references to the tune "Springfield Mountain." It is typical in style of the period of ballets and scores for radio, film and student musicians. Works of this type and period make extensive use of folk-music idioms and of actual folk songs such as:

a. The Shaker tune, "Simple Gifts," in *Appalachian Spring;*
b. "Bury Me Not on the Lone Prairie" in *Billie the Kid;*
c. The *Four Dance Episodes* for orchestra from the ballet, *Rodeo,* titled "Corrale Nocturne," "Buckaroo Holiday," "Saturday Night Waltz," and "Hoedown" with their quotations of cowboy tunes.

The Symphony, no. 3 represents the fourth period return to nonprogrammatic writing, but the musical content is strongly based on the third-period ballet style. I is in the characteristic contemplative style of Copland. It opens with a long stately line unaccompanied in E. This line, typical of Copland, involves octave transpositions, prominence of perfect fourths and fifths, triadic outlines and reiteration of short figures which return to a focal point.

A second theme introduced by violas and a third theme initially stated by trombones are of the same general character as the first. Each theme is in turn developed to a climax aided by the enrichment of the texture resulting from accumulation of voices and chord members.

Themes 1 and 2 then appear together, and theme 1 appears in a free augmentation for the final majestic climax. The movement closes with a statement of the first phrase of theme 1.

II is a scherzo with trio in which the scherzo (though not so named) returns in expanded form with the trio theme. The themes and treatment are reminiscent of the folk dances from the earlier ballets.

The trio melody (in 3/4 meter) returns in canon form interrupting the recapitulation of the scherzo section. The movement closes with the main scherzo melody presented in augmentation in loud orchestral unison.

The opening sections of both II and III include motives derived from the first and third themes respectively of I.

III, Andantino, is designed as follows:

a. Meditative introduction based on theme 3 of I;
b. a slightly faster dancelike section based on a diatonic theme in E which is of the type found in II of the *Piano Sonata* and the *Piano Variations* (Variations 15, 16 17);
c. a third section involving pandiatonic ostinato patterns and development of triadic motives which have evolved from the previous material;
d. a return of the thematic material of the second section (b) but with different tonal treatment;
e. return of the introductory thematic material to complete a freely designed arch form A B C B A.

The finale, IV, has an introduction, the *Fanfare for the Common Man*, which Copland wrote during World War II. The first theme of the movement proper is a sprightly triadic tune, diatonic in D, which is immediately developed in brilliant fashion through several keys to a climax. At this point the fanfare theme is stated in augmentation.

Then theme 2 follows. It is in 7/8 time, 3/8 plus 2/4. It is treated to harmonization by parallel triads in D.

A further contrapuntal development of motives from the fanfare and theme 1 ensues.

Theme 1 is recapitulated in Db in conjunction with the fanfare motives in augmentation.

Theme 1 of I then returns followed by theme 2 of IV in a massive chorale-like statement and the work closes with a grand peroration on theme 1 of I. This movement exemplifies Copland's mastery of the contrapuntal combination and development of thematic material.

It is quite natural that Copland with his method of expressing himself in clear, open textures and sparsely accompanied lines should adopt the serial technic. And because his style so well fits serial considerations his later works involving the tone row still have the Copland "sound."

The Piano Quartet in three movements consists of an Allegro II framed on either side by short, slow movements. The work is based on an eleven tone row.

I is a small sonata-type design. The row is used in its original form in various transpositions and also in inversion. The middle (development) section is devoted mainly to a treatment of the intervallic pattern of the ninth, tenth and eleventh tones of the row.

II, Allegro giusto, is based on a theme formed from the retrograde inversion of the row. This movement should be analyzed for its formal design.

In III he uses the row in such a way as to maintain that conflict between major and minor thirds so characteristic of his style. Compare this to I of the Piano Sonata.

The Piano Fantasy is a major piano work involving the serial technic but not adhering strictly to the twelve-tone system. The form, as implied by the title, is autogenetic or a spontaneous growth from germ ideas. The rhythms, textures, sonorities and thematic contours are in the familiar Copland style.

The *Nonet* for three violins, three violas and three cellos (1960) is a one-movement work with contrasting sections. The work opens and closes with the same material in slow, solemn style with the faster rhythmic expression confined to the central portions, a design rather typical in Copland's music. There is a return to a fairly diatonic style of writing and an emphasis on fourths and fifths in the harmony and melodic intervals.

SUGGESTED WRITTEN ASSIGNMENTS

1. Analyze II of the Piano Sonata.
2. Study the transcription of *El Salón México* for two pianos by Leonard Bernstein and compare it with nos. 4, 5 and 6 (Copacabana, Ipanema, and Gavea) from *Saudades do Brazil* (Souvenirs of Brazil), a suite of Latin-American dances for piano by Darius Milhaud. Both composers exemplify in these works rather direct and uncomplicated bitonal writing.
3. Write a short piece for piano (32 measures) based on a simple dance pattern in which the right hand is in one key and the left-hand accompaniment is in another key.
4. Write a short piece (32 measures) for woodwind quartet or quintet in fast 5/8 and/or 7/8 meter involving the manipulation of a rapid five- or six-note motive in a rather lean texture. The motive should be tossed about from instrument to instrument, and the various devices of octave transposition, contrary motion (inversion of the motive),

expansion of intervals and rhythmic augmentation should be employed.

5. Write a short (16 measures) piano piece in slow, meditative style using block harmonies and a three- or four-note motive as illustrated in Example 128 or 129.

BIBLIOGRAPHY

BERGER, ARTHUR, *Aaron Copland*, New York: Oxford University Press, Inc., 1953.

COPLAND, AARON, *Our New Music*, New York: McGraw-Hill Book Company, 1941.

SMITH, JULIA, *Aaron Copland*, New York: E. P. Dutton & Co., Inc., 1955.

EXAMPLE 128
COPLAND
MUSIC FOR THE THEATRE
Suite for Small Orchestra
I. PROLOGUE
(Measures 24-36)

EXAMPLE 129
COPLAND
MUSIC FOR THE THEATRE
Suite for Small Orchestra
III. INTERLUDE
(Measures 36-44)

EXAMPLE 130
COPLAND
PIANO VARIATIONS
Theme (Complete)
Var. II (Complete)
Var. IV (Complete)
Coda (Measures 10-11)

EXAMPLE 131
Copland,
EL SALÓN MÉXICO
(First 17 Measures)

ᴦ

CHARLES IVES

1874-1954

The concept of style can hardly be applied to the music of Ives because his music is an undisciplined, incongruous and unpredictable sequence and mixture of tonal material, atonality, polytonality, tone clusters, impressionistic effects, unmetrical and polymetrical rhythms, dissonance and intentional banality.

Ives inherited his interest in musical experimentation from his father. He was a rugged individual, independent of external musical concerns, who wrote music as an avocation and as an outlet for his own mystical and philosophical nature: descriptive, nationalistic music which shows his unconcern for difficulties of performance, unity or consistency of style, or for any kind of musical convention or artistic restraint.

He attacked all the conventions of musical expression at once and through his fecund imagination produced a body of rambling, rhapsodic works which are unique in the literature. Though he had musical training his relative isolation from the central current of musical evolution and his concern with the descriptive and philosophical possibilities of music caused him to compose from a spontaneous and intuitive point of view.

Yet Ives was a significant innovator in the evolution of western music.

He wrote most of his works between 1888 and 1927 and was one of the first to employ such twentieth-century devices or idioms as:

a. Tone clusters (see Example 132);
b. atonality;
c. polytonality;
d. polymetrical, unmetrical and asymmetrical rhythmic effects;
e. arbitrary and extreme dissonance.

His importance for this reason is highly overrated because his employment of these original rhythms and textures is entirely intuitive and unsystematic. His music is important mainly as a unique and fantastic conglomeration of idioms uninfluenced by and without influence on the mainstream of western musical styles.

EXAMPLE 132 (page 377)
"Majority," a song

As an indication of his musical impracticality he stated in connection with the publication of his *114 Songs* (1922) that some could not be sung. Though there are few difficulties which today's performers cannot surmount, a study of certain of these songs, his Concord Sonata for piano, and some of his orchestral works will reveal what he meant.

1. Tone clusters are a common ingredient in Ives' music. The clusters in frames are to be played by the forearm.

2. All tones are natural unless preceded by an accidental; that is, accidentals apply only to the tones which immediately follow.

3. Ives indicates that it is preferable for a unison chorus to sing the song because it is almost impossible for a single voice to hold its own against the piano.

4. This song which consists throughout of the same kind of complex, dissonant chordal formations as seen in this example ends on a simple V I cadence in F.

5. The introduction before the entrance of the voice has no meter signature and only an occasional bar line is inserted, apparently to define certain patterns to the eye.

6. Like the song "Majority" (Example 132) nearly all the one hundred fourteen songs involve text painting in that the accompaniment and the vocal line describe as literally as possible in musical terms the meaning of the text; for example, the chord clusters, many notes, to represent the concept of many or

majority. Also unexpected rhythmic pauses and out-of-tune harmonic effects to suggest the faltering performances of untrained musicians are found in Ives' music.

Literal description and impressionistic effects are the quintessence of Ives' artistic approach.

Throughout the *114 Songs* Ives has inserted various remarks regarding directions for performance, his political views, the reason for including the song, or casual thoughts associated with the particular song. Actually his writings generally are a good clue to his artistic intent and are quite direct and interesting.

The songs contain all sorts of interesting effects, some of which are listed below according to the number of the song in the edition of *114 Songs*, which he published himself. Nearly all the later songs, except a few which are of a studied banality and simplicity, have vocal lines which are not overly difficult set to accompaniments which are tonally and rhythmically very complex and abstruse. The later, more complex songs, those written after 1900, are among the first seventy. Most of the songs after No. 70 were written before 1900 and are generally quite conventional harmonically and melodically.

Tone clusters are prominent in 1, 11 and 22. In 27 they are used for a primitive percussive effect.

A great number of the songs written later are unmetrical, with no meter signature, such as Nos. 21, 27, 30 and with no bar lines such as Nos. 11 and 26.

Some are very short, only one, two, or three lines, such as Nos. 9, 12, 13, 26, 33, 34, 41, 64.

No. 6 has a meter signature of 4½/4 time.

No. 10 contains a passage in which the singer speaks the words in melodrama style, and in one complex passage Ives states that the notes are only an approximate indication, that the time is the main point.

Other songs with directions for optional methods of performance or for ad libitum or improvisational approaches are Nos. 15, 21, 27, 57, 96 and 97. In No. 37 there is no meter signature or bar lines. The performer is directed to mark off the measures to suit his taste. In No. 39 the pianist is directed to play as indistinctly as possible to produce an impressionistic haziness.

Borrowed melodies occur in several songs such as Nos. 16 (a tune of Geo. F. Root), 17 (the theme from *Prelude to the Afternoon of a Faun* by Debussy is quoted at the word *faun*), Nos. 38 and 44-47 (based on hymn tunes), No. 50 (includes a mélange of fragments of Civil War songs) and Nos. 54 and 56.

Humor and intentional triteness are expressed in Nos. 28, 32, 53 and 96.

The following are to be noted:

Parallel dominant formations in No. 10; changing meters in No. 14; double pedals in Nos. 15 and 77; clear bitonality in No. 18; parallel fourths in No. 22; augmented triads in No. 29; whole-tone dominant in No. 70; quartal harmonies in No. 64; and canon between the voice and piano throughout No. 111.

Texts run from the best to the most mediocre American and British poetry, and there are settings of Latin, German and French texts also. The text is omitted from No. 72 because permission had not been obtained to reprint it.

Examples and Suggestions for Further Study of the Music of Ives

The Concord Sonata for piano (1909-1915) is a group of four musical portraits of nineteenth-century New England transcendental writers: I, Emerson, II, Hawthorne, III, The Alcotts, IV, Thoreau, and is of transcendental difficulty.

The various movements include quotations (sometimes literal) from gospel hymns, parlor songs and patriotic tunes, such as "Columbia, the Gem of the Ocean"; "Shall We Gather at the River"; "Jesus, Lover of My Soul"; and "Here Comes the Bride." The opening motive of the Beethoven Fifth Symphony reappears throughout the work as a kind of motto theme. In III the player is instructed to use a heavy, 14¾-inch board to play tone clusters. Nearly every unusual procedure employed by Ives is exemplified in this work.

Though his interest is in free handling of harmonies and rhythm rather than on counterpoint or specific forms there is a fugue in III of his Symphony, no. 4 (1916), and in Symphony, no. 1, I is a sonata form and III a scherzo. His setting of Psalm 67 is bitonal throughout, the sopranos and altos have the key signature of C and the tenors and basses the key signature of g minor (2 flats).

The second number of *Three Places in New England* for orchestra titled *Putnam's Camp, Redding, Connecticut* includes a musical description of two bands marching toward each other and passing while playing two different pieces in different keys, meters and tempi.

This effect of independent musical groups is in *The Unanswered Question* (1908), which involves a string group playing simple diatonic chords in the background, while a trumpet soloist plays in another key and four flutes in a third key.

Ives used asymmetric and polymetric effects as well as pandiatonicism before Stravinsky; he used atonality and polytonality before Schoenberg and Milhaud; he used tone clusters before Cowell; he employed chance musical effects before Cage; he employed studied simplicity and banality before Thomson; he used American folk melody before Copland. All this is a credit to his originality and imagination. But his music finally reached public awareness too late to have had an influence on these composers.

Suggested Written Assignments

1. Compare Virgil Thomson's *Variations on Sunday School Tunes* for organ with Ives' treatment of Civil War tunes in the song, "He is There" (No. 50) or with his treatment of hymn tunes in other works.

2. Compare Schumann's setting of the poem, *Ich Grolle Nicht*, with Ives' song on the same poem (No. 83).

3. Examine Ives' setting of Psalm 67 and compare his bitonal technic with Milhaud and Copland.

Bibliography

Bellomann, Henry, "Charles Ives, The Man and His Music," *Musical Quarterly*, January, 1933.

Carter, Elliot, "Ives Today: His Vision and Challenge," *Modern Music*, May-June, 1944.

Chase, Gilbert, *America's Music*, New York: McGraw-Hill Book Company, 1955.

Cowell, Henry and Sidney, *Charles Ives and His Music*, New York: Oxford University Press, Inc., 1955.

EXAMPLE 132
IVES
"MAJORITY"
A Song
(Piano Introduction)

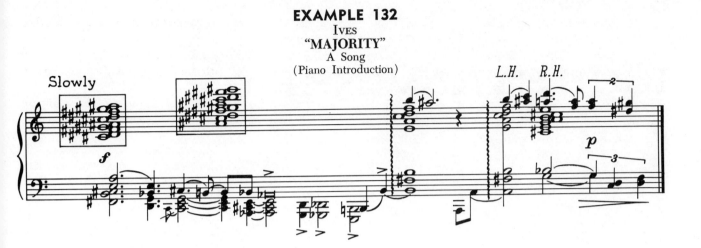

CHAPTER 30

IGOR STRAVINSKY

1882-

Schoenberg, Bartók, Stravinsky and Hindemith are the four composers who are generally considered to have had the greatest influence on the course of musical styles in the first six decades of the twentieth century.

Each composer in his own way had a strong impact on one or more of the components of musical organization: tonality, rhythm, harmony, melody and/or form. For example, Schoenberg replaced the traditional concept of tonality by the serial or twelve-tone row organization, whereas Stravinsky immobilized or froze tonality by suspending the qualities of tendency, tonal pull and resolution in his harmonic and melodic organization. Thus, the tonal structure of Stravinsky's music is rigid and static so that his forms become a series of separate, tonally motionless tableaux. The lack of dynamism and direction in tonal organization is then somewhat counteracted by an emphasis on rhythmic commotion and instrumental color.

Thus, the obvious rhythmic intensity in Stravinsky's music providees the needed quality of motion which tends to compensate for the fixity of tonal organization; but it is a kind of motion analogous to the motion of hamsters on a treadmill, much movement without going anywhere or static frenzy.

Stravinsky achieves this quality of tonal solidity through pandiatonicism—free use of the scale tones without regard for their tonal pull or directional tendencies toward one another—and through constant use of osinati, one after another.

Stravinsky's rhythmic inventiveness, his vivid orchestral scenes and imaginative harmonic combinations have had great effect on contemporary composers. Also, his articulateness in speaking and writing on music and his ability to remain current by modifying his compositional style in keeping with the require-ments of the times have played an important role in his musical eminence.

Throughout the various style changes, from expressively violent ballets such as *Le Sacre du Printemps,* to the unpretentious simplicity of *Pulcinella,* to the use of classic formal procedures as in *Symphony in C,* to the adoption in *Agon* of the serial technic (which he had earlier condemned), Stravinsky always sounds like Stravinsky—much to his credit.

The apparent contradictions in his writings on music happily do not transfer to his musical instinct and artistic intuition.

Though he is generally called a neoclassicist such categorization applies only tenuously. The classical forms involve (1) the tension or pull between tonalities, (2) the natural transition from one tonal center to another through harmonic progression, (3) the balance between suspense and resolution of tendency tones and rest tones (4) unified by the evolution, development or proliferation of basic thematic or rhythmic motives and figures. Stravinsky's music can hardly be considered to coincide with these elements of classic procedure. However, his music does have certain external similarities to classical sound (18th-century style) in that (1) it is not romantic in expression, (2) it is carefully calculated, controlled and ordered, (3) it has a textural clarity associated with classical thought. Classicism as referring to ancient Greece is evident in the choice of subjects of such works as *Oedipus Rex* (opera-oratorio, 1927), *Apollon Musagète* (ballet, 1928) and *Perséphone* (1934); but this is of course no reference to musical style.

EXAMPLE 133 (pages 383, 384)
Petroushka, Scene I

1. This work of 1911 offers a clear exemplification of pandiatonicism. The entire work consists of

378

a series of contrasting sections. Each section involves a characteristic dance rhythm and texture and is based usually on an ostinato pattern moving within a specific tonal orbit. The emphasis on Russian folk-music idioms shows its direct relationship to Mussorgsky, Examples 77, 80, 81 and 84.

2. There is little or no attempt to connect one idea or tonal block to another, each part is an independent, generally static entity. Themes representing the main characters of the ballet reappear from time to time to provide an element of continuity.

3. The ballet is in four large scenes. This example is taken from the dance at the close of the first scene.

4. M. 1-8 involve a repetitive melodic motive typical of the Russian folk-dance idiom, harmonized with parallel chord formations reminiscent of impressionism and placed in a series of V⁷-I progressions in C. Notice the free use of all the notes of the scale over V⁷.

5. M. 9-20 are an ostinato in G producing a sustained dominant effect. Notice the alternation between V⁹ and I $^6_4$ (with added tones) and avoidance of resolution to tonic.

6. The melodic component of m. 9-20 is a rhythmic patter on five notes having the effect of commotion rather than tonal direction.

7. The combination of the ostinato and this melodic patter in the upper staff produces an effect of much rhythmic activity but in a harmonic and tonal "dead center."

EXAMPLE 134 (page 384)
Petroushka, Scene IV

This and Examples 135-138 are all excerpted from the fourth scene.

1. Here a four-beat ostinato (bracketed) is superimposed in a six-beat meter. The ostinato (lower staff) involves octave doublings not shown in this reduction, which includes the essential harmony.

2. The ostinato is based on the dominant seventh chord on F♯ with diminished 5th (C♮) and contains two tritones: C-F♯ and A♯-E. Compare the harmonic effect of this with Example 77 from Mussorgsky.

3. This pattern carries on with the addition of voice doublings and additional melodic lines for nine measures, which lead after an additional two measures into the idea of Example 135.

EXAMPLE 135 (page 385)
Petroushka, Scene IV

1. Here the "white key" notes are used in pandiatonic freedom. Note the "mirroring" or contrary motion of the LH in relation to the RH. This "white key" pattern continues with some variation of contour

and range and with the addition of a new melodic idea for a total of twenty-two measures, using only the notes of the C scale throughout. It then alternates with another section in a new rhythmic and melodic pattern but still involving only the notes of the scale of C.

2. Chordal structures in parallel motion form a common device in impressionistic music. Could you argue that the intent and effect is different in this case, however?

EXAMPLE 136 (page 385)
Petroushka, Scene IV

1. These are the opening measures of this dance and define the tonal limits of the entire section. The addition of melodic fragments does not change this tonal color.

2. As in Example 133 (m. 9-20) the entire passage is poised motionlessly on the dominant.

EXAMPLE 137 (page 385)
Petroushka, Scene IV

1. Here again a "patter" melody weaves asymmetrically around five tones. The irregular rhythmic pattern and awkward interruption of the chords produce an intentionally burlesque effect.

2. Notice the diatonic character and the emphasis on fourths and fifths in the chords.

3. This type of material extends for seventeen measures and leads into Example 138.

EXAMPLE 138 (pages 386-389)
Petroushka, Scene IV

1. Here is pandiatonic pandemonium representing the commotion of a carnival of dancing.

2. The entire passage uses only the tones of the E♭ scale with a shift to diatonic A♭ toward the close of the example.

3. Compare the melody in Example 137 with the melody in the upper staff of this example.

4. Notice the variety of patterns—scale segments, quartal-type chords, arpeggios and trills—all based on the E♭ scale and used in a manner which is independent of chord or scale-tone function.

5. Identify the various lengths of the ostinato patterns by placing brackets over them. Note that the melody in the upper staff is also repeated.

6. This kind of writing is frequently found in the music of Eric Satie, for example, the ballets, *Parade* (1917), *Mercure* (1924) and *Relâche* (1924). Such music consisting of separated blocks of tonally immobile but highly rhythmic sound is associated with cubism in painting. This cubistic element is present throughout the works of Stravinsky, though less evident in the serial works which involve greater linearity.

Examples and Suggestions for Further Study
of the Music of Stravinsky

Limitation of space allows a discussion of only a few works selected from the great number and variety of Stravinsky's oeuvre.

In the music of many twentieth-century composers there is an emphasis on intellectualization of the composing process; there is much rationalization regarding how and why a piece came to be written; there is a seeking for erudition to be somehow associated with the subjects of musical works and their construction. Though such attitudes are not new in the world of music, their predominance would seem to imply that they are serving to fill a vacuum which was left when certain elements of musical lyricism, artistic necessity, sentiment, tonal organization and harmonic considerations became old fashioned.

This emphasis on organizational aspects over emotional effect is typical of Stravinsky and has been one of his greatest influences on younger composers. Stravinsky believes that order and discipline in the sonorous scheme take precedence over emotional elements.

Thus, Stravinsky has often applied specific features of other composers, other periods or other musical types as a basis for the tonal organization and instrumental color of his works. Yet his own musical individuality is always predominant in all his works. He believes that limiting himself to certain resources engenders creative freedom. Therefore, nearly every work is written for a different combination of instruments and/or voices so that the ensemble is unique to the particular kind and limits of expression with which each composition is concerned. The variety of media, forms, stylistic influences and subjects in Stravinsky's works is illustrated in the following representative list:

The Firebird (ballet, 1910) shows the influence of Russian nationalism and his teacher, Rimsky-Korsakov. This work and *Le Rossignol* (The Nightingale) (1914) also show the influence of French impressionism.

Petroushka (1911), *Rite of Spring* (1913) and *Les Noces* (The Wedding) (1923) are also for dance and are based on Russian subjects, but elements of Stravinsky's individuality—pandiatonicism, dissonant sonorities, primitive rhythmic drive, ostinati and static tonal blocks—are predominant.

Works involving themes of other composers are:

Pulcinella (ballet, 1919) based on themes of Pergolesi, but the harmonic, rhythmic and orchestral treatment are typical Stravinsky. A work of studied simplification involving elements of the "wrong note" style.

Mavra, opera buffa (1922) inspired by the style of Rossini.

The *Fairy's Kiss* (ballet, 1928) based on Tchaikovsky themes.

Four Norwegian Moods (1942) for orchestra based on Grieg themes.

It is natural that his interest in rhythm would have led him into brief encounters with the limited elements of ragtime and jazz in such works as *Ragtime* (1918) for eleven instruments and *Piano-Rag Music* (1919) and *Ebony Concerto* (1945) for dance band.

Elements of jazz appear in *L'Histoire du Soldat* (The Soldier's Story) (1918), the *Octet* (1923) for wind instruments and the *Capriccio* (1929) for piano and orchestra.

It is typical of Stravinsky to resurrect old forms or the names of old forms or types and apply them to his work. Reference to eighteenth-century Viennese classicism is implied in Symphony in C (1940), Symphony in Three Movements (1945) and the opera, *The Rake's Progress* (1951).

Baroque forms and texture are applied in the Piano Sonata (1924) and the Octet (1923), which includes a sinfonia, a set of variations and a variety of textures and rhythms ranging from Bach to Offenbach to jazz.

The use of contrapuntal textures and technics such as canon and fugue increases from 1923 on.

The Septet (1953) for three strings, three winds and piano is in three movements as follows:

I is sonata design.

II is a passacaglia involving a free type of serial organization and a pointillistic texture possibly influenced by Webern.

III is a gigue involving much fugal imitation. All three movements are based on a theme stated in the opening of I.

Sets of variations occur as movements in other larger works such as *Pulcinella*, the Octet, Concerto for Two Pianos (1935), *Jeu de Cartes* (Card Game) (ballet, 1936), *Danses Concertantes* (1942), Sonata for Two Pianos (1944), and the Ebony Concerto.

Several works involving voices are set to Latin texts. Latin, a language of ritual and convention, allows Stravinsky (and also Orff) to break the words into separate syllables and treat them as sounds independent of their literal meaning. This static, disconnected use of words is fitting for harmonically static, disconnected blocks of sound. In fact, in his opera-oratorio, *Oedipus Rex*, even the characterizations and staging maintain this static quality—the characters wear the Greek masks (static facial expression) and stand motionless (static tableau). Here Stravinsky invokes Hellenistic classicism.

The Symphony of Psalms (1930) for chorus and orchestra is generally considered one of Stravinsky's most effective works, possibly because the musical message prevails over the musical manner. The Latin text, the orchestra without violins and violas in which wind sound predominates, and the handling of part writing show Stravinsky in a Renaissance mood.

The Mass (1948) for chorus and double wind quintet recalls the Gothic style of Machaut. Here the aural effect of interweaving voices in imitation reminiscent of Gothic *Stimmtausch*, the narrow pitch range and busy rhythmic character is like the visual effect of ants crawling over one another in a narrow tunnel of an anthill.

As with Copland, Stravinsky's adoption of serial technic was inevitable and was predicted by Debussy as early as 1917. His interest in precise manipulation of materials and in essaying various forms and styles would naturally lead to the serial approach, the popular technic of mid-twentieth century. After all, the tone row has captivated most contemporary composers, and tracing tone rows has become the favorite indoor sport of music students.

Stravinsky gradually approached an extensive employment of serial technic through a series of works which partially involve serial organization. Even serially ordered works still bear the individuality of the Stravinsky sound because:

a. Static harmonic effects still pervade the texture;
b. ostinati and pedals are still present;
c. asymmetrical and polymetrical rhythmic organizations are still common;
d. themes outline harmonies, the rows themselves have harmonic and tonal implications, certain tones are emphasized to produce a sense of tonal center.

As usual, Stravinsky is not doctrinaire in his adherence to the serial system. In his Cantata (1952) for soprano and tenor soloists, women's chorus and small instrumental ensemble he applies the serial concept to an eleven-tone row which involves repetitions so that there are only six different tones. This work like many of his row-oriented works involves sections based on row organization alternating with interludes or ritornelli which are not serially organized.

The work is a seven-part setting of anonymous sixteenth-century poetry. Parts 1, 3, 5 and 7 are the same music set to a different stanza of the same poem. Parts 2 and 4 are vocal solos which Stravinsky calls Ricercare I and Ricercare II, a term applied to seventeenth- and eighteenth-century instrumental music. Part 6 is a vocal duet so that the seven parts have an ABACADA design. Only part 4 (C) is serially constructed.

The Septet (1953), already referred to, falls in the line of works leading finally to extensive utilization of serial technic.

In Memoriam Dylan Thomas (1954) for tenor, string quartet and four trombones is a serial work on a five-tone row and in three parts:

    I. Prelude, consisting of canonic passages alternating antiphonally between the four trombones and the string quartet.
    II. Setting of a Dylan Thomas poem for tenor with instrumental ritornelli before, between the lines of the poem and at the close.
    III. Postlude, consisting of the material of the Prelude presented in reverse order.

The arch design with a central focal point balanced on either side by formal elements in symmetrical relationship is found in greater or less degree in several of the later works such as the Cantata, the Septet, *In Memoriam* and *Canticum sacrum* (1956) for chorus, soloists and orchestra composed mostly of winds (no violins or cellos).

The latter is in five movements forming an arch design with V a *retrograde* version of I similar to *Ludus Tonalis* by Hindemith in which the Postludium is a *retrograde inversion* of the Preludium.

III, the central movement is the largest, and the relationship of materials presents an arch effect within the movement.

Thus, the general outward design is:

    I Chorus and orchestra
    II Tenor solo
    III Solos, chorus, orchestra (arch design)
    IV Baritone solo
    V Chorus and orchestra (retrograde of I)

Only the three middle movements are serially conceived—using twelve-tone rows—possibly Stravinsky's first use of a complete twelve-tone series.

Agon (ballet, 1954-1957) is a mixture of serial and nonserial writing and involves row segments of six, eight and twelve tones. The rows are typically arranged to provide harmonic implications and the usual interludes are present.

Threni (1958) for chorus and orchestra is based entirely on one twelve-tone row which is subjected to all kinds of modifications such as segmentation into four groups of three tones and change of order such as 1, 3, 5, 7, 9, 11, 12, 10, 8, 6, 4, 2 (again an arch effect) in addition to the conventional retrograde and inverted forms and transposed versions. Stravinsky's interest in the static, ritual element is seen in the fact that he even sets to music the Hebrew letters which identify the verses of text as they appear in the Vulgate Bible.

The Movements (1959) for piano and orchestra illustrate how Stravinsky has been able to assimilate certain outward characteristics of the serial styles of Webern, Boulez and Stockhausen. This is seen in the (a) pointillistic texture involving octave displacement over a wide range, (b) complex serial organization, (c) nonmetrical rhythmic quality, (d) emphasis on the tritone and an atonal sound, (e) brevity, abstruseness and compactness of form. The five movements separated by four interludes total only one hundred ninety-three measures. Thus, Stravinsky has aligned himself with some of the latest approaches to the organization of musical tones.

Elements common in these later serial compositions include:

a. Shorter forms;
b. use of arch design for groups of movements;
c. small binary and ternary forms within movements;
d. ritornelli and interludes used as binding and unifying elements;
e. pointillistic texture: octave displacement and brief entrances of instruments to play short, rhythmically complex figures;
f. emphasis on contrapuntal texture and devices but balanced by sustained pedals and by ostinati.

Suggested Written Assignments

1. Write a passage for piano (16 measures) according to the following specifications:

a. Use only the white keys;
b. Use 5/8 meter;
c. Write on three staves for three players at one piano;
d. The lower staff contains a four-beat ostinato bass pattern;
e. The middle staff consists of parallel triads or sevenths in a scalewise, six-beat pattern;
f. The upper staff is a single melodic line, of a range not to exceed a fifth, which repeats after eight measures.

2. Connect the previous passage to another passage with the same general texture but in a new scale, a new meter and with new ostinato patterns.
3. Write a short (32 measures) dance-type composition for four wind instruments and some percussion, using one of the dances from *L'Histoire du Soldat* as a model.
4. Analyze the last movement (III) of the Symphony of Psalms.

Bibliography

Lang, Paul Henry, *Stravinsky, A New Appraisal of His Work*, New York: W. W. Norton & Company, Inc., 1963.

Lederman, Minna, Ed., *Stravinsky in the Theatre*, New York: Pellegrini and Cudahy, 1949.

Mann, Theodore Henry, *Form and Tonality in the Late Music of Igor Stravinsky*, San Francisco State College Thesis, 1964.

Myers, Rollo, *Introduction to the Music of Stravinsky*, London: Dennis Dobson, 1950.

Stravinsky, Igor and Robert Kraft, *Conversations with Igor Stravinsky*, New York: Doubleday & Company, Inc., 1959.

Stravinsky, Igor, *Poetics of Music*, New York: Vintage Books, 1956.

Strobel, Heinrich, *Stravinsky: Classic Humanist*, New York: Merlin Press, 1955.

Tansman, Alexandre, *Igor Stravinsky*, New York: G. P. Putman's Sons, 1949.

Vlad, Roman, *Stravinsky*, London: Oxford University Press, 1960.

White, Eric, *Stravinsky: A Critical Survey*, New York: Philosophical Library, Inc., 1948.

EXAMPLE 133
Stravinsky
PETROUSHKA
SCENE I, RUSSIAN DANCE
(First 20 Measures)

EXAMPLE 134
Stravinsky
PETROUSHKA
SCENE IV, BEAR DANCE
(First 2 Measures)

EXAMPLE 135
STRAVINSKY
PETROUSHKA
SCENE IV, BEAR DANCE
(Measures 12-13)

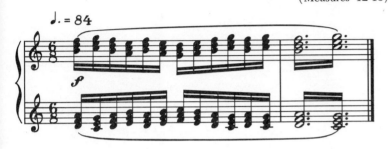

EXAMPLE 136
STRAVINSKY
PETROUSHKA
SCENE IV, DANCE OF THE COACHMEN AND GROOMS
(First 4 Measures)

EXAMPLE 137
STRAVINSKY
PETROUSHKA
SCENE IV, THE MASQUERADERS
(Measures 28-36)

EXAMPLE 138
STRAVINSKY
PETROUSHKA
SCENE IV, THE MASQUERADERS
(Measures 45-59)

CHAPTER 31

PAUL HINDEMITH

1895-1963

In contrast to Stravinsky's impersonal, ritualistic concept of music, Hindemith believed that music has a moralistic or ethical significance and power to humanize the individual and society, and that the composer has the high obligation of fulfilling the best potentials of the art. In his life and his compositions he consistently strove to exemplify his philosophy of the composer's role, his theories of composition and the meaning of music.

His philosophy of the role of music derives from Plato and Boethius, and his musical style descends from the music of the Reformation through Bach, Schumann, Brahms and Reger.

His mature style (excluding much of his music before 1930) may be characterized as neobaroque in texture, though, in addition to baroque forms, he often employs classic formal designs with modifications consistent with his tonal language. As with Bach his counterpoint is entirely directed by harmonic considerations organized around tonal centers. The concept of tonic in Hindemith applies to the gravitational center of all twelve notes of the chromatic scale and not just scales in the diatonic sense. Assuming C as tonic the other eleven tones are related to C according to the interval each tone forms with C in the following order: C →G, F, A, E, E♭, A♭, D, B♭, D♭, B, F♯. Thus, in his theory the intervals from simple to complex are involved in this order also: from perfect fifth, to perfect fourth, to thirds and sixths, to seconds and sevenths and finally the tritone. The tonalities of the twelve fugues in *Ludus Tonalis* follow this order, and Hindemith attaches symbolic significance to this order of tonal relationships in the song cycle, *Das Marienleben* (The Life of Mary) (1948).

He also evolved a theory of chord structures and relationships which is based on this order of tones and intervals and which takes into account all kinds of formations including quartal, polychordal and other combinations.

Thus, his music involves dissonant contrapuntal and harmonic texture founded on tonal centers which are manifested in clearly defined cadences to a triad, open fifth, unison or octave.

Chords with tritones or tones distantly related to tonic produce more tension than chords with the simpler intervals (perfect fourths and fifths) or with tones more closely related to tonic. Thus, most Hindemith cadences produce a strong effect of resolution from suspension or tension to release or conclusiveness.

His melodic lines and vertical structures are based strongly on perfect fourths and fifths. (See Examples 140-142.) Where there are frequent changes of harmony or tonal center these usually take place at the point of stepwise motion in the melody. (See the examples of Hindemith.) Cadences often involve stepwise approach by contrary motion to the final chord or tone as in the sixteenth-century *clausula vera*. (See Examples 140 and 141.)

In movements in sonata design the relationship between the key centers of the first and second themes is often a whole or half step. (See discussion of specific works.)

As in Bartók and later works of Stravinsky the arch design is frequently found. Hindemith employs this arch concept in a variety of ways:

1. In the opera *Hin und Zurück* (Here and Back) the order of dramatic events is reversed at the midpoint.
2. In some sonata movements, for example, in the Sonata for flute and piano (1936), the themes return in reverse order in the recapitulation.
3. In *Ludus Tonalis* the Postludium is an exact visual retrograde inversion of the Preludium.

Again, as in Bach, there is a quality of strong, forward, metrical flow in Hindemith's music and, at the same time, much diversity and interest in rhythmic patterns. He makes frequent use of 9/8 and 3/2 meters. This is in contrast to the novel asymmetrical or fragmentary rhythmic patterns found in much twentieth-century music.

Though his music often has a chromatic look because of frequent shifts of tonal center involving many accidentals, the emphasis on perfect intervals in the harmonic and melodic organization effects a diatonic aural quality. There is little melodic chromaticism but more of a modal quality in the linear components.

This music is the product of the application of a remarkable intellect to a specific system of composition, and it ranges from objective pieces written for practical purposes of instruction to works of universal appeal, works in which romantic expressiveness, classic order, baroque ebullience and renaissance imagery are fused to form an original, moving and ethically oriented style.

EXAMPLE 139 (page 397)
Symphony Mathis der Maler, I

The three movements of this symphony (suite) extracted from the opera, *Mathis der Maler* (Matthias, the painter) are named after three paintings by the hero of the opera, Matthias Grünewald (1460-1528). Hindemith's musical reference to these three paintings which Grünewald painted for the famous Isenheim altar at Colmar, Alsace, is symbolic rather than descriptive. The titles are:

I. *The Angelic Concert*
II. *The Entombment*
III. *The Temptation of St. Anthony*

The letters identifying tonality in Hindemith's music simply refer to the tone which is tonic and not to mode (such as major or minor) because the twelve tones of the chromatic scale are within the orbit of that tonic. Also, such letters indicate only the opening tonal center and do not imply a complete section with that tone as tonic.

1. The design of I is along sonata lines as follows:

Introduction opens in G and includes the quotation of a medieval religious song called "Three Angels Sang," stated three times, in F, A and D♭.

(Exposition) Theme 1 enters in G and is treated in contrapuntal imitation. This example quotes the first eight measures. Theme 2 enters in F♯ (note the half-step relationship). Theme 3

enters in G and could be considered a closing theme.

(Development) Themes 1 and 2 are treated in contrapuntal combination. This could be considered the development section.

(Recapitulation) The introduction tune returns in 3/2 meter combined with theme 2 in 2/2 meter. The former is again stated three times in the same tonalities but with the third statement in augmentation. Theme 1 returns in A♭. (Notice the half-step relationship to theme 1 originally.) Theme 3 returns in E♭.

The coda deals with theme 2 in G.

2. According to this analysis of the form of I is the arch design involved? What elements of symmetry do you find in this design?

3. The tonal center of this example is G. Play the example stopping on beat three of m. 5 then 6 then 7 playing G after each stop to confirm this.

4. Beginning with m. 8 there is a temporary shift toward C which is confirmed by resolution to the tones C and G in the next measure (not quoted).

5. Check this analysis with Hindemith's own analysis in his book, *The Craft of Musical Composition*, page 220, for points of disagreement. What do you think?

6. Examine both the vertical (harmonic) and horizontal (melodic) intervallic relationships in this example of four-voice texture. What intervals predominate at strong rhythmic points?

7. How do strong melodic points relate to the tonal center?

8. Transpose Hindemith's order of tonal relationship shown for a tonic of C on page 390 to G and then study the example in light of that order. Notice the shifting emphasis toward C in m. 8.

II of this work is a rather free abab song-form design. The second b part is much varied from the first b part.

III is in several sections and includes four main thematic ideas (ABCD) plus quotation of the old hymn *Lauda Sion Salvatorem* (Praise Zion That Shall Save Us). The design is as follows:

Introduction (m. 1-18). See m. 417-506.
Theme A (m. 19-86) includes eleven of the twelve tones of the chromatic scale.
Theme B (m. 87-130). Note the string patterns based melodically on perfect fourths which are repeated somewhat like ostinati.

Theme C (m. 131-183).

Theme D (m. 184-223).

Theme C varied (m. 224-294).

Theme D varied (m. 295-363).

Theme A (m. 364-394) in the original tonality but rhythmically altered.

Coda in three sections. The first section is a fugato (m. 395-454). The first three entrances of the subject have the same intervallic relationship, successive fifths, as in the exposition of the Fugue, IV, of the Third Sonata for Piano (1936). The second section includes the hymn quotation combined with continuation of the fugato material plus a four-measure ostinato melody from the introduction in the horns (m. 455-506). The third section is a closing chorale-fanfare which Hindemith titles *Alleluia* (m. 507-523).

EXAMPLE 140 (page 397)
First Piano Sonata, I

Hindemith wrote three piano sonatas in 1936. The first one is in five movements in the following general design:

I is an exposition of two themes: the first in A, the second in E. This example quotes the first ten measures and Example 141 quotes the last thirteen measures of this movement.

II is the slow movement, a march in ABA rondo form.

III is an elaborate movement combining elements of scherzo and trio with a sonata-type development.

IV is a recapitulation of the themes of I in reverse order, theme 2 in D followed by theme 1 in D. The final cadence (last five measures) of both I and IV are exactly the same.

V is a long rondo design, ABCDBA coda. Notice the arch-form element. The material of sections C and D is somewhat related to A and B. Also the material at the close of the first appearance of B is recalled in the close of the movement. What design is implied by these elements?

1. This example (the first 10 measures of I) comprises the first statement of theme 1. An extended restatement of the theme opening and closing in A covers m. 11-22.

2. Notice that the first statement closes on D♯ (m. 10), the most distantly related tone from A, the interval of a tritone away.

3. The 10 measures fall into a melodic and harmonic pattern of $2 + 2 + 2 + 4$ measures.

4. Analyze the voice movement at cadence points. What kind of sound is the final vertical formation of each cadence? What is the tonal center at each cadence?

5. Does Hindemith apply his order of tonal relationships in building tension as the period progresses?

6. What are the most common melodic intervals? What type of chord formation appears most frequently?

EXAMPLE 141 (page 398)
First Piano Sonata, I

1. The last thirteen measures of I illustrate Hindemith's approach to a final cadence, from the tension of distant and dissonant tonal relationships to the utter repose of a major triad.

2. The thirteen measures consist of a $4 + 4 + 5$ design. IV closes with the same thirteen-measure design, the last five measures being exactly the same.

3. In the last three measures notice the contrary motion in the outer voices leading to the cadence. Compare Hindemith's voice leading in this example to the Vaughan Williams Example 117. Note the harmonic, melodic and cadential similarities of the two styles.

4. Apply Hindemith's order of tonal relationships in a comparison of the tonality of cadence points with the final tonal center.

5. Note the chords outlined by the melody in m. 2, 6 and 10.

EXAMPLE 142 (page 398)
Piano Duet Sonata, I

This Piano Duet Sonata (1938) and the Sonata for two pianos (1942) are probably Hindemith's best-known piano works.

1. The first movement is in sonata form. The exposition consists of theme 1 in E and theme 2 in C. The development is short and devoted primarily to a treatment of theme 2. This example quotes the first eight measures of theme 2 at its entrance in the development section. The recapitulation consists of the return of themes 1 and 2 both in E. A five-measure extension of the final cadence closes the movement.

2. The first seven measures of the upper voice of this example (to the end of the 8va) is a restatement of theme 2 one step higher than its first appearance in the exposition and with a slight rhythmic change in m. 2.

3. Try to identify nonharmonic tones in this example as opposed to the basic harmonies.

4. Identify shifts of tonal center. What tone is tonic in m. 1 and in m. 7?

5. Compare the chord formations in this example with those in the previous Hindemith examples.

6. The line in the lower staff of m. 7-8 (bracketed) refers to the second part of theme 2.

II is a humorous scherzo involving ingenious syncopations. It is in song form and trio design. The song form returns beginning with part b, and the movement closes with a recalling of the close of the trio.

III is in three sections: a fugato involving several motives, a contrasting, more homophonic, middle section based on one of the fugal motives, and a return of the fugato with a new counter-motive and changed order of presentation of materials. The first idea is last to return, a hint of the arch design.

Examples and Suggestions for Further Study of the Music of Hindemith

A sampling of the many works of Hindemith will provide a rather comprehensive insight into his style. Evidence of his practical utilitarian attitude toward the composer's responsibility lies in the types of pieces and titles he gave them.

a. He wrote a sonata and/or concerto for nearly every orchestral instrument.

b. For groups of pieces he used titles such as *Tafelmusik* (table music, a term used by Teleman), *Abendkonzert* (evening concert), *Morgenmusik* (morning music), *Trauermusik* (funeral music), *Kammermusik* (chamber music), which includes pieces for all kinds of instrumental groups, and *Tanzstücke* (dance pieces).

His interest in symbolism and philosophical speculation is manifested in many works such as *Mathis der Maler* and *Das Marienleben*, already cited, and the symphony, *Die Harmonie der Welt* (1951), which was expanded into an opera by the same name in 1957. This symphony, *The Harmony of the Universe* (as well as the later opera), is inspired by the life of Johannes Kepler (1571-1630), the German astronomer, and the three movements are named after the three aesthetics discussed by Boethius (c. 474-525) in his treatise *De Institutione Musica* as follows:

    I. *Musica Instrumentalis*
    II. *Musica Humana*
    III. *Musica Mundana*

Hindemith's formal designs are usually very clearly delineated because:

a. Sections are clearly defined by cadences;

b. Each theme (usually the equivalent of a period) is immediately repeated after it is first introduced;

c. The contrapuntal nature of the texture and the subsequent use of imitation provide frequent hearings of a given theme.

Both classic and baroque forms are found in multi-movement works.

In sonata movements and rondo movements the key relationship between themes is often a half step or whole step, for example, the second theme may appear a half step below tonic in the exposition and a half step above tonic in the recapitulation. Also, the arch form concept is often employed to a greater or lesser degree in that some themes may be presented in reverse order on their return. The cyclic design is found in works such as *Ludus Tonalis*, Third Sonata for Piano, *Symphonia Serena* (1946) and *Apparebit Repentina Dies* (1947) for chorus and brass.

Baroque forms such as fugue, passacaglia and concerto grosso are frequently used. In fugal expositions the successive entrances of the subject (answer) are usually a fifth above (e.g., C G D) or a fifth below (e.g., C F B♭) the previous entrance. A fourth entrance will be on the tone of a previous entrance, however.

other keyboard sonatas

The Second Sonata for Piano (1936) is in three movements:

I is a sonata. Themes 1 and 2 are in G and F and return in G and C respectively. Theme 2 soon moves to G for the close of the movement.

II is similar to a five-part song form (abaca).

III consists of a slow introduction followed by a rondo: ABACA. The theme of section C is derived from the theme of A. The A theme is similar to a three-part song form.

The Third Sonata for Piano (1936) is in four movements:

I is a sonata with arch design and half-step relationship between themes as follows: Theme 1 in B♭, 2 in A, development, theme 2 in B, 1 in B♭. This effect of polarity in which the second theme appears an equal distance on either side of theme 1 is rather common in Hindemith.

II is a scherzo and trio form.

III is an ABA rondo form. Section B is a fugato which reappears in IV as the second subject of a large double fugue. In IV the exposition of the first subject consists of entrances on B♭, F and C. Both subjects are treated together in the final section of the fugue.

The Sonata for Two Pianos (1942) is an unusual five-movement work:

I is titled *Chimes* and exploits piano resonance.

II is an arch-form sonata with a fugue for the development:

> Exposition—Theme 1 in C, theme 2 in A.
>
> Development—a four-voice fugue on theme 1 with the voices entering on F, E, F♯ and F, another example of tonal polarity.
>
> Recapitulation—Theme 2 in G, theme 1 in C.

III is a double canon in which the two voices of the first piano are strictly imitated by the second piano one measure behind and one octave lower.

IV is called a recitative, referring to an anonymous medieval poem inscribed at the beginning.

V is a large, triple fugue.

The sonata, no. 1 for organ (1937) is in baroque formal design throughout. There are two movements employing the elements of fugue and free fantasia. The second and third organ sonatas should be analyzed as interesting formal designs.

sonatas for orchestral instruments

The following sonatas for solo instruments with piano exhibit arch form and/or polarity of key relationships between themes.

Two sonatas for violin and piano illustrate these points. Both I and II of the Sonata for Violin and Piano (1935) are examples. In I, themes 1 and 2 first appear in E and E♭ and reappear in reverse order in the recapitulation, 2 in F and 1 in E. In II themes 1 and 2 appear in E and E♭ and return reversed, theme 2 in F and theme 1 in E.

The Sonata in C for Violin and Piano (1939) is in three movements:

I is a sonata in arch form. Themes 1 and 2 are introduced in C and B♭ and return in reverse order, theme 2 in D and 1 in C, exhibiting whole-step relationship compared to half-step relationship in the previous work.

II is a lively movement in 5/8 meter preceded and followed by a slow section:

Section:	Slow	A	B	C	A	C	B	Slow
Tonality:	E	E♭	E	F♯	G	C	F	E

III is a triple fugue. In the exposition of the first subject the voices enter on C, B♭, A, G. The third subject is treated in contrary motion prior to the combining of all three subjects in the final section.

In I of the Sonata for Flute and Piano (1936) themes 1 and 2 first appear in B♭ and G♯ and return in C and B♭.

In the Sonata for Viola and Piano (1940) themes 1 and 2 first appear in F and E and return in F♯ and E.

The Sonata for Oboe and Piano is in two movements.

I is a sonata with episode replacing development as follows:

Theme:	1	2	3	4	(Episode)	2	1	3
Tonality:	G	F♯	E		Fugato	A♭	G	G

II combines slow movement and finale in the following design involving baroque contrapuntal treatment of material:

	A	Slow
Lively	B	Derived from A
	C	Reminiscent of I
	D	
	E	
	A	Slow
Lively	B	Fugato
	E	
	D	

concertos

Three representative examples of Hindemith's several concertos for solo instruments with orchestra are the Cello Concerto, no. 2 (1940), the Piano Concerto (1945), and *Der Schwanendreher* (viola concerto, 1935).

The Cello Concerto is in three movements:

I is based on three themes treated in the following sequence:

> 1, 2, 3, closing theme, development of 2, cadenza dealing with all three themes, recapitulation of themes 3, 1 and closing theme.

II again combines the elements of slow movement and scherzo in an unusual design consisting of three large sections:

Section 1 is in 9/8 meter, andante and consists of two statements of theme A.

Section 2 is in 9/8 meter also but molto vivace, three times as fast as the previous tempo. Two themes, B and C, are stated in various ways in alternation (BCBCB).

Section 3 consists of the continuation of themes B and C in the solo cello at the same tempo (molto vivace) against theme A stated in the orchestra in its original tempo. Thus, three measures of 9/8 in the cello's tempo equal one measure of 9/8 in the orchestra's tempo.

III is a march with trio (ABA form). The A section includes three themes.

The Piano Concerto is in three movements:

I is a sonata with arch design.

II is a sonata.

III is a medley in five sections: canzona, march, valse lente, caprice and *tre fontane* (medieval dance). Each is a characteristic treatment (variation) on the same tune.

Der Schwanendreher (1935), "The Swan-turner," is a concerto for viola and small orchestra consisting of cellos, double basses, winds and tympani. It is in three movements and based on renaissance folk songs of Germany. III is a set of seven variations on a mocking song about the man who turns swans on a spit in the kitchen and from which the work gets its name. This work is a good example of Hindemith's treatment of folk tunes.

Hindemith's application of concerto grosso style is found in such works as Concert Music for Brasses and Strings (1930), Concerto for Woodwinds, Harp and Orchestra (1949), Concerto for Orchestra (1925) and Philharmonic Concerto (1932) (theme and six variations for orchestra).

Hindemith wrote three ballet scores, two of which are *Nobilissima Visione* (1937, on St. Francis of Assisi), and *The Four Temperaments* (1944, a theme and four variations for piano and strings).

The orchestral suite (1938) from the former ballet is in three movements.

I Introduction and Rondo
II March and Pastorale
III Passacaglia

The third part of the cantata for chorus and brass, *Apparebit Repentina Dies*, "The Day of Repentance Appears" (1947), is a passacaglia. The introductory motive of part one reappears in part four in cyclic fashion.

Besides the concertos for orchestra and symphonies based on operas, Hindemith wrote a Symphony for Concert Band (1951), a Symphony in E♭ (1940) and *Symphonia Serena* (1946).

The latter work is Hindemith at his best. A variety of moods, forms and styles are displayed in its four movements.

I is a sonata with the themes returning in reverse order. The development is devoted to theme 1 and involves canonic treatment. The return of theme 2 is orchestrated with colorful use of percussion.

II is a march with contrasting trio (ABA) based on a Beethoven theme. It is scored for winds and percussion only.

III is for strings alone. It consists of three sections:

Section one is a piece for strings arco.
A violin cadenza echoed by an off-stage violin connects section one to two.
Section two is a piece for pizzicato strings.
A viola cadenza is echoed by an off-stage viola (in the opposite wings).
The two violas and two violins of the previous cadenza join at the close of this interlude and lead to section three.
Section three consists of sections one and two played together.
This movement is comparable to II of the Cello Concerto, no. 2 and also to the String Quartets, nos. 14 and 15, of Milhaud which are written to be played first as independent works and then together as an Octet.

IV is a sonata with theme 1 of I being recalled in the development section. The movement opens and closes with a short fanfare.

Another large orchestral work which contains the traditional Hindemith optimism, joy and vitality is *Symphonic Metamorphoses* on themes by von Weber (1943). It is a brilliant work in four parts, displaying great virtuosity.

Among his many chamber works which include six string quartets is an early suite for woodwind quintet called *Kleine Kammermusik* (Little Chamber Music) (1922). This along with a Piano Suite, 1922 (based on jazz idioms) is representative of Hindemith's early works. It is clever, satirical, brash music typical of much that was written in the early 1920s.

The witty character in this music is found throughout Hindemith's works. The third of the five short movements involves an ingenious two-measure ostinato in three instruments, serving as accompaniment to the melody in the other instruments.

Though Hindemith's harmonic theory does not admit the concept of polytonality there are nevertheless many passages in his music involving simultaneous melodies or harmonic strata in the orbits of two different tonalities. A few of many examples of this polytonal counterpoint are:

a. String Quartet, no. 3 at the beginning of III.
b. Symphony in E♭ in III.
c. Piano Duet Sonata in II.
d. Kleine Kammermusik.

Polymetric effects are also frequent as in the (First) Concerto for Piano and Twelve Solo Instruments, op. 36, no. 1 (*Kammermusik* No. 2) (1924) in which 3/8 and 4/4 occur simultaneously, in the Cello Concerto, no. 2, II, already cited, and in *Mathis der Maler*, I, where 3/2 appears against 2/2.

Suggested Written Assignments

1. Write a three-voice fugal exposition with entrances on C, G and A, using a theme in Hindemith style beginning with two ascending fourths.
2. Analyze IV, the basso ostinato movement, of the Concerto for Orchestra or one of the passacaglia movements of Hindemith for an understanding of his technic of writing variations over a ground.
3. Analyze the trio of II of the Piano Duet Sonata for block harmonic writing and compose a short piece (24 measures) in similar texture.
4. Analyze the fugal writing in a choral work such as *When Lilacs Last in the Dooryard Bloomed* (1946) or *Apparebit Repentina Dies*. Note the entrance intervals, the countersubjects, treatment of episodes and stretto effects.
5. *Ludus Tonalis* (Tonal Diversions) is a handy compendium of Hindemith's fugal technics. A careful study of the various contrapuntal devices employed in these twelve fugues as well as other fugues such as the double and triple fugues already cited will provide an understanding of an important twentieth-century linear style.
6. For insight into Hindemith's handling of unaccompanied voices analyze his *Six Chansons* (1943).

Bibliography

Hindemith, Paul, *A Composer's World*, Cambridge: Harvard University Press, 1952.

————, *The Craft of Musical Composition* vol. I, New York: Associated Music Publishers, 1942.

Landau, Victor, *The Harmonic Theories of Paul Hindemith*, Ann Arbor: University of Michigan Press, 1958.

Strobel, Heinrich, *Paul Hindemith*, Mainz: Schott, 1948.

EXAMPLE 139
HINDEMITH
SYMPHONY MATHIS DER MALER
I. ANGELIC CONCERT
(Measures 39-46)

EXAMPLE 140
HINDEMITH
FIRST PIANO SONATA
I
(First 10 Measures)

EXAMPLE 141
HINDEMITH
FIRST PIANO SONATA
I
(Last 13 Measures)

Copyright 1936 by B. Schott's Söhne, Mainz. Renewed 1963. Used by permission.

EXAMPLE 142
HINDEMITH
PIANO DUET SONATA
I
(Measures 91-98)

Copyright 1939 by B. Schott's Söhne, Mainz. Used by permission of Associated Music Publishers, Inc., sole U.S. agents.

CHAPTER 32

BÉLA BARTÓK

1881-1945

Bartók is probably the most important nationalist composer of the twentieth century. He succeeded in fusing eastern (Central European) melody and rhythm with western technics. He adopted the modal melodies, *parlando rubato* rhythms and primitive drive of ancient Finno-Ungrian and Turkish-Tartar folk music to the tonal organization of West European musical culture; that is, he combined the elements of primitive Hungarian, Rumanian, Bulgarian, Slovakian, Arabian and Turkish folk music with the contrapuntal tradition of the late baroque, the classical forms of thematic development and the twentieth-century concept of nonfunctional harmony.

Like Mussorgsky with Russian folk-music elements and Vaughan Williams with English folk songs, Bartók brought back to life the indigenous music of his people. He did not, however, simply force this eastern musical language into the traditional shapes and tonalities of western music, nor did he simply dress borrowed folk songs in western garb. Instead, as a result of his vast and pioneering research in ethnomusicology, he was able to fuse the spirit of this primitive folk music with the stream of western musical evolution and by a process of musical syncretism to develop a highly personal and original style. (It should be understood that the true Hungarian and Central European folk music referred to here has little relationship to the gypsy melodies which Liszt and Brahms used under the name Hungarian.)

General aspects of his music are outlined as follows:

MELODY:

1. Modes, gapped and artificial scales, especially those scales which emphasize the tritone such as Lydian (augmented fourth from 1 to 4) and Locrian (diminished fifth from 1 to 5). This emphasis on the tritone is part of the Asiatic influence in Hungarian (Magyar) folk melody. (Example 147)
2. Melodic motives and themes which consist of small intervals moving about a central tone (e.g. G♯ B♭ A) or chromatic figures combined with whole steps. See the String Quartet, no. 4, I, principal motive, or the fugue theme of Music for Strings, Percussion and Celesta, I.
3. Use of devices. Melodic forms governed by arbitrary tonal pattern or even visual pattern. (Example 143)
4. Use of short motives or figures tossed about in a nonthematic manner for the effect of mood or color.
5. Use of the usual contrapuntal manipulations such as contrary motion.
6. Occasional use of the twelve tones of the chromatic scale in a theme. (Example 143)
7. Pounding repetitions of a tone or alternation between two tones is a frequent melodic feature.

RHYTHM:

1. The constantly shifting rhythms, asymmetrical meters, rubatos and hesitations of Hungarian folk music are reflected in much of Bartók's music particularly that based strongly on folk themes. (Example 146)
2. Primitive driving rhythms of folk dances as in *Allegro Barbaro* or Examples 148-149.
3. Improvisational or rhapsodic passages which are almost nonrhythmic or at least nonmetrical for the sake of emphasis on timbre are contrasted to the savage, percussive rhythms as in Rumanian Dance, no. 1, op. 8a (See Example 148) or III of Music for Strings, Percussian and Celesta.
4. Use of asymmetrical combinations such as dividing 10/8 meter into $3 + 2 + 2 + 3$ or 9/8 into $4 + 2 + 3$ (eighth notes).

5. The rhythms, inflections and accentuation of the Hungarian language are reflected in Bartók's rhythmic style.

HARMONY:

1. Harmonization of melodies by parallel chord structures, for example, all sevenths or all quartal chords. (Example 146)
2. Doubling melodies in sevenths, seconds, fifths or some other specific interval. See Concerto for Orchestra, II.
3. Chord clusters, complex dissonance, arbitrary harmonic clashes resulting from pursuit of a preconceived pattern. The element of device or artifice is strong in Bartók's music. Though there is much manipulation of melodic, harmonic and rhythmic patterns, the musical result seldom seems sacrificed.
4. Nonfunctional use of chords and use of polytonal sonorities.
5. Characteristic melodic intervals are also emphasized in chord structure, that is, tritones, diminished thirds, minor ninths, diminished octaves and major sevenths (equivalent of minor seconds).
6. Chords evolved from simultaneous use of major and minor triads.

TONALITY:

1. Bartók's music is tonal in the sense that certain tones through repetition or other emphasis form points of reference around which the music is organized. Again, because Bartók, like Hindemith, makes free use of the twelve tones around a single tone as center, capital letters will refer to that tone without implying a specific mode. Major, minor or modality will be specifically indicated where intended.
2. The tritone relationship between tonal centers is frequent. (Example 143)
3. Many early and late works are more tonal in the traditional sense than works of the middle years, the 1920s and 30s. Like Hindemith, Schoenberg, Prokofiev and others, Bartók wrote in an extremely harsh, complex and uncompromisingly astringent style in his middle years but returned to a mellower, more universal and less radical expression in his late works.

FORM:

1. Classical formal designs are most frequent: sonata, rondo, scherzo and trio. There is clear demarcation between formal sections. It should be understood that Bartók uses the sonata design, for example, only as a framework on which to hang thematic material. The classic sonata form was based on major-minor tonality which does not exist in the Bartók sense of tonality. In other words, Bartók superimposes a different tonal organization on the old framework of the sonata deprived of the dynamism of functional harmony.
2. Use of arch design in regard both to relationship of themes within movements and to relationship of movements as a group.
3. Cyclic principle sometimes employed through use of motto themes.
4. Development of trenchant rhythmic and/or melodic motives in the tradition of the Viennese classic school, especially Beethoven. His formal designs and style of thematic development should make Bartók a neoclassicist, but this term is not customarily applied to him, perhaps because the term itself is too limited by its rather exclusive application to the styles influenced by Stravinsky.

Actually Bartók uses a great variety of tonal resources to encompass in his music a wide range of moods, from savage emotion to tender nostalgia, from brutal irony to humorous parody. Complex nontonal contrapuntal textures, especially canonic imitations, are placed beside simple homophonic settings. Passages of rapid harmonic change and vigorous rhythmic character are juxtaposed with static scenes in which instrumental color predominates over a harmonically progressionless and rhythmically motionless texture. His imaginative use of instrumental color and particularly his virtuoso writing for percussion, strings and piano contributed a variety of new possibilities and technics in writing for these instruments.

Because of the common element of Asiatic influence in both Russian and Hungarian folk music and because of their contemporaneity one can find certain similarities in the music of Prokofiev, Stravinsky and Bartók. Compare the melodic lines of Prokofiev's middle period (Second Piano Concerto) with the melodies of Bartók's middle period (Violin and Piano Sonatas), or compare Russian inspired works of Stravinsky with Bartók works in which rhythm is the prominent element. Though there was little direct influence between Bartók and the two Russians, yet the interest of all three in primitive resources produced some similar results.

Bartók's position as a piano virtuoso and piano teacher for most of his life is reflected in his many works for the instrument written throughout his career. His *Mikrokosmos* (1937), a six-volume set of graded piano pieces, is not only an encyclopedia of pianistic technics but also a compendium of twentieth-century compositional devices epitomizing particularly Bartók's own approaches to composing. It is probably this century's most important single contribution to the pedagogy of contemporary piano technic and musical device.

EXAMPLE 143 (pages 409, 410)
Fourteen Bagatelles, Op. 6, II

There are many collections of short piano pieces which illustrate Bartók's treatment of folk tunes and exemplify in a simple manner various tonal, rhythmic, melodic and harmonic characteristics of his style.

The Fourteen Bagatelles, op. 6 (1908), constitute an early display of Bartók's individuality. These fourteen short piano pieces exemplify various Bartók idioms which he develops throughout his oeuvre.

I illustrates duotonality: The RH is in four sharps, the LH in four flats.

II (this example) illustrates the following:

1. The major second ostinato. Major and minor seconds find frequent emphasis in both melody and harmony.
2. Typical melodic device. Notice the device in m. 3-5 of alternating tones on either side of the ostinato, ascending by half steps above and descending by half steps below, to include by this half-step expansion all the twelve tones of the octave.
3. Considering the ending of the piece, m. 24-30, the tonal center would appear to be Db both in the last seven measures and the first six measures. In that case the tonal center of m. 17-20 would be G. Thus, the three statements of this melodic pattern would be in Db, G and Db, a tritone relationship and regularly exploited by Bartók.
4. The two augmented triads outlined in the arpeggio of m. 7 (brackets) form a tonal progression to eb minor (m. 8). How would you analyze this harmonic progression?
5. Notice the modulatory quality of m. 9-10 and the duotonal effect between the RH and LH in m. 10. The use of scale segments as in m. 10 is typical.
6. What is the tonal center of m. 11-14?
7. Note the repetition of rhythmic and melodic figures in m. 11-14. Of what kind of music is this repetition characteristic?
8. M. 15-16 are modulatory. Compare to m. 9-10.

III is devoted to a chromatic ostinato as background for a melody emphasizing ♯4 of the scale.

EXAMPLE 144 (page 411)
Fourteen Bagatelles, Op. 6, IV

IV is a rather straightforward transcription of a folk song.

1. Notice that the first phrase is first harmonized by triads, then on its repetition by parallel sevenths in the LH, which form an occasional ninth with the RH tones.
2. The modal quality is evident throughout, but it is important to observe the G♯ in m. 8 and 12. This ♯4 of the scale is typical of Hungarian folk music and an outstanding melodic tone in the Bartók style.
3. What is the mode? Explain the voice leading of the G♯-F♯ in m. 8 and 12. Does this sound like other national folk music in tonality, in melodic line and/or in form?

V is a Slovakian folk song against repeated chords in a traditional tonal (modal) setting reminiscent of Mussorgsky, Example 84.

VI through IX should be analyzed for their characteristic tonal and rhythmic devices.

EXAMPLE 145 (pages 411, 412)
Fourteen Bagatelles, Op 6, X

X consists of a series of patterns or devices such as a specific, single harmonic formation in parallel motion, an ostinato pattern or a melodic figuration. The first twenty-two measures quoted here show four of these patterns:

1. In m. 1-5 the interval of a minor ninth is exploited in parallel motion in the outer voices and the inner two voices move in minor thirds. Exceptions are the two major ninths in m. 4.
2. In m. 5-7 augmented triads in the RH form minor-major seventh chords with the LH tones.
3. In m. 10-14 the chords are all formed from the six tones of the whole-tone scale (whole-tone dominants).
4. In m. 15-22 the ubiquitous tritone, bitonality and ♯4 appear over ostinato figures.
5. The first thirteen measures are unified mainly by the rhythmic figure, ♪ ♩ ♪ .
6. What is the effect of m. 8-9?
7. The last eight measures contain four characteristic features of Bartók:

    a. The ostinato on a perfect fifth, probably influenced by Hungarian bagpipe music;

    b. the diminished octave and tritone in the RH figure of m. 17-18;

    c. the bitonality of F♯ major against C in m. 19;

    d. the D♮ which is ♯4 against the Ab triad in m. 20-22.

8. Another characteristic melodic figure is the falling fourth preceded by a rising half step which is repeated sequentially in m. 3-4. See Music for Strings, Percussion and Celesta, IV, m. 210-230 and m. 262-270 as well as elsewhere for other examples of this figure.

9. This piece continues with a series of other sections exploiting specific devices combined with some of the melodic material already introduced in the first twenty-two measures.

EXAMPLE 146 (pages 412-414)
Fourteen Bagatelles, Op. 6, XI

1. This piece deals with two themes in an aba design.
2. Again, the tonal character is based on devices:

   a. Parallel quartal harmonies in the RH of m. 1-17, part a;

   b. manipulation of a four-note figure by rhythmic and intervallic modification and by change of harmonization, m. 30-60, part b.

3. A feature of this piece is the unusual rhythmic character. The effect of rubato is written in by the rests over the bar lines, indicating the length of pause between specific measures, and by the frequent accelerations, retardations and sudden tempo changes indicated. A spasmodic improvisatory effect is created by these constant hinderances to an even metrical flow. Again this rhythmic character is typical of some of the folk idioms which influenced Bartók. The composer indicates that sostenuto means a sudden retardation.

4. M. 19-33 constitute a transition from part a (m. 1-18) to part b (m. 34-60). Notice how the four-note melodic figure of part b is anticipated in m. 30-32.

5. In part b a variety of chord formations are used as punctuating harmony under the RH line.

6. Part a is restated in modified form beginning at m. 61.

7. Notice the typical scale formations of unrelated segments in m. 25-28 and the device of parallel major thirds in m. 20-25.

XII is one of those Bartók pieces in which fleeting melodic figures and static harmonies float in an improvisatory, almost rhythmless format.

XIII is a doleful melody over an ostinato consisting of the eb minor triad, then of the a minor triad, then of an alternation between the two, again illustrating the tritone relationship.

XIV is a whimsical waltz, a parody.

EXAMPLE 147 (pages 414, 415)
Sketches, Op. 9, V

The Sketches, op. 9, (seven short piano pieces, 1910) are harmonically less daring than the Bagatelles.

1. V displays two characteristics of Rumanian folk song:

   a. Pentatonic scale, B Mixolydian with two and six of the scale missing.

   b. constant repetition of melodic figures, the three predominant melodic figures throughout being those of m. 1, 2, and 3.

2. Bartók provides a variety of harmonies to go with these melodic figures. In m. 19 he uses the F major triad, a tritone from B.

3. Notice in the final cadence the D♮ to D♯, a minor-major effect.

4. Compare the repetitions and modal aspects of this melody with Example 148 and with the Mussorgsky and Stravinsky examples.

EXAMPLE 148 (pages 415-418)
Rumanian Dances, Op. 8a, I

The first of the Two Rumanian Dances, op. 8a (1910) is one of Bartók's most popular piano solos.

1. This is one of those frenzied, barbaric dances consisting of a rhythmic, melodic idea carried through a series of repetitions and modifications accompanied by gradually increasing tonal and rhythmic intensity and harmonic weight. It is the relentless drive of one idea which accumulates density on its way toward a climax. This effect is directly comparable to Example 84 of Mussorgsky.

2. The principal theme is a four-measure phrase consisting of two motives, each repeated, thus: 1,1, 2,2 (m. 3-6). Recall that this kind of phrase is often found in the music of Mussorgsky, Debussy, Ravel and Stravinsky.

3. These motives are modified in a variety of ways: by free melodic inversion of figures, many different harmonizations, expansion and contraction of intervals and by fragmentation and elaboration of small figures. Also in the central section of the work (not quoted but occurring between this excerpt and Example 149) the motives are treated in a completely contrasting mood, a mood in which the rhythmic drive is interrupted by a sonorous improvisation, after which the rhythmic drive resumes.

4. Each statement of the theme usually consists of the four-measure phrase repeated. Each statement is connected by a transition or extension based once on the ostinato figure (m. 11) and every other time on the rhythmic-melodic figure of the first and/or last beat of m. 3; thus: introduction (m. 1-2), theme in C (m. 3-10), transition (m. 11), theme alternating between E♭ and G♭ (m. 12-19), transition (m. 20-25), theme alternating between E♭ and C (m. 26-33), extension (m. 34-36), theme in C♯ (m. 37-40), in E (m. 41-44), transition (m. 45-50), second motive of theme in C (m. 51-52), extension (m. 53) and transition (m. 54-59), second motive in C (m. 60-61), extension (m. 62-63).

5. Compare the transition, m. 45-50 with the transition in m. 54-59. How are they alike? How do they differ?

6. Notice in the original version (m. 3-6) of the theme the ♯4 (F♯) and the alternation between ♭2 and ♮2. With what mode does such a melodic idea seem most nearly related?

7. Notice the free inversion (contrary motion) of the thematic figures in the version at m. 12-19. Why A♭♭ and F♭ in m. 14-15? Why not G and E?

8. In m. 22-25 the prolongation of the B E F♯ figure builds suspense for the brilliant resolution to B♭ E♭ G at m. 26.

9. In m. 26-27 the E♭ tonality gives the melody a Mixolydian character. Notice that Bartók exploits the diminished third B♮-D♭ on the last beat of m. 27, 28 and 31 where the resolution is to C. What is the last chord in each measure of m. 26-33?

10. In m. 37-44 the theme is modified so that it begins on one instead of three or five of the scale. Notice the emphasis on the minor seventh of the scale both in the melody and harmony of this passage. What modes are most strongly indicated here?

11. The transitions at m. 45-50 and m. 54-59 are good examples of Bartók's free use and mixture of scale inflections derived from eastern folk melody.

12. M. 51-52 and m. 60-61 illustrate still further imaginative harmonic treatments of the second motive of the theme. Analyze the harmonic and tonal formations of these measures. Notice the diminished third again in m. 60-61.

EXAMPLE 149 (pages 419-421)
Rumanian Dances, Op. 8a, I

After the contrasting middle section (m. 64-75), the rhythmic drive resumes.

1. The section from m. 76 through 96 is in the nature of a development section because the tonal center shifts more often, every one or two measures, and the theme is much more greatly modified by change of contour, interval expansion and fragmentation.

2. In this section (m. 76-96) the thematic statements are pairs of measures consisting of one thematic motive repeated, thus: first motive in E (m. 76-77), first motive in G (m. 78-79), second motive in E♭ (m. 80-81), second motive in b minor (m. 82-83), transition (m. 84-86), second motive in A major (87-88), transition 89-96.

3. The transition (m. 89-96) begins with tonal shifts on each beat (m. 89), moves through various dominant-type formations (m. 90-91) and arrives at a passage of alternating harmonies implying the key of F♯ major, m. 92-96. The use of half-diminished

seventh chords (incomplete dominant ninths or VII⁷ chords) in m. 92-95 is reminiscent of Debussy. Notice that certain tones in the RH form unresolved appoggiaturas with these chords. In m. 96 the same figure, B E F♯, is used to lead into the recapitulation of the theme in E♭. The tones G♯ and C♯ are added in the LH chords, to build even more tension, however. Compare m. 96 with m. 22-25 of Example 148.

4. The section beginning at m. 97 with the return of the theme in E♭ as originally at m. 26 (Example 148) and continuing through m. 111 is like a recapitulation. The remainder of the work (not quoted) is like a coda consisting of a gradual diminuendo to the character of the opening measures and a final sudden rush to a loud final reiteration of the first motive, reminiscent of a Beethoven ending.

5. In m. 97-111 the full theme is again stated. What keys are used in these statements? What modes are indicated?

6. Notice the diminished third in m. 103, 104 and 107. What is the chord on beat four of m. 107?

7. What scales are implied in m. 108-111? How are the clusters in the LH derived?

8. Observe the use of unrelated scale segments in the transition passages of both this and Example 148. This shifting from one scale to another is idiomatic.

9. M. 105 consists of one quarter rest. This is the same effect as the rests between measures in Example 146. Extra pulses such as this appear frequently in Bartók.

Examples and Suggestions for Further Study of the Music of Bartók

Bartók's earlier works (1903-1908) involve some romantic-impressionistic influences as well as the direct effect of nationalist interest. Works written during the period, 1908-1926, are more dissonant, complex tonally and more personal in their intent. By the early thirties Bartók had evolved his mature, more universally directed style, and after 1927 most of his best-known works were written. During this latter period the linear element in his music becomes important and is balanced with homophonic textures.

piano music (solo)

Besides the *Mikrokosmos* there are many collections of short piano pieces which display all aspects of his style.

Important collections of this type include *Ten Easy Pieces* (1908), *Three Burlesques* (1910), *Four*

Dirges (1910), *Eight Improvisations on Peasant-songs* (1920) and *Out-of-Doors* (1926).

Allegro Barbaro (1910) is, as the name implies, a savage dance based on a pentatonic tune and exploiting dissonant harmonic formations around an F♯ center. It is in ternary form.

The Sonatina (1915) is really a suite. I is titled *Bagpipes* and is a ternary form. II is *Bear Dance* and consists of a period repeated and extended by repetition of the last phrase. III consists of two dances: a Turkish dance and witches' dance.

The Suite for Piano (1916) consists of four movements in dance style. II and III are song form and trio designs.

The Sonata (1926) is in three movements:

I is a sonata form on Hungarian themes. The second theme is an example of bitonality, g♯ minor against C Lydian.

II is a song form. III is a rondo, the main theme of which is predominantly Mixolydian.

chamber music

The six string quartets represent the quintessence of Bartók's writing and are, as a group, perhaps the most significant works in this medium since Brahms.

The First Quartet (1908) is in three movements with subtle thematic relationships. I is a slow fugue interrupted by a homophonic middle section. II is a sonata with arch design: Themes return in reverse order in the recapitulation. An improvisation passage precedes III like an introduction. III is a bright finale: Two principal themes derived from motives in the previous movement are introduced and treated in contrapuntal combination. A third, adagio theme interrupts. Then the first theme is treated in graceful homophonic style and developed in fugal style. A varied recapitulation follows in which the themes are further developed and the adagio theme reappears. It is a movement of great energy and variety with polytonal passages.

The Second String Quartet (1917) closes with a slow, lento, third movement. I is a sonata and a good example of Bartók's lyric style. Note the emphasis on the tritone in the return of theme 1 and elsewhere. II is a barbaric movement in free rondo design. There is a drumming effect of repeated tones and alternating between two tones, especially the minor third. Contrasting tranquil passages occasionally interrupt the wild rhythmic drive. III is a slow, expressive movement in four sections with the theme of each section returning compressed in the coda.

The Third Quartet (1927) is more astringent than the lyric Second Quartet and formal objectivity

dominates. The process of development, especially contrapuntal manipulation, permeates the quartets and other works from this point on to an even greater degree. Because there is less concern for vertical sonorities in the preoccupation with linear manipulation one finds more reliance on devices, patterns and imitative effects in the works of this period.

The first of the two movements is Moderato and in ABA form. It involves manipulation of figures consisting of small intervals. These small intervals are expanded by inversion and octave transposition. II follows without a break and is a sonata design followed by a return of the themes of I greatly transformed and a coda on themes of II. The development contains a fugue, and the transitions include many coloristic string effects found increasingly in later Bartók. This two-movement quartet is another example of a recombination of elements of the classic sonata seen in works from Haydn to the present.

Though the Fourth Quartet (1928) is possibly a more personal expression, the use of contrapuntal devices—retrograde and inverted forms of themes—the exploitation of instrumental potentialities, linear emphasis and vertical dissonance continue. There are five movements which form an arch design in their relationship: I related to V, II to IV and III contrasting to the others.

I is a sonata design based on themes with small intervals, particularly the minor second which is predominant both melodically and harmonically. A motto theme which is heard again in V is highly developed in I. II and IV are fast scherzo and trio movements which share similar thematic material. The trios of both exploit the diminished third and minor second intervals. Considering the tonal center of I and V to be C, the arch form is further emphasized by the fact that the tonal center of II is E and of IV is A♭, a major third above and below C.

III is one of those improvisatory movements in which tone color and instrumental effects are exploited over a motionless harmonic and rhythmic background.

IV should be studied for the masterful canonic writing.

V is in three sections:

a. The principal theme and its inverted form are introduced and developed in homophonic and canonic textures.

b. The motto theme from I is recalled and developed canonically.

c. The principal theme of V returns for further contrapuntal manipulation with the motto theme in a complex fabric of imitation involving "mirroring" (simultaneous contrary motion) and retrograde and inverted forms of the theme. V closes like I with a brusque statement of the motto theme.

In the Fifth Quartet (1934) Bartók's interest in constructive devices (as opposed to expressive considerations) is even more pronounced. The five movements are in arch form similar to the Fourth Quartet. I is related to V; II is related to IV, but both are slow movements instead of scherzi; and III is the scherzo.

I is a sonata in which the arch form is carried to its ultimate within the movement. In the recapitulation the themes return not only in reverse order but also each is inverted.

II is an ABA design with themes of A returning in reversed order. Thematic material of IV is again related to that of II.

III is a scherzo and trio exploiting asymmetrical Bulgarian rhythms. Meters used in this movement include:

$$\frac{4 + 2 + 3}{8} \qquad \frac{3 + 2 + 2 + 3}{8}$$

$$\frac{2 + 3 + 2 + 3}{8} \qquad \frac{2 + 3 + 3 + 2}{8}$$

There is much use of mirroring and imitation by contrary motion in III.

IV exploits coloristic effects including triple-stop pizzicato-glissandos.

V is a brilliant contrapuntal finale in the following design:

Introduction (m. 1-13)
Theme 1, part 1 (m. 14-54)
Theme 1, part 2 (m. 55-74)
Theme 1, part 2 inverted (m. 75-93)
Transition (m. 93-109)
Theme 1, part 1 inverted (m. 110-149)
Introduction material (m. 150-156)
Transition derived from Theme 1 (m. 157-201)

Theme 2 is treated throughout in canonic imitation (m. 202-345). In m. 224-242 a motive of the theme is treated in double imitation through sequential repetitions; the first violin and viola state the motive in simultaneous contrary motion and are imitated by the second violin and cello in simultaneous contrary motion (mirroring) for nine sequential repetitions.

Transition and return of introduction theme (m. 346-368)

Fugue on a subject derived from theme 1 of I (369-484). The last full entry of the subject is inverted (m. 420-430 in the cello).

Transition (m. 484-527) based on fragments of the fugue material
Introduction theme (m. 527-546)

Theme 1, part 1 in canon by contrary motion and later combined with part 2, the first transition motive, and a motive of theme 2 (m. 546-698). This recapitulation section builds to a climax and is suddenly interrupted by an incongruous passage of organ-grinder music (699-720). Theme 1, part 2 is harmonized by I and V^7 chords in A major to be played mechanically. It is like a childish reaction to the constant contrapuntal involutions of the movement.

Coda (m. 721-828) composed of various thematic elements treated contrapuntally in increasing tempo

What formal design does this movement most nearly represent? Notice how frequently twentieth-century composers employ the cyclic principle by recalling a theme from the first movement in the finale and giving it a fugato treatment.

In the Sixth Quartet (1939) the cyclic relationship of movements is even more emphasized. The four movements are connected by a motto theme which becomes the basis of the finale which in turn recalls themes from I.

In addition to the many other unusual string instrument effects previously used by Bartók the use of quarter tones appears in III.

The two Sonatas for Violin and Piano (1921-1922) reveal the same concern with objective organization of form as seen in the quartets. These works involve complex harmony—polytonal effects resulting from simultaneous chord streams in separate tonal spheres.

The Sonata for Two Pianos and Percussion (1937) further demonstrates Bartók's preoccupation with instrumental color and especially his virtuosity in handling percussion instruments (including piano). All the devices of polytonality, canonic imitation of various types, mirroring, chord streams and complex rhythms of the piano concertos are found in this outstanding work.

Contrasts (1938) for violin, clarinet and piano consists of two dance movements separated by a central contrasting movement. For III the violin is tuned to G♯ D A E♭, a twentieth-century example of scordatura.

orchestral works

There are several excellent early works for orchestra such as two orchestra suites (1905-1907), *Two Portraits* (1907), *Two Pictures* (1910) and *Dance Suite* (1923), but Bartók's best-known orchestral works are those of his last ten years.

The Music for String Instruments, Percussion and Celesta (1935) includes piano and harp as part of the ensemble. The four movements effectively display Bartók's technics of counterpoint, orchestration and design and are universal in their appeal.

I constitutes an unusual fugal design on a typical Bartók subject made up of narrow intervals. The subject enters on A and the subsequent entrances form a pattern alternating between fifths above A and fifths below A, thus:

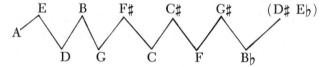

Notice the tritone A to E♭ traversed in this series of entrances. Inverted entrances of the subject then lead back to A. The final cadence on a unison A is approached by two mirrored voices resolving through the diminished third G♯, B♭ to A. Notice that the imitation of the subject is not always exact but based sometimes on the general shape and rhythm of the subject.

II is a sonata design with close dissonant canons and fugato in the development. The opening motive of the fugue subject of I is recalled and developed. Here as in other works Bartók requires a percussive pizzicato in which the strings are pulled hard enough to snap back on the fingerboard and also pizzicato glissandos.

III is characterized by exploitation of instrumental timbres: amorphous rustlings and shimmerings of sound. Yet the organization of the movement is an arch, ABCDCBA, and the motive of I again is used. Note the use of tympani glissando. Compare this music with the pointillistic style of Webern. How are the two kinds of music alike? How do they differ?

IV is a rondo based on folk-dance idioms and includes references to the theme of I. The design is A B A C D E D F G A.

The Concerto for Orchestra (1944) and the Third Piano Concerto (1945) exemplify Bartók's return to a more direct tonal organization, a more universally approachable, less subjective style. Yet the constructive and coloristic devices are still present. In the Concerto for Orchestra, I is a sonata design. The introduction (later recalled) and theme 1 are based strongly on the interval of a perfect fourth. Theme 2 consists mainly of the alternation of two tones a major second apart.

II is an example of device writing which, as usual, produces delightful results. It is called *Game of Pairs* and is an A B A design as follows.

A is a series of whimsical tunes. Each tune is played by a different pair of wind instruments doubling the tune at a specific interval: bassoons in minor sixths, oboes in minor thirds, clarinets in minor sevenths, flutes in perfect fifths and muted trumpets in major seconds.

B is a brass chorale.

A comprises the return of all the tunes but with more elaborate accompaniment or addition of instruments to the original pair, for example, a third bassoon in running passages against the original duet, and a pair of clarinets in minor thirds playing the tune in simultaneous strict contrary motion to the oboes in minor thirds. A few raps on a side drum without snares form the introduction and conclusion to this marvelous invention.

III, *Elegy,* is one of the best examples of Bartók's declamatory style. It is based on derivations from material of I.

IV, *Interrupted Intermezzo,* is a mixture of whimsey and boisterous parody. It is A B A C B A design. The theme of A dwells on the interval of the augmented fourth, and B is a nostalgic kind of waltz tune fitted into asymmetrical rhythmic patterns. The interruption is the C section. Here mocking versions of the march theme from Shostakovich's Seventh Symphony (I) are interrupted by instrumental effects which sound like gales of sarcastic laughter.

V is another brilliant example of Bartók's contrapuntal and orchestral ingenuity. It includes references to themes of the opening of I, whirling perpetual motions, fugatos against colorful ostinati and all kinds of canonic devices.

concertos

There are three earlier rhapsodies for solo instrument with orchestra: two for violin soloist (1928) and one for piano (1904). The best-known solo concertos however are the three concertos for piano (1926, 1931 and 1945) and the Violin Concerto (1938).

The Second Piano Concerto is a remarkable work which is a veritable catalog of pianistic and orchestral devices. One should not fail to study this work which is so rich in twentieth-century harmonic, melodic and tonal devices, just a few of which are:

a. Polytonality;
b. harmonic counterpoint—one stream of parallel chords or intervals against another—involving all kinds of canonic imitation and mirroring;
c. tremolos or multiple trills composed of white-key chord clusters alternating with black-key clusters;
d. complex rhythmic texture.

The ostinato pattern, composed of the alternate tones of a minor third, which is prominent in III of this work, is also found in other works such as the Second String Quartet (II) and the Music for Strings, Percussion and Celesta, II.

The Third Piano Concerto is Bartók's last work and illustrates best of all his later trend toward lyric and tonal simplicity and directness. The piano is treated more as a lyric instrument in contrast to its percussive role in previous works. The contrapuntal ingenuity is still present but the sonorities are less complex and more tonally directed. I is a sonata. Theme 1 is in E, and some of the material from the second-theme group returns in inverted form. II is quite tonal and closes with a cadence one would expect in Hindemith. It is an ABA design. The B section is devoted to shimmering tremolos and other impressionistic effects. III is a rondo design involving fugal and canonic development of themes and return of some material in inverted form. Notice the use of parallel major seconds comparable to the use of chords in fifths in II of the Second Piano Concerto.

The Violin Concerto (1938) is another example of Bartók's wizardry with instrumental colors and effects. I is a sonata design involving much modification of themes in the recapitulation. Theme 1 appears in augmentation and also inversion in the development. Theme 2 utilizes all twelve tones of the chromatic scale. II is a theme and six variations. The two principal themes of III are directly related to those of I.

The following list locates just a few of the unusual effects which Bartók uses in this work, many of which also appear in other works:

1. Second theme built on twelve tones, I (m. 73-75)
2. Quarter tones for solo violin, I (m. 303-308)
3. Glissandos for:
   Solo violin, I (m. 91 and 265-267)
   Tympani, I (m. 72 and 294), III (m. 589-591)
   Harp, I (m. 67-70 and 280-283 and frequently elsewhere); chord glissando, III (m. 222-230)
   Trombones, I (m. 294-297), III (m. 205-208)
   String section, I (m. 364-367), III (m. 44); slow glissando, III (m. 228-230)
4. Sul ponticello, tremolo and glissando in strings, I (m. 36-38)
5. Trombone flutter-tongue, I (m. 113)
6. Notated glissando—solo violin, I (m. 69-70)
7. Percussive pizzicato (with string snapping against fingerboard), I (m. 373-376)
8. Notes on snare drum at the edge of the head, I (m. 373-376), II (m. 106-112), III (m. 177-181)
9. Tympani, col legno (with wooden sticks), II (m. 106-112)
10. Strings, col legno, III (m. 122-125)
11. Trumpet and horn glissandos through harmonics, III (m. 604-608)
12. Cymbals played with edge of penknife blade, III (m. 126-145)
13. Triangle with thin wood sticks, III (m. 135-138)
14. Trumpet and trombones with cardboard mutes, III (m. 202-204)

SUGGESTED WRITTEN ASSIGNMENTS

1. Both Bartók and Hindemith use chords of superimposed fourths or fifths (quartal and quintal harmonies) but not in the same ways. Analyze the Bartók, Second Piano Concerto, II, and the Hindemith, *Ludus Tonalis* (Interlude, No. 8) and compare the uses of such harmonies by the two composers.
2. Compare the Music for Strings, Percussion and Celesta, II, m. 200-241, with Stravinsky, Symphony in Three Movements, I, m. 21-53 in regard to:
   a. instrumental color
   b. harmonic content
   c. rhythm

3. Write short (eight-measures) exercises involving the following devices:
   a. For piano, a melody in thirds in the RH stated simultaneously in contrary motion by the LH in thirds (mirroring).
   b. For four wind or string instruments, a double canon of two mirrored voices imitated at the octave by two other mirrored voices two beats behind.
   c. A canon for piano, parallel chords in the RH consisting of two perfect fifths (e.g. C G D) imitated in contrary motion two beats later in the LH.
   d. An ostinato of major seconds with a theme using minor seconds and tritones.

4. Analyze a movement of the Divertimento for String Orchestra (1940).

5. The Second Piano Concerto of both Bartók and Prokofiev occupies a similar position in regard to each composer's piano works. The percussive aspects of piano style are exploited in each work. Discuss the similarities and differences in style and artistic intent in the two works.

BIBLIOGRAPHY

BARTÓK, BÉLA, *Studia Memoriae Beloe Bartok Sacra*, London: Bossey & Hawkes, 1959.

BATOR, VICTOR, *The Béla Bartók Archives; History and Catalog*, New York: Bartók Archives Publication, 1963.

FASSETT, AGATHA, *The Naked Face of Genius: Béla Bartók's American Years*, Boston: Houghton Mifflin Company, 1958.

HARASZTI, EMIL, *Béla Bartók*, Paris: The Lyrebird Press, 1938.

STEVENS, HALSEY, *The Life and Music of Béla Bartók*, New York: Oxford University Press, Inc., 1953.

EXAMPLE 143
BARTÓK
FOURTEEN BAGATELLES, OP. 6
II
(Complete)

EXAMPLE 144
BARTÓK
FOURTEEN BAGATELLES, OP. 6
IV
(Complete)

EXAMPLE 145
BARTÓK
FOURTEEN BAGATELLES, OP. 6
X
(First 22 Measures)

EXAMPLE 146
BARTÓK
FOURTEEN BAGATELLES, OP. 6
XI
(Complete)

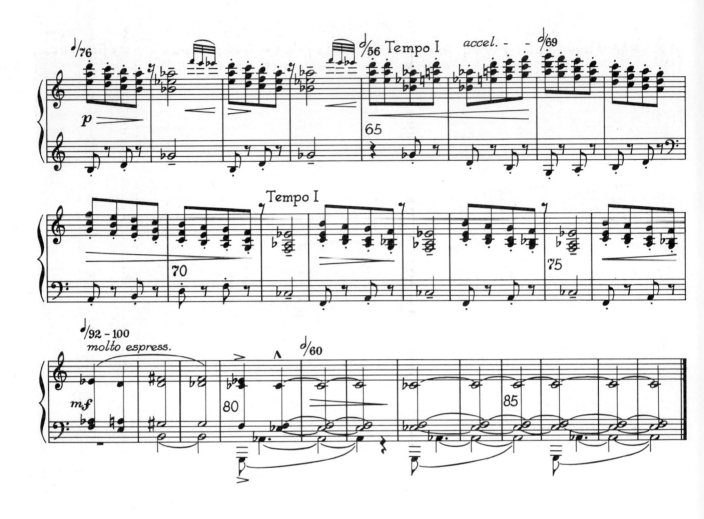

EXAMPLE 147
BARTÓK
SKETCHES, OP. 9
V–RUMANIAN FOLKSONG
(Complete)

EXAMPLE 148
BARTÓK
RUMANIAN DANCES, OP. 8a
I
(First 63 Measures)

EXAMPLE 149
BARTÓK
RUMANIAN DANCES, OP. 8a
I
(Measures 76-111)

CHAPTER 33

ARNOLD SCHOENBERG

1874-1951

Through chromatic shifts from one dominant-function chord to another and through various forms of deceptive progression, Wagner maintained a constant tonal suspense. This emphasis on suspense was continued by such composers as Strauss and early Schoenberg but in the Wagnerian tradition which involved chromatic textures of traditionally derived harmonies in a tonal organization. However, the prevailing artistic mood in Germany at the close of the nineteenth century was one of morbid obsession with subjectivity, intense emotion to the point of hysteria, which demanded in music even more emphasis on unresolved dissonance. The idea of dying German romanticism seemed to be that if a great amount of emotional suspense and dissonance is good, then 100 per cent dissonance and emotional intensity is even better.

Thus dissonance for the sake of constant emotional intensity began to dominate musical texture to the extent that tonality in the conventional sense simply disappeared and the term *atonality* was applied to this kind of music. The term applied to this movement in the arts in general is *expressionism*: expression of the innermost turmoil of the soul.

The foremost musical exponents of this dissonant, atonal, hysterical movement were Schoenberg and Berg. The former had moved from a style based on Wagnerian chromaticism exemplified in such works as *Verklaerte Nacht,* op. 4 (Transfigured Night; 1899) and *Pelléas and Mélisande,* op. 5 (symphonic poem; 1903) to a style based on dissonant atonality exemplified in such works as Five Pieces for Orchestra, op. 16 (1909) and *Pierrot Lunaire,* op. 21 (1912).

Without the cohesive element of tonality works of this period depend on contrapuntal devices, vocal texts or miniature dimensions for formal coherence. Schoenberg saw the need for some sort of tonal or-

ganization to replace the former concepts of tonality. During the period of 1915 to 1923 he developed the twelve-tone row technic.

In this system the twelve tones of the chromatic scale are placed in an arbitrarily chosen order which becomes the basis on which a piece is organized and replaces the dynamism of harmonic relations in the tonal system. Thus the sequence of the twelve different tones regardless of their register and the characteristics and relationships inherent in that particular order of tones whether transposed, inverted and/or reversed supplant the pull of a single tone as center.

The twelve-tone row system is an an application of serial technic which in turn is a broader term applying to the use of any given order of tones as the basis of a composition. Serial technic in general involves a sequence of any number of tones which serves as the organizing factor for thematic development, harmony and tonal orientation. Works such as the Bartók, Fourth Quartet (I especially), the Stravinsky, *In Memoriam Dylan Thomas* and, to some extent, the Copland, *Piano Variations,* involve the serial technic but are not twelve-tone row pieces.

Though there are many details of procedure and usage which vary with the composer and composition involved the principles common to most twelve-tone row styles are the following:

1. The row consists of all twelve tones of the chromatic scale arranged in a particular order, no tone omitted and no tone repeated in the row.
2. In addition to its original (prime) form (P) the inverted, retrograde and retrograde-inversion forms (I, R and RI) are available and all four forms can be transposed to any tone of the chromatic scale. Thus, all four forms of any row may begin on any tone of the twelve-tones of the chromatic scale for a total of forty-eight available forms.

422

3. The row can be used to generate both vertical (chord) formations and horizontal (melodic) lines.

4. Though the order of a row is normally not to be broken by returning to a tone once left before its normal position arrives in the next statement of the row, still a tone may be retained and repeated in a given voice so long as no other tone intervenes in that voice.

5. A row may be broken into smaller segments or cells to allow for more flexibility in repetition or in sustaining a vertical formation.

The examples of twelve-tone row music will illustrate these principles in action.

EXAMPLE 150 (page 427)
Klavierstück, Op. 33a

A simple and direct use of the untransposed row in prime form is shown in Example 151. One who is beginning the study of the row technic should analyze that example before working with the present excerpt which illustrates a more complex row texture.

1. This work composed in 1929 is the first of two piano pieces in op. 33. It is forty measures long and based upon the following row:

Right Hand
P

2. The excerpt includes measures 19-25. The right hand is formed from the untransposed retrograde (R) and prime (P) forms of the row. The left hand is formed from the retrograde-inversion (RI) and inversion (I) forms of the row transposed up a perfect fourth, tone 1 is E♭(D♯) instead of B♭:

Left Hand
I (Transposed)

Notice that the last half (tones 7-12) of this row contains the same tones as the first half of the untransposed P form though not in the same order. The obverse is also true of course. The use of these two rows simultaneously avoids octave doubling.

3. Notice that tones 1 and 2 appear in neither row in measure twenty. The R in the right hand and the RI in the left hand both move backward to tone 3 of their respective forms, and then at beat four in

m. 20 the order is changed to the forward forms, P and I, starting on tone 3 of each row.

4. The right-hand figure of m. 20 consists of a segment of the row, tones 3, 4, 5, 6, stated forward and backward and likewise the left-hand figure consists of tones 4, 5, 6 reiterated to produce a sustained vertical formation.

5. Notice that the same type of thing happens in m. 21-22 with different segments of the row forms.

6. Tone 12 (A♮) of the I form does not appear in the left hand of measures 21-22.

7. Tones 1 and 2 of each row form (both R and I) finally appear in m. 23. Since the first three tones of the row form perfect fourths or fifths it is possible that Schoenberg omitted them from the previous four measures to provide a strong, fresh, contrasting quintal formation at m. 23.

8. Notice in m. 23-25 that there is another segmental treatment of each row form, only the first six tones are used in each form and then repeated. Tone 4 (B) the last note in the right hand of m. 25 is followed in m. 26 by tones 5 and 6 (A-F♯) simultaneously.

9. By repeating segments of the row form Schoenberg maintains certain vertical forms over several beats and with rhythmic variety and flexibility.

10. The composer follows such procedures throughout the work. A careful analysis of the entire piece will reveal many interesting "tonal" relationships achieved by careful manipulation of row forms and segments. The emphasis on certain intervals inherent in the row and the reiteration of sonorities make this work hardly less tonal than other works not labeled with the term *atonal*. It should be recalled that Schoenberg did not subscribe to the term *atonality* in connection with his music.

11. It can be argued that this work follows sonata design. See George Perle, *Serial Composition and Atonality*, an excellent work on the subject.

Examples and Suggestions for Further Study of the Music of Schoenberg

It is difficult and somewhat futile to make generalizations about serial works. Simply identifying the row on which such a work is based reveals nothing about construction, color or emotional character of the work. To categorize a work as being based on the twelve-tone row means very little because there have evolved many styles which are based on the row technic. Schoenberg, Berg, Webern, Riegger, Krenek, Stravinsky and Copland have all used the row technic but each in his own way and with a different result. The row technic probably has inherent within it as many ramifications of style as the realm of major tonality. Therefore, each work can be understood stylistically only through careful analysis of the result of application of the row.

Schoenberg's early works (before 1908) in the post-Wagnerian chromatic style are still as popular as any of his later works. The best known of these is *Verklaerte Nacht*, a long, one-movement tone poem of contrasting moods unified by recurring themes in the Liszt-Wagner manner. It was written originally for string sextet and later transcribed for string orchestra. It, along with the *Gurre-Lieder* (the songs of Gurre, a mythological castle; 1901), represent the apogee of late German romanticism. The latter is for huge orchestra, multiple choruses and soloists.

The First String Quartet, op. 7 (1905), like *Verklaerte Nacht* is an intensely emotional one-movement work lasting forty-five minutes. It is also based on the general principle of thematic transformation in the best tradition of Liszt, Wagner and Mahler.

The Second String Quartet, op. 10 (1908) is a transitional work showing Schoenberg's interest in further expanding the tonal limits and in the association of words with his emotional style of expression. The last two movements of the quartet include a soprano soloist in settings of poetry by Stefan Georg.

The second period in Schoenberg's work (1908-1912) would include those compositions in the atonal, expressionist style. It should be remembered that throughout his life and various outward changes of approach to composition Schoenberg was an intense romanticist who believed that the goal of the composer was to transmit his emotions to the listener. The fact that he applied his intellect to the development of a new system of tonal organization does not deny his romantic credo. Style characteristics of this period, along with dissonance and atonality, are (1) brevity, (2) thematic significance abandoned to manipulation of small motives or figures, (3) complex horizontal lines involving skips of tritones, major sevenths, minor ninths and octave displacements, (4) unusual instrumental combinations and colors, (5) accent on emotional intensity, concentration of

form and expression, and on timbre, (6) resulting use of the extreme registers of instruments, unusual effects (flutter tonguing, glissando) and instruments of high register (piccolo, glockenspiel). These characteristics generally prevail in later Schoenberg and the works of Berg and Webern and their disciples.

Serial concepts are apparent in the Three Pieces for Piano, op. 11 (1908). Here small three-tone cells are manipulated both horizontally and vertically to produce a sense of cohesiveness. These three pieces deserve careful analysis, particularly the first, which was written after the second.

The Five Pieces for Orchestra, op. 16 (1909), exemplify Schoenberg's use of orchestral color in combination with atonal textures. The elimination of the contrast of consonance and dissonance and the consequent dissolution of the effect of traditional cadences, phrases and periods result in music which has the temporal flow of prose rather than the rhythmic quality of poetry. The rhythmic drive and momentum of a Bartók or Prokofiev is absent from this music. This lack of poetic meter, of specific melodic idea, of tonal gravitation and harmonic clarity places the criteria for musical comprehension on entirely new bases. What are these bases?

These five pieces comprise greatly contrasting moods. The third is noteworthy as an example of what Schoenberg calls *Klangfarbemelodie* (tone-color melody). Here the accent is on changes of timbre in a texture which is rhythmically, harmonically and melodically motionless. Changes of color replace changes of pitch. This emphasis on timbre at the sacrifice of rhythm, melody and harmony is an important factor in the generation of the fragmentational, pointillistic styles of Webern, late Stravinsky and a generation of composers since 1950.

These five pieces should be carefully studied as music which had a great influence on present musical styles.

Both *Erwartung* (Expectation; 1909) and *Die Glückliche Hand* (The Lucky Hand; 1913) are stage works based on expressionist subjects, fascination with morbid, nightmarish emotional states.

Pierrot Lunaire (Looney [moonstruck] Pierre; 1912) carries the atonally conceived vocal writing of the previous two works to its logical extreme, a kind of recitation involving wide-pitch inflections but not actually singing on specific pitches. This Schoenberg called *Sprechstimme* (speaking voice).

This work consists of miniature settings of twenty-one poems by Albert Giraud for speaker, piano, flute (doubling on piccolo), clarinet (doubling on bass clarinet), violin (doubling on viola) and cello. Here Schoenberg employs contrapuntal devices, later associated with twelve-tone row music, to provide formal coherence. Such devices include passacaglia, retrograde canons and the strict arch effect in which the second half of a piece is a retrograde version of the first half. This work is thought to have inspired Stravinsky to write the *Three Japanese Lyrics* (1913) and Ravel to write *Trois poèmes de Stéphane Mallarmé* (1913) which are also for voice and an unusual instrumental group.

The third period of Schoenberg's work, 1923-1933, follows the period, 1915-1923, in which he developed the row system and includes his first compositions involving that system.

With the row technic as an organizational factor Schoenberg could now construct more extended forms based on objective considerations rather than emotional intensity for their effect. The Variations for Orchestra, op. 31 (1928), is an outstanding work of this period. There are many analyses of this work (see bibliography) which can be helpful in gaining an insight into this type of expression. Careful study of it will reveal the manifold procedures which Schoenberg developed in connection with this method of composing. In the finale he develops the B A C H (B♭ A C B♮) motive first stated in the introduction. The motto idea as unifying factor is important also to this style of writing.

The Wind Quintet, op. 25 (1924), and the Third String Quartet, op. 30, (1926) are other important works of this period.

A continuing interest in spinning larger forms from the row germ is seen in the works after 1933, when he lived in the United States. In works of this period there is a fusion of row technics with conventional forms and tonal procedures. As with Bartók and Hindemith, Schoenberg tends to back away from the earlier subjective and astringent expression and adopts a more universally communicative mode.

The Piano Concerto, op. 42 (1942) illustrates many features of this period. It is in four connected movements, each involving the adaptation of conventional formal designs to row technics. I is a sonata design in which the row is used melodically to form the principal theme which is recalled in cyclic fashion in the finale. The ideas are often stated in regular phrase patterns as in the first sixteen measures of I. The possibilities inherent in the row are expanded by the use of segments or cells of the row independently. Thus in the principal row theme with which the work opens tones 9, 10, 11 are repeated before 12 is introduced, and later in the work the first six tones in prime (P) order are followed by the last six tones in retrograde (R) order to form virtually a new row.

II is a scherzo with contrasting trio; III is a theme and five variations with coda; IV is a rondo design with the theme of I recalled at the close.

The Fourth String Quartet is another work in which the four forms of the row are expressed melodically as thematic material for development. This use of the row is typical in the music of Riegger and is found in other serial composers' works also. Where the elements of sonata design and the row as theme are employed in such atonal music as this the needed effect of contrast is dependent on variety in rhythm, texture and dynamics.

Schoenberg's impact on the course of music is as great as any in history. Facets of the row technic have been adopted by many later composers, and each has applied his own individual talents in extracting from the row that which he believes music should say.

SUGGESTED WRITTEN ASSIGNMENTS

1. As a study of the evolution of the row technic through Schoenberg's works it is suggested that the following works be analyzed in the order given:

   a. A section of *Verklaerte Nacht* or the First String Quartet.
   b. The opening section of the Kammersymphonie, op. 9 (1906).
   c. The Litany (III) of the Second String Quartet.
   d. The first of the Three Piano Pieces.
   e. No. 8, "Night," from *Pierrot Lunaire*.
   f. Prelude from Suite for Piano, op. 25 (1924); analysis in Eschman (see bibliography, page 5).
   g. *Klavierstück*, op. 33a. Analysis in Perle (see bibliography, page 426).
   h. First movement of the Piano Concerto.

2. Compare the orchestral resources which Schoenberg uses for his tone poem *Pelléas and Mélisande* with Debussy's orchestra for his opera on the same subject. Both works were written at almost exactly the same time.

3. Analyze or study an analysis of a work by Alban Berg such as the first or last movement of the Lyric Suite for string quartet (1926) and a work by Anton Webern such as the Symphony for Small Orchestra, op. 21, I (1928) or the first movement of the Variations for Piano, op. 27 (1936). How do these composers' row technics compare with Schoenberg's? Compare the music of these three composers in regard to emotional quality (expres-

siveness), to structural facets (texture, melody, rhythm, form, contrapuntal devices) and to the general aural impression (degree of tonality or atonality; degree to which the row emerges aurally as an organizing factor).

BIBLIOGRAPHY

LEIBOWITZ, RENÉ, *Schoenberg and His School*, New York: Philosophical Library, Inc., 1949.

NEWLIN, DIKA, *Bruckner, Mahler, Schoenberg*, New York: King's Crown Press, 1953.

PERLE, GEORGE, *Serial Composition and Atonality*, Berkeley: University of California Press, 1963.

RUFER, JOSEPH, *Composition with Twelve Notes*, London: Rockliff, 1954.

————, *The Works of Arnold Schoenberg*, New York: Free Press of Glencoe, 1963.

SCHOENBERG, ARNOLD, *Style and Idea*, New York: Philosophical Library, Inc., 1950.

SLONIMSKY, NICOLAS, *Music Since 1900*, New York: Coleman-Ross, 1949.

STUCKENSCHMIDT, HANS H., *Arnold Schoenberg*, New York: Grove Press, Inc., 1960.

WELLESZ, EGON, *Arnold Schoenberg*, New York: E. P. Dutton & Co., Inc., 1947.

EXAMPLE 150

SCHOENBERG

KLAVIERSTÜCK, OP. 33a

(Measures 19-25)

CHAPTER 34

ERNST KŘENEK

1900-

Křenek is a member of that line of composers of this century whose stylistic changes follow a familiar pattern of influences, from (a) the late romantic style of Strauss and Mahler, to (b) experiments in the areas of expressionistic atonality, in jazz and in the neoclassic idioms to (c) the twelve-tone row technic of Schoenberg to (d) the post-Webern serial technic in which intervals, durations, dynamics and texts are subjected to serialization and finally to (e) electronic music. This is a natural sequence of events for a composer born in 1900 and growing up in Vienna.

He is a prolific composer and wrote many successful works before adopting the row technic with his opera *Karl V* in 1933. He has been influential in promoting appreciation of row music not only as a composer but also as a teacher and writer. Besides two books dealing with composition technic he wrote the Twelve Short Piano Pieces, op. 83 (1938), which demonstrate the use of the row in a direct and instructive, but musical manner similar on a smaller scale to Bartók's intent in writing the *Mikrokosmos*.

EXAMPLE 151 (page 432)
Twelve Short Piano Pieces, Op. 83, IV, The Moon Rises

All twelve pieces in op. 83 are based on the same tone row; each piece is based on a different form or different forms of the row, thus:

1. P	7. P + RI
2. I	8. I + R
3. R	9. I + RI
4. RI	10. P + R + RI
5. P + I	11. P + I + R
6. P + R	12. P + I + R + RI

1. *The Moon Rises* is no. 4 based entirely on the RI (retrograde inversion) form of the row with no transposition. For the sake of simplicity the row tones in the example have been numbered 1 to 12. Actually in relation to the original row they would be reversed (12 to 1); but since this is the only form of the row used in this piece, the 1 to 12 numbering provides for easier analysis. Write the row on which this piece is based, and then from it write the original row form (Prime).

2. The numbers in circles with arrows pointing to E♭ indicate each beginning of the row.

3. Notice that a previous row often overlaps the beginning of the next row, particularly in m. 7-8 where tones 11 and 12 of statement (3) overlap the first nine tones of statement (4). Notice that this makes possible the prolonging of the tones of the D♭ triad through three measures (m. 7-9).

4. There are several illustrations of the rule that a tone may be repeated out of sequence provided that it remains in the same voice:

   a. In m. 1, tones 1, 2, 3 are repeated after 4.

   b. In m. 2, tone 4 is repeated though tones 1-7 have intervened.

   c. In m. 3, tone 1 of statement (2) occurs simultaneously with tones 11-12 of statement (1) and is repeated on the fourth beat with 3-4 after 2 has already sounded.

   d. In m. 9, tone 9 (C) is repeated after two-beats rest. Here tones 10, 11, 12 intervene in the right hand before tone 9 is repeated with tones 1, 2, 3 of statement (5).

   e. In m. 8-9, D♭ is followed by A♭ and then returns with the D♭ triad in the right hand of m. 9. Does this repetition of D♭ differ from the manner in which the other repetitions come about?

   f. In m. 10, in the right hand the tones B C B C are "allowable," otherwise trills would be impossible. Note the similar situation in m. 13.

5. Trace each statement of the row noting the repetitions of tones and the way they are introduced.

How would you explain the entrance out of sequence of B♭-D in m. 13?

6. There are a total of twenty measures in the piece and the last chord consists of the last four tones of the row. Do you find any tonal implications in the example? Do certain features inherent in the row emerge to provide a specific aural character? In other words, are there any rhythmic, melodic or harmonic motives recognizable to the ear which are traceable to the nature of the row itself?

EXAMPLE 152 (page 432)
Symphonic Elegy for String Orchestra

In most of his twelve-tone row works written during the period of 1935 to 1947 the following characteristics are present:

a. Melodic, harmonic and rhythmic figures or motives reappear in conjunction with certain tones of the row in such a way that the listener is subconsciously if not consciously aware of the row as an inner generator of the work.

b. Melodic ideas have a contour and form which might be associated with tonal music. While there is the usual octave transposition of this kind of music, still the principal motives have an expressive character which seems to imply a balance of harmonic and nonharmonic tones even though the texture is atonal.

c. The rows themselves are usually constructed with some element or elements of symmetry involved as in this example. This Symphonic Elegy was written in 1946 in memory of Webern. It is an excellent work with which to introduce twelve-tone row, atonal music to the uninitiated listener because the logic of its construction emerges aurally as an intrinsic part of its expressive beauty, a result to be hoped for but not always found in any row work.

1. The row which generates this piece is symmetrically conceived. There are two segments of six tones. The second segment of six tones is the RI form of the first six transposed a fifth lower. Thus, the basic shape of the first six tones is simply restated in different form in the second six tones.

2. Write the entire twelve-tone row in its four forms beginning on E♭. Note that the inversion of the entire row ends on B♭, a fifth higher. What relationships can you draw from a comparison of the various forms of the entire row and of the six-note segments? Note that with regard to the entire row

the R form is the same shape as the I form, and the RI form is the same shape as P form.

3. You will see in the next example that, because the row ends a perfect fifth above or below the starting tone (depending on the form used), Křenek uses the last tone as the first of a new row transposed down a fifth (or up a fifth).

4. Also observe that the row divides into three groups of four tones each, the middle group forming two major thirds a perfect fifth apart, and the outer groups are, of course, the retrograde inversion of one another. It will be seen in the next example how he uses these four-note motives.

EXAMPLE 153 (pages 433-435)
Symphonic Elegy

1. As preparation for the study of this example copy on manuscript paper the P form of the row on E♭ and the eleven transpositions of it, one below the other, each starting a perfect fifth below the preceding one.

2. The first thirty-one measures comprise twelve statements of the row, each succeeding statement being a perfect fifth below the preceding one. Thus, the last tone (12) of each row is the first tone of the next. Each time the row is in P form. Not until m. 36, with the entrance of the I form on B, is any but prime form used. Use your sheet of row transpositions to help in tracing the various rows.

3. The brackets in m. 1-4 identify important figures or motives which appear throughout the work as unifying elements like motto themes. Notice in this excerpt alone how these ideas recur, in exact form, or rhythmically or intervallically modified. Identify such reappearances and indicate which are exact and which are modified and how.

4. The beginnings of rows are identified with arrows. In m. 14-15 you will note that three rows are being stated simultaneously. These rows cross over one another from staff to staff in a rather complex web. For example, in m. 14 the E♭ in the first violin and the D-F♯ in the double basses are part of the same row.

5. In m. 20-21 the row order is broken and tones 9, 10 appear before 7, 8. Where is this?

6. Observe in m. 24-31 how Křenek holds and repeats tones from the row beginning in m. 23 and from the last row to effect a sonorous climax at the close of this section with the return to E♭ in m. 31.

7. M. 32-33 show the two-note figure of m. 1-2, opening a new section in which the row is used in its other form (R and I, which are the same shape in this row). This second section is somewhat like a varied restatement of the first thirty-one measures,

emphasizing a different motivic element but closing in much the same way as the first section. The general design of the entire work is as follows:

SECTION 1—m. 1-31.

SECTION 2—m. 32-86.

TRANSITION—m. 87-99. Here segments of the row are used, tones 9-12 of P (m. 87-92) and 9-12 of R (m. 92-96).

SECTION 3—m. 100-149. A contrasting andante exploiting new motives derived from both row forms.

TRANSITION—m. 150-167. Here the opening ideas are restated but in a different order. The four-note row segments are rotated so that the second and third segments exchange places, thus:

1 2 3 4	9 10 11 12	5 6 7 8
Segment	Segment	Segment
1	3	2

Complex rotations of row segments involving the application of mathematical operations have become a common technic in the later serial writing not only of Křenek but also of many other composers as well.

SECTION 4—m. 168-280.

This vivace section involves development of the opening motives and serves as a kind of scherzo. The R (or I) form of the row is used as an ostinato played pizzicato by the double basses (m. 168-191). The second segment (tones 5-8) receives special treatment in m. 234-244 (see Example 154), and the section then closes with a greatly augmented (rhythmically, dynamically and emotionally) statement of the opening six measures starting on B♭ instead of E♭ so that the statement closes on E♭.

SECTION 5—m. 281-325.

This is a slow meditative section starting andante and slowing soon to adagio. The row is modified toward the end with occasional tones interpolated out of order. This last section is a moving close, fitting for an elegy and reminiscent in its treatment of texture and fragmentation of motives to the close of the Funeral March of Beethoven's Symphony, no. 3. This work should be analyzed because it is effective music in which the expressive element, the message, is inextricably bound with technic. The row sounds through both as a generating factor and as an aesthetic result.

EXAMPLE 154 (page 436)
Symphonic Elegy

1. These measures are quoted to show an effect derived from segment two (tones 5-8).

2. The twelve tones of the chromatic scale appear in these measures but hardly in row form.

3. The tones in m. 245-246 are the lower tones of the major thirds in the previous measure (244).

4. Do you find a recurring pattern in m. 240-244?

Examples and Suggestions for Further Study of the Music of Křenek

One of Křenek's early successes is his opera, *Jonny Spielt Auf!* (Johnny Plays!; 1927), based on jazz idioms in a parodistic style typical of the twenties.

Křenek has written many serial works since 1933. The following are suggested as examples to study for a fuller understanding of his style.

The Sonata for Violin and Piano (1945) is in three movements involving motives and themes which are clearly defined through manipulation of row segments. Observe the method of notating the canons in I.

The Organ Sonata, op. 92, no. 1 (1941) is a one-movement work in rondo design. A theme involving an arch effect in which the second half is the retrograde of the first half recurs throughout. Again the Křenek lyric quality is evident.

The Piano Sonata, no. 3 (op. 92, no. 4; 1943) is a four-movement work based on a symmetrically constructed row composed of four segments of three tones each. The segments are rotated in various orders, forms and transpositions to produce a unified work with a variety of expressive qualities.

I is a sonata design.

II is titled Theme, Canons and Variations.

III is a short, piquant scherzo.

IV is a lyric-dramatic adagio with passages having definite tonal implications.

The Piano Sonata, no. 4 (1948) is also a four-movement work and involves cyclic recall of various themes. Again three-tone segments derived from the basic row are combined in various ways. The entire row appears as such only occasionally. I is a sonata design. II is a three-part form. III is an ABACABA rondo. IV is a slow minuet with five variations. This exemplifies Křenek's ability to apply advanced serial technics to traditional types and forms with aesthetically satisfying results.

In his *Sestina* for voice and instrumental ensemble (1957) he has placed not only pitches but also durations, spacing (register), density, speed and dynamics under serial control. The tones of the basic row are rotated according to a preset formula which in turn affects other elements of the musical fabric. This placing of all the musical elements under serial operation has been the concern of many serial composers in the past twenty years and has led many of them including Křenek to experimentation in the field of electronic music, where total control can be more precisely and intricately established.

Suggested Written Assignments

1. Analyze nos. 1, 7, 10 and 12 of Twelve Short Piano Pieces.
2. Analyze the second movement of the Piano Sonata, no. 3 (op. 92, no. 4) for an understanding of the technic of rotation of row segments. The basic row is D C G Bb F E G♯ A D♯ B C♯ F♯.
3. Construct three twelve-tone rows involving the kind of symmetry found in the Křenek rows.
4. Write a short piece (16 measures) for piano involving only one or two row forms.

Bibliography

Křenek, Ernst, *Music Here and Now*, New York: W. W. Norton & Company, Inc., 1939.
————, *Studies in Counterpoint*, New York: G. Schirmer, 1940.
See general references on contemporary composers.

EXAMPLE 151
KŘENEK
TWELVE SHORT PIANO PIECES, OP. 83
IV—THE MOON RISES
(First 14 Measures)

EXAMPLE 152
KŘENEK
SYMPHONIC ELEGY FOR STRING ORCHESTRA
(Tone Row of the Work)

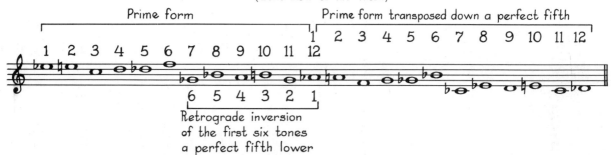

EXAMPLE 153

KŘENEK

SYMPHONIC ELEGY

(First 33 Measures)

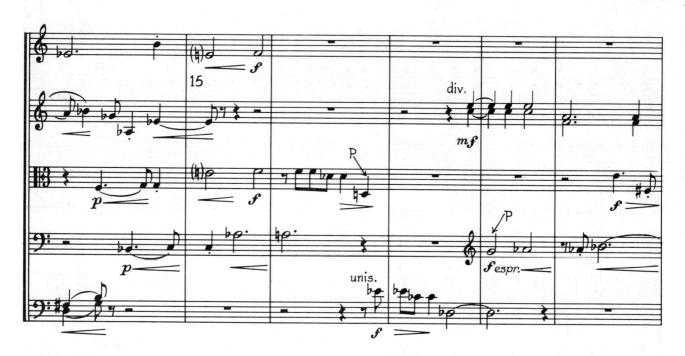

EXAMPLE 154
KŘENEK
SYMPHONIC ELEGY
(Measures 240-246)

CHAPTER 35

WALLINGFORD RIEGGER

1885-1961

Riegger uses the twelve-tone row as an organizing factor in a style which has the rhythmic energy and drive, the thematic delineation, formal definition and textural clarity of the classical tradition. In contrast to Schoenberg's, Berg's and Webern's use of the row to evolve intensely personal, abstruse and subjective expressions, Riegger incorporates the row into a robust, objective idiom characterized by formal directness, lyric warmth, rhythmic impulsion and instrumental color. Though Riegger's music is atonal and dissonant the traditional methods of construction have been little disturbed by injection of the twelve-tone row technic.

He maintains strict adherence to row principles only when they suit the conditions of the musical idea and abandons the row when he feels it interferes with the natural expression of the particular work.

In much serial music the themes, rhythmic ideas and forms are so abstruse or nonexistent that the dissonant aspect obtrudes with undue force in the absence of other elements to attract and hold the attention of the listener.

On the other hand, Riegger's music has an immediate appeal because its classical balance of form and content tend to place the elements of dissonance and atonality in true perspective, as intrinsic to the idiom and not as effects drawing attention out of proportion.

In other words, atonality and dissonance are so inevitably integrated with the many traditional features in Riegger's music that they do not emerge aurally as ends in themselves. The themes, rhythms and formal designs are so significant and so directly set forth that the listener is attracted to them and is, therefore, less conscious of dissonance and atonality as such.

Like other composers of his generation, Riegger did not begin writing atonal music until rather late in life. His first important work in this category is *Study in Sonority* for ten violins or any multiple thereof (1927).

EXAMPLE 155 (pages 441, 442)
Symphony No. 3, I

Riegger is best known for his works for orchestra and instrumental ensembles. His instrumental writing exhibits a transparency resulting from clear definition of lines, a blending of timbres without producing a blurred or turgid quality and soloistic rather than tutti employment of orchestral resources. In this work which is typical of his style complex dissonances are usually placed in high rather than low registers, and doublings are at a minimum; the prevailing texture is two- or three-voice counterpoint with chords used for rhythmic punctuation, and extreme dissonance and thickening of texture occur mainly at climax points.

In certain climaxes in this work the dissonance becomes so harsh that it takes on a percussive quality at which points pure percussive timbre and rhythm in the form of bass drum, snare drum and cymbals take over. These passages exhibit the propulsion of pitch relationships to such a degree of tension that only rhythmic noise remains to express the savage excitement. This effective modulation from textures of definite pitch to sheer noise is an impelling feature of Riegger's style.

1. Riegger often makes very clear the row he is using in a piece by identifying it on a separate staff on the first page as in the String Quartet, no. 1, op. 30 (1938), or by laying it out in the beginning as a principal theme, as in this work. Copy on manuscript paper the basic row which is stated by the oboe in m. 4-5. For later reference, also write the inversion of this row beginning on E instead of F. This first movement is a sonata design.

2. In m. 1-3 tones 4-7 of the row form an introductory motive which appears other places in the movement.

3. The basic row is stated in the presentation of the principal theme by the oboe, m. 4-5. It is partially restated by the flute and oboe together in m. 6-8.

4. In m. 8 the bassoon hints at the introductory motive.

5. These first ten measures serve as an introductory statement of the main thematic material. The movement proper, a sonata, begins with the allegro at m. 11 where the theme is presented in measured tremolo pattern in the first violins (m. 11-22).

6. In m. 23-25 the oboe, then clarinet, then flute state the row theme in the tempo of the introduction.

7. In m. 26-39 the allegro is resumed. The cellos state the inversion (I) form of the row theme transposed down a half step in measured tremolo. It is then taken up by the violas, and a segment (tones 10, 11, 12, 8, 9) is then repeated in a pattern by the upper strings and woodwinds. Short chords in the brass punctuate the thematic statements.

EXAMPLE 156 (pages 443-447)
Symphony No. 3, I

1. This excerpt (m. 40-53) illustrates the prime (P) untransposed form of the row in the brasses against the inverted (I) form one half step lower in the strings.

2. In m. 41-44 the trombones and horns have what motive?

3. The canonic entrances in the strings lead to the vertical formation in the second half of m. 43. How does the chord in the woodwinds come about?

4. The canonic entrances of the strings in m. 44-46 lead into chromatic lines in m. 47-48. Compare the string chords in m. 47-48 with the woodwind chords in m. 48. This type of formation is common in Riegger as well as much other atonal music.

5. What tones of the inverted form of the row are used to form the string chords in m. 49-51?

6. In m. 50-53 the intervals in the brass lines resulting from octave transposition of tones are typical of atonal music. The emphasis is on tritones and intervals that are a half step larger or smaller than an octave. This melodic formation is typical not only of Riegger but also of many other serial composers.

7. In m. 53 compare the last two tones of the horns with the last two tones of the trombones. Can you explain the rotation of tones 8 and 9?

8. Notice the chord formations in the woodwinds on the last beat of m. 53.

9. From these short examples what conclusions could you draw regarding Riegger's method of employing the twelve-tone row? Though these few measures are not sufficient to illustrate all facets of Riegger's row technic, they do indicate certain tendencies which can be found throughout his music.

10. Riegger continues with his treatment of the row theme through m. 80. Notice in m. 60-70 the use of snare drum, bass drum and cymbals as an extension of dissonance and, of course, for rhythmic impulse.

11. A new idea, a second theme, involving high chords in the strings appears at m. 81.

12. The development is a long one beginning at m. 99 with fragments of theme 1 (the row theme) being tossed about among the woodwinds and concluding at m. 179 where the introductory motive is again introduced.

13. The recapitulation starts at m. 185 with an almost exact restatement of the exposition for several measures. The second theme is omitted and an extended fugato based on the row theme beginning at m. 213 serves as a coda.

II (the slow movement) is based on a theme from an earlier work. It is an ABA form. The B section is a fugato. Parallel major seconds combined with tritones and chromatic lines form the principal harmonic ingredients of the A sections.

III is a scherzo typical of Riegger in its mood of brittle wit and good-natured sarcasm. It has the following interesting form.

Introduction (m. 1-5): Statement of principal motives of theme 1 in fragmentary humorous fashion.

Introduction (m. 6-12): Statement of motives of the second theme which is based on the whole-tone scale.

Section A (m. 13-79): Scherzo on theme 1 which is a twelve-tone row. The P form is used in combination with the I form beginning one-half step higher.

Section B (m. 80-183): A bright fugato based on a jaunty eleven-measure subject, the first seven measures of which are derived from theme 1 and the last four from theme 2. Thus, the closing measures of the subject have a whole-tone scale outline.

At the close of this section (m. 185-195) the theme 1 motives are stated by the whole orchestra in augmentation.

Introduction repeated (m. 196-207): The first five measures of the movement are almost exactly repeated (m. 196-200), and the second section (m. 201-207) is a repetition of m. 6-12 with some transpositions.

Section C (m. 208-276) is devoted to further development of the last four measures of the fugato theme, the whole-tone scale motive. Thus, the entire movement is based on the leaping motive of theme 1 and the whole-tone scale motive of theme 2, thus:

Introduction: theme 1 then theme 2
Section A: theme 1
Section B: themes 1 and 2 combined
Introduction repeated
Section C: theme 2

EXAMPLE 157 (page 448)
Symphony No. 3, IV

IV is a passacaglia and fugue based on the themes shown in this example.

1. The passacaglia theme includes within its seven tones the intervallic elements which have pervaded the work: chromaticism, augmented octave, major seventh and tritone.

2. The fugue theme is, of course, derived from the passacaglia theme and adds great emphasis to the tritone.

3. The passacaglia section (m. 1-135) displays Riegger's remarkable technic of rhythmic manipulation and contrapuntal variation. There are twenty-six statements of the theme.

4. The fugue lasts one hundred forty-four measures, then the passacaglia theme returns at m. 280 and is further developed both as a thematic idea as well as an ostinato in the last eighty-eight measures. Thus, the movement is a large ABA design. Note the isolated statements of the passacaglia theme midway through the fugue.

5. Notice the use of percussion to accent the elements of dissonance and rhythmic drive in the last twenty-three measures.

6. In the original version of the work Riegger provided an additional nineteen measures which brought the work to a quiet close with a cyclic restatement of the row theme of I. Because they are anticlimactic these last nineteen measures are usually omitted in performance.

Examples and Suggestions for Further Study of the Music of Riegger

Examination of Riegger's works will reveal a highly original and effective use of dissonance and twelve-tone row procedures.

Like Bartók and Křenek, Riegger wrote a set of piano pieces to illustrate aspects of contemporary compositional practices. This set of twelve pieces is titled *New and Old* (1947) and is provided with analyses and explanation of terms relating to the devices illustrated. Riegger, in the preface, states that "the title is meant to focus attention on the continuity of musical evolution." Actually all of his music as a combination of traditional and original elements admirably exemplifies the continuity of musical evolution.

In his String Quartet, no. 1, op. 30 (1938), each of the four movements is based on one of the forms of the basic row: I on P, II on R, III on I and IV on RI.

The String Quartet, no. 2, op. 43 (1948) is an expressive work making free use of row principles. The four movements are interrelated by thematic derivations and returns. Each succeeding movement opens with the motive or chord with which the preceding movement ends. The themes of I are recalled in III and IV. Traditional formal designs prevail for the most part.

The *Dichotomy* for chamber orchestra (1932) receives its title from the fact that it is based on two opposing tone rows.

The *Music for Brass Choir* (1949) for ten trumpets, eight horns, ten trombones, two tubas and timpani exploits huge brass sonorities including tone clusters of ear-splitting dissonance and power.

Other significant works of Riegger include the popular *New Dance* (1942) for orchestra and transcribed for two pianos; the Concerto (Sextet), op. 53 (1956), for piano and woodwind quintet; the Symphony, no. 4 (1957); the Variations for Piano and Orchestra (1953) and the Variations for Violin and Orchestra (1954). These latter two works, commissioned by the Louisville (Ky.) Symphony Orchestra, show Riegger at his best and should be heard and studied.

SUGGESTED WRITTEN ASSIGNMENTS

1. Compare Riegger's use of the twelve-tone row with Křenek's and Schoenberg's technics in regard to:

    a. Construction of the row itself;
    b. vertical formations;
    c. horizontal (melodic) formations;
    d. shifts from voice to voice;
    e. employment of two or more forms simultaneously;
    f. thematic evolvements;
    g. rhythmic patterns;
    h. texture.

2. Analyze a work of Riegger's such as the String Quartet, no. 1, *Dichotomy*, or the Sextet.
3. Write a row theme and derive ten melodic and rhythmic variations from it.
4. Write a three-voice fugal exposition using a row theme as subject.

BIBLIOGRAPHY

COWELL, HENRY, "Wallingford Riegger," *Musical America*, December, 1948.

GOLDMAN, RICHARD F., "The Music of Wallingford Riegger," *Musical Quarterly*, January, 1950.

See general references on contemporary composers, especially American composers.

EXAMPLE 155

RIEGGER

SYMPHONY NO. 3

I

(First 10 Measures)

EXAMPLE 156
RIEGGER
SYMPHONY NO. 3
I
(Measures 40-53)

EXAMPLE 157
RIEGGER
SYMPHONY NO. 3
IV
Passacaglia Theme
(Measures 1-5)

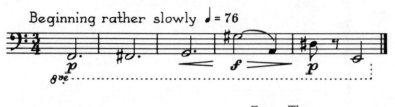

Fugue Theme
(Measures 127-134)

Copyright 1949, 1957 by Associated Music Publishers, Inc., New York. Used by permission.

CHAPTER 36

CURRENT TRENDS

The present variety of technics of composing and of aesthetic concepts of music as an art covers a wide range. This is an age of extremes in approaches toward writing music.

One extreme is represented in works in which the serial process has been extended toward complete numerical control over every aspect of the musical gesture.

The opposite extreme is represented by works in which the elements of pure chance and/or improvision largely replace the role of the composer and meaningful manipulation of materials is largely abandoned. In such works the "composer" establishes only a suggestion, pattern or framework of musical possibilities and leaves their order, juxtaposition and/or general evolvement to chance or the momentary choice of the performer. Works based extensively or wholly on chance can be entertaining or draw attention in the sense of an Olsen and Johnson comedy or a similar random series of events, but they can hardly be considered seriously as artistic endeavor. Perhaps the "composer" who provides the indeterminite situation for such random happenings hopes that an aesthetic effect will by chance come to pass, but this is hoping to make virtue out of chaos.

Then there are those works which represent the broad middle range between the extreme positions. These compositions are based usually on new approaches to traditional procedures or on a conservative, eclectic combining of various tested elements, and they are products of a belief that music as an art should have an appeal which is reasonably universal and direct.

Some composers, as we have seen, have employed various technics at various times.

Electronically generated and mutated musical sound furnishes a new dimension in current musical expression. Works in this medium also display a wide variety of technics ranging likewise from serial to chance concepts.

Present serial music recalls the works of Guillaume de Machaut (1304?-1377), which were based on numerical symbolism, and also the canonic writing of Johannes Ockeghem (? -1495) and other composers of the Netherlands school of the late-fifteenth century. The pointillistic texture of these current serial works recalls the hocket style of medieval polyphony (13th and 14th centuries).

Actually, many of the terms of traditional music cannot be applied with their customary meanings to present serial styles. The fragmentation of the horizontal line among the various instruments over several octaves tends to stretch the traditional significance of the term *melody*. Constantly changing meters, speeding-up of the beat, elimination of bar lines, a fluid or indeterminate notation of rhythmic durations and vastly increased complexity of rhythmic patterns tend to destroy the conventional concepts of beat, meter and tempo.

The emphasis on serial rotation of intervals and avoidance of the conventional vertical formations have caused the term *harmony* to be replaced by some such term as *vertical density*. In each of the following works the composer has sought to create significant music through applying numerical relationships to various elements of the musical gesture. These works represent a projection, expansion and further development of the ideas of Schoenberg and Webern and are direct descendants of the works of these two composers.

Besides the late works of Stravinsky and Křenek the following should be studied:

Pierre Boulez (1925-), *Le Marteau sans maître* (1955), for voice and instrumental ensemble; Third Piano Sonata (1957); *Doubles* for orchestra (1958).

Karlheinz Stockhausen (1928-   ), *Zeitmasse* for five woodwinds (1956).

Milton Babbitt (1916-   ), Composition for Twelve Instruments (1948); String Quartet, no. 2 (1954); Composition for Tenor and Six Instruments (1960); and Three Compositions for Piano (1948).

Two works in which chance and/or performer's choice control the order of events and even the nature of the events themselves are listed below. It should be understood that the degree of chance in a work depends on the number of elements which the composer has determined and the number he has left undetermined. Some works may contain both serially controlled sections and sections to be improvised.

John Cage (1912-   ) is one of the foremost exponents on chance music. His later works employ a variety of media including taped sound and random noises. An example of this type of work is his *Aria with Fontana Mix.*

Zyklus (Cycle; 1959) by Stockhausen is a work for one percussionist. The music consists of sixteen pages of notation which are spiral bound so that there is no beginning and no end. The performer standing in a circle of percussion instruments starts where he chooses in the music but must complete a cycle of the sixteen pages and must turn 360 degrees clockwise or counterclockwise during the performance.

Such works cannot be studied except in performance because a score, if it exists, can predict little about the performance which is different on each occasion.

Also electronic music can be studied only from recordings, unless one wishes to pursue the technics of creating electronic music in which case the score is a set of plans developed by the composer to be realized by the electronic "performer." Since the live performer is eliminated in this music, the composer can exercise complete control over the music and make it as complex as his ingenuity and electronic device will allow.

The term *musique concrète* has been applied to works which result from electronic modification of natural musical sounds or noises. Representative works of this type include: The *Veil of Orpheus* by Pierre Henry, and *Rhapsodic Variations for Tape Recorder and Orchestra* (1954) by Vladimir Ussachevsky and Otto Luening.

The latter two composers as well as Babbitt, Stockhausen, Luciano Berio and many others are presently active in the development of music which results from electronically generated sound.

The traditional concepts of music as an expressive force are combined with creative individuality in the styles of many twentieth-century composers such as Roger Sessions (1896-   ), Elliott Carter (1908-   ), Luigi Dallapiccola (1904-   ), Carl Orff (1895-   ) and other contemporaries discussed in previous chapters. These composers represent the eclectic middle range and, though they may be influenced by certain elements of extreme technics, do not abandon the message of music in the search for mathematical order or constant surprise.

It is interesting to note that to the casual and often to the attentive listener music under complete serial control may sound quite as haphazard as music based on chance. Thus, the two extremes seem to merge, at least aurally, and close the circle. From what point or points on the circle will the future course of music depart?

INDEX OF CHORDS AND VARIOUS TONAL DEVICES

The list of examples under each category is representative of that category and does not include every appearance of that chord or device to be found in the book.

The boldface numbers indicate the number of the example, and the numbers which follow refer to the measures in that example where the item is to be found. No measure numbers are given when the item is to be found frequently throughout the example.

To avoid confusion in terminology the categories of chords are identified by their spelling with reference to the key of C major or c minor as the case may be.

The examples listed under a given heading include various inversions of the chord or chords as well as fundamental position.

Secondary Dominant Formations

OF II

V of II (A C♯ E in C)
 7—45, 50
 24—114
 75—4

V⁷ of II (A C♯ E G in C)

1—98	40—14	57—5
4—14	41—5	72—3, 7,
9—49	48—5	17, 19
11—22	51—60, 64	73—20
31—37	52—81, 100, 105	75—4

V⁹ of II (A C♯ E G B♭ in C)
 52—105, 109
 60—15
 101—18

VII of II (C♯ E G in C)
 1—30, 116
 18—6, 14, 104
 45—12

VII⁷ of II (C♯ E G B♭ in C)

3—32, 38	7—45, 50
4—25, 54	14—82

26—16
28—21
52—86

61—17
72—4, 8

OF III

V⁷ of III (B D♯ F♯ A in C)

9—30	49—12
19—69	52—85
31—5, 17	57—7, 8

VII⁷ of III (D♯ F♯ A C in C)
 57—7

OF IV

V of IV (C E♮ G in c minor)

19—61, 65, 67	24—21

V⁷ of IV (C E G B♭ in C or c)

1—17, 45, 126, 131	21—(60-61), (74-75),
3—11	(78-79), (221-222),
4—136	(235-236), (239-240),
5—5	297
7—29, 67, 69	22—12, 22
9—28, 48	24—47
13—68, 229, 237, 256, 265,	26—2, 4, 12
273, 283	27—29

Neapolitan Chord Formations
(chords built on flat two of the scale)

Nondominant Diminished Seventh Chord Resolutions

Chords Involving Augmented Sixths

Modal Passages

Passages Based on the Whole-Tone Scale

Passages Involving the Eight-Tone Symmetrical Scale

Bitonal Passages

Pedal Point or Rhythmic Figure

Ostinato

Canon

INDEX OF MUSICAL WORKS

Those works represented by musical examples are indicated by an asterisk *. The pages which include the principal discussion of the examples are shown in *italics* following the example number, and the pages on which the actual music appears follow in **bold face** type. Other references to the work appear in standard type.

GENERAL INDEX